D1716317

Jeffrey L. Larsen
227 Oak Grove Street #201
Minneapolis, MN 55403

Computer-Aided Design

Dean L. Taylor
Cornell University

ADDISON-WESLEY PUBLISHING COMPANY
Reading, Massachusetts • Menlo Park, California • New York • Don Mills,
Ontario • Wokingham, England • Amsterdam • Bonn • Sydney
Singapore • Tokyo • Madrid • San Juan • Milan • Paris

This book is in the Addison-Wesley series in **Mechanical Engineering**

Cover: Photo courtesy of Jon Davis, General Electric Company.

Adobe Illustrator is a registered trademark of Adobe Systems Incorporated.
AutoCAD is a registered trademark of AutoDesk, Inc.
CADAM is a registered trademark of CADAM, Inc.
CATIA is a registered trademark of Dassault Systemes of Canada.
CMS is a registered trademark of International Business Machines.
CA-CricketGraph is a trademark of Computer Associates International, Inc.
HOOPS is a registered trademark of Ithaca Software.
MACSYMA is a trademark of Symbolics, Inc., Cambridge, MA.
Mathematica is a registered trademark of Wolfram Research, Inc.
PATRAN is a registered trademark of PDA Engineering.
PostScript is a registered trademark of Adobe Systems Incorporated.
UNIX is a registered trademark of AT&T.
VMS is a registered trademark of Digital Equipment Company.

Library of Congress Cataloging-in-Publication Data

Taylor, Dean, 1949-
    Computer aided design / Dean Taylor.
        p.   cm.
    Includes bibliographical references and index.
    ISBN 0-201-16891-X
    1. Computer-aided design. I. Title.
    TA174.T39 1992
    620'.0042'0285—dc20   91-23895
                                                           CIP

    2 3 4 5 6 7 8 9 10-MA-95 94 93 92 91

To Kathy and Laurie

Color Plate Insert Credit List

Plate 1. Surface plot for pressure distribution within fluid film of crank end of a connecting rod, with zero pressure shaded red. Courtesy of Gary LaBouff.

Plate 2. Iteration map for Newton's method applied to Project 3.1. Courtesy of Scott A. Burns, University of Illinois at Urbana-Champaign.

Plate 3. Patch Representation of joystick handle. Courtesy of Silicon Graphics, Inc.

Plate 4. Shaded surface of joystick handle. Courtesy of Silicon Graphics, Inc.

Plate 5. Two-dimensional color map.

Plate 6. Pressure distribution over surface of transport aircraft. Courtesy of Douglas Aircraft Company, McDonnell Douglas Corporation.

Plate 7. Color shaded surface stress distribution for human femur. Courtesy of Cornell-HSS Program in Biomechanical Engineering.

Plate 8. Contoured surface stress distribution for a mechanical part. Courtesy of PDA Engineering.

Plate 9. Surface distribution of von Mises stress. Courtesy of PDA Engineering.

Plate 10. Temperature distribution during molding of plastic part. Courtesy of Cornell Injection Molding Project.

Plate 11. A three-dimensional rendering of a mechanical part. The colors show different levels of stress for complex loading conditions calculated with PATRAN P/Stress, a stress analysis program. Surface rendering allows the stresses on the surface of the part to be visualized. Created by Pixar. Data courtesy of Mr. Harris Hunt, PDA Engineering. ©1987 Pixar. All rights reserved.

Plate 12. A three-dimensional rendering of a mechanical part. The colors show different levels of stress for complex loading conditions calculated with PATRAN P/Stress, a stress analysis program. Volume rendering allows the internal stresses within the part to be visible. Created by Pixar. Data courtesy of Mr. Harris Hunt, PDA Engineering, ©1987 Pixar. All rights reserved.

Plate 13. Surface representations of isocontours for volume filling data. Low pressure (white), low streamwise velocity (yellow), outward ejections of low-speed fluid (red), and wallward sweeps of high-speed fluid (lavender).

Plate 14. Three-dimensional instantaneous velocity vectors, with blue representing low pressure and magenta representing high pressure.

Plate 15. Injection molding sequence, $T = T_4$. Courtesy of Richard Ellson, Kodak Research Scientist; Donna Cox, Visualization Research Artist; Ray Idaszak, Visualization Research Programmer; National Center for Supercomputer Applications.

Plate 16. Two dimensional velocity vector plot using marker arrows. Courtesy of PDA Engineering.

Plate 17. Three dimensional velocity vector plot using market arrows. Courtesy of PDA Engineering.

Plate 18. Pressure distribution on fan with flow ribbons. Courtesy of Douglas Aircraft Company, McDonnell Douglas Corporation.

C O N T E N T S

Chapter 5
Simulation   *141*

Chapter 6
Optimization   *189*

Chapter 10
Databases and Data Structures   405

P R E F A C E

This book is the result of a course (MAE 389, Computer-Aided Design) that the author has taught for 12 of the past 15 years in the Mechanical and Aerospace Engineering School at Cornell University. Computer-aided design has been evolving rapidly as a field, with changes in hardware and software tools available. However, a core of material has developed that will serve the student in future years as hardware and software continue their rapid change. Unfortunately, that core of material has been available only by using three or four separate books, an unsatisfactory solution for an undergraduate course. The objective of this book is to present the fundamentals of computer-aided design, showing its analytical rigor and algorithmic nature independent of specific software implementation.

The objective of the book is not to teach any particular CAD program. Focusing on a specific program would be counter to the trends in this field and would also limit the scope of material. In order to use existing software effectively and create usable macros or programs, students must understand the computing environment and the underlying algorithms. The objective is to produce knowledgeable CAD users who can quickly learn a specific program within a specific environment and who, understanding the fundamental concepts and limitations of techniques and data structures, can utilize that program to the "limits of the envelope."

The author's basic philosophy is programming oriented and project oriented. Exercises have been included in the book to help guide readers who may be using the book outside of a formal classroom setting. The projects in the book are taken from real situations and use realistic values as much as possible. One subgoal of this book is to provide a set of realistic interconnected design problems. The projects have been chosen so that the course can satisfy ABET design course objectives with the addition of appropriate reports and supplementary material.

Project courses are particularly challenging when combined with a substantial amount of formal material. A single large project is attractive because of the scope it makes possible, but a series of individual projects is also attractive because of the more uniform workload for the students. The course at Cornell has been based on a series of related projects, as reflected in the book.

A course could be organized in several ways from this book. If the only prerequisite is a programming course, then the CAD course might include Chapters 2, 3, 5, 6, and 7. However, if the students have already taken a numerical methods course (in addition to a programming course), the CAD course could be based on Chapters 4, 5, 6, 7, 9, and 10. If the existing curriculum includes courses in finite-element analysis, simulation or optimization, these chapters can be replaced with material from Chapters 8, 10, and 11. The author has also taught a second course using the more advanced material in Chapters 7, 8, 9, 10, and 11.

The prerequisite for the course at Cornell is the College of Engineering Introductory Computing course (taught in PASCAL on Apple Macintosh). However, the majority of the students have also taken an introductory numerical methods course (taught in FORTRAN). The CAD course uses material from Chapters 4, 5, 6, 7, and 9. Students are assigned a very simple initial project (usually from Chapter 2) to familiarize themselves with the computing environment (the operating system, editor, and compiler, and the input/output and file system operations). This is followed by the sailboat projects from Chapters 5, 6, 7, and 9. By the end of the semester, the students have produced a working simulation of a sailboat, performance predictions, and a graphical representation of the hull. The final project is to tie all of this together and participate in a class regatta. A communications package is provided so that each student's program can be advised of the other students' boat locations. The situation is similar to that of multiple-machine, multiple-aircraft flight simulators. Although the regatta is clearly a competition, the students' grades are determined by participation rather than by order of finish.

Commercial programs are available for all the material covered in this book (although no single program spans the entire range). Although a course could be organized using three or four commercial packages, the course offered at Cornell is oriented to programming, and students are expected to create programs to complete the design tasks. Obviously, one does not create such programs from scratch, so a collection of software should be provided. This is similar to the situation in industry, where some software will be available but must be adapted to the immediate task. Depending upon the material covered and projects assigned, the class should be provided with a complete numerical methods library (including curve-fitting, splines, polynomial root-finding, matrix decomposition, variable time step integration, and unconstrained and constrained optimization), a hierarchical graphics package at the level of PHIGS or GL, a geometry package, an interactive graphing and plotting program, a contour plotting and/or surface plotting program, and a menu creation program. The author has been able to obtain or create public domain alternatives for many of these. Students are also encouraged to make use of programs on personal computers (generally Macintosh at Cornell) for plotting, spreadsheet and prototyping, and document preparation.

This book, and the course that has used it, assumes that the students have previous experience in programming, understand an operating system and file system, and can learn programming productivity tools such as a full screen editor and debugger. The students are therefore expected to pick up the particular environment for this course with moderate effort. Specifically, the course uses the UNIX operating system. The course could be taught in many alternative languages. A procedural compiled language is most appropriate. The author has recently chosen to teach in C, although FORTRAN is certainly a viable alternative. Given the project orientation of the book, and the excellent interlanguage procedural calling capability, a course could be offered in both languages, with each student making an individual choice.

The course at Cornell uses Silicon Graphics UNIX workstations, and students prepare projects in C. With some compromise in graphics capability, almost any UNIX workstation could be used. For the course as offered at Cornell, current personal computers are not sufficiently powerful. The primary difficulty is the lack of virtual memory, which imposes constraints on program and data size. This is a problem if students are to use efficiently a collection of programs and software that is not designed to work together.

I am indebted to the following reviewers who helped at various times throughout the book's development: Thomas R. Chase, University of Minnesota; Mark S. Ganter, University of Washington; Mark Henderson, Arizona State University; David A. Hoeltzel, Columbia University; K. Khozeimeh, George Washington University; Gary L. Kinzel, Ohio State University; Arvid Myklebust, Virginia Polytechnic Institute; Thomas Phelps, University of Missouri—Columbia; Donald R. Riley,, University of Minnesota; and Robert R. Ryan, University of Michigan.

I want to thank my colleagues at Cornell—Don Bartel, Jack Booker, and Paul Dawson—who have provided stimulation and support. Much of my approach to CAD developed from discussions with graduate students over many years: Randy Bartlett, David Bell, Michael Butler, Shirish Chinchalkar, Av Edidin, Steve Fontes, Paul Hauck, Kumar Hebbale, Pat Hollis, Bill Horn, Diana Hauser, Nobuhisa Kamikawa, B. R. Kumar, Govirdaraj Kuntimad, Xuehai Li, Mike McCarthy, Masa Moriyama, Dev Prabhu, Ganesh Subbarayan, Scott Walter, DaZong Wang, and Richard Warkentin. As do all university faculty, I owe a tremendous debt to the students I have been able to work with. I would like to express my appreciation to the teaching assistants and students of MAE 389 and 489 during the past 15 years.

Pat Hollis provided much of the material for Chapters 3 and 4. Paul Dawson provided projects for Chapter 4. Jack Booker provided the material for the annotated bibliography for Chapters 4 and 5. Ganesh Subbarayan provided material for Chapter 6. Paul Hauck provided the material for the annoted bibliography for Chapters 7 and 8.

I want to express appreciation to Gary Weigand, who taught me about graphics programming, and to acknowledge the staff of CADIF, which has provided the computing environment for this class in recent years. I also want to thank Mike Piplani and John Lottey. I would also like to acknowledge IBM, which has supported the IMAP research lab for many years.

I would like to thank Ginny Giles, who helped prepare the manuscript, and Teresa Howley, who helped prepare the illustrations. My thanks to my editor, Don Fowley, and associate editor Laurie McGuire, whose gentle prods saw the project to completion. Thanks also to Kristina Williamson and Melissa G. Madsen, who provided an extensive and valuable edit of the entire manuscript.

This book was prepared in TEX, and the majority of the figures were prepared in Adobe Illustrator.

D. L. T.

C H A P T E R

1
Introduction

1.1 DEFINITION

It is difficult to imagine a book on computer-aided design that does not begin by defining design. On the other hand, engineers who have dealt with design realize how difficult it is to define. At the most fundamental level, design can be defined as problem solving. This, however, is not sufficiently precise. The difficulty is underscored by the following definition: "specification of dimensions, materials, and operations of devices to meet functional requirements." This focuses attention on devices, highlighting the importance of specification as the result and functional requirements as the starting point.

Because design is so difficult to define with precision, we will be content with a characterization of design and computer-aided design. Design is usually viewed as cyclic. The process is shown in Fig. 1.1 as a block diagram that is reminiscent of feedback control loops. One begins with a specification of functional requirements and an initial design specification. Some analysis is used to predict the performance of the specific design being considered. This performance is then compared to the functional requirements. Based on this comparison, the design specification is changed by a redesign process. This cyclic process continues until satisfactory performance is achieved.

Alternatively, design is often described as the reverse of analysis (as shown in Fig. 1.2). Note that the same blocks are employed, but the emphasis is on beginning with functional requirements and ending with a design specification. Given an initial design specification, analysis is used to predict performance. Based on the comparison of performance to the functional specifications, the design specification is modified. In Fig. 1.2, the analysis step (in the back-facing portion of the loop) is needed only to produce the performance prediction for comparison. It is this idea of inversion of analysis that leads to the description of design as *synthesis*.

The design process continues until performance and functional requirements converge. There are several ways to achieve this. Using an analogy with iterative computer algorithms, convergence occurs when the design

1

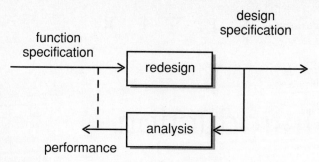

Figure 1.1 Design as a cyclic process.

variation from cycle to cycle is below specified limits. Alternatively, convergence can be obtained by reducing below specified limits the difference between performance and requirements. If the functional requirements are ranges (rather than specific target values), then convergence can be achieved simply by getting the performance variables into the desired range.

The subject of computer-aided design concerns the productivity tools that facilitate the design process. CAD can be useful in both parts of the design cycle, both analysis and synthesis (redesign). Much of this book will address how CAD can be used in analysis. Presently, CAD is not particularly effective in the initial synthesis of a design or in the redesign portion of the design loop; however, it is highly useful in providing efficient ways to help the designer revise the design. A simple sequence of new commands can cause a wide range of changes throughout the design. For example, an alteration in shaft diameter may produce subsequent changes in gear diameter, thickness, and even tooth profile. Actually, these changes are, in effect, a preprogrammed result of some functional relationship between the parameters. (In fact, the parameterization of the problem is a major step in design specification.) If the CAD programs were instrumental in both determining the underlying relationships and producing the initial change in shaft diameter, the process would be more correctly described as computer-automated design rather than computer-aided design. In this book, we will

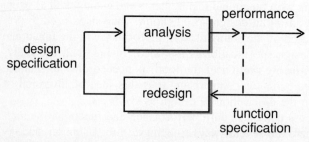

Figure 1.2 Design emphasized as different from analysis.

concentrate on the productivity tools useful for the analytical and descriptive parts of the the design loop.

Design questions include:

- How is function specified?
- How is behavior specified?
- How is the design specified?
- How is the process specified?
- How is the initial design obtained?
- How is redesign achieved?

Finally, design has been described as the exercise of creativity. A major objective of computer-aided design is to enable the engineer to exercise creativity. In problem solving, creativity has been compared to the cavalry charge in nineteenth-century military operations. To be effective, the cavalry charge required extensive practice and preparation, as well as perfect timing; in addition, it could be used effectively only once. Design creativity shares these traits so the purpose of CAD systems is to allow the engineer to fully exploit creativity at the critical moment.

The multidimensional computer-aided design makes it holographic in nature. Thus, it is impossible to lay out a linear cut through the topic. The field can be categorized by the various types of design, design techniques, and application areas, or by classification of the various computational tools available. The objective of this chapter is to provide several different views of design that can be referred to when individual topics are covered later in this book. Section 1.2 discusses a taxonomy for the various types of design. Section 1.3 discusses the characteristics of computers, and Section 1.4 uses these characteristics to classify the software packages useful to CAD. In Section 1.8 we will use these characteristics to classify the components of CAD software.

1.2 TYPES OF DESIGN

A scientific approach to any subject frequently involves the development of a taxonomy, an orderly classification of the members of a set according to their relationships. Simplified, a taxonomy provides a road map or framework for organizing large amounts of information. One can classify design problems by the stages of the product design cycle in which they occur:

- Innovation, invention
- Conceptual design
- Configuration design
- Parametric design
- Detail design (component design)

Throughout the book, design problems will be illustrated by example, rather than by definition. Note that the theoretical boundaries between the stages are not distinct.

Consider the development of compact-disk technology. The *innovation* stage is the initial conception of the product (digital storage of music in a package suitable for the consumer market). The *conceptual design* would involve issues such as sensing modalities (laser scanning) and packaging for the digital data (disk versus tape). This might also involve choice of disk material and how the binary data are to be marked on the disk. The initial choice of disk size, disk rotation speed, track spacing, and bit spacing along a track may occur here or during configuration design. *Configuration design* involves choosing the methods for loading and unloading the disks, the method for turning the disk (DC motor, stepper motor, direct drive, gear drive, etc.), and the methods for moving the laser scanning head (stepper motor, voice coil, etc.). The number and arrangement of components also are determined. *Parametric design* includes finalization of disk size, disk rotation speed, track spacing, bit spacing along a track, and the size of the motor and the head scanning mechanism. Values for all key design parameters are set. During *detail design* each part's design is completed in sufficient detail for manufacturing and all other phases of operation. Detail design produces the final, complete description of each component.

A look at any product should make it clear that the distinctions between these phases of design are not distinct in practice, either. Furthermore, just as each type of design is iterative, the process itself is iterative. Detail design may require a change in a parameter value that was set in the parameter design stage. This would require a return to that level of design, followed by resolution of any associated parameter changes and then continuation of the detail design. This phenomenon can be observed at any stage. However, the design process is usually structured to minimize such reversions to previously adressed, more general problems.

Computer-aided design provides different types of productivity tools for each of these types of design, although little is provided for innovation and invention. At this stage, general-purpose presentation and documentation, including sketching, transparency and slide production, and word processing, are most useful. More assistance is available in conceptual design; however, little conceptual design has been implemented in formal mechanical CAD systems. Here, expert-system techniques may prove helpful in the development of conceptual designs. The central problem is determining an appropriate, precise, and machine-readable description for conceptual designs.

It is at the configuration design stage where the benefits of computer assistance begin to make an impact. Designers can develop data structures for configurations and simulate the behavior of systems. In addition, CAD systems can be programmed to generate configurations. However, current CAD tools are most effective at parametric design. At this stage, the problems become more mathematical, including functional relationships, constraints, and performance prediction. CAD systems are adept at solving such simulation and optimization problem. The last stage, component design, is strongly supported by analytical tools such as the finite-element method. These methods are often too computation-intensive to be used in parametric design and also require more detail than is available at that stage. In detail design, computer-aided drafting is the primary productivity tool.

1.3   THE ROLE OF THE COMPUTER IN DESIGN

The objective of this book is to illustrate how computer software can assist or aid design. In this section we consider the computer characteristics that can be exploited and used in CAD.

Thinking about the role of the computer in the design process can give insight when new applications are being considered. The discipline of computer science can identify many generic actions or operations. Relative to computer-aided design, these operations can be grouped under three broad functions:

- Calculation
- Bookkeeping/record keeping
- Visualization

The calculation activity of computation is probably the oldest use of CAD. CAD is particularly helpful with extremely large amounts of floating-point operations, which are intolerable using calculators. The importance of calculation is seen in the early computer language FORTRAN (FORmula TRANslation). Optimization and simulation applications also depend upon calculation.

The extensive memory and mass storage capabilities of computers help in bookkeeping/record-keeping activities. These capabilities, which have the flavor of formal computer science, are often overlooked by mechanical engineers in computer-aided design. Bookkeeping/record-keeping functions are characterized by complex relationships between information and the management of large volumes of numbers. Calculations are not completely absent; but if they do occur, they will be limited to either many small, unrelated calculations or a massive calculation that can actually be viewed as many small steps.

The latter is one way to look at finite-element analysis. Although equations for any specific element are relatively simple, it is the simultaneous solution that leads to the complexity. In the extremely early days of finite-element analysis, the problems were solved by rooms of people processing information through mechanical calculators. Each person received a program sheet with numbers, operations, and fields for the results. These results were combined with those of other calculations and passed along in another program sheet to another calculator. Thus it is easy to see how the data management aspects of computers were instrumental in the success of finite-element analysis. Finite-element techniques will be discussed in Chapter 4.

The recent invention of spreadsheet programs exploits the record-keeping nature of computers. The calculation in most spreadsheet programs is very simple. The record-keeping power of computers has also made possible even more recent applications that perform symbolic algebraic manipulation.

At the most simple level, record keeping can be viewed as any manipulation of data other than calculation, such as storage, retrieval, or sorting. Such information includes

- Product data

- Design process data

- CAD system data

Examples of product-related data are geometric information, connectivity data, attributes for drafted output (color, line style, notes), and production plans. Design process information can include pointers to results, numerical accuracy, number of iterations, previous design values considered, and other aspects of the design history. Examples of CAD system data are the representations open on the screen, number and location of windows, viewpoints within windows, menu options selected, values that have been chosen to override default values, and other aspects of the user interface.

A dynamic system simulation program can be used to further demonstrate the distinctions between product, process, and CAD system information. Product data required would be differential equations, number of state variables and their names, sets of values for physical parameters (and their names), and sets of initial conditions and associated responses. The process information would include type of numerical integration scheme used, time step size used, and numerical accuracy. Historical data for the design process would include the sequence of parameter values and initial conditions that had been considered. The CAD system information would include the number and location of windows open on the screen. Some of these windows might contain graphs of the response of the system over time, so the CAD system data would identify what responses and state variables had been plotted, what scales were used, what line types and colors and/or marker symbols were used, and what hard-copy parameters had been set.

Because of the development of electronic representations for graphic images, combined with the capability to manipulate large amounts of data rapidly, computers can be used to transfer information visually. It is true that graphics involves extremely intensive calculation; however, the objective of these calculations is ultimately what color to set for each pixel on the screen (the background is also a color). The actual value of the color is almost never used arithmetically in the design process. All of the computation is focused on producing the screen image.

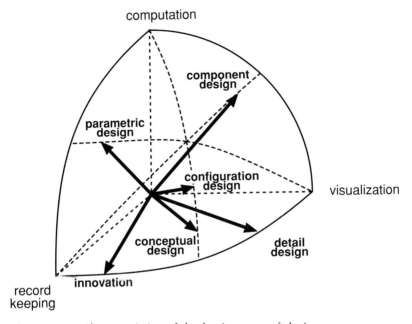

Figure 1.3 Characteristics of the basic types of design.

If the three functions of the computer are plotted as orthogonal axes, then the different types of design can be drawn as vectors, each type of design depending upon a different combination of the three basic functions. Figure 1.3 illustrates each type of design in relation to the three basic functions. Each type of design is a vector whose point lies on a unit sphere. Note that parametric design uses both computation and record keeping but requires little visualization. On the other hand, component design that would require extensive finite-element analysis uses computation and visualization but does not make use of the record-keeping strengths. Component design is shown separate from detail design to distinguish between the heavy calculation requirements of analysis and the less demanding requirements of drafting.

1.4 HISTORICAL BACKGROUND

The contribution made by each role of the computer can be seen in the history of computer-aided design and the sequence of the development of applications. The applications of computer-aided design have developed in three stages:

- Early
  - Finite-element method
  - Simulation of dynamic systems
  - Optimization

- Later
  - Graphics
  - Geometry
- Most recently
  - Algebraic manipulation
  - Spreadsheets
  - Combinations (electronic notebooks)

Originally, computer applications for mechanical engineers were developed to solve problems in structural stress analysis, simulation, and optimization. All three used numerical methods that already existed but were impractical without speed and the ability to manipulate large amounts of data. The aerospace industry was one of the earliest users of these methods.

As computer applications developed, the amounts of data increased to such a level that graphic display was necessary. Soon thereafter, applications to create and manipulate geometry began. Much of the development effort dealing with geometry focused on drafting, which in this instance includes both the two-dimensional geometry of the drawing and the lines associated with dimensioning, cross-hatching, and notes.

Drafting is inherently two-dimensional, and so the development in this area pursued questions of user interface and data structures rather than pure questions of geometry. The amounts of data created by commercial engineering operations (literally thousands of drawings) created pressure to solve problems in database methods (the manipulation of large amounts of data that are shared by several programs and users).

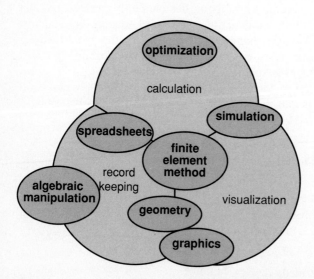

Figure 1.4 Relationship among CAD applications
and aspects of computation.

The descriptive needs of analysis (primarily structural finite-element methods and fluid flow analysis) and manufacturing (NC programming) drove the development of methods for three-dimensional geometry.

Figure 1.4 shows how CAD's strengths have used the three basic functions of the computer. Comparing Fig. 1.4 to Fig. 1.3 reveals a general correspondence between the types of design and the traditional CAD techniques.

1.5   CHARACTERISTICS OF DESIGN

Having discussed types of design, the role of the computer, and the historical development of CAD programs, it is necessary to discuss additional characteristics of design that have not yet been addressed. This discussion is not intended to be a complete taxonomy of design characteristics but is meant to highlight those attributes not yet discussed that are particularly important to computer-aided design. The reader should watch for these aspects as we cover different topics through the book:

- Iterative versus direct
- Synthesis (initial design) versus redesign
- Incremental design
- Remapping
- Hierarchy
- Decomposition and recursion versus iteration
- Self-reference

Iterative versus Direct

Generally, numerical methods are characterized as either iterative or direct. Since these descriptions also apply to algorithms in general, the techniques of computer-aided design can be categorized in this fashion as well. For example, most design problems that lead to parameter optimization are usually approached in an iterative fashion. Characteristics of iterative methods are concerns with convergence criteria and ways to obtain the initial starting point. Because design is usually described as iterative, the iterative paradigm is applied to most CAD tools. However, if direct techniques are available, the feedback loop in Fig. 1.2 can be replaced by a straightforward computation of the design. Examples of direct algorithms include most of the computations involved in computer graphics.

Synthesis versus Redesign

Design problems are always either initial design or redesign. Although it seems clear that the overwhelming majority of design problems involve redesign, there is no concrete information on the topic. Redesign follows the iterative paradigm quite closely, with the same concerns of convergence. The generation of the starting point is usually neglected in redesign: the previous design serves as a starting point, and the primordial design receives little attention. If the data structure for a design is defined, a very primitive design can be generated within that data structure by any arbitrary brute-force method. Frequently, this can be achieved simply by coding specific numeric values into the data structure, hence the term "hand-packed." The initial design problem is most difficult in those areas where a hand-packed design is not available. Given a starting point, the CAD tools can be used to redesign a configuration that would be much too difficult to reach initially and/or to generate by hand.

Incremental Design

Problems that primarily involve redesign can also be called incremental design. These problems focus more on design changes than on the underlying design. The result is variant design, with two types of data: default and variant. The standard design is characterized by the default values. These are combined with the overriding or variant values to describe the complete design. Notice how the structure of the data is different from a simple, straightforward design description. The situation is further complicated by the number of variants to be tracked. In a variant design situation, usually several variants must be considered. This can reflect the need to develop a family of products, all variants on a fundamental concept (for example, a class of hydraulic actuators). Alternatively, several variants may be maintained and developed in detail, with the full expectation that a single variant will be selected for manufacture later in the design process. A variant design process is analogous to developing a tree of possible solutions and maintaining some subset of all possible designs as the design proceeds. Periodic pruning will reduce the tree but usually leaves a number of variants.

The coordination of change is central to incremental design. All of the general questions raised earlier about design now can be applied to change: How is change specified? How is change in performance and behavior specified? How is the incremental process specified? Given incremental design change, how is the resulting design realized or instantiated?

Remapping

As design proceeds, it often involves change that is more sweeping than incremental. This change from one representation to another is more like a translation into another language than a simple iterative evolution of the value of a parameter. For example, a general geometry for an aircraft wing might be expressed as plan-form and cross-section. Later, the internal structure is elaborated in terms of stringers, ribs, and stiffening panels. Still later, the specific cross-section of the stringers is set. Finally, manufacturing information is added. The process can be seen as involving increasing levels of detail and information. Alternatively, this can be expressed as a decreasing amount of abstraction. Note that the iterative process of incremental design, in which the model type does not change but the specific parameters (or possibly number of parameters) do change, is distinctly different from remappping. The remapping aspect has been described as a widening cone of design. Iteration at certain levels can be described as looping; remapping can be defined as proceeding from relatively simple to relatively complex models with more information content.

Hierarchy

Design problems frequently can be characterized by a hierarchical structure. Both natural and artificial objects display this structure. Hierarchy can be used to as impose an organization to the problem; however, multiple hierarchies are required because there is no unique hierarchy that can be used in all problems. Rather, hierarchy is always context-dependent.

Consider the example of a computer workstation as a product. To simulate the performance of the device, a functional hierarchy is useful. Such a hierarchy might divide the workstation into memory, input/output, central processing unit, and mass storage. An alternative hierarchy is based on physical distinction: card cage, boards, connectors, wiring harness, and power supply.

Decomposition and Recursion

The two algorithmic approaches of decomposition and recursion are related to hierarchy and variant design. Decomposition is a solution procedure where the initial problem is replaced by a set of simultaneous smaller problems. This is analogous to building the hierarchy tree mentioned previously. The power of decomposition is that the technique then can be applied to each new problem. Decomposition is not often applied in the three traditional CAD analytical problems of optimization, simulation, and finite-element analysis, but it is most useful in organizing the process aspect of the design problem. This can be seen in the development of manufacturing process plans.

Consider the machining of a part with several pockets and holes. The first step is to decompose the machining requirements into those features that can be machined with the same tool, such as holes of the same diameter and pockets that can use the same end-mill. The next step is to decompose those sets into features that can be independently machined, such as individual holes and separate pockets. The following step is to determine the cutter path for each pocket or hole.

The key characteristic of decomposition is that the subproblems are independent. However, the subproblems need not be of the same type as each other or as the parent problem. In the more limited case where the parent and all siblings are of the same type, the technique of recursion is applicable. For example, recursion is appropriate for a system that is a collection of subsystems if a subsystem is itself a collection of subsystems.

Recursion is fundamentally different from iteration. In an iterative approach, a fully defined solution is changed sequentially to a better solution. There might be 100 variables, each of which has a value from the first iteration. Conversely, in a recursive approach, the first level of recursion is not a complete solution. It is only as deeper and deeper levels of recursion are reached that the details of the solution (in effect, its information content) are developed. Both recursion and iteration algorithms require convergence criteria, but the nature of the criteria are fundamentally different. Iterative convergence is usually based on some error metric being reduced below a target value. The criteria can, however, be tightened afterwards, and then the algorithm can be cycled "a few more" iterations. Recursive convergence is not based on an error metric but usually on a logical test; that is, "Is the problem solved?" Consider the classical example of recursion in the calculation of factorials. The recursion stops when the level of 1! is reached because 1! is considered to be known. In constructing hierarchies, recursive convergence is reached when any level can no longer be subdivided.

Another example can be drawn from geometry. Attempting to represent an arbitrary curve by a series of straight lines is an example of the iterative style of convergence. (This is a more simple version of the tessellation of surface patches discussed in Chapter 9.) The recursive approach would define a curve as a collection of curves, connected end to end. Each subcurve would itself be a curve and therefore a collection of curves. This recursion would proceed until certain fundamental atomic entities, such as straight lines, circular arcs, or conic sections, were detected.

Self-Reference

Self-reference is a slightly different twist on the concept of recursion. Self-reference is meaningful at the higher level of CAD system architecture. Advanced design techniques and software development tools must be considered in the design of design systems.

Process Aspect of CAD

Neither the design problem nor the design-solution method can be considered in isolation. The CAD system combines both and demonstrates the fundamental characteristics of each. For example, a process viewpoint is highly useful in organizing the CAD system. In this case, the system is viewed as a flowchart or as a continuous-flow process analogous to manufacturing processes at the factory or refinery level. Various parts of the process are analogous to the processing units in a refinery. It is not sufficient to know the current design; it is also necessary to know both the previous designs and the previous CAD modules used to generate that design. This historical or trajectory information is necessary if design changes force "back-tracking" to explore other alternatives. In fact, such back-tracking is just a further extension of the trajectory through design space.

From this viewpoint, the CAD system might be represented by a graph of CAD components and possible data paths between programs. The design trajectory is a particular path that has been used. The graph is roughly analogous to a flowchart for a computer program; the design trajectory is a particular path through that flowchart.

A computer program exists within a defined computer language. If CAD is considered analogous to a program, then the developer can generalize and conceptualize an underlying 'language' or structure describing the process.

State-Machine Aspect of CAD

The alternative to the process viewpoint is the state-machine aspect of CAD, which draws upon the state-machine model of generalized computing. This model consists of a set of states, each state having a set of acceptable values. In addition the model includes specification of the circumstances that would change the value of one or more states. These are the state-transition rules. In this perspective of CAD, a complete description of the problem consists of the set of current values and the transition rules. This model views the CAD system as a set of data values existing within a defined data structure.

1.6   DESIGN PARADIGMS

Several paradigms have been proposed, either formally or informally, to describe the design process. These paradigms can be useful in developing an overview of CAD systems:

- Design as search
- Design as optimization
- Design as compilation
- Design as constraint satisfaction

Design has been characterized as search, which assumes that a design consists of a set of variables, each with a set of acceptable values. In such a situation, it is relatively easy to specify different designs. The design process "simply" involves choosing between these competitive designs. Most often, this can be described as a "generate and test" process. Designers can propose various strategies, depending upon how much organization can be imposed on the space of designs. Expert systems tend to be based on this paradigm and use guided search, depth-first search, breadth-first search, and other approaches.

In addition, design has been characterized as optimization. Of course, optimization is search, but search limited within a tightly structured design space. This paradigm emphasizes the use of the objective function to measure the quality of the design. Furthermore, optimization handles constraint functions. Optimization can take place within continuous space and/or within discrete space (the latter is descriptive of combinatorial problems). In this paradigm, the analytical step in Fig 1.2 predicts design performance, and the redesign step chooses the optimization algorithm's next test point.

Unlike the iterative nature of the previous two paradigms, design as compilation encompasses any algorithm that is direct or explicit. Compilation is essentially a mapping process, in which an entity (usually a program) is mapped from a higher-level language, such as FORTRAN or C, into a lower-level language (i.e., the assembly language for a particular processor). Compilation is not iterative, although some compilers may require multiple passes through the program. The source and target languages are essential to compilation, and each must be well defined.

Yet another paradigm simply presents design as constraint satisfaction. The design consists of a set of values, and the function can be computed from these values. However, there are also many constraint relationships that must be satisfied. Here, design becomes the process of determining values that satisfy all constraints.

All of these paradigms are useful in obtaining a global, strategic overview of the CAD process and how CAD's components can be used to solve design problems.

1.7 BROADER DESIGN TOPICS

Computer-aided design techniques have been applied to an increasing number of design problems. Each new area coins a different terminology: design for manufacture, design for assembly, design for analysis, life-cycle design, and quality-function deployment. It is beyond the scope of this text to describe the approach used in each, let alone compare and contrast these methods. However, each method can be seen to rely upon one or more of the computer strengths listed previously: calculation, bookkeeping, and visualization. In fact, it is these strengths that have enabled the development of the methods.

In all of these methods, a model or representation of the design is defined. This model can be used to determine some performance characteristic in the domain of interest, whether it is assembly, manufacturing, or some other field. Because the design model is well defined, the performance characteristic can be determined with a computer algorithm. Furthermore, another algorithm can be used to vary the design and track the variations. The designer is relieved from mind-numbing accounting schemes and allowed to focus on the creative aspects of the design problem.

1.8   COMPONENTS OF CAD

Computer-aided design systems require a collection of procedures and subroutines to provide the range of functions needed. These procedures are usually collected into software libraries that can be used to categorize the functionality needed. In many of these areas, standards are developing that enhance portability between different hardware platforms. Effective system development almost mandates the use of libraries in the following areas:

- Numerical methods
- Graphics
- Geometry
- Interface package
- Database manager
- Data structures toolbox

Figure 1.5 shows how these libraries utilize the strengths of the computer. Each of these is discussed in later chapters. Here, we will only briefly discuss each so as to put them all in perspective.

Numerical methods libraries provide calculation function in many areas. Although other topics may be included, a comprehensive library will include

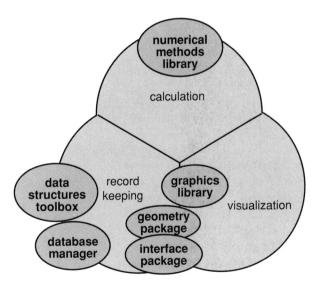

Figure 1.5   Relationship among components of
CAD and aspects of computation.

these functions:

- Function manipulation
  - Interpolation
  - Extrapolation
  - Integration
  - Differentiation
  - Root finding
  - Least squares
  - Spline fitting
- Matrix manipulation
  - Multiplication
  - Decomposition (inversion)
  - Eigenvalue extraction
- Integration of differential equations
- Optimization algorithms

Graphics packages produce the images and text that appear on the screen and on hard-copy output. Although graphic images usually contain geometric information, much of this functionality is reserved for a separate library. Although graphics packages mainly provide visualization capability they also include record keeping in the organization of the image produced. Understanding and using graphics packages also requires understanding and using material that could be called data structures. Graphics usually involves only a limited scope of numerical calculation, although the amount of calculation can be quite intensive.

The geometry of even one part is complex enough to require extensive data structures; the geometry of a product or a collection of parts is even more so. The role of the geometry manager is to create and manipulate the data structures that contain geometric information. Depending on implementation, the geometry library may support points, lines, surface patches of several types, solid primitives, and volumetric data. The geometry package should allow the developer and user easily to create specific instances of the geometric elements and search the data for explicit information (coordinates) and implicit information (distance between entities, intersections, etc.). The geometry library is a collection of subroutine calls that, when combined with an appropriate interface as defined in the interface package, begins to form a complete application. The geometry library is kept separate, however, because other programs may also need to manipulate geometric information. If the only available geometry library is packaged into a complete application, then other programs will have extreme difficulty using it.

Often the interface package actually consists of these four separate software libraries:

- Window manager
- Menu manager

- Interactive-device manager
- Help text manager

The window manager governs the multiple windows often used by separate programs and thus is intimately involved with the specific hardware and operating system used. In contrast, the menu manager is more limited in scope, handling the specific graphic representations for dials, scroll bars, and other menu elements. It will use the data structures toolbox and the graphics package. The interactive-device manager handles communication with peripheral devices such as a mouse, a tablet, or a joystick. This package takes care of specific hardware concerns such as word size and baud rate, as well as more general concerns about format or about how the information is encoded. For example, this package allows the user to obtain tablet x, y data with a single procedure call. Finally, the help text manager is a special-purpose database program to facilitate the creation and maintenance of the large amount of textual information within an interactive program.

Information is made useful by organization. The database manager and the data structures toolbox are two types of applications or libraries that organize the information within a CAD system. The database manager is actually a separate program that maintains the large amounts of data used by several application programs. CAD systems are only now beginning to make use of database management programs. On the other hand, the data structures toolbox creates and manipulates a wide variety of useful data structures within individual CAD programs. As will be discussed later, libraries such as the geometry library, the graphics support package, and the menu manager are special-purpose data structure toolboxes.

A useful CAD system environment will have most, if not all, of these libraries available to the user as well as the CAD developer. In fact, a rich CAD environment will be so flexible as to blur the distinction between the user and the developer. As users become more familiar with the system, they will begin to use the programming aspects of the system to customize the interface and to implement new functions.

1.9 OBJECTIVES OF THIS BOOK

The basic goal of this book is to develop a general view of CAD beyond any application area or specific CAD package. Rather than acquiring specific training in a particular program, we will seek a broader understanding of the fundamental components and associated algorithms. Therefore, there will be a significant component of software development. The object is not just a CAD user, but an informed, intelligent CAD user who can be an effective CAD modifier. The material that follows forms the groundwork for educating the CAD software developer. Virtually every chapter can be seen as an introduction to topics for which more advanced books and courses are available.

It is worth commenting on the mechanical engineering aspect of the examples and projects. CAD for mechanical engineers differs significantly from CAD for electrical engineers (probably the only other major engineering area of CAD). Mechanical engineering design is more concerned with three-dimensional geometry and lacks the well-developed representations of function that are available to digital design for electrical engineers. More recently, we have seen the development of CAD systems for architectural applications and software engineering. The former has many uses for mechanical engineers because of its treatment of geometry, visualization, and user interfaces. The latter is particularly interesting to developers of CAD systems for mechanical engineers because ultimately a CAD system is a software product. In subsequent chapters we will try to look beyond the specific; we will consider the generic aspects of each topic and place the material in context.

Underlying Theme

In exploring the generic nature of the subject matter, it is always necessary to seek ways to generalize processes, data, or algorithms for broader use. In particular, the reader should always consider the contrasting attributes of data and process: The data viewpoint centers around data structure (arrays, lists, trees, graphs, etc.) and data content. The alternative process viewpoint focuses on algorithms, program constructs that can be utilized (loops, branches, procedures, etc.), and fundamental actions that are necessary and sufficient.

However, the division is never clear, and insight frequently can be gained by forcing a shift in viewpoint. For example, an algorithm can be expressed as a flowchart, which is a type of graph, which in turn is a type of data format, and then the operations of data manipulation can be applied to that graph. This allows the CAD user to generalize the algorithm to something that can be saved, manipulated (parameterized and changed), and reapplied later. This is the advantage of using an algebraic program such as Macsysma or Mathematica for algorithm testing and development. As far as these programs are concerned, the algorithms being tested are data.

Conversely, a data structure, as for a piece of geometry, can be viewed as the process by which the entity (geometry) is created. Processes contain constructs such as loop, branch, test, and subprocedures. In a drawing of a gear, each individual tooth is better considered as a call to a subprocedure than as a unique set of lines.

Observed from a vantage point where data and process are similar, it becomes apparent that simple use of any CAD system can be considered as programming. Most engineers recognize development of a segment of FORTRAN code as programming. However, that same section of code is simply a particular instance of data located within a well-defined data structure within the system of the text editor, compiler, and operating system. The development of a design within a CAD system is the creation of a particular program within a well-defined programming language.

This generalization to a broader view, known as meta-design, enables more powerful use of current CAD packages, more creative combination of existing software, and the development of innovative solutions.

1.10   ANNOTATED REFERENCES

Ammeraal, Leendert. *Programs and Data Structures in C.* New York: Wiley, 1987.

Booch, G. *Object Oriented Design with Applications.* Menlo Park, Calif.: Benjamin/Cummings, 1991.

Borse, G. J. *FORTRAN 77 and Numerical Methods for Engineers.* Boston: PWS Engineering, 1985.

Comprehensive, integrated approach.

Encarnacao, J., and Schlechtendahl, E. G. *Computer Aided Design—Fundamentals and System Architecture.* New York: Springer-Verlag, 1983.

Etter, D. M. *Structured Fortran 77 for Engineers and Scientists.* Menlo Park, Calif.: Benjamin/Cummings, 1987.

Comprehensive, emphasizing structure.

Finger, S., and Dixon, J. R. "A Review of Research in Mechanical Engineering Design, Part I: Descriptive, Prescriptive, and Computer-Based Models of Design Processes," *Research in Engineering Design,* Vol. 1, No. 1 (1989), pp. 51–68.

Finger, S., and Dixon, J. R. "A Review of Research in Mechanical Engineering Design, Part II: Representations, Analysis, and Design for the Life Cycle," *Research in Engineering Design,* Vol. 1, No. 2 (1989), pp. 121–138.

Hurt, James. "A Taxonomy of CAD/CAE Systems," *Manufacturing Review,* vol. 2, no. 3, (September 1989), pp. 170–178.

Presents a classification scheme for commercial programs, considering geometric dimensionality and topology and support for various types of engineering analysis.

Hubka, Vladmir, Andreason, M. M., and Edder, W. Ernst. *Practical Studies in Systematic Design.* Boston: Butterworths, 1988.

Hubka, V., and Edder, W. E. *Theory of Technical Systems: A Total Concept Theory for Engineering Design.* New York: Springer-Verlag, 1988.

Katzan, H. *Fortran 77.* New York: Van Nostrand Reinhold, 1978.

Comprehensive, concise reference.

Kernighan, B. W., and Ritchie, D. M. *The C Programming Language.* 2d ed. Englewood Cliffs, N. J.: Prentice-Hall, 1988.

The classic reference for the language. For readers with programming experience.

Metcalf, M. *Effective FORTRAN 77.* Oxford: Clarendon Press 1985.

Authoritative, professional language reference.

Middendorf, William H. *Design of Devices and Systems*, 2d ed. New York: Marcel
Dekker, 1990.

Very broad view of design questions.

Pahl, G., and Beitz, W. *Engineering Design: A Systematic Approach*. New York:
Springer-Verlag, 1988.

Press, W. H., Flannery, B. P., Teukolsky, S. A., and Vetterling, W. T. *Numerical Recipes
in C: The Art of Scientific Computing*. New York: Cambridge University Press,
1988.

Sedgewick, Robert. *Algorithms*. Reading, Mass.: Addison-Wesley, 1983.

Shoup, Terry. *A Practical Guide to Computer Methods for Engineers*. Englewood
Cliffs, N.J.: Prentice-Hall, 1976.

*Focuses on numerical and analytical methods more so than CAD. Has many good
problems, many tables listing (then) available programs.*

Spillers, William R., ed. *Basic Questions of Design Theory*. New York: North Hol-
land, 1974.

*Collection of early papers in design theory. Includes civil, chemical, mechanical,
electrical, mathematics, and socio/urban design.*

Suh, Nam P. *The Principles of Design*. New York: Oxford University Press, 1990.

Tomiyama, T., and Yosikawa, H. "Metamodel: A Key to Intelligent CAD Systems,"
Research in Engineering Design, Vol. 1, No. 1 (1989), pp. 19–34.

Vetterling, W. T., Teukolsky, S. A., Press, W. H., and Flannery, B. P. *Numerical Recipes
Example Book (FORTRAN)*. New York: Cambridge University Press, 1985.

Coordinated examples with Press et.al.

Vetterling, W. T., Teukolsky, S. A., Press, W. H., and Flannery, B. P. *Numerical Recipes
Example Book (C)*. New York: Cambridge University Press, 1988.

Coordinated examples with Press et.al.

The following publications should be read regularly by CAD developers.

ACM Transactions on Graphics. Association for Computing Machinery, monthly.

Computer Aided Engineering. Penton Publishing, monthly trade journal.

Computer Aided Engineering Journal. Institute of Electrical Engineers and Institute
of Production Engineers. British monthly trade journal.

Computer Graphics. Special Interest Group on Computer Graphics, Association for
Computing Machinery, monthly.

Engineering with Computers. Springer-Verlag, quarterly international journal for
computer-aided mechanical and structural engineering.

International Journal for Numerical Methods in Engineering. Wiley, monthly.

Journal of Mechanical Design. ASME, quarterly.

Research in Engineering Design. Springer-Verlag, quarterly.

SIGGRAPH Proceedings. Association for Computing Machinery, annual.

2

Functions

2.1 INTRODUCTION

The techniques for manipulating the functional dependence between two variables are found at the most fundamental level of computer-aided design. Although functions can be approached either analytically or numerically, this chapter will focus on numerical aspects of function representation and manipulation. (Analytical techniques now appearing in many CAD packages are beyond the scope of this book; however, Chapter 10, Data Structures and Chapter 11, User Interfaces, provide a good introduction to analytical techniques.) Readers with background in numerical methods will find this chapter to be a quick review of the material. Also, this material is frequently included in examples and exercises in engineering programming courses.

Numerical function representation does not separate easily from the material presented in Chapter 9, Geometry, because many of the techniques for generating geometry are similar to curve fitting. Also, important operations for geometry manipulation, such as integration, differentiation, and root finding, are fundamental to function representation. This chapter focuses primarily on one-dimensional problems, although the sections covering least-square approximation and root finding are multi-dimensional.

The following examples illustrate the importance of functional representation:

1. The pressure distribution in a fluid journal bearing can be determined from Reynolds equation. The forces are obtained by *integration*, $F = \int p$. The stability of the bearing depends upon the bearing stiffness and damping coefficients, which are obtained by *differentiation*: $\partial F / \partial x$; $\partial F / \partial y$; $\partial F / \partial \dot{x}$; $\partial F / \partial \dot{y}$.

2. In aircraft design, one of the preliminary steps of aerodynamic analysis is to calculate the pressure distribution over the airfoil. If the shape of the airfoil is described by a sequence of point coordinates, the chamber line slope at any point is obtained by *differentiation*, $\partial \eta / \partial x$. This can

21

be used to determine the pressure distribution, p. *Integration*, $F = \int p$, yields the net aerodynamic forces, and the functional dependence of the aerodynamic forces upon the angle of attack, $\partial F / \partial \alpha$, can determine the stability of the aircraft.

3. Heat-transfer problems are frequently solved by finite-difference methods, yielding a temperature distribution $T(x, y, z)$. The heat flux at any point can be found by *differentiation*, $q = \partial T / \partial x$, and the total heat flow can be found by *integration*, $Q = \int_A q \, dA$.

4. The torque-speed curve for a motor may be given as a set of experimental data values. A simulation will require torque at arbitrary speed values, necessitating a *curve fit*.

5. Stress may be calculated at specific locations in an elastic body. Prediction of stress at other locations will require *interpolation*.

6. Using the principles of mechanics, performance variables can be determined as analytic functions of design variables. For example, in a fluid film bearing, torque loss, lubricant heat rise, minimum film thickness, and load number are functions of design parameters. Achieving specified constraints can require the solution of simultaneous algebraic equations (*root finding*).

This chapter will discuss numerical function representation from the traditional view of a single-valued function of one or two variables. It will include the fundamental operations of

- Interpolation/curve fitting
- Differentiation
- Integration
- Root finding

The fundamental concept in functional representation is *analytical substitution*. Assuming that the actual function is unknown, the goal is to determine constants C_i and functions f_i or g_i such that $y = f(x)$ can be represented by either

$$y = \sum_{i=1}^{n} C_i f_i(x)$$

or

$$y = \sum_{i=1}^{n} g_i(x) y_i$$

where the y_i are values at specified points. All of the methods that follow will use one of these two forms; the application determines which is more desirable. For a repetitive evaluation of the same function at many different values of x, the first form is better because the overhead in calculating C_i need not be repeated. However, the second form more efficiently evaluates several different functions at the same value of x, because a new curve (and new values of y_i) can be easily substituted without recalculating $g_i(x)$.

Example 2.1: Two Forms of a Linear Fit. Given two points (x_1, y_1) and (x_2, y_2), the linear fit $(y = ax + b)$ can be expressed in either of the following forms. The first is

$$y = \frac{y_1 x_2 - y_2 x_1}{x_2 - x_1} + \frac{y_2 - y_1}{x_2 - x_1} x$$

which is an analytical approximation in the first form mentioned above, where

$$C_1 = \frac{y_1 x_2 - y_2 x_1}{x_2 - x_1} \qquad f_1(x) = 1$$

$$C_2 = \frac{y_2 - y_1}{x_2 - x_1} \qquad f_2(x) = x$$

Alternatively,

$$y = (\frac{x_2 - x}{x_2 - x_1}) y_1 + (\frac{x - x_1}{x_2 - x_1}) y_2$$

which is an analytical approximation written in the second form, where

$$g_1(x) = \frac{x_2 - x}{x_2 - x_1}$$

$$g_2(x) = \frac{x - x_1}{x_2 - x_1}$$

Any functions can be used for the analytical substitution, but some are more useful than others. The ordinary polynomials are most frequently used, but Legendre, Chebyshev, and Lagrange polynomials also have applications. In addition, the trigonometric functions (sine, cosine) lead to Fourier analysis.

The reader should be careful: Many but not all of the formulae that follow assume equal spacing in x (centered at x_0). Furthermore, they may only apply at "key points" of x_i and not at arbitrary values of x. This warning also applies to formulae provided by reference books.

2.2 INTERPOLATION

CAD frequently uses both interpolation and curve fitting. For instance, many functions of interest to engineers only exist in tabular form (e.g., viscosity as a function of temperature, modulus of elasticity as a function of density). Often the data are obtained experimentally and not derived using mechanics.

Sometimes, mechanics can indicate the form of the function (such as exponential or cubic) although the true function itself is unknown. Historically, one role of engineering handbooks has been presentation of this kind of data.

Curve fitting is a more general problem than interpolation; its goal is to determine a usable analytical function that fits reference points in some way. This technique is referred to as analytical substitution. Interpolation is the evaluation of that function at a specific intermediate point. If the function needs to be integrated for some reason, then the analytical approximation is obviously more useful than any number of intermediate values. Similarly, the slope can be determined from an analytical function at any location, whereas the classical finite-difference formulae can only provide derivatives at the data points. On the other hand, if only a single intermediate value is needed, it can usually be obtained more efficiently by interpolation rather than by determining a complete analytical approximation.

These techniques have developed recently in the computer graphics field, because it is possible to store a rather complex geometry that can be evaluated at arbitrary locations using only a few defining points.

There are five types of curve fitting:

1. Pass through all points exactly, using a single complicated function.
2. Pass through all points exactly, using several simple equations.
3. Pass through all points exactly, with an aesthetically pleasing shape.
4. Pass through the first and last points, using intermediate points to "shape" or "influence" the curve.
5. Pass through no points specifically, but achieve a "best fit" of a single, relatively simple equation.

The first four types are various kinds of splines; the fifth is the province of least-squares analysis. We will begin with the first type, noting, however, that it is a limiting case for the least-squares approach (i.e., fitting a 10th-order polynomial through 11 points).

Polynomial

Given $n + 1$ points it is possible to determine a unique nth-order polynomial which passes through these points. If $P_n(x)$ denotes an nth-order polynomial, then exactly solving the polynomial at $n + 1$ points leads to

$$y_0 = P_n(x_0) = a_n x_0^n + \cdots + a_1 x_0 + a_0$$
$$y_1 = P_n(x_1)$$
$$\vdots$$
$$y_n = P_n(x_n)$$

Rearranging to isolate the $n+1$ unknown coefficients $(a_n, a_{n-1}, \ldots, a_1, a_0)$ leads to the following linear problem

$$
\begin{bmatrix}
x_0^n & x_0^{n-1} & \cdots & x_0 & 1 \\
x_1^n & x_1^{n-1} & \cdots & x_1 & 1 \\
\vdots & \vdots & \ddots & \vdots & \\
x_n^n & x_n^{n-1} & \cdots & x_n & 1
\end{bmatrix}
\begin{Bmatrix}
a_n \\
a_{n-1} \\
\vdots \\
a_1 \\
a_0
\end{Bmatrix}
=
\begin{Bmatrix}
y_0 \\
y_1 \\
\vdots \\
y_n
\end{Bmatrix}
$$

Chapter 3 will discuss ways to solve such matrix problems. In general, for very large n, this matrix will be ill conditioned, and so this method should be used with caution. That is, the coefficients may not be accurately determined for high-order polynomials due to numerical problems. However, this formulation is useful in the derivation of lower-order fits, particularly for equally spaced data.

Example 2.2: Fourth-order Polynomial Through Equally Spaced Points.
The coefficients for a fourth-order polynomial through five equally spaced points can be determined in closed form as follows:

$$ y = P_5(x) = a_4 x^4 + a_3 x^3 + a_2 x^2 + a_1 x + a_0 $$

If the points are equally spaced with spacing h and the numbering is centered on 0, such as $(-2h, h, 0, h, 2h)$, and $(y_{-2}, y_{-1}, y_0, y_1, y_2)$, then

$$
\begin{bmatrix}
16h^4 & -8h^3 & 4h^2 & -2h & 1 \\
h^4 & -h^3 & h^2 & -h & 1 \\
0 & 0 & 0 & 0 & 1 \\
h^4 & h^3 & h^2 & h & 1 \\
16h^4 & 8h^3 & 4h^2 & 2h & 1
\end{bmatrix}
\begin{bmatrix}
a_4 \\
a_3 \\
a_2 \\
a_1 \\
a_0
\end{bmatrix}
=
\begin{Bmatrix}
y_{-2} \\
y_{-1} \\
y_0 \\
y_1 \\
y_2
\end{Bmatrix}
$$

The inverse of this matrix has been determined in closed form and yields

$$ a_0 = y_0 $$

$$ a_1 = \frac{1}{12h}(y_{-2} - 8y_{-1} + 8y_1 - y_2) $$

$$ a_2 = \frac{1}{24h^2}(-y_{-2} + 16y_{-1} - 30y_0 + 16y_1 - y_2) $$

$$ a_3 = \frac{1}{12h^3}(-y_{-2} + 2y_{-1} - 2y_1 + y_2) $$

$$ a_4 = \frac{1}{24h^4}(y_{-2} - 4y_{-1} + 6y_0 - 4y_1 + y_2) $$

Note that the actual values of the variable x have been lost in the assumption of equal spacing centered on zero; therefore, only the values for y appear in the equations.

Lagrangian Interpolation

Determining an exact fit with a high-order polynomial involves the solution of a linear problem, which requires a numerical-methods procedure, because the matrix is not invertible in closed form (i.e., the inverse cannot be written analytically) and is ill-conditioned. However, by expending the effort to calculate the coefficients, the interpolating polynomial can be evaluated rather quickly at intermediate points. Is it possible to find alternative functions that bypass the solution of the matrix problem? This is the role of the Lagrange polynomials. Consider $n + 1$ polynomials, each of order n:

$$\Pi_0(x) = (x - x_1)(x - x_2) \times \cdots \times (x - x_n)$$

$$\Pi_1(x) = (x - x_0)(x - x_2) \times \cdots \times (x - x_n)$$

$$\Pi_2(x) = (x - x_0)(x - x_1) \times \cdots \times (x - x_n)$$

$$\Pi_i(x) = \prod_{j=0, j \neq i}^{n} (x - x_j)$$

The symbol Π_i is used to denote a polynomial formed by a product, with the subscript denoting the missing term. Now, instead of fitting

$$y = a_0 + a_1 x + \cdots + a_n x^n$$

consider fitting

$$y = a_0 \Pi_0(x) + a_1 \Pi_1(x) + \cdots + a_n \Pi_n(x)$$

As before, the polynomial must match the key points:

$$y_k = a_0 \Pi_0(x_k) + a_1 \Pi_1(x_k) + \cdots + a_n \Pi_n(x_k) \qquad k = 0, \ldots, n$$

However, note that the basis functions are constructed to be zero at all key points except one:

$$\Pi_i(x_j) = 0 \qquad i \neq j$$

This simplifies the problem to

$$y_k = a_k \Pi_k(x_k) \qquad k = 0, \ldots, n$$

or

$$a_k = \frac{y_k}{\Pi_k(x_k)} \qquad k = 0, \ldots, n$$

Each unknown coefficient can be determined independently, without the solution of the matrix equation. Alternatively, one could say that the matrix equation turns out to be diagonal and hence trivial to invert. Therefore,

$$y(x) = y_0 \frac{\Pi_0(x)}{\Pi_0(x_0)} + y_1 \frac{\Pi_1(x)}{\Pi_1(x_1)} + \cdots + y_n \frac{\Pi_n(x)}{\Pi_n(x_n)}$$

or in more compact notation,

$$y(x) = \sum_{i=0}^{n} y_i \prod_{j=0, j \neq i}^{n} \left(\frac{x - x_j}{x_i - x_j} \right)$$

Note that no savings has occurred in computational time for interpolation because each term of the curve fit has a large number of differences and products. Furthermore, these values must be recomputed for different values of x, even for the same curve.

Nonparametric Cubics

A common method for curve fitting involves successive fittings of cubic polynomials over each interval (except, of course, for the first and last intervals). In practice, several cubics are better than one large polynomial (such as 16th order) because they are easier to evaluate at any specific intermediate point. In addition, high-order polynomials tend to display many inflection points that usually do not provide good engineering fits, even though mathematically they fit the N points exactly (higher-order polynomials tend to "wiggle"). Complicated functions are also susceptible to round-off errors.

Four pairs of points, (x_i, y_i), $i = -1, 0, 1, 2$, are used to determine a cubic polynomial

$$y = a_0 + a_1 x + a_2 x^2 + a_3 x^3$$

that is then used over the range $x_0 \leq x \leq x_1$. Another useful form for the cubic fit is the local form; each term is based on $x = x_0$ instead of $x = 0$:

$$y = b_0 + b_1(x - x_0) + b_2(x - x_0)^2 + b_3(x - x_0)^3$$

The four unknowns a_0, a_1, a_2, a_3 can be determined in several ways. The straightforward approach leads directly to the solution of a full 4×4 matrix:

$$\begin{bmatrix} 1 & x_{-1} & x_{-1}^2 & x_{-1}^3 \\ 1 & x_0 & x_0^2 & x_0^3 \\ 1 & x_1 & x_1^2 & x_1^3 \\ 1 & x_2 & x_2^2 & x_2^3 \end{bmatrix} \begin{Bmatrix} a_0 \\ a_1 \\ a_2 \\ a_3 \end{Bmatrix} = \begin{Bmatrix} y_{-1} \\ y_0 \\ y_1 \\ y_2 \end{Bmatrix}$$

This cannot be carried further in general and requires inversion of each particular 4×4 matrix. Note that limiting the situation to equal spacing in x would allow us to proceed further analytically.

Lagrange interpolation allows the coefficients to be found more easily, at the expense of a more complicated function reserved for later evaluation.

$$\begin{aligned} y = \ & c_{-1}(x - x_0)(x - x_1)(x - x_2) \\ & + c_0(x - x_{-1})(x - x_1)(x - x_2) \\ & + c_1(x - x_{-1})(x - x_0)(x - x_2) \\ & + c_2(x - x_{-1})(x - x_0)(x - x_1) \end{aligned}$$

where

$$c_i = \frac{y_i}{\displaystyle\prod_{j=-1, j \neq i}^{2} (x_i - x_j)}$$

Note, cubic fits for adjacent panels provide a curve that is only continuous (C^0), with discontinuities in slope at each point. Figure 2.1 shows 10 points with exact polynomial and piecewise cubic Hermite interpolation (Table 2.1 provides these coordinates). Note that the ninth-order polynomial passes through the points exactly, but provides a rather poor fit. Cubic interpolating polynomials have been determined for each interval or panel. These are only drawn for the active range of each interval. However, in Fig. 2.1b, three adjacent panels are shown over a larger range. For example, the curve for the third panel is determined from the four points x_1, x_2, x_3, x_4 and is intended for use over the range $x_2 < x < x_3$. Figure 2.2 shows an enlarged view of the cubic fits for these three adjacent panels. Even at this scale, the slope discontinuities are difficult to see. Note the trade-off between

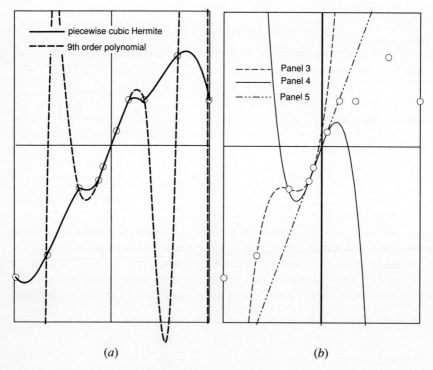

piecewise cubic Hermite

9th order polynomial

Panel 3

Panel 4

Panel 5

(a)   (b)

Figure 2.1 Alternative fits for 11 data points.

x	y
−6.0	−3.0
−4.0	−2.5
−2.0	−1.0
−0.81	−0.81
−0.5	−0.5
0.31	0.31
1.0	1.0
2.0	1.0
4.0	2.0
6.0	1.0

Table 2.1   Data for Fig. 2.1.

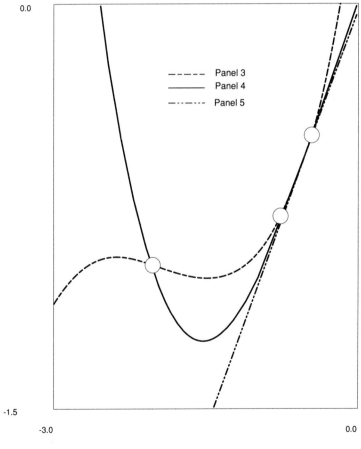

Figure 2.2   Enlarged view of fourth interval in Fig. 2.1.

calculation and data storage. Ten x, y pairs can be replaced by 10 coefficients $(a_0, \ldots, a_9)$ or by nine sets of four cubic coefficients $(a_0, \ldots, a_3)_1$, $(a_0, \ldots, a_3)_2, \ldots, (a_0, \ldots, a_3)_9$.

Assuming that slopes were known at x_0, x_1, the cubic panel could have been fit between x_0 and x_1, matching exactly the value and slope at each endpoint (y_0, y_0', y_1, y_1') rather than four points. This is called *piecewise cubic Hermite interpolation*. Using the local form for the cubic, the coefficients can be evaluated by requiring

$$y_0 = y(x_0)$$
$$y_0' = y'(x_0)$$
$$y_1 = y(x_1)$$
$$y_1' = y'(x_1)$$

yielding

$$b_0 = y_0$$

$$b_1 = y_0'$$

$$b_2 = \frac{3(y_1 - y_0)}{(x_1 - x_0)^2} - \frac{2y_0' + y_1'}{x_1 - x_0}$$

$$b_3 = \frac{-2(y_1 - y_0)}{(x_1 - x_0)^3} + \frac{y_0' + y_1'}{(x_1 - x_0)^2}$$

While this is conceptually attractive, usually a tabular function does not provide information on derivatives. If the slopes at each point are developed numerically, it is called *piecewise cubic Bessel interpolation*.

$$y_0' = \frac{y_1 - y_{-1}}{x_1 - x_{-1}}$$

$$y_1' = \frac{y_2 - y_0}{x_2 - x_0}$$

Note that if the slopes are chosen consistently for all panels, either of the preceding equations will result in a C^1 curve (one that has continuous values for slope).

The effects of any changes are somewhat localized. Changing y_i or x_i only affects four cubic functions or "intervals." The local or global extent of changes to basis points becomes more important in geometry representation than in functional representation.

The end panels require special consideration. One possibility is to fit the cubic using the four points x_0, x_1, x_2, x_3. Of course, this is simply the cubic for the second panel between (x_1, x_2). Another alternative arbitrarily sets a slope for the end, in which case the cubic would be determined from dy/dx (evaluated at x_0), x_0, x_1, x_2. This is useful if the slope were known to be zero or periodic (matching dy/dx evaluated at x_n). The third possible method adds a phantom point x_{-1} at a location chosen by the analyst. This arbitrary manual intervention is often used in geometry creation.

Parametric Space Curves

Moving to higher dimensions such as a curve in 3-space or a function of two or more variables complicates the situation. A function of two variables can be thought of as a surface, and so that topic will be discussed in Chapter 9, Geometry. However, the topics presented in Chapter 9 are also useful to higher-order function approximation. The reader can use the material developed there for higher-dimensional "curve" fitting.

Returning to space curves, when viewing y and z as functions of x,

$$y = y(x)$$
$$z = z(x)$$

the preceding sections apply. An alternative method develops a space curve at the intersection of two surfaces:

$$g(x, y, z) = 0$$
$$h(x, y, z) = 0$$

The strength of these approaches is that the representation can be maintained in analytical form.

Although the analytical approaches to curve definition have great value, they also have serious limitations. The resulting curves are not independent of the axes chosen to evaluate them. Vertical tangents may not be possible. For instance, the cubic functions just developed do not permit vertical tangency $(dy/dx = \infty)$. Finally, and most importantly, the basic equations may not easily represent the multi-valued nature of the curve.

Parametric representation is the solution to these limitations:

$$x = x(t)$$
$$y = y(t)$$
$$z = z(t)$$

where t can be thought of as a path-length coordinate or distance along the curve.

For example, a helix with radius r and pitch p is given by

$$x = r \cos t$$
$$y = r \sin t$$
$$z = pt$$

Note that an infinite number of representations are possible, depending on the scale desired along the path. The scale for t is frequently chosen as $0 \le t \le 1$ over the range of interest.

The preceding section on nonparametric cubics can now be reinterpreted as three cubic functions for x, y, z, respectively. For simplicity, let

$$
\begin{array}{ll}
t = -1 & \text{at point } -1 \\
t = 0 & \text{at point } 0 \\
t = 1 & \text{at point } 1 \\
t = 2 & \text{at point } 2
\end{array}
$$

then,

$$
\begin{aligned}
x &= b_{x0} + b_{x1}t + b_{x2}t^2 + b_{x3}t^3 \\
y &= b_{y0} + b_{y1}t + b_{y2}t^2 + b_{y3}t^3 \\
z &= b_{z0} + b_{z1}t + b_{z2}t^2 + b_{z3}t^3
\end{aligned}
$$

Note that under these assumptions the general cubic and the local cubic reduce to the same form. In this context, the straightforward cubic fit through four points leads to

$$
\begin{Bmatrix} b_{x0} \\ b_{x1} \\ b_{x2} \\ b_{x3} \end{Bmatrix} =
\begin{bmatrix}
0 & 1 & 0 & 0 \\
-\frac{1}{3} & -\frac{1}{2} & 1 & -\frac{1}{6} \\
\frac{1}{2} & -1 & \frac{1}{2} & 0 \\
-\frac{1}{6} & \frac{1}{2} & -\frac{1}{2} & \frac{1}{6}
\end{bmatrix}
\begin{Bmatrix} x_{-1} \\ x_0 \\ x_1 \\ x_2 \end{Bmatrix}
$$

Lagrange interpolation over equally spaced points leads to

$$
c_{x,-1} = -\frac{1}{6}x_{-1}
$$

$$
c_{x0} = \frac{1}{2}x_0
$$

$$
c_{x1} = -\frac{1}{2}x_1
$$

$$
c_{x2} = \frac{1}{6}x_2
$$

In general, values for $dx/dt, dy/dt, dz/dt$ will not be available, so piecewise cubic Hermite interpolation is impractical. However, piecewise cubic Bessel interpolation leads to

$$
x_0' = \frac{x_1 - x_{-1}}{2}
$$

$$
x_1' = \frac{x_2 - x_0}{2}
$$

Then

$$b_{x0} = x_0$$

$$b_{x1} = -\frac{1}{2}x_{-1} + \frac{1}{2}x_1$$

$$b_{x2} = x_{-1} - \frac{5}{2}x_0 + 2x_1 - \frac{1}{2}x_2$$

$$b_{x3} = -\frac{1}{2}x_{-1} + \frac{3}{2}x_0 - \frac{3}{2}x_1 + \frac{1}{2}x_2$$

or

$$\begin{Bmatrix} b_{x0} \\ b_{x1} \\ b_{x2} \\ b_{x3} \end{Bmatrix} = \begin{bmatrix} 0 & 1 & 0 & 0 \\ -\frac{1}{2} & 0 & \frac{1}{2} & 0 \\ 1 & -\frac{5}{2} & 2 & -\frac{1}{2} \\ -\frac{1}{2} & \frac{3}{2} & -\frac{3}{2} & \frac{1}{2} \end{bmatrix} \begin{Bmatrix} x_{-1} \\ x_0 \\ x_1 \\ x_2 \end{Bmatrix}$$

Note that the evaluation of (x, y, z) can be cast as a matrix multiplication

$$\begin{Bmatrix} x & y & z \end{Bmatrix} = \begin{Bmatrix} 1 & t & t^2 & t^3 \end{Bmatrix} \begin{bmatrix} b_{x0} & b_{y0} & b_{z0} \\ b_{x1} & b_{y1} & b_{z1} \\ b_{x2} & b_{y2} & b_{z2} \\ b_{x3} & b_{y3} & b_{z3} \end{bmatrix}$$

and so

$$\begin{Bmatrix} x & y & z \end{Bmatrix} = \begin{Bmatrix} 1 & t & t^2 & t^3 \end{Bmatrix} \begin{bmatrix} 0 & 1 & 0 & 0 \\ -\frac{1}{2} & 0 & \frac{1}{2} & 0 \\ 1 & -\frac{5}{2} & 2 & -\frac{1}{2} \\ -\frac{1}{2} & \frac{3}{2} & -\frac{3}{2} & \frac{1}{2} \end{bmatrix} \begin{bmatrix} x_{-1} & y_{-1} & z_{-1} \\ x_0 & y_0 & z_0 \\ x_1 & y_1 & z_1 \\ x_2 & y_2 & z_2 \end{bmatrix}$$

As we will discuss in Chapter 7, it is becoming more common for engineering workstations to have custom hardware which performs 4×4 matrix multiplication. This means that the parametric curves, as written above, can be evaluated extremely quickly.

■ **EXERCISE 2.1:** Determine closed-form expressions for the coefficients of a quadratic polynomial that was fit through three equally spaced points centered on zero.

■ **EXERCISE 2.2:** Simplify the Lagrangian interpolation formula for equally spaced values of x. Show that if $n = 5$, the result is the same as in Example 2.2.

■ **EXERCISE 2.3:** What curve is described by

$$x = e^{-t} \cos 12\pi t$$

$$y = e^{-t} \sin 12\pi t$$

$$z = e^t$$

2.3   LEAST-SQUARE CURVE FITTING

As discussed at the beginning of this chapter, one form of curve fitting attempts to use a single rather simple function to approximate several points without passing through any of the points exactly. This "best fit" is achieved by minimizing an error criterion for the curve. Consider M points and an approximating curve of

$$y = f(x)$$

Each point x_i, y_i will produce an error E_i (sometimes called a residual), which may be defined as

$$E_i = y_i - f(x_i)$$

and the entire error vector can be written as

$$\mathbf{E} = \left\{ \begin{array}{c} E_1 \\ E_2 \\ \vdots \\ E_M \end{array} \right\}$$

The goal is to determine $f(x)$ such that the norm of $\mathbf{E}$ is minimized. The selection of a norm is central to the process because $\mathbf{E}$ must be converted from a vector to a scalar for minimization. Different approximations are obtained depending on the choice of the norm (and on the choice of the error). Three common norms that can be used are

$$\text{norm}(\mathbf{E}) = \max_i |E_i(x)|$$

$$\text{norm}(\mathbf{E}) = \sum_i |E_i(x)|$$

$$|\mathbf{E}|^2 = \sum_{i=1}^{M} w_i E_i^2(x)$$

Example 2.3: Consider a straight line fit to M points:

$$y = ax + b$$

The goal is to determine a, b such that

$$y_i \simeq ax_i + b$$

Using the vertical deviation from the line as the definition for the error,

$$E_i = y_i - ax_i - b$$

and using the square norm of $\mathbf{E}$,

$$|\mathbf{E}|^2 = \sum (y_i - ax_i - b)^2$$

This must be minimized by variation of a and b. At the minimum value, the partial of the norm with respect to the variables must be zero:

$$0 = \frac{\partial |\mathbf{E}|^2}{\partial a} = -2 \sum x_i (y_i - ax_i - b)$$

$$0 = \frac{\partial |\mathbf{E}|^2}{\partial b} = -2 \sum (y_i - ax_i - b)$$

This produces two equations in the two unknowns a, b, which can be written as

$$\sum x_i y_i = a \sum x_i^2 + b \sum x_i$$
$$\sum y_i = a \sum x_i + b \sum 1$$

or written in matrix notation as

$$\begin{bmatrix} \sum 1 & \sum x_i \\ \sum x_i & \sum x_i^2 \end{bmatrix} \begin{Bmatrix} b \\ a \end{Bmatrix} = \begin{Bmatrix} \sum y_i \\ \sum x_i y_i \end{Bmatrix}$$

Each summation is over M data points. Solving this matrix equation yields the least square values for a, b.

Ordinary Polynomials

The least square fit of an Nth-order polynomial can be determined by generalizing from the preceding example:

$$y = a_0 + a_1 x + a_2 x^2 + \cdots + a_N x^N$$

The error to be minimized is

$$\text{minimize} \quad \sum_{i=1}^{M} (y_i - a_0 - a_1 x_i - a_2 x_i^2 - \cdots - a_N x_i^N)^2$$

The necessary conditions for the minimum are

$$0 = \frac{\partial |\mathbf{E}|^2}{\partial a_k} = -2 \sum_{i=1}^{M} (y_i - a_0 - a_1 x_i - a_2 x_i^2 - \cdots - a_N x_i^N) x_i^k$$

$$\text{for} \quad k = 0, 1, 2, \ldots, N$$

Rearranging as before into matrix formulation yields

$$\begin{bmatrix} \sum 1 & \sum x_i & \cdots & \sum x_i^N \\ \sum x_i & \sum x_i^2 & \cdots & \sum x_i^{N+1} \\ \vdots & \vdots & \ddots & \vdots \\ \sum x_i^N & \sum x_i^{N+1} & \cdots & \sum x_i^{2N} \end{bmatrix} \begin{Bmatrix} a_0 \\ a_1 \\ \vdots \\ a_N \end{Bmatrix} = \begin{Bmatrix} \sum y_i \\ \sum y_i x_i \\ \vdots \\ \sum y_i x_i^N \end{Bmatrix}$$

Therefore, an Nth-order least-square fit requires the solution of an $N + 1 \times N + 1$ matrix problem.

Arbitrary Functions

Any set of basis functions, not just normal polynomials, can be used to describe the approximating function. The previous section used functions $f_i = x^i$. Consider $N + 1$ arbitrary functions $f_i(x)$ and the approximation

$$y = a_0 f_0(x) + a_1 f_1(x) + a_2 f_2(x) + \cdots + a_N f_N(x)$$

The least-square optimization can be stated as

minimize w.r.t. a_k

$$\sum_{i=1}^{M} [y_i - a_0 f_0(x_i) - a_1 f_1(x_i) - a_2 f_2(x_i) - \cdots - a_N f_N(x_i)]^2$$

The necessary conditions for the minimum are

$$0 = \frac{\partial E}{\partial a_k} \qquad k = 0, \ldots, N$$

or

$$0 = -2 \sum_{i=1}^{M} f_k(x_i) \left[y_i - a_0 f_0(x_i) - a_1 f_1(x_i) - a_2 f_2(x_i) - \cdots - a_N f_N(x_i) \right]$$

$$\text{for} \quad k = 0, 1, 2, \ldots, N$$

Rearranging into matrix notation gives

$$\begin{bmatrix} S_{00} & S_{01} & \cdots & S_{0N} \\ S_{10} & S_{11} & \cdots & S_{1N} \\ \vdots & \vdots & \ddots & \vdots \\ S_{N0} & S_{N1} & \cdots & S_{NN} \end{bmatrix} \begin{Bmatrix} a_0 \\ a_1 \\ \vdots \\ a_N \end{Bmatrix} = \begin{Bmatrix} T_0 \\ T_1 \\ \vdots \\ T_N \end{Bmatrix}$$

where

$$S_{kj} = \sum_{i=1}^{M} f_k(x_i) f_j(x_i)$$

$$T_k = \sum_{i=1}^{M} y_i f_k(x_i)$$

The ease of solution will depend upon the basis functions.

Orthogonal Series Expansion

The numerical complexity of the least-square problem decreases significantly for orthogonal functions. Specifically, the problem can be formulated so that the resulting matrix is diagonal. To better understand the results, consider first the technique for series expansion of a function using orthogonal basis functions. Note that in most cases, series expansion is the same as a least-square fit of N terms through N points, in other words, $N + 1 = M$.

$$F(x) = \sum_{j=0}^{\infty} a_j f_j(x)$$

If the basis functions are orthogonal, which means,

$$\int_a^b f_j(x) f_k(x)\, dx = 0 \qquad j \neq k$$

then the unknown coefficients can be determined as

$$a_j = \frac{\int_a^b F(x) f_j(x)\, dx}{\int_a^b f_j^2(x)\, dx}$$

For a set of M equally spaced discrete points, the integration can be changed to a summation:

$$a_j = \frac{\sum_{j=1}^{M} F(x) f_j(x)\, dx}{\sum_{j=1}^{M} f_j^2(x)\, dx}$$

The denominator can be precalculated, and each coefficient can be determined individually. The orthogonality condition means that the off-diagonal terms (S_{jk}) in the resulting matrix equation that was developed in the previous subsection will be zero.

$$\int_a^b f_j(x) f_k(x)\, dx = \sum_{j=1}^{M} f_j(x_j) f_k(x_j)\, dx = 0$$

Thus the Nth-order problem is diagonal and trivial to solve. It is important to remember that orthogonality is defined over a specific range (a, b), and that functions are not orthogonal over arbitrary ranges.

Legendre Polynomials

The preceding standard least-squares polynomial fit used basis functions $(f_j(x) = x^j)$ that are not orthogonal. If the function to be approximated is mapped into the interval $-1 \leq x \leq 1$ and the points are equally spaced in x, then it is possible to avoid the matrix inversion by using Legendre polynomials, which happen to be orthogonal over that range:

$$P_0(x) = 1$$

$$P_1(x) = x$$

$$P_2(x) = \frac{3x^2 - 1}{2}$$

$$P_3(x) = \frac{5x^3 - 3x}{2}$$

$$P_4(x) = \frac{35x^4 - 30x^2 + 3}{8}$$

$$P_{n+1} = \frac{(2n + 1)x P_n - n P_{n-1}}{(n + 1)}$$

Legendre polynomials provide a basis for rapid curve fitting because each coefficient can be determined independently. This is an advantage if one wishes to increase the order of an existing polynomial fit.

Chebyshev Polynomials

The final candidate for basis functions are the Chebyshev (Tschebysheff) polynomials. These are chosen so as to give a maximum value of ± 1 over the range $-1 \leq x \leq 1$.

$$T_0 = 1$$

$$T_1 = x$$

$$T_2 = 2x^2 - 1$$

$$T_3 = 4x^3 - 3x$$

$$T_4 = 8x^4 - 8x^2 + 1$$

$$T_{n+1} = 2x T_n - T_{n-1}$$

This basis is used to yield solutions with equally distributed error instead of the usual results, which contain larger errors near the ends of the range.

Fourier Series

The coefficients of the classical Fourier series,

$$y = \frac{a_0}{2} + \sum_{j=1}^{\infty} a_j \cos \frac{2\pi j}{L} x + \sum_{j=1}^{\infty} b_j \sin \frac{2\pi j}{L} x$$

$$a_j = \frac{2}{L} \int_0^L y(x) \cos \frac{2\pi j x}{L} \, dx$$

can be determined in a similar fashion. Harmonics of sine and cosine are orthogonal over the range $0, 2\pi$—something useful to remember when deriving the equation for a_j. The discrete evaluation is also orthogonal, given $2N$ points that are equally spaced over the interval $0, 2\pi$, and the discrete Fourier coefficients are given by

$$A_j = \frac{1}{N} \sum_{i=0}^{2N-1} y(x_i) \cos \frac{2\pi j x_i}{L}$$

This equation shows the connection between least-square curve fitting and Fourier series expansion. However, the reader should be warned that the preceding equation is not the most efficient method for calculating Fourier coefficients unless only a few low harmonics are of interest. If the number of samples is an integer power of two, 2^M, the Fast Fourier Transform (FFT) can calculate the coefficients substantially faster than the Fourier transform as developed above. Most numerical methods libraries include the FFT procedure.

Nonlinear Least Squares

All of the preceding sections have dealt with linear least-square problems. The linearity in linear least squares refers to the system of equations that results from the minimization criteria. A linear least-square problem does not necessarily mean a straight-line fit. Some function approximations, however, do not lead to a linear system of equations. Specifically, a nonlinear least-square problem results if $\partial^2/(\partial a_i \partial a_j) \neq 0$.

For example, consider experimental data taken from an exponential decay problem. Based on physical considerations, it is known that the shape of the functions should be

$$y(x) = a e^{-bx}$$

The error can be written as

$$E = \sum (y_i - a e^{-bx_i})^2$$

The necessary conditions for minimization yield

$$0 = \frac{\partial E}{\partial a} = -2 \sum x_i e^{-bx_i}(y_i - a e^{-bx_i})$$

$$0 = \frac{\partial E}{\partial b} = 2 \sum x_i(y_i - a e^{-bx_i}) e^{-bx_i}$$

This must be solved to find the values of a, b. There are two approaches to solving this problem:

1. Solve it as a true system of N nonlinear equations.
2. Shift to some form that will give a linear form for the unknown coefficients.

The latter approach recognizes that an exponential curve is a straight line on a log plot. A shift to a linear occurrence of the unknown coefficient

$$\ln y = \ln a - bx$$

leads to a linear least-square problem. This will give the best fit in a $\ln y$ versus x plot. Although solving the least-square problem in log space will not give the same value for b as solving the nonlinear equation, it is often acceptable.

Another example of shifting to a more acceptable shape involves the identification of the natural frequency and damping ratio for a second-order system from experimental data. That is, what is ω_n and ζ such that

$$H_{x/y} = \frac{1}{1 - \omega^2/\omega_n^2 + 2j\zeta(\omega/\omega_n)}$$

In a polar plot of $H_{x/y}$, the ideal frequency response of a second-order system is a circle, which can be rather easily fit.

Many problems, however, require a solution of the nonlinear equations. This can sometimes be constructed without resorting to numerical methods packages. For instance, consider the step response from non-zero initial conditions of a first-order system, which can be written as

$$y = a + be^{cx}$$

In this case, the unknowns are a, b, and c, from which the initial value $y(0)$, the final value $y(\infty)$, and the time constant $1/c$, can be determined. The necessary conditions for minimization yield three equations in three unknowns:

$$0 = \sum_{i=1}^{M}(y_i - a - be^{cx_i})$$

$$0 = \sum_{i=1}^{M}(y_i - a - be^{cx_i})(-e^{cx_i})$$

$$0 = \sum_{i=1}^{M}(y_i - a - be^{cx_i})(-x_i be^{cx_i})$$

If a value were known for a, the problem could be converted to a linear problem in $\ln b$ and c:

$$\ln(y - a) = \ln b + cx$$

This motivates the following approach:

1. Guess at a

2. Fit preceding for c and $\ln b$

3. Update a using $0 = \partial E/\partial a = \sum -2(y - a - be^{cx})$ and loop

An alternative is to

1. Guess at c
2. Fit a and b
3. Change c using $\partial E/\partial c = \sum -2bx\,e^{cx}(y - a - be^{cx})$

We will explore the topic of root finding later in Section 2.7.

Example 2.4: How to Fit a Circle. Given several points which are thought to lie on a circle, what are x_c, y_c, r such that

$$(x - x_c)^2 + (y - y_c)^2 = r^2$$

The equation of the circle can be rewritten as

$$(r^2 - y_c^2 - x_c^2) + 2x_i x_c + 2y_i y_c = x_i^2 + y_i^2$$

To obtain a form with linearly occurring unknown coefficients, write the equation as

$$z + 2x_i x_c + 2y_i y_c = x_i^2 + y_i^2$$

The unknowns are x_c, y_c, and z. Once they are known, r can be determined easily.

■ **EXERCISE 2.4:** Many interactive programs for personal computers or workstations can perform least square fits to various orders using various basis functions. Fortunately, these programs provide graphing tools also. Create a data set of 10 points and explore different orders of polynomial fit. Investigate sensitivity to changes in data points. Look for pathological and limiting cases.

2.4 SPLINES

Historically, the *spline* is a thin flexible strip (often wooden) that was passed through a number of heavy weights and allowed to take up its natural intermediate shape. The intermediate shape could then be transferred to a workpiece. This step was part of the process known as lofting a curve. The term lofting comes from the time when the shapes for boat hulls and sails were created at full scale in a loft over the workshop. The intermediate shape of the physical spline can be calculated by analyzing the strip as a beam passing through a number of frictionless pinned joints. Curvature, the second derivative, is related to the bending moment, so if no moment input is allowed at the pins, then the slopes and curvature will be continuous for the length of the spline. This method leads to aesthetically pleasing curves, although the drawback is that no single section can be determined independently. This may pose problems if the technique is used on tabular data that may be frequently modified. In contrast, the methods discussed earlier simply would have required recalculation of the four coefficients for four sections, two to each side of any change.

Consider a situation with $M + 1$ points $(x_i, y_i, i = 0, \ldots, M)$ and therefore M panels. Define $q_i(\tilde{x})$ for each panel

$$q_i(\tilde{x}) = a_{0i} + a_1^i \tilde{x} + a_{2i}\tilde{x}^2 + a_{3i}\tilde{x}^3$$

Note that $\tilde{x}$ is a local normalized variable defined within each panel such that $0 < \tilde{x} < 1$ within each panel. The M panels contain $4M$ constants and thus $4M$ constraints that must be identified. Half of these constraints result from requiring panels to match at the control points:

$$q_i(1) = y_i = q_{i+1}(0)$$

The next $2M - 2$ constraints come from matching slopes and curvature at each control point:

$$q_i'(1) = q_{i+1}'(0)$$
$$q_i''(1) = q_{i+1}''(0)$$

There are only $2M - 2$ constraints here because the end points cannot be matched in this way. Typically each of the final two constraints chosen are one of the following: (a) specified slope, (b) zero curvature (free moment boundary condition), or (c) continuous closed curve.

As one might expect, carefully choosing the form of the cubic used in each panel reduces the algebraic complexity. A proper choice can satisfy some of the constraints trivially. The following form as presented by Shoup ensures that each cubic panel passes through the control points:

$$
\begin{aligned}
q_i(\tilde{x}) = {}& y_i\tilde{x} + y_{i-1}(1 - \tilde{x}) \\
& + \Delta x_{i,i-1}\left(b_{i-1} - \frac{\Delta y_{i,i-1}}{\Delta x_{i,i-1}}\right)\tilde{x}(1 - \tilde{x})^2 \\
& - \Delta x_{i+1,i}\left(b_i - \frac{\Delta y_{i,i-1}}{\Delta x_{i,i-1}}\right)\tilde{x}^2(1 - \tilde{x})
\end{aligned}
$$

where

$$\Delta x_{ij} = x_i - x_j \qquad \Delta y_{ij} = y_i - y_j$$

The slope constraint also is satisfied automatically by this form. Now only $M + 1$ constants remain to be evaluated ($b_i, i = 0, \ldots, M$). The curvature requirement leads to a single equation at each internal point and a special form of that equation for each end point. Assuming zero curvature (free end) results in a matrix of tri-diagonal form that can be easily solved by Gaussian elimination, or iteration (because the matrix is diagonally dominant):

$$
\begin{bmatrix}
2 & 1 & 0 & \cdots & 0 & 0 \\
\Delta x_{21} & 2\Delta x_{20} & \Delta x_{10} & \cdots & 0 & 0 \\
0 & \Delta x_{32} & 2\Delta x_{31} & \cdots & \vdots & \vdots \\
\vdots & \vdots & \vdots & \ddots & \vdots & \Delta x_{M-1,M-2} \\
0 & 0 & 0 & \cdots & 1 & 2
\end{bmatrix}
\begin{Bmatrix}
b_0 \\ b_1 \\ \vdots \\ b_M
\end{Bmatrix}
=
\begin{Bmatrix}
\Delta y_{10}/\Delta x_{10} \\ \vdots \\ c_i \\ \vdots \\ \Delta y_{M,M-1}/\Delta x_{M,M-1}
\end{Bmatrix}
$$

where

$$c_i = \frac{\Delta y_{i,i-1} \Delta x_{i+1,i}}{\Delta x_{i,i-1}} + \frac{\Delta y_{i+1,i} \Delta x_{i,i-1}}{\Delta x_{i+1,i}}, \qquad i = 2, \ldots, M-1$$

Requiring a continuous closed curve yields a matrix that is almost tri-diagonal, with the exception that entries at positions $(1, M+1)$ and $(M+1, 1)$ are nonzero.

The method as presented in theory will develop difficulties in practice because of steep slopes or multi-valued curves. The fundamental cubic simply cannot represent these features. Two modifications can be used to avoid these difficulties. For each panel, *local axis transformation* is developed, using a coordinate system based on the end of the panel and defined by the slope of a straight line between points i and $i+1$. Then the cubic equation is developed in the local reference frame, denoted by ξ, η. To evaluate the coordinates of points along the spline requires the value θ in addition to the constants b_i. Note, that the coordinates (ξ, η) must be transformed back into (x, y) space for use. Also note that the adjacent control points must be transformed into (ξ, η) to determine the coefficients.

The local axis transformation is not sufficient to produce splines for arbitrary control points because each panel, being cubic, must be single valued. The more general solution is a parametric representation. In this case, the indices, rather than simply being integers, can be interpreted as a measure of path length. All problems with slopes or multiple values disappear.

$$x = x(s)$$
$$0 \le s \le M$$
$$y = y(s)$$

with control points (x_i, y_i, s_i), $i = 0, \ldots, M$. For convenience, s_i is usually assigned the value $s_i = i$. However, this is in no sense required.

The spline has been developed here with cubic panels as the basis. It is possible to extend the concept to higher-order interpolation functions that would provide higher-order continuity (i.e., beyond C^2). The student may understand this better by reducing order instead of increasing it. A series of straight lines connecting the points can be interpreted as a first-order spline. Further discussion of splines, B-splines, and Bezier curves can be found in Chapter 9.

■ **EXERCISE 2.5:** Choose a set of 10 ordered (x, y) pairs, and assign a value of $s = 0, 1, \ldots, 9$ to each pair, in order. Then develop the parametric cubic spline. Using any available graphing or plotting tool, observe the resulting curve. Finally, explore for pathological and limiting cases. Note, that if 3-D graphics utilities are available, use triplets (x, y, z) and generate a space curve.

2.5   DIFFERENTIATION

The objective of numerical differentiation is to approximate the derivative of an unknown function, given only certain discrete evaluations of the function. Although there are several approaches to this topic, we will use the method of analytical approximation to develop a function that can be analytically differentiated.

Consider first the problem of approximating the first derivative of a function at a specific point. From calculus, this is known to be the limit

$$\frac{dy}{dx} = \lim_{\epsilon \to 0} \frac{y(x + \epsilon) - y(x)}{\epsilon}$$

This formula can be used to approximate the derivative by choosing a value of ϵ (most probably the spacing of the data). This will be a first order approximation, whether ϵ is chosen positive or negative. The best way to understand the derivation of higher-order derivatives is to start with an analytical approximation. Note that this approach will lay the groundwork for the derivation of differentiation formulae either for nonequally spaced data or for differentiation intermediate to the control points. These extensions are left as an optional exercise for the reader.

Consider a fourth-order approximation to the first derivative of y, given $y_{-2}, y_{-1}, y_0, y_1, y_2$ and equal spacing h. Note that given the assumption of equal spacing, the actual values for $x_{-2}, x_{-1}, x_0, x_1, x_2$ are irrelevant. A fourth-order approximation to the function can be written as

$$y = P_4(x) = a_4 x^4 + a_3 x^3 + a_2 x^2 + a_1 x + a_0$$

where a_4, a_3, a_2, a_1, a_0 are given in Example 2.2. The derivative at *any* location is approximated by

$$\frac{dy}{dx} = 4a_4 x^3 + 3a_3 x^2 + 2a_2 x + a_1$$

and specifically at x_0 by

$$\left.\frac{dy}{dx}\right|_0 = a_1 = \frac{1}{12h}(y_{-2} - 8y_{-1} + 8y_1 - y_2)$$

This can be written as $1/(12h)$ and $(1, -8, 0, 8, 1)$, an operator molecule to be applied at the desired location in the table of y values. Figures 2.3–2.6 show operator molecules for various order approximations to first, second, third, and fourth derivatives.

Applying the molecules at the beginning or end of a data set reveals an obvious problem: The molecules extend beyond the data set. This leads to the need for nonsymmetric operators. Almost 100 percent of the operators in use are either symmetric or biased entirely to the left or right. The slope of the fourth-order approximating polynomial can be evaluated at the end of

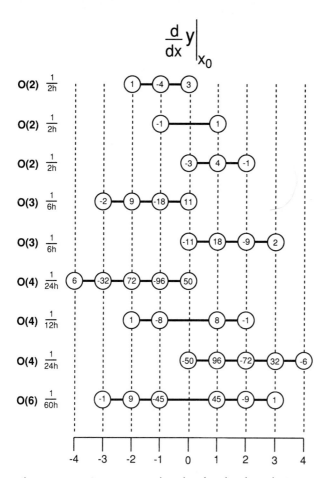

Figure 2.3 Operator molecules for the first derivative.

the interval as

$$\frac{dy}{dx}\bigg|_2 = 4a_4(2h)^3 + 3a_3(2h)^2 + 2a_2(2h) + a_1$$

which yields

$$\frac{dy}{dx}\bigg|_2 = \frac{1}{24h}(6y_{-2} - 32y_{-1} + 72y_0 - 96y_1 + 50y_2)$$

However, differentiation formulae are always written as applying at the point where $x = 0$. This is easily achieved by shifting the indices of the previous equation:

$$\frac{dy}{dx}\bigg|_0 = \frac{1}{24h}(6y_{-4} - 32y_{-3} + 72y_{-2} - 96y_{-1} + 50y_0)$$

This is seen to be one of the $O(4)$ operators in Fig. 2.3.

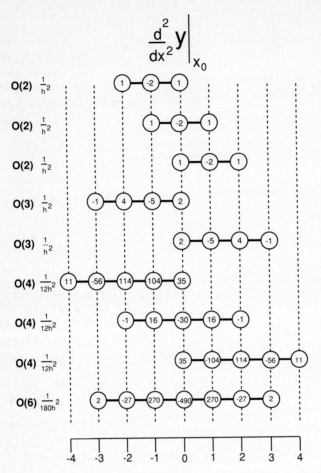

Figure 2.4 Operator molecules for the second derivative.

Although not commonly used, double-sided but nonsymmetric molecules can be derived. For instance, at x_1,

$$\left.\frac{dy}{dx}\right|_1 = 4a_4h^3 + 3a_3h^2 + 2a_2h + a_1$$

Once again, substituting for a_i from Example 2.2 and shifting the indices yields

$$\left.\frac{dy}{dx}\right|_0 = \frac{1}{12h}(-y_{-3} + 6y_{-2} - 18y_{-1} + 10y_0 + 3y_1)$$

Additional mention of numerical differentiation can be found in Section 4.10, which discusses finite-difference operators for the solution of field equations. For now, the reader should note that the molecules presented are one-dimensional finite-difference operators.

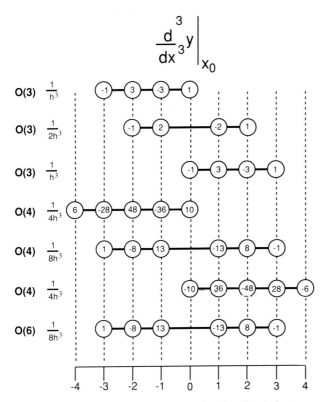

Figure 2.5   Operator molecules for the third derivative.

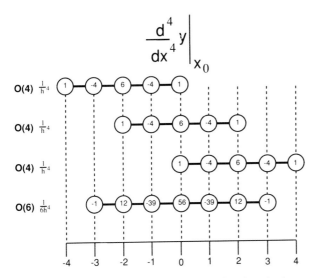

Figure 2.6   Operator molecules for the fourth derivative.

■ **EXERCISE 2.6:** Derive a second-order forward-based approximation to the second derivative.

■ **EXERCISE 2.7:** Derive a second-order approximation to the first derivative dy/dx evaluated at $x = 0.75h$.

■ **EXERCISE 2.8:** Derive a second-order central-based approximation to the second derivative for nonequally spaced values of x. Use the notation $(-a, y_{-1})$, $(0, y_0)$, (b, y_1).

2.6 INTEGRATION BASED ON LAGRANGE INTERPOLATION

The integral of an unknown function, represented by n points, can be determined by integrating the analytical approximation. If Lagrange interpolation is used, then the integral can be written as

$$\int_a^b f(x)\,dx = \int_a^b \sum_{i=0}^n \prod_{j=0, j \neq i}^n \left(\frac{x - x_j}{x_i - x_j} \right) y_i \, dx$$

As a specific example, when using three centrally located and equally spaced points (h), the Lagrange interpolation can be written as

$$\sum_{i=-1}^1 \prod_{j=-1, j \neq i}^1 = \frac{x(x - h)}{2h^2} y_{-1} + \frac{(x - h)(x + h)}{-h^2} y_0 + \frac{(x + h)x}{2h^2} y_1$$

which rearranges to

$$\sum_{i=-1}^1 \prod_{j=-1, j \neq i}^1 = \frac{y_{-1} - 2y_0 + y_1}{2h^2} x^2 + \frac{y_1 - y_{-1}}{2h} x + y_0$$

Note that this is exactly the same result as would be found by fitting a cubic polynomial through the three points. Continuing and integrating over the two panels $(-h, h)$ yields

$$\int_{-h}^h = \frac{h}{3}(y_{-1} + 4y_0 + y_1)$$

This forms the basis for the well-known Simpson's rule. The integral over a range (a, b) requires an odd number of points (counting the ends), which gives an even number of panels. Repetitively applying the preceding formula gives

$$\int_a^b f(x)\,dx = \frac{h}{2}(y_0 + 4y_1 + 2y_2 + 4y_3 + \cdots + 2y_{n-2} + 4y_{n-1} + y_n)$$

An alternative derivation of Simpson's rule follows:

$$\int_{-h}^{h} f(x)\, dx = w_{-1}y_{-1} + w_0 y_0 + w_1 y_1$$

where the w values are constants, to be determined by requiring the preceding formula to give the exact result for the following three cases:

$$f(x) = 1$$
$$f(x) = x$$
$$f(x) = x^2$$

That is,

$$\int_{-h}^{h} dx = 2h = w_{-1}y_{-1} + w_0 y_0 + w_1 y_1$$

$$\int_{-h}^{h} x\, dx = 0 = w_{-1}y_{-1} + w_0 y_0 + w_1 y_1$$

$$\int_{-h}^{h} x^2\, dx = \frac{2}{3}h^3 = w_{-1}y_{\,1} + w_0 y_0 + w_1 y_1$$

The order of accuracy of the integration is determined by the order of accuracy of the analytical approximation. Like the differentiation molecules, the formulae can also be presented as molecules.

2.7   ROOT FINDING

This section discusses finding the real roots of a single transcendental equation. Although simultaneous equations are much more common, we begin the discussion with single-equation solution for simplicity. As we will see later, the Secant Method, Newton's Method, and Successive Approximation will generalize easily. Complex roots can be viewed as roots of two simultaneous equations. Polynomials use specialized techniques such as the Lin-Bairstow method because the number of roots are known and, if complex, occur in conjugate pairs.

The objectives of a root-finding technique are fast, guaranteed convergence to all roots. Unfortunately, this is impossible to achieve, mainly because of the uncertainty about the number of roots to an arbitrary function. Fortunately, most problems have a range or interval of interest that can narrow the search. Furthermore, in design situations one is often performing redesign or parameter studies, and so good estimates might be available.

In beginning with an unknown function, one technique simply scans the range at specific points, evaluating the function and looking for a sign change. However, the reader can imagine the difficulties in determining a step size without missing two closely spaced roots. This technique can be used to scan $-\infty$ to $+\infty$ by rewriting the function, using $z = 1/x$, and/or employing a logarithmic scan (rather than equally spaced).

The common root-finding algorithms include

- Interval halving
- False position
- Secant method
- Newton's method

Interval Halving

A sign change in the function value indicates the presence of a root. The *binary chop* method samples the midpoint and retains the resulting half-size interval known to contain the root indicated by the sign change. Although this algorithm is extremely easy to implement, it also suffers from many disadvantages.

The greatest disadvantage is having to initially identify an interval that straddles a root. For example, two roots relatively close together are extremely difficult to detect. Given an odd number of roots in the interval, only one will be found. Finally, algorithms will converge on the pathological case of a pole, [i.e. $1/(x - 3)$].

False Position

This algorithm uses more information than simply the sign of the function value. Given a sign change $f_1 f_2 < 0$, if $|f_2| < |f_1|$, a point closer to x_2 is a better guess than the midpoint. Using straight-line interpolation between x_1, x_2, the root is estimated as

$$x_3 = x_1 - f_1 \frac{x_2 - x_1}{f_2 - f_1}$$

This is another application of analytic approximation. Given x_3 and the resulting f_3, the dilemma centers on narrowing the interval: Which side should be kept? The conservative technique will always straddle the root by maintaining a sign change between the ends of the new interval.

$$\text{if } f_3 f_2 < 0 \quad \text{then } x_1 \Leftarrow x_3$$
$$\text{if } f_3 f_2 > 0 \quad \text{then } x_2 \Leftarrow x_3$$

If the root is near one side, that side will remain pinned as shown in Fig. 2.7. The *modified false-position method* attempts to correct this disadvantage by arbitrarily adjusting the height of the end of the interval which does not move. For the case shown in Fig. 2.7, at the end of each iteration

$$x_1 \Leftarrow x_3$$
$$f_1 \Leftarrow f_3$$
$$f_2 \Leftarrow \frac{1}{2} f_2$$

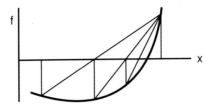

Figure 2.7 False position.

The root bracketing is never lost, but the analytical approximation (the linear interpolation) becomes less meaningful because one endpoint is no longer on the curve. Furthermore, the reader can consider the program logic required to account for changes in the end that is "pinned."

Secant Method

A significant improvement of the false-position method uses the new point x_3 and the lowest of the two endpoints, working on the assumption that they are closer to the zero function value at the root:

$$\text{if } f_1 < f_2 \text{ then } x_2 \Leftarrow x_1$$
$$\text{and } x_1 \Leftarrow x_3$$

Although the guarantee of bracketing the root is lost, convergence is faster. This is the basis for the *secant method*. In addition, this self-starting method does not require an initial sign change—a feature that is more important than convergence.

Newton-Raphson

Interestingly, the most well-known method played a central role in Newton's development of calculus. The Newton-Raphson method is often used when an analytical expression for the slope is available and when a reasonably good estimate of the root is known. The method uses a straight line tangent to the curve at the test location. Rather than two function evaluations, the function value f_1 and local slope f_1' are used.

$$x_2 = x_1 - \frac{f_1}{f_1'}$$

This method converges extremely quickly. However, this method is at a major disadvantage if $f(x)$ is not differentiable. For example, in engineering CAD, f may not be a function but the result of a numerical algorithm. Of course, one can approximate the local slope by a finite-difference formula (as discussed earlier in this chapter); the result is the secant method.

Important characteristics to remember are that Newton's method is self-starting, handles poles, and doubles accuracy every iteration. Unfortunately,

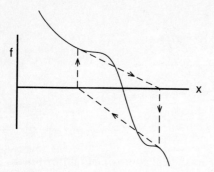

Figure 2.8 Newton's method may oscillate about a root.

Newton's method can oscillate about a root (Fig. 2.8). This can be corrected by using a second-order method based on a quadratic approximation. The iteration formula is

$$x_{n+1} = x_n - \frac{f_n}{f_n' - f_n f_n''/2f_n'}$$

Second-order (or higher) analytical approximations are seldom used in CAD. In most cases, f_n'' is not available. One can envision methods based on any of several possible approximations to the second derivative [i.e. (f_n, f_n', f_{n-1}) or (f_n, f_n', f_{n-1}')]. A pitfall for second-order root-finding techniques is that a quadratic can have two roots or even no real roots (complex valued roots).

Successive Approximations

This technique is very commonly seen in various forms. Instead of $f(x) = 0$, the problem is rearranged as $y = F(x)$, $x = G(y)$. The solution procedure cycles between these two equations. For example:

$$bx \cos x - \sin x = 0$$

is rearranged as

$$y = bx \cos x$$
$$x = \sin^{-1} y$$

However, this pair of equations is unstable, showing that the nonuniqueness of the rearrangement is a problem.

The standard form for successive approximation expresses $f(x) = 0$ as $x = F(x)$:

$$y = F(x)$$
$$x = y$$

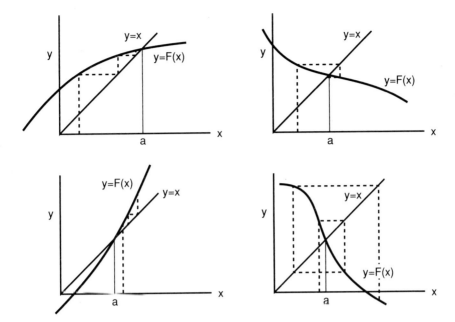

Figure 2.9 Successive approximation displays four types of behavior.

The convergence criteria can be proven to depend upon the slope at the root, $F'(a)$. Specifically, the algorithm converges if $-1 < F'(a) < 1$. The four modes of convergence are shown in Fig. 2.9. This method may converge, diverge, or settle into a cycle, and may miss some roots when more than one occur.

The divergence can be handled by modifying the technique to use a relaxation factor. The iteration

$$x_{n+1} = F(x_n)$$

can be viewed as

$$x_{n+1} = x_n + \Delta x$$

where

$$\Delta x = F(x_n) - x_n$$

The update step can be corrected to

$$x_{n+1} = x_n + \alpha \Delta x$$

However, the correct value for α must be determined. This algorithm can be shown to converge if

$$\alpha = \frac{1}{1 - F'(\xi)} \quad \text{where } x_n < \xi < a$$

Of course the value of ξ is not known. If $F'(x_n)$ is used in the preceeding equation ($\xi = x_n$), this algorithm is equivalent to Newton's method. In a procedure similar to the secant method, $F'(\xi)$ can be approximated as

$$F'(\xi) \approx \frac{F(x_n) - F(x_{n-1})}{x_n - x_{n-1}}$$

■ **EXERCISE 2.9:** Plot values of roots of

$$bx = \tan x$$

for values of $0 < b < 3.0$

■ **EXERCISE 2.10:** Prove the convergence criteria for the method of successive approximation.

2.8 COMPLEX ROOTS AND POLYNOMIALS

Complex roots can be handled in two ways. First, the previous algorithms can simply be coded with variables declared as complex. This is particularly easy in FORTRAN with Newton's method. Second, each complex equation $0 = w(z)$ can be written as two equations in two unknowns, letting $w = u + iv$ and $z = x + iy$. Then for both real and imaginary parts of w to equal zero implies

$$0 = u(x, y)$$
$$0 = v(x, y)$$

However, polynomials are usually treated differently because the number of roots can be known a priori. If the polynomial coefficients are real-valued, then the roots are known to be either real or complex conjugate pairs. One extremely well-behaved polynomial algorithm is known as the Lin-Bairstow method. This first-order method extracts roots two at a time by finding quadratic factors $x^2 + ax + b$. The polynomial is deflated to order $N - 2$ by synthetic division:

$$P_{n-2}(x) = \frac{P_N(x)}{x^2 + ax + b}$$

The remainder from this step is a good measure of the accuracy of the quadratic factor. The coefficients of $P_{n-2}(x)$ are determined and the algorithm is repeated until $N/2$ quadratic factors are determined. Finally, the roots are extracted from each quadratic factor. This algorithm avoids the use of complex variables.

The Lin-Bairstow algorithm is not difficult to develop from scratch. However, most numerical methods libraries will provide polynomial root solvers.

2.9   SUMMARY

Engineering design frequently depends upon the assumption of functional dependence between variables. This chapter has reviewed the basic numerical methods for functional manipulation including interpolation, differentiation, and integration. One-dimensional root finding has been discussed, and the material for multiple-dimension root finding follows well from Chapter 3's discussion of matrix systems. Key points to remember from this chapter include the parametric cubic representations and the linear least-square techniques.

Most CAD systems will provide numerical methods libraries for the topics discussed. If this is not the case, there are good routines that have been published (see Annotated References). The reader should also explore various spreadsheet, graphing, and "engineering spreadsheet" programs. The equations presented can be easily programmed in these environments and many numerical examples can be studied. The reader is strongly urged to develop experience with these techniques on several sets of data.

2.10   ANNOTATED REFERENCES

Acton, F. S. *Computer Methods that Work*. New York: Harper & Row, 1970.

Broad introduction with a very readable style. Excellent discussion of root finding and other numerical methods.

Adey, R. A. and Brebbia, C. A. *Basic Computational Techniques for Engineers*. New York: Wiley, 1983.

Limited to matrices and numerical integration/differentiation.

Conte, S. D. and deBoor, C. *Elementary Numerical Analysis*. New York: McGraw-Hill, 1977.

Broad introduction.

Dahlquist, G., Bjorck, A., and Anderson, N. *Numerical Methods*. Englewood Cliffs, N. J.: Prentice-Hall, 1974.

Forsythe, G. E., Malcom, M. A., and Moler, C. B. *Computer Methods for Mathematical Computing*. Englewood Cliffs, N.J.: Prentice-Hall, 1977.

This is a classic book for numerical methods algorithms, including least squares, splines, integration, root finding, optimization, and matrix decomposition. Contains FORTRAN listings of very good subroutines in each area. Of particular note to this chapter are SPLINE and SEVAL.

Gerald, C. F. and Wheatley, P. O. *Applied Numerical Analysis*. 4th ed. Reading, Mass.: Addison-Wesley, 1989.

Broad introduction.

Ketter, R. L. and Prawel, S. P. *Modern Methods of Engineering Computation.* New York: McGraw-Hill, 1980.

Useful reference for integration and differentiation operators. Good first introduction to finite-difference method.

Press, W. H., Flannery, B. P., Teukolsky, S. A., and Vetterling, W. T. *Numerical Recipes in C: The Art of Scientific Computing.* New York: Cambridge University Press, 1988.

Shoup, T. E. *A Practical Guide to Computer Methods for Engineers.* Englewood Cliffs, N.J.: Prentice-Hall, 1979.

Very broad and very practical introduction to methods and codes. Useful review of existing programs and packages. Good development of splines.

2.11   PROJECTS

Project 2.1   Interpolation of Sail Forces

Problem Statement   Develop a procedure or subroutine that will produce the driving and heeling forces for a mainsail as a function of angle to the wind.

Problem Data   The experimental data for this project are given in Project 6.1.

Analysis   A sail can be viewed as an airfoil, operating at some angle of attack to the wind. Any simulation of sailing performance will require a constitutive relationship for sail forces as a function of geometric parameters. Obtaining an analytical prediction for lift and drag as a function of angle of attack is difficult, however, for a particular sail, nondimensionalized lift and drag coefficients have been measured experimentally. These data are provided in Figure 6.34 in Project 6.1.

Project 2.2   Sail Shape Analytical Approximations

Problem Statement   Develop analytical approximations for the angle of attack and camber as function of height for both the mainsail and the jib.

Problem Data

13.86 m	Length at the water line
21.0 m	Total hull length
0 m	Position of mast
+4.77 m	Coordinate of waterline
−9.09 m	Coordinate of waterline

Mainsail			Jib			
z	α	Camber	z	α	Chord	Camber
2.2	4.0°	0.01	0.5	17°	7.84	0.07
5.1	6.2°	0.09	3.3	19°	6.36	0.13
8.2	9.0°	0.13	6.2	26°	5.00	0.18
11.2	11.5°	0.11	9.1	32°	3.86	0.19
14.3	17.0°	0.14	11.9	34°	2.27	0.15
17.4	21.7°	0.10	14.8	36°	0.79	0.14
20.5	20.5°	0.14	19.0	top of forestay		
23.4	45.0°	0.25				
25.0	mast height					

Table 2.2   Sail measurements.

+8.0 m	Coordinate of bow
−13.0 m	Coordinate of stern
+7.05 m	Coordinate of foot of forestay
10.0 m	Boom length
6.8 m	Foot of jib
25 m	Mast height
19.0 m	Forestay height (at mast)

Analysis   The data given in Table 2.2 are extracted from experimental measurements of sail shape for a mainsail and jib, as presented graphically in Marchaj. Note that each sail was raised and measured independently.

Comments   These data are used in Project 9.2 to develop a geometric (patch) representation of the sail. These data can be used in Project 8.6 to develop a pressure distribution for visualization.

Project 2.3   Aircraft Performance Envelope

Problem Statement   Determine the velocity envelope as a function of the altitude of a long-endurance aircraft at a given weight.

Analysis   The velocity envelope is the minimum and maximum velocity at steady level flight. These velocities occur when the power available from the engine is equal to the power required to maintain a steady level flight (the product of total drag and forward velocity):

$$\eta_{\text{prop}} P_{\text{eng}} = P_{\text{reg}} = DV$$

The drag is found from the drag coefficient,

$$D = \frac{\rho_{air} V^2 s c C_d}{2}$$

where drag includes parasitic drag and induced drag due to the lift:

$$C_d = C_{d\_par} + \frac{C_L^2}{\pi \eta_{wing} \frac{s}{h}}$$

Finally, the plane will operate at an angle of attack that produces a lift coefficient sufficient to support the plane at the particular velocity. Hence,

$$W = L = \frac{1}{2} \rho_{air} V s c C_L$$

Solving for C_L gives

$$C_L = \frac{2W}{\rho V^2 s c}$$

Substitution and elimination of terms leads to

$$\left(\frac{\rho_{air} s c}{2}\right)^2 C_{d\_par} V^4 - \frac{1}{2} \rho_{air} s c \eta_{prop} P_{eng} V^2 + \frac{W^2}{\pi \eta_{wing} \frac{s}{h}} = 0$$

The lift coefficient has an upper bound beyond which the wing stalls. If $C_L = C_{L\max}$, then

$$V_{stall} = \sqrt{\frac{2W}{C_{L\max} \rho_{air} s c}}$$

The density of air at altitude can be calculated from the following formula:

$$\rho_{air} = \rho_o \left(1 - \frac{\lambda h}{T_o}\right)^{g/\lambda R - 1}$$

Project Data

h	m	Current altitude
λ	6.5×10^{-3} K/m	Adiabatic Lapse Rate
ρ_o	1.23 kg/m^3	Density of air at sea level
R	287.0 J/kg K	Gas constant for air
g	9.8 m/s^2	Gravity
T_o	288.2 K	Temperature at sea level
P_{eng}		Power developed by engine
η_{prop}		Propeller efficiency
D		Total drag

V	Forward Velocity
ρ_{air}	Density of air at altitude
C_d	Drag coefficient
s	Span
c	Chord
C_{d_par}	Parasitic drag coefficient
C_L	Lift coefficient
η_{wing}	Wing efficiency
L	Lift
W	Weight

Comments   Several methods could be used to solve the resulting nonlinear equation. Which ones are more appropriate, given that the equation must be solved repetitively at successively increasing altitude? The results should be checked to ensure that the velocity makes sense physically.

Alternate parameter studies involve the study of power available as a function of altitude versus power required as a function of altitude.

Project 2.4   Gas Turbine Performance

Problem Statement   The objective of this project is to use a computer program to investigate the performance characteristics of a gas turbine. Pratt and Whitney, General Electric, and other manufacturers use a similar approach. The performance as represented by power output and fuel consumption depends upon the cycle, properties of the working fluid, pressure ratio, and turbine inlet temperature. Generally, turbine inlet temperature is constrained by the materials and manufacturing processes available; the designer must select the pressure ratio.

Plot efficiency versus the pressure ratio for turbine inlet temperatures ranging from 800°F to 2,200°F. Also, plot the net power output versus the pressure ratio for those temperature values. For a desired output of 4,000 kW, select the best pressure ratio, assuming temperature is limited to 1,400°F. How much improvement is gained by going to 1,800°F?

Problem Data

p_1	15	psia	Compressor inlet pressure
T_1	40°	R	Compressor inlet temperature
T_2		° R	Compressor outlet temperature
T_3		° R	Turbine inlet temperature
T_4		° R	Turbine outlet temperature
h		Btu/lb	Enthalpy

r			Compressor pressure ratio (out/in)
W_{net}			Net work
η			Efficiency
η_t	0.85		Turbine efficiency
η_c	0.83		Compressor efficiency
ρ		lb/ft^3	Working fluid density
Q	40,000	ft^3/min	Volumetric flow rate
k	1.4		

Analysis The gas turbine cycle is shown in Fig. 2.10. Assuming adiabatic (without gaining or losing heat) compressor turbine processes:

$$\frac{T_2}{T_1} = \frac{T_3}{T_4} = r^{(k-1)/k}$$

The thermal efficiency for any fluid is given by

$$\eta = \frac{(h_3 - h_4)\eta_t - (h_2 - h_1)/\eta_c}{h_3 - h_{2'}}$$

Assuming constant k, the efficiency is given by

$$\eta = \frac{(T_3 - T_4)\eta_t - (T_2 - T_1)/\eta_c}{T_3 - T_{2'}}$$

The value of $T_{2'}$ is obtained from the definition of compressor efficiency:

$$T_{2'} = \frac{T_2 - T_1(1 - \eta_c)}{\eta_c}$$

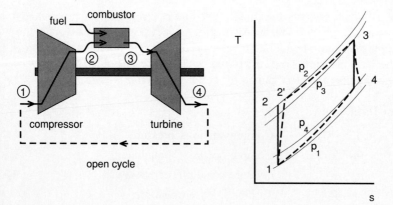

Figure 2.10 Gas turbine cycle.

The temperatures T_2 and T_4 can be eliminated to give an overall efficiency of

$$\eta = \left(\frac{\eta_t T_3 - T_1 r^{(k-1)/k} / \eta_c}{T_3 - T_1 - T_1 (r^{(k-1)/k} - 1)/\eta_c} \right) \left(1 - \frac{1}{r^{(k-1)/k}} \right)$$

The net work can be determined from

$$W_{net} = Q\rho\,[(h_3 - h_4)\eta_t + (h_1 - h_2)/\eta_c]$$

An approximation to the properties of the working fluid (air) is

$$h = 0.219T + (0.342 \times 10^{-4})T^2 - (0.293 \times 10^{-8})T^3$$

You will need to determine a function for inlet air density. A useful conversion will be 1 kW = 56.87 Btu/min.

Optional Exercises Using increased turbine inlet temperature will require higher-cost, more exotic materials (single crystal blades, ceramic blades, etc.) and manufacturing processes. Develop an economic model for the cost savings resulting from improved efficiency and generate an economic trade-off analysis.

Project 2.5 Determining Joint Centers in Finger Joints

Problem Statement Finger joints may be damaged by arthritis to such an extent that most hand function is lost. As a result, the patient's ability for self-sufficiency and independence in normal daily activities may be greatly impaired. The damaged joints may be replaced by artificial joints that restore function and relieve pain.

When designing internal artificial finger joints, it is very important to locate the joint center properly. In general, the center of the artificial joint should be as close to the center of the normal joint as possible. If this is done, the forces in the tendons will have normal moment arms with respect to the joint center, and as a result, the forces and moments about the joint will be more nearly normal. Consequently, the kinematics of the replaced joint and the function of the entire finger will be improved.

In general, human or animal joints have joint axes that move with respect to the bones. That is, the joint function cannot be replaced exactly by a fixed pin joint. However, in the finger, a fixed axis is a reasonable approximation. The center of the joint (x_c, y_c) may be estimated by experimentally determining the motion of a point on one side of the joint (P_1) with respect to a reference frame M fixed to the other side of the joint.

To determine the displacement of P_1 and P_2 relative to M, M is fixed with respect to external x, y axes; markers are attached to the two points P_1 and P_2, and the joint is moved through its range of motion. X-rays or photographs are used to record the positions of the markers with respect to the axes. These images can be digitized to determine the x, y coordinates of the markers for various flexion angles.

Data from a simulated experiment are given in Table 2.3. It has been found that the paths described by these data are very nearly circular. Two paths are generated, one with a nominal radius of 50 mm and the other with a radius of 90 mm. You are to find the radii of the two circles with a common center that best fit these data using a least-squares curve-fitting procedure. This procedure will also locate the approximate center of the joint.

Analysis   The equation of the circle for the first path is given by

$$R_1^2 - y_c^2 - x_c^2 + 2x_i x_c + 2y_i y_c = x_i^2 + y_i^2$$

and for the second path by

$$R_2^2 - y_c^2 - x_c^2 + 2x_i x_c + 2y_i y_c = x_i^2 + y_i^2$$

These equations are of the form

$$z_1 + 2x_i x_c + 2y_i y_c = x_i^2 + y_i^2$$

and

$$z_2 + 2x_i x_c + 2y_i y_c = x_i^2 + y_i^2$$

Table 2.3 lists values for x_i, y_i. The unknowns to be determined are x_c, y_c, z_1, and z_2. Once they are known, R_1 and R_2 are easily determined.

Using the preceding equations and the data from Table 2.3, a set of 18 equations is obtained in terms of the four unknowns. This equation may be written in the form

$$\mathbf{AX = B}$$

where $\mathbf{A}$ is an 18 × 4 matrix, $\mathbf{X}$ is a 4 × 1 column vector, and $\mathbf{B}$ is an 18 × 1 column vector. Clearly there are more equations than unknowns. It

x_1 (mm)	y_1 (mm)	x_2 (mm)	y_2 (mm)
12	66	12	105
21	64	28	104
29	61	43	99
37	58	57	92
44	53	69	83
51	48	81	72
55	40	89	60
59	32	97	46
61	24	101	31

Table 2.3   Finger joint measured data.

can be shown that the solution $\mathbf{X}$, which satisfies this set of equations in the least-squares sense, may be determined by solving the equation

$$\mathbf{A}^T\mathbf{A}\mathbf{X} = \mathbf{A}^T\mathbf{B}$$

Your task is to form this equation and solve it, using both the data given and library subroutines devised for matrix multiplication and the solution of simultaneous algebraic equations.

Project 2.6   Squeeze Film Damper Forces

Problem Statement   Squeeze film dampers are often used on turbomachinery such as aircraft engines to control vibrations of the shaft and blades at high speed. A squeeze film damper is similar to a journal bearing except that the journal does not rotate; it only translates within the clearance space. The antifriction rotation usually is provided by roller bearings within the journal. The roller bearings also ensure fail-safe operation in case oil pressure is lost. Because the squeeze film damper has no inherent load-carrying capability, centering springs are usually provided to maintain a nominal clearnace. The viscous film dissipates energy and allows operation through one or more shaft critical speeds.

Solving dynamics problems for systems that include hydrodynamic bearings requires calculation of the forces exerted by the bearing on the rotor system. Given shaft displacements and velocities, a determination of forces can be described as an impedance calculation [i.e., $\vec{F} = f(x, y, \dot{x}, \dot{y})$].

Develop a procedure to determine $\vec{F}$ given $x, y, \dot{x}, \dot{y}$. Then, plot $\vec{F}$ (or its components) for the cases of (a) pure radial squeeze [β constant, $\vec{F} = f(\epsilon, \dot{\epsilon})$] and (b) pure circular motion [$\epsilon, \dot{\beta}$ constant, $\vec{F} = f(\epsilon, \dot{\beta})$].

Analysis   The squeeze film system is as shown in Fig. 2.11. The Reynolds equation for a constant viscosity incompressible fluid can be written in polar-cylindrical coordinates as

$$\frac{\partial}{\partial\theta}\left(h^3\frac{\partial p}{\partial\theta}\right) + R^2\frac{\partial}{\partial z}\left(h^3\frac{\partial p}{\partial z}\right) = \frac{12\mu R^2 V_s}{C^3}\cos(\alpha + \theta)$$

where h is the normalized film thickness defined by $h = 1 + e\cos\theta$, z is the axial position variable, $e = r/C$ is the radial eccentricity, θ is the polar coordinate angle based on the eccentricity vector, and β is the polar coordinate for the end of the shaft.

The magnitude of the velocity of the center of the shaft is V_s and α is the angle between the velocity vector and the eccentricity vector (positive from V to e counterclockwise). The Ocvirk solution (for a short film) is obtained by neglecting the first term on the left and solving for $p(\theta, z)$. This function can be integrated axially to eliminate z and yields the following

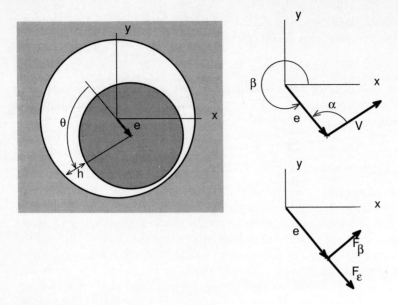

Figure 2.11 Squeeze film damper.

average pressure definition:

$$P(\theta) = \frac{-\mu L^2 V_s \cos(\alpha + \theta)}{C^3 h^3}$$

Forces applied to the shaft can be determined by a circumferencial integration of the pressure distribution:

$$F_\epsilon = RL \int P(\theta) \cos \theta \, d\theta$$

$$F_\beta = RL \int P(\theta) \sin \theta \, d\theta$$

this can be nondimensionalized to

$$F_\epsilon = -V_s 2 \mu L \left(\frac{R}{C}\right)^3 \left(\frac{L}{D}\right)^2 \int \frac{\cos(\alpha + \theta) \cos \theta}{(1 + e \cos \theta)^3} \, d\theta$$

$$F_\beta = -V_s 2 \mu L \left(\frac{R}{C}\right)^3 \left(\frac{L}{D}\right)^2 \int \frac{\cos(\alpha + \theta) \sin \theta}{(1 + e \cos \theta)^3} \, d\theta$$

Although these integrals can be solved analytically, this is a good introduction to numerical integration as used for finite-length bearings.

Project 2.7   Sizing of Impact-Absorbing Automobile Bumper

Problem Statement   Consider a car with an impact-absorbing bumper. Your design assignment is to determine the values of a linear spring and damper that minimize the maximum acceleration experienced by the vehicle. The problem is complicated by the requirement that a vehicle with a mass of 1,500 kg traveling at a velocity of 12 m/sec must be stopped within a distance of 0.6 m.

Analysis   The system can be modeled as a single-degree-of-freedom system shown in Fig. 2.12. The governing differential equation is

$$1,500\ddot{x} + b\dot{x} + kx = 0$$

where

$$x(t_0) = 0$$
$$\dot{x}(t_0) = 12 \text{ m/sec}$$
$$x(t_1) = 0.6 \text{ m}$$
$$\dot{x}(t_1) = 0$$

The time of maximum deflection t_1 is to be determined.

Suggested Problem Formulation

1. Determine an equation for the response $x(t)$. Any basic vibration or system dynamics book will have this.
2. Find the equation that determines the time of maximum displacement, (t_1).
3. Use (2) in (1) to get an equation for x_{max}.
4. If specific values for x_{max}, k, and m, are given, then b can be found from the third step. This will require finding the root of a nonlinear equation.

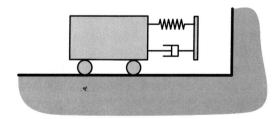

Figure 2.12   Simple dynamic model of impact-absorbing bumper.

5. The previous step can be viewed as producing $b = f(k)$ with x_{max} and m specified. This can be graphed by solving Step 4 repeatedly for several values of k. You can check your results by calculating the value of k when $b = 0$. (Hint: All the kinetic energy will become potential energy if none is dissipated.) If you slowly decrease k from this value, you will always have a good estimate of the root in Step 4 to use as a starting point.

6. Since you have a good idea where the root is, an accelerated method such as Newton's is a good choice.

7. As a matter of tactics, you should consider finding the value of $\sqrt{1 - \zeta^2}/\zeta$ versus k and then converting $\sqrt{1 - \zeta^2}/\zeta$ to b. Note that ζ is the traditional damping ratio for a single-degree-of-freedom system.

8. *Caution:* What happens when the system gets overdamped?

9. While functioning as a design engineer, you should also look ahead to ways to decide between the various combinations of values that lead to 0.6 m. Have the program calculate the maximum deceleration for each set of k and b that you determine.

Options   As a test of program generality, repeat for constraints of x_{max} = 0.4 m and x_{max} = 0.8 m maximum deflection.

Project 2.8   Spring Selection for Automotive Suspension

Problem Statement   An idealization of a classic independent suspension for an American passenger car is shown in Fig. 2.13. Design the front coil spring to fit within a space 7 inches in diameter and 18 inches long (it may be smaller than this space). The front end's natural frequency should be about 60 cycles per minute, and the spring must be able to take (to be conservative) an infinite number of loadings caused by an emergency braking stop.

The mass carried by the suspension is usually referred to as the sprung mass. The mass of the tire, rim, brakes, bearings and spindles, and so on, is collectively referred to as the unsprung mass.

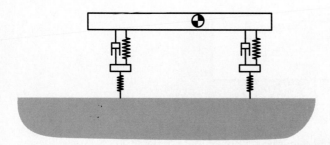

Figure 2.13 Lumped parameter vehicle suspension model.

Project Data

Chevrolet, vintage 1958

97 lb$_m$	Front unsprung mass, per wheel
311 lb$_m$	Rear unsprung mass, total
3,962 lb$_m$	Sprung mass, with two passengers in the front seat
9.79 ft	Wheelbase
13,775 lb$_f$/ft	Tire stiffness, per tire
0.8	Tire/road maximum coefficient of friction
	Location of c.g. of sprung mass:
4.17 ft	Behind the front wheel centers
1.73 ft	Above ground

Project 2.9   Thermocouple Curve Fit

Problem Statement   Table 2.4 is a thermocouple conversion table for temperature as a function of voltage in millivolts. There is a NIST curve fit for

(°C)	0	2	4	6	8
0	0.000	0.078	0.156	0.234	0.312
10	0.391	0.470	0.549	0.629	0.709
20	0.789	0.830	0.951	1.032	1.114
30	1.196	1.279	1.361	1.444	1.528
40	1.611	1.695	1.780	1.865	1.950
50	2.035	2.121	2.207	2.294	2.380
60	2.467	2.555	2.643	2.731	2.819
70	2.908	2.997	3.087	3.176	3.266
80	3.357	3.447	3.538	3.630	3.721
90	3.813	3.906	3.998	4.091	4.184
100	4.277	4.371	4.464	4.559	4.654
110	4.749	4.844	4.939	5.035	5.131
120	5.227	5.324	5.420	5.517	5.615
130	5.712	5.810	5.908	6.007	6.105
140	6.204	6.303	6.403	6.502	6.602
150	6.702	6.803	6.903	7.004	7.106
160	7.207	7.309	7.411	7.513	7.615
170	7.718	7.821	7.924	8.027	8.131
180	8.235	8.339	8.443	8.548	8.652
190	8.757	8.863	8.968	9.074	9.180

Table 2.4   Thermocouple data: copper versus copper-nickel (thermoelectric voltage in absolute millivolts).

voltage as a function of temperature, but there is no available curve fit for temperature as a function of voltage, which would be needed for a sensor calibration. Use the first column (temperatures in increments of 10°C) to generate an approximation for use in an algorithm that calculates temperature, given voltage. Evaluate your fit at intermediate temperatures using the voltages given in the other columns. Note that a typical table from a reference book will contain values at increments of 1°C over the range of −270°C to 400°C.

C H A P T E R

3
Systems of Equations

3.1 INTRODUCTION

Solving simultaneous equations is one of the more common numerical problems encountered in analytical CAD techniques. This problem occurs directly in the analysis of systems that are obviously a collection of individual parts. Each part is well understood, but the coupling is such that simultaneous treatment leads to a system of equations. If the behavior of each part is linear, the simultaneous equations lead to a matrix problem.

In many cases the system can be idealized as a graph, with the individual parts forming edges. Equilibrium or conservation at each node will give rise to a separate equation. A structural truss is obviously such a system, but the factory-floor product-flow analysis that occurs in manufacturing plants can also be formulated this way. Multiple-domain dynamic systems (electrical, fluid, magnetic, mechanical) frequently are modeled by lumped parameters.

Two other types of problems lead to systems of equations: finite-element and finite-difference analyses. In these cases, a field problem (as described by a partial differential equation) is broken down into a set of simultaneous equations. It is important to remember that in field problems, the object being analyzed is not naturally divided into discrete parts. However, at the heart of both of these analytical methods is the solution of a set of simultaneous equations. Finite-element methods will be thoroughly discussed in Chapter 4. Finite-difference methods, on the other hand, will not be discussed in any detail because they are not as widely applied (although they are extremely valuable for certain fluid flow and heat transfer problems). Furthermore, the discussion of finite element methods includes the single most important application of matrix methods and is therefore sufficient.

The objective of this chapter is to discuss ways of solving systems of equations. Section 3.2 opens with a discussion of the analysis of trusses, then the treatment of individual members is presented. In Section 3.3, a *system matrix* is assembled from the contributions of each individual member. An extensive example illustrates the global stiffness matrix assembly and the treatment of boundary conditions. This example results in a set of linear equations (the matrix problem). In Section 3.4, both noniterative and iterative methods of solution are presented. However, less detail is provided for the noniterative methods (e.g., Cholesky decomposition), because these are commonly taken from a numerical methods library. In contrast, the iterative methods are more likely to be coded by the CAD system developer than to be taken from a library. Therefore these algorithms are presented in more detail to help the user understand the aspects of the problems being solved. (The reader should refer to specialized texts for a more detailed discussion of numerical methods.) Section 3.7 summarizes and compares the methods.

If the components of the system are nonlinear, the result is a system of simultaneous equations not expressible in matrix form. Section 3.5 discusses the solution of such problems. This material is a direct extension of the root-finding methods discussed earlier in Section 2.7.

The iterative methods for matrix and nonlinear problems frequently display convergence problems. The over/underrelaxation technique can be used to correct these problems. This method is applicable to both types of problems and is discussed in Section 3.6.

This chapter will not cover the eigenvalue problem, a significant computational procedure involving matrices. In analytical CAD, this problem will be encountered in the study of dynamic response of systems or in finite-element analysis of dynamic (rather than static) problems. The reader is referred to the literature on that topic.

3.2   SIMPLE TRUSS SYSTEM

A simple pinned truss is an ideal example of a multicomponent system that leads to a matrix equation. The individual components are clearly identifiable, and the mechanics of the system are well understood. The system of equations is assembled by considering equilibrium, compatibility, and constitutive equations. In the next example, observe how a careful accounting scheme (notation) eases problem formulation. The example has been limited to two dimensions for clarity, but the extension to three dimensional trusses is straightforward.

The truss shown in Fig. 3.1 could represent a crane made of bars pinned at the joints. The truss members are assumed to be capable of carrying only tensile or compressive loads. Nodes are numbered in a roman font; elements are numbered in a **bold** font. The vector force $\vec{F}$ at any node can be stored as a two-component column vector $\mathbf{F}$ expressed in either a reference frame oriented relative to the element (ξ, η) or a global reference frame (x, y). A $^{\text{pre}-\text{super}}$script will denote the reference frame. The nodal

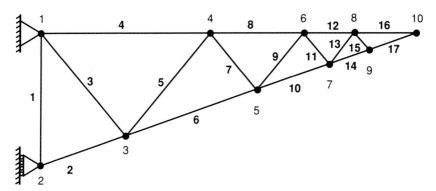

Figure 3.1 A simple truss.

force is therefore $^\xi\mathbf{F}$ with resolutes (F_ξ, F_η) or $^x\mathbf{F}$ with resolutes (F_x, F_y). Similarly the displacements $\vec{\delta}$ are $^\xi\boldsymbol{\delta}$, $(\delta_\xi, \delta_\eta)$ or $^x\boldsymbol{\delta}$, (δ_x, δ_y).

The sum of the elemental forces at each node gives the applied external load at that node. For example, if the only external load is $\vec{W}$ on node 7, and if the structure is to remain stationary, then the horizontal and vertical forces at node 3 must be in equilibrium, (Fig. 3.2):

$$F_{3x}^3 + F_{3x}^4 + F_{3x}^5 + F_{3x}^6 = 0 \qquad F_{3y}^3 + F_{3y}^4 + F_{3y}^5 + F_{3y}^6 = 0$$

Each element makes its own contribution to the set of nodal forces. The bold superscript (e.g., ^{5}) on the forces distinguishes the forces from each element that affects the node. Note that for $\theta_\mathbf{m}$ and $k_\mathbf{m}$ the element is indicated by subscript. In most cases, however, the subscript denotes the node number and the direction of the force resolute.

In general, where F_{ix} and F_{iy} are the external applied loads at node i, *equilibrium* gives

$$\sum_j F_{ix}^\mathbf{j} = F_{ix} \qquad \sum_j F_{iy}^\mathbf{j} = F_{iy}$$

where j ranges over all the elements incident upon node i.

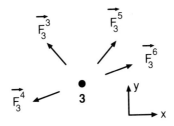

Figure 3.2 Forces at node 3.

The *compatibility relations* mean we don't need to superscript the deflections δ_{ix} and δ_{iy} since the deflections of all the elements at any node must all be the same, otherwise the truss is coming apart.

The *constitutive equations* relate the nodal forces to nodal displacements. Consider the case of Element **5**, in Fig. 3.3. For generality, we can denote this as element **m** and one end of this element as i and the other as j. From simple elasticity theory, the relation between force and displacement for axial tension-compression of a uniform bar is $\Delta = PL/(AE)$ where P is the load, A is the cross-sectional area, L is the length, and E is Young's modulus.

For the specific element being considered, simple elasticity theory relates the forces and displacements in the local reference frame:

$$F_{i\xi} = \frac{EA}{L}(\delta_{i\xi} - \delta_{j\xi}), \qquad F_{i\eta} = 0$$

$$F_{j\xi} = \frac{EA}{L}(\delta_{j\xi} - \delta_{i\xi}), \qquad F_{j\eta} = 0$$

Denoting the common term EA/L as $k_{\mathbf{m}}$, or the stiffness of the **m**th element, and using matrix notation, the constitutive equation can be written as

$$\begin{Bmatrix} F_{i\xi} \\ F_{i\eta} \\ F_{j\xi} \\ F_{j\eta} \end{Bmatrix} = \begin{bmatrix} k_{\mathbf{m}} & 0 & -k_{\mathbf{m}} & 0 \\ 0 & 0 & 0 & 0 \\ -k_{\mathbf{m}} & 0 & k_{\mathbf{m}} & 0 \\ 0 & 0 & 0 & 0 \end{bmatrix} \begin{Bmatrix} \delta_{i\xi} \\ \delta_{i\eta} \\ \delta_{j\xi} \\ \delta_{j\eta} \end{Bmatrix}$$

The constitutive equation naturally occurs in the ξ, η local element reference frame. The equilibrium equation is written in the x, y global reference

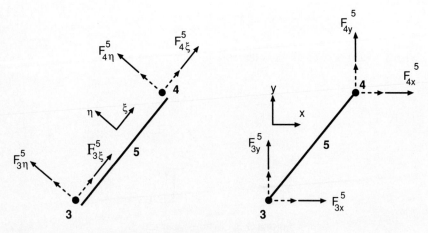

Figure 3.3   A typical truss element.

frame. The transformation between the two is

$$\begin{Bmatrix} F_x \\ F_y \end{Bmatrix} = \begin{bmatrix} \cos\theta & -\sin\theta \\ \sin\theta & \cos\theta \end{bmatrix} \begin{Bmatrix} F_\xi \\ F_\eta \end{Bmatrix}$$

If $^{x/\xi}\mathbf{R}$ denotes the 2×2 rotation matrix from ξ, η to x, y and $^\xi\mathbf{F}$ denotes the vector force $\vec{F}$ in the ξ, η reference frame, then

$$^x\mathbf{F} = {}^{x/\xi}\mathbf{R}^\xi\mathbf{F}$$

and the constitutive equation can be written as

$$\begin{Bmatrix} F_{ix} \\ F_{iy} \\ F_{jx} \\ F_{jy} \end{Bmatrix} = \begin{bmatrix} {}^{x/\xi}\mathbf{R}i & [0]_{2\times2} \\ [0]_{2\times2} & {}^{x/\xi}\mathbf{R} \end{bmatrix} \begin{bmatrix} k_m & 0 & -k_m & 0 \\ 0 & 0 & 0 & 0 \\ -k_m & 0 & k_m & 0 \\ 0 & 0 & 0 & 0 \end{bmatrix} \begin{bmatrix} {}^{\xi/x}\mathbf{R} & [0]_{2\times2} \\ [0]_{2\times2} & {}^{\xi/x}\mathbf{R} \end{bmatrix} \begin{Bmatrix} \delta_{ix} \\ \delta_{iy} \\ \delta_{jx} \\ \delta_{jy} \end{Bmatrix}$$

This equation is more commonly written as

$$\mathbf{F^m} = \mathbf{k^m}\boldsymbol{\delta}_{ij}$$

where the *elemental stiffness matrix* $\mathbf{k^m}$ can be shown to be

$$\mathbf{k_m} = \frac{AE}{L}\Bigg|_m \begin{bmatrix} \cos^2\theta_m & \cos\theta_m\sin\theta_m & -\cos^2\theta_m & -\sin\theta_m\cos\theta_m \\ \cos\theta_m\sin\theta_m & \sin^2\theta_m & -\cos\theta_m\sin\theta_m & -\sin^2\theta_m \\ -\cos^2\theta_m & -\cos\theta_m\sin\theta_m & \cos^2\theta_m & \cos\theta_m\sin\theta_m \\ -\sin\theta_m\cos\theta_m & -\sin^2\theta_m & \cos\theta_m\sin\theta_m & \sin^2\theta_m \end{bmatrix}$$

The element orientation θ_m can be found from the nodal coordinates:

$$\theta_m = \tan^{-1}\left(\frac{y_j - y_i}{x_j - x_i}\right)$$

The nodal displacement and force vectors are defined as

$$\boldsymbol{\delta}_{ij} = \begin{Bmatrix} \delta_{ix} \\ \delta_{iy} \\ \delta_{jx} \\ \delta_{jy} \end{Bmatrix} \qquad \mathbf{F^m} = \begin{Bmatrix} F^m_{ix} \\ F^m_{iy} \\ F^m_{jx} \\ F^m_{jy} \end{Bmatrix}$$

After all the elements are assembled to form the truss structure, the elemental equations can also be assembled into one structural equation:

$$\mathbf{F} = \mathbf{k}\boldsymbol{\delta}$$

where the displacement and force vectors are now

$$\boldsymbol{\delta} = \begin{Bmatrix} \delta_{1x} \\ \delta_{1y} \\ \vdots \\ \delta_{Nx} \\ \delta_{Ny} \end{Bmatrix} \qquad \mathbf{F} = \begin{Bmatrix} F_{1x} \\ F_{1y} \\ \vdots \\ F_{Nx} \\ F_{Ny} \end{Bmatrix}$$

The structural stiffness matrix **k** is of size $2N \times 2N$, where there are N nodes in the structure. It is assembled by considering both the connectivity of the structure and that the sum of forces at any joint equals the applied load at the joint. The major step here is to determine how each elemental stiffness matrix contributes to the structural stiffness matrix used in the system equation.

3.3 GLOBAL STIFFNESS MATRIX ASSEMBLY

Now that we have discussed the mechanics of the individual members of a truss, we can consider how the system behaves as a whole. The process of assembling the global stiffness matrix is best understood by a detailed example. The reader will note the importance of careful notation for bookkeeping purposes.

Consider three truss members connected at three nodes, subjected to the loads shown in Fig. 3.4. Assume that the area and Young's modulus are the same for all three members. We know that each elemental stiffness matrix $\mathbf{k^m}$ is given by

$$\left.\frac{AE}{L}\right|_m \left[\begin{array}{cccc} C_\theta^2 & C_\theta S_\theta & -C_\theta^2 & -S_\theta C_\theta \\ C_\theta S_\theta & S_\theta^2 & -C_\theta S_\theta & -S_\theta^2 \\ -C_\theta^2 & -C_\theta S_\theta & C_\theta^2 & C_\theta S_\theta \\ -S_\theta C_\theta & -S_\theta^2 & C_\theta S_\theta & S_\theta^2 \end{array}\right]_m$$

This is the same elemental matrix given in Section 3.2, using the abbreviated notation of C_θ, S_θ for $\cos\theta, \sin\theta$ respectively, with θ being θ_m. Thus for element **1** ($\theta_1 = 60°$, $L_1 = 2.0$), the stiffness matrix is

$$\mathbf{k^1} = \frac{AE}{2}\left[\begin{array}{cccc} 0.250 & 0.433 & -0.250 & -0.433 \\ 0.433 & 0.750 & -0.433 & -0.750 \\ -0.250 & -0.433 & 0.250 & 0.433 \\ -0.433 & -0.750 & 0.433 & 0.750 \end{array}\right]$$

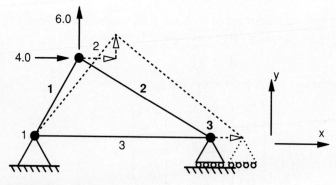

Figure 3.4 A simple truss.

The matrix equation relating the forces on element **1** to the deflections of nodes 1 and 2 is

$$\mathbf{F}^1 = \left\{ \begin{array}{c} F^1_{1x} \\ F^1_{1y} \\ F^1_{2x} \\ F^1_{2y} \end{array} \right\} = \mathbf{k}^1 \left\{ \begin{array}{c} \delta_{1x} \\ \delta_{1y} \\ \delta_{2x} \\ \delta_{2y} \end{array} \right\}$$

Similarly, the elemental stiffness matrix for element **2** is

$$\mathbf{k}^2 = \frac{AE}{3.464} \begin{bmatrix} 0.750 & -0.433 & -0.750 & 0.433 \\ -0.433 & 0.250 & 0.433 & -0.250 \\ -0.750 & 0.433 & 0.750 & -0.433 \\ 0.433 & -0.250 & -0.433 & 0.250 \end{bmatrix}$$

The matrix equation relating the forces on element **2** to the deflections of nodes 2 and 3 is

$$\mathbf{F}^2 = \left\{ \begin{array}{c} F^2_{2x} \\ F^2_{2y} \\ F^2_{3x} \\ F^2_{3y} \end{array} \right\} = \mathbf{k}^2 \left\{ \begin{array}{c} \delta_{2x} \\ \delta_{2y} \\ \delta_{3x} \\ \delta_{3y} \end{array} \right\}$$

Finally, for Element **3**,

$$\mathbf{k}^3 = \frac{AE}{4} \begin{bmatrix} 1 & 0 & -1 & 0 \\ 0 & 0 & 0 & 0 \\ -1 & 0 & 1 & 0 \\ 0 & 0 & 0 & 0 \end{bmatrix}$$

and

$$\mathbf{F}^3 = \left\{ \begin{array}{c} F^3_{1x} \\ F^3_{1y} \\ F^3_{3x} \\ F^3_{3y} \end{array} \right\} = \mathbf{k}^3 \left\{ \begin{array}{c} \delta_{1x} \\ \delta_{1y} \\ \delta_{3x} \\ \delta_{3y} \end{array} \right\}$$

These relations describe the forces and deflections of each element.

We can also write an equilibrium equation for the forces acting at each node; that is, the sum of the elemental forces at each node must equal the applied load at the node (see Fig. 3.5). Considering the horizontal and vertical forces at each node gives the following equations:

$$F^1_{1x} + F^3_{1x} = F_{1x} = ?$$
$$F^1_{1y} + F^3_{1y} = F_{1y} = ?$$
$$F^1_{2x} + F^2_{2x} = F_{2x} = 4$$
$$F^1_{2y} + F^2_{2y} = F_{2y} = -6$$
$$F^2_{3x} + F^3_{3x} = F_{3x} = 0$$
$$F^2_{3y} + F^3_{3y} = F_{3y} = ?$$

The forces (F_{1x}, F_{1y}, F_{3y}) are the unknown external loads caused by the boundary supports. To obtain the overall structural stiffness matrix, it is necessary to assemble the three elemental stiffness matrices using the preceding nodal force relations. The goal is to get a single relation of the form

$$
\begin{Bmatrix} F_{1x} \\ F_{1y} \\ F_{2x} \\ F_{2y} \\ F_{3x} \\ F_{3y} \end{Bmatrix} = \mathbf{k} \begin{Bmatrix} \delta_{1x} \\ \delta_{1y} \\ \delta_{2x} \\ \delta_{2y} \\ \delta_{3x} \\ \delta_{3y} \end{Bmatrix}
$$

So, splitting the applied forces at each node into the elemental forces:

$$
\begin{Bmatrix} F_{1x} \\ F_{1y} \\ F_{2x} \\ F_{2y} \\ F_{3x} \\ F_{3y} \end{Bmatrix} = \begin{Bmatrix} F_{1x}^1 \\ F_{1y}^1 \\ F_{2x}^1 \\ F_{2y}^1 \\ 0 \\ 0 \end{Bmatrix} + \begin{Bmatrix} F_{1x}^3 \\ F_{1y}^3 \\ 0 \\ 0 \\ F_{3x}^3 \\ F_{3y}^3 \end{Bmatrix} + \begin{Bmatrix} 0 \\ 0 \\ F_{2x}^2 \\ F_{2y}^2 \\ F_{3x}^2 \\ F_{3y}^2 \end{Bmatrix}
$$

$$
= \begin{bmatrix} k_{11}^1 & k_{12}^1 & k_{13}^1 & k_{14}^1 & 0 & 0 \\ k_{21}^1 & k_{22}^1 & k_{23}^1 & k_{24}^1 & 0 & 0 \\ k_{31}^1 & k_{32}^1 & k_{33}^1 & k_{34}^1 & 0 & 0 \\ k_{41}^1 & k_{42}^1 & k_{43}^1 & k_{44}^1 & 0 & 0 \\ 0 & 0 & 0 & 0 & 0 & 0 \\ 0 & 0 & 0 & 0 & 0 & 0 \end{bmatrix} \begin{Bmatrix} \delta_{1x} \\ \delta_{1y} \\ \delta_{2x} \\ \delta_{2y} \\ \delta_{3x} \\ \delta_{3y} \end{Bmatrix}
$$

$$
+ \begin{bmatrix} k_{11}^3 & k_{12}^3 & 0 & 0 & k_{13}^3 & k_{14}^3 \\ k_{21}^3 & k_{22}^3 & 0 & 0 & k_{23}^3 & k_{24}^3 \\ 0 & 0 & 0 & 0 & 0 & 0 \\ 0 & 0 & 0 & 0 & 0 & 0 \\ k_{31}^3 & k_{32}^3 & 0 & 0 & k_{33}^3 & k_{34}^3 \\ k_{41}^3 & k_{42}^3 & 0 & 0 & k_{43}^3 & k_{44}^3 \end{bmatrix} \begin{Bmatrix} \delta_{1x} \\ \delta_{1y} \\ \delta_{2x} \\ \delta_{2y} \\ \delta_{3x} \\ \delta_{3y} \end{Bmatrix}
$$

$$
+ \begin{bmatrix} 0 & 0 & 0 & 0 & 0 & 0 \\ 0 & 0 & 0 & 0 & 0 & 0 \\ 0 & 0 & k_{11}^2 & k_{12}^2 & k_{13}^2 & k_{14}^2 \\ 0 & 0 & k_{21}^2 & k_{22}^2 & k_{23}^2 & k_{24}^2 \\ 0 & 0 & k_{31}^2 & k_{32}^2 & k_{33}^2 & k_{34}^2 \\ 0 & 0 & k_{41}^2 & k_{42}^2 & k_{43}^2 & k_{44}^2 \end{bmatrix} \begin{Bmatrix} \delta_{1x} \\ \delta_{1y} \\ \delta_{2x} \\ \delta_{2y} \\ \delta_{3x} \\ \delta_{3y} \end{Bmatrix}
$$

Substituting for numerical values leads to

$$
\begin{Bmatrix} F_{1x} \\ F_{1y} \\ 4 \\ 6 \\ 0 \\ F_{3y} \end{Bmatrix} = AE \begin{bmatrix} 0.375 & 0.2165 & -0.125 & -0.2165 & -0.25 & 0 \\ 0.2165 & 0.375 & -0.2165 & -0.375 & 0 & 0 \\ -0.125 & -0.2165 & 0.3415 & 0.0915 & -0.2165 & 0.125 \\ -0.2165 & -0.375 & 0.0915 & 0.4472 & 0.125 & -0.0722 \\ -0.25 & 0 & -0.2165 & 0.125 & 0.4665 & -0.125 \\ 0 & 0 & 0.125 & -0.0722 & -0.125 & 0.0722 \end{bmatrix} \begin{Bmatrix} 0 \\ 0 \\ \delta_{2x} \\ \delta_{2y} \\ \delta_{3x} \\ 0 \end{Bmatrix}
$$

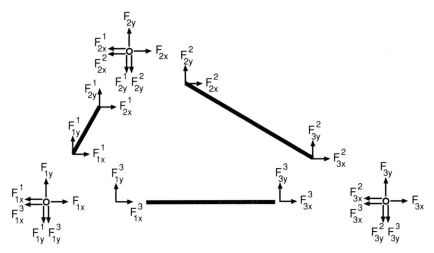

Figure 3.5 Forces acting at each node and on each element.

Handling Boundary Conditions

Let us examine the truss and the resulting system of six equations. Note that joint 1 is pinned while joint 3 is free to move only horizontally. Thus the boundary conditions are $\delta_{1x} = \delta_{1y} = \delta_{3y} = 0$, and the three unknown deflections are δ_{2x}, δ_{2y}, and δ_{3x}. In addition, there are three known forces and three unknown reaction forces for a total of six equations in six unknowns (three forces and three deflections). However, these unknowns are not isolated on one side of the equation. We need to rearrange the equation $\mathbf{F} = \mathbf{k}\delta$ to account for these boundary conditions.

Given that there are three unknown forces and three unknown deflections, one method of solving the equations would rearrange the equations *partitioning* the problem into subproblems, each with all the unknowns on one side. This is accomplished by performing row and column interchanges and partitioning the matrix to achieve the following form:

$$
\begin{Bmatrix} 4 \\ 6 \\ 0 \\ \hline F_{1x} \\ F_{1y} \\ F_{3y} \end{Bmatrix} = AE
\left[\begin{array}{ccc|ccc}
0.3415 & 0.0915 & -0.2165 & -0.125 & -0.2165 & 0.125 \\
0.0915 & 0.4472 & 0.125 & -0.2165 & -0.375 & -0.0722 \\
-0.2165 & 0.125 & 0.4665 & -0.25 & 0 & -0.125 \\
\hline
-0.125 & -0.2165 & -0.25 & 0.375 & 0.2165 & 0 \\
-0.2165 & -0.375 & 0 & 0.2165 & 0.375 & 0 \\
-0.0722 & -0.125 & 0 & 0 & 0.125 & 0.0722
\end{array} \right]
\begin{Bmatrix} \delta_{2x} \\ \delta_{2y} \\ \delta_{3x} \\ \hline 0 \\ 0 \\ 0 \end{Bmatrix}
$$

This matrix equation always has the form

$$
\begin{Bmatrix} \text{loads} \\ \text{supports} \end{Bmatrix} = \begin{bmatrix} \mathbf{k} & \mathbf{k_S} \\ \mathbf{k_S} & \mathbf{k_D} \end{bmatrix} \begin{Bmatrix} \text{deflections} \\ \{0\} \end{Bmatrix}
$$

$$
\begin{Bmatrix} \mathbf{F_L} \\ F_S \end{Bmatrix} = \begin{bmatrix} \mathbf{k} & \mathbf{k_S} \\ \mathbf{k_S} & \mathbf{k_D} \end{bmatrix} \begin{Bmatrix} \delta \\ \{0\} \end{Bmatrix}
$$

This matrix equation is solved in two steps:

$$\{\text{loads}\} = \mathbf{k}\{\text{deflections}\}$$
$$\{\text{supports}\} = \mathbf{k_S}\{\text{deflections}\}$$

In the example, this becomes

$$\begin{Bmatrix} 4 \\ 6 \\ 0 \end{Bmatrix} = AE \begin{bmatrix} 0.3415 & 0.0915 & -0.2165 \\ 0.0915 & 0.4472 & 0.125 \\ -0.2165 & 0.125 & 0.4665 \end{bmatrix} \begin{Bmatrix} \delta_{2x} \\ \delta_{2y} \\ \delta_{3x} \end{Bmatrix}$$

and

$$\begin{Bmatrix} F_{1x} \\ F_{1y} \\ F_{3y} \end{Bmatrix} = AE \begin{bmatrix} -0.125 & -0.2165 & -0.25 \\ -0.2165 & -0.375 & 0 \\ -0.0722 & -0.125 & 0 \end{bmatrix} \begin{Bmatrix} \delta_{2x} \\ \delta_{2y} \\ \delta_{3x} \end{Bmatrix}$$

Note that finding deflections requires solving a matrix equation; then, the support forces are obtained by simple matrix multiplication.

Alternatively, we can find an approximate solution using a trick commonly referred to as *blasting*. We modify the equations associated with the boundary condition deflections by first letting the external forces at these locations be zero, and then setting the diagonal elements of the stiffness matrix for these equations to a large number, such as 10^8. We are essentially replacing the fixed supports by very stiff springs. Using a very large stiffness factor forces the deflections to be very small. The support deflections will be orders of magnitude smaller than any other deflections, so they can be considered equivalent to zero. There are no external forces applied to these "fixed" nodes. Thus the modified matrix equation becomes

$$AE \begin{bmatrix} 10^8 & 0.2165 & -0.125 & -0.2165 & -0.25 & 0 \\ 0.2165 & 10^8 & -0.2165 & -0.375 & 0 & 0 \\ -0.125 & -0.2165 & 0.3415 & 0.0915 & -0.2165 & 0.125 \\ -0.2165 & -0.375 & 0.0915 & 0.4472 & 0.125 & -0.0722 \\ -0.25 & 0 & -0.2165 & 0.125 & 0.4665 & -0.125 \\ 0 & 0 & 0.125 & -0.0722 & -0.125 & 10^8 \end{bmatrix} \begin{Bmatrix} \delta_{1x} \\ \delta_{1y} \\ \delta_{2x} \\ \delta_{2y} \\ \delta_{3x} \\ \delta_{3y} \end{Bmatrix} = \begin{Bmatrix} 0 \\ 0 \\ 4 \\ 6 \\ 0 \\ 0 \end{Bmatrix}$$

Note that the 10^8 overpowers the other elements in their rows so that the corresponding δ must be very small (negligible).

We then solve for the δ's, in this case,

$$\delta = \frac{1}{AE} \begin{Bmatrix} 0 \\ 0 \\ 9.795 \\ 10.963 \\ 1.608 \\ 0 \end{Bmatrix}$$

To find the unknown forces, we then have to go back to our elemental stiffness equations, using $\mathbf{F}^m = \mathbf{k}^m\boldsymbol{\delta}$ to find each element's contribution to the nodal force. Then the support reactions are

$$F_{1x} = F_{1x}^1 + F_{1x}^3 = -4.000$$
$$F_{1y} = F_{1y}^1 + F_{1y}^3 = -6.232$$
$$F_{3y} = F_{3y}^2 + F_{3y}^3 = 0.232$$

3.4 SIMULTANEOUS LINEAR EQUATIONS: MATRIX PROBLEMS

The preceding sections have dealt with formulation of the matrix problem, commonly written as $\mathbf{Ax} = \mathbf{b}$, where $\mathbf{A}$ is the "system matrix" and $\mathbf{b}$ is the "forcing vector." In this section, several algorithms for solving this problem will be discussed.

Cramer's Rule

The first method taught to solve simultaneous equations in many linear algebra courses is Cramer's Rule. In this formula, let Δ denote the determinant of the matrix $\mathbf{A}$: $\Delta = |\mathbf{A}|$.

Also, let Δ_i denote the determinant of the matrix obtained by replacing the ith column of $\mathbf{A}$ with $\mathbf{b}$ (nonhomogeneous loading). Cramer's Rule states that the system of linear equations $\mathbf{Ax} = \mathbf{b}$ has a unique solution if and only if $\Delta \neq 0$, and

$$\mathbf{x} = \frac{1}{\Delta}\left\{\begin{array}{c} \Delta_1 \\ \vdots \\ \Delta_n \end{array}\right\}$$

This algorithm is extremely computation-intensive, requiring $(n + 1)$ evaluations of $n \times n$ determinants. Each determinant requires approximately $n!$ multiplications. Neglecting additions, the overall algorithm complexity is $(n + 1)n!$.

It is not uncommon to see problems with $n = 200$ through $n = 1000$. The reader will remember that n is the number of degrees of freedom. To observe how rapidly the number of operations gets out of control, consider Table 3.1, which approximates the computation time for a computer with a

Size	Number of Multiplications	Time
5×5	720	216 μs
10×10	4×10^7	12 s
15×15	2.1×10^{13}	6×10^6 s (70 days)
20×20	5.11×10^{19}	1.53×10^{13} s (4.8×10^5 years)

Table 3.1 Solution time using Cramer's Rule.

300-ns multiplication cycle. Obviously, Cramer's Rule is useless for realistic problems, even if computer speed improved by orders of magnitude.

Table 3.1 provides an excellent example of the need for algorithm complexity analysis. Although we will not focus on it in this book, all CAD designers can benefit from at least a cursory use of complexity analysis. Many times the straightforward approach, although manageable for small examples, will become unusable for realistic problems. The CAD system developer is well-advised to find out early and seek alternative algorithms.

A Caution about Matrix Inversion

The linear-system solution is often written as

$$\mathbf{x} = \mathbf{A}^{-1}\mathbf{b}$$

and so the solution process is referred to as inverting the matrix $\mathbf{A}$. The reader will be able to find procedures in numerical methods libraries for determining the inverse of a matrix. Given the inverse, matrix multiplication leads to the solution. The reader is warned that in almost all cases, this method will be less efficient than Gaussian elimination and the other algorithms that will be discussed in this section. Because the notation $\mathbf{A}^{-1}$ is extremely convenient, it is frequently used. In practice however, matrix inverses are virtually never explicitly determined.

Gaussian Elimination

The aim of Gaussian elimination is to use appropriate row operations to convert the original system of equations

$$\begin{bmatrix} a_{11} & a_{12} & a_{13} & \cdots & a_{1n} \\ a_{21} & a_{22} & a_{23} & \cdots & a_{2n} \\ \vdots & & \ddots & & \vdots \\ a_{n1} & a_{n2} & a_{n3} & \cdots & a_{nn} \end{bmatrix} \begin{Bmatrix} x_1 \\ x_2 \\ \vdots \\ x_n \end{Bmatrix} = \begin{Bmatrix} b_1 \\ b_2 \\ \vdots \\ b_n \end{Bmatrix}$$

into upper triangular form:

$$\begin{bmatrix} a_{11} & a_{12} & a_{13} & \cdots & a_{1n} \\ 0 & a'_{22} & a'_{23} & \cdots & a'_{2n} \\ 0 & 0 & a'_{33} & \cdots & a'_{3n} \\ \vdots & & & \ddots & \vdots \\ 0 & 0 & 0 & \cdots & a'_{nn} \end{bmatrix} \begin{Bmatrix} x_1 \\ x_2 \\ \vdots \\ x_n \end{Bmatrix} = \begin{Bmatrix} b'_1 \\ b'_2 \\ \vdots \\ b'_n \end{Bmatrix}$$

The lower triangle of zeros is produced by a sequence of row operations. For example, the zero in location a_{21} is obtained by replacing each element in the second row by

$$a'_{2i} \Leftarrow a_{2i} - \frac{a_{21}}{a_{11}} a_{1i} \quad \text{for } i = 1, \ldots, n$$

$$b'_2 \Leftarrow b_2 - \frac{a_{21}}{a_{11}} b_1$$

Applying a similar operation sequentially to rows 3 through n produces the first column of zeros. The appropriate multipliers are $a_{31}/a_{11}, a_{41}/a_{11}, \ldots, a_{n1}/a_{11}$. The algorithm is then applied to the resulting $n - 1 \times n - 1$ matrix. This *forward elimination process* repeats for the smaller square matrix left in the lower right-hand corner until only a single entry remains. A full lower triangle of zeros will have been produced.

The solution is obtained by a *backward substitution*, which uses the last equation to find x_n, the $n - 1$ equation to find x_{n-1}, and so forth:

$$x_n = \frac{b'_n}{a'_{nn}}$$

$$x_{n-1} = \frac{1}{a_{n-1,n-1}} (b'_{n-1} - a'_{n-1,n} x_n)$$

Note that when using this order, only one variable is unknown in each row.

The amount of effort required can be compared to Cramer's rule by determining the number of operations required as a function of the problem's size. An operation count shows that Gaussian elimination for an $n \times n$ matrix requires $\approx n^3/3$ operations, including the backward substitution, as compared to the $(n + 1)n!$ necessary for Cramer's rule. The 20×20 matrix from Table 3.1 is seen to take 2,667 operations or 8×10^{-4}s. A $7,000 \times 7,000$ matrix only requires ≈ 9.5 hours.

A procedure from a numerical methods library will usually consider some or all of the following issues:

- Each successive zero in the lower triangle is produced by a division by the diagonal element of **A**. Numerical accuracy is improved if this entry is large. A diagonally dominant matrix meets this criteria.

- Row pivoting or row and column pivoting can be used to ensure that the largest possible entry is used, thus maximizing numerical accuracy.

- Ill conditioning occurs if two of the equations (rows) are almost identical. This can be detected in some algorithms and is reported as the condition number of the matrix.

- In the case of banded or sparse matrices, much of the lower triangle is already zero and so substantial computation can be saved. Banded matrices have zero entries except for the diagonal and a number of sub- and superdiagonals. A sparse matrix has very few nonzero entries (compared to the n^2 total entries), but these entries are not necessarily located near the diagonal.

- If the matrix is banded with b nonzero off-diagonals, the complexity reduces to $n(2b + 1)^2 + n^2$.

Although ill-conditioned problems occur, most engineering problems are well behaved. Many engineering systems lead to diagonally dominant matrices. This is usually a result of the mechanics of the underlying governing differential equation, a topic that will be discussed in Chapter 4. Also, in many cases these matrices will be rather tightly banded ($b = n/10$). Banding is primarily a function of the topology of connections. In finite-element problems, elements usually connect adjacent nodes, so the resulting matrix is usually banded. The order in which nodes are numbered significantly affects the resulting bandwidth.

Although Gaussian elimination is efficient and stable, if the non-homogeneous vector (the forcing vector) changes, the process must be completely repeated. In most engineering situations, the matrix **A** represents the system and the vector **b** represents the external loading. It is not uncommon for designers to need to consider a variety of loading conditions applied to the same system. Gaussian elimination is inefficient in this case.

Cholesky Decomposition

The Cholesky decomposition is also referred to as *L U decomposition*, because the matrix **A** is replaced by the product of two matrices, one a lower triangular matrix and the other an upper triangular matrix. The objective of the Cholesky decomposition algorithm is to determine **L** and **U** such that

$$
\mathbf{A} = \mathbf{LU} = \begin{bmatrix} l_{11} & 0 & \cdots & 0 \\ l_{21} & l_{22} & & 0 \\ \vdots & & \ddots & 0 \\ l_{n1} & l_{n2} & \cdots & l_{nn} \end{bmatrix} \begin{bmatrix} u_{11} & u_{12} & \cdots & u_{1n} \\ 0 & u_{22} & & u_{2n} \\ \vdots & & \ddots & 0 \\ 0 & 0 & \cdots & u_{nn} \end{bmatrix}
$$

Because the matrix **A** has n^2 entries and the matrices **L** and **U** have $n^2 + n$ nonzero terms, there are n terms which are arbitrary. This is usually resolved by arbitrarily requiring $l_{ii} = 1$. Alternatively, the diagonal terms can be made identical, $l_{ii} = u_{ii}$. In the case of a symmetric positive definite matrix (commonly encountered in engineering problems), this results in $\mathbf{U} = \mathbf{L}^{\mathrm{T}}$. Usually, **L** and **U** are stored in a single matrix (in other words, the zeros are not stored).

The procedure for determining **L** and **U** will not be discussed in detail here. It is very similar to Gaussian elimination, primarily involving carefully storing the multipliers from the elimination steps. Furthermore, a designer will probably never code the L U decomposition algorithm, but use instead a procedure from a numerical methods library.

Once **L** and **U** are determined, the solution for any **b** is obtained by a *forward elimination* and a *backward substitution*. Given

$$\mathbf{LUx} = \mathbf{b}$$

solve for **z** from **Lz** = **b**:

$$
\begin{bmatrix}
l_{11} & 0 & \cdots & 0 \\
l_{21} & l_{22} & & 0 \\
\vdots & & \ddots & 0 \\
l_{n1} & l_{n2} & \cdots & l_{nn}
\end{bmatrix}
\begin{Bmatrix}
z_1 \\ z_2 \\ \vdots \\ z_n
\end{Bmatrix}
=
\begin{Bmatrix}
b_1 \\ b_2 \\ \vdots \\ b_n
\end{Bmatrix}
$$

The first equation determines z_1; each successive equation introduces only a single unknown variable. Use **z** to solve for **x** from **Ux** = **z** as in Gaussian elimination:

$$
\begin{bmatrix}
u_{11} & u_{12} & \cdots & u_{1n} \\
0 & u_{22} & & u_{2n} \\
\vdots & & \ddots & 0 \\
0 & 0 & \cdots & u_{nn}
\end{bmatrix}
\begin{Bmatrix}
x_1 \\ x_2 \\ \vdots \\ x_n
\end{Bmatrix}
=
\begin{Bmatrix}
z_1 \\ z_2 \\ \vdots \\ z_n
\end{Bmatrix}
$$

Because the decomposition can be saved for later use, a numerical library will provide one procedure to determine the L U decomposition and another to solve for **x**. The matrices **L** and **U** essentially represent the inverse of **A**.

Successive Approximation: Jacobi Method

An alternative to the direct methods is an iterative algorithm. The simplest is the *Jacobi method*, which is a method of successive approximation. The fundamental step changes the equation **Ax** = **b** or **Ax** − **b** = 0 into **x** = **f** + **Gx**. This resulting form can be cycled iteratively until convergence is achieved.

Beginning with

$$\mathbf{Ax} = \mathbf{b}$$

the main step is to decompose **A** into two matrices, the diagonal **D** and nondiagonal **B**.

$$\mathbf{A} = \mathbf{D} + \mathbf{B}$$

where

$$
\mathbf{D} =
\begin{bmatrix}
a_{11} & \cdots & 0 \\
\vdots & \ddots & \vdots \\
0 & \cdots & a_{nn}
\end{bmatrix}
\quad \text{and} \quad
\mathbf{B} =
\begin{bmatrix}
0 & \cdots & a_{1n} \\
\vdots & \ddots & \vdots \\
a_{n1} & \cdots & 0
\end{bmatrix}
$$

The matrix equation can then be rewritten as

$$\mathbf{Dx} = \mathbf{b} - \mathbf{Bx}$$

However, $\mathbf{D}$ is trivial to invert (the inverse of a diagonal matrix is obtained by inverting each diagonal entry).

$$\mathbf{x} = \mathbf{D}^{-1}\mathbf{b} - \mathbf{D}^{-1}\mathbf{Bx}$$

or

$$\mathbf{x} = \mathbf{f} - \mathbf{Gx}$$

where

$$\mathbf{f} = \left\{ \begin{array}{c} b_1/a_{11} \\ \vdots \\ b_n/a_{nn} \end{array} \right\} \quad \text{and} \quad g_{ij} = \left\{ \begin{array}{ll} a_{ij}/a_{ii} & \text{if } i \neq j \\ 0 & \text{if } i = j \end{array} \right.$$

After denoting the iterations by a superscript $x^{(i)}$, the algorithm can be re-written as

$$\mathbf{x}^{(i+1)} \Leftarrow \mathbf{f} - \mathbf{Gx}^{(i)}$$

Note that to minimize operations, $\mathbf{f}$ and $\mathbf{G}$ should be calculated once before the iteration begins.

The Jacobi method can be shown to converge if $\mathbf{A}$ is diagonally dominant. Diagonally dominant means the diagonal term is greater than or equal to the sum of the off-diagonal entries in the row. Because most field problems lead to matrices that are symmetric and diagonally dominant, the method is widely applicable.

Note also that many problems give rise to sparse matrices. The iterative method is particularly efficient in these cases because the multiplication of the zero terms in $\mathbf{G}$ is not necessary. Similarly, a banded matrix can be dealt with very efficiently.

Gauss-Seidel

An improvement on the Jacobi method, the *Gauss-Seidel method* usually provides faster convergence. The only difference from the Jacobi method is earlier use of the new terms in $\mathbf{x}^{(i+1)}$. Although the Jacobi algorithm indicates a single step to find $\mathbf{x}^{(i+1)}$, in actuality each element $x_j^{(i+1)}$ is calculated individually. Specifically, when calculating $x_j^{(i+1)}$, the method uses the new values of $x_k^{(i+1)}$ where $k < j$. This can be written as

$$x_j^{(i+1)} = f_j - \sum_{k=1}^{j-1} G_{jk} x_k^{(i+1)} - \sum_{k=j+1}^{n} G_{jk} x_k^{(i)}$$

In effect, this can be achieved by storing $x^{(i+1)}$ and $x^{(i)}$ in the same location.

The iterative methods can be further accelerated by the use of relaxation factors. This is discussed for all iterative methods in Section 3.8.

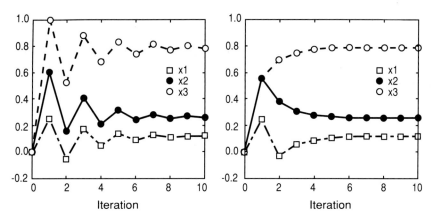

Figure 3.6 Iteration sequence for Jacobi and Gauss-Seidel algorithms.

Example 3.1: Iterative Solution. Figure 3.6 shows the iteration cycle for both the Jacobi and Gauss-Seidel methods applied to a very simple matrix problem.

$$\begin{bmatrix} 4.00 & 2.00 & 0.00 \\ 2.00 & 10.00 & 4.00 \\ 0.00 & 4.00 & 5.00 \end{bmatrix} \begin{Bmatrix} x_1 \\ x_2 \\ x_3 \end{Bmatrix} = \begin{Bmatrix} 1 \\ 6 \\ 5 \end{Bmatrix}$$

Both methods started from the trivial {0}. Note how much more quickly the Gauss-Seidel method converged.

3.5 SIMULTANEOUS NONLINEAR EQUATIONS

Section 2.7 discussed root finding for one equation, but design problems do not often lead to a single transcendental equation. Rather, the usual result is a system of equations $\mathbf{f}(\mathbf{x}) = 0$. Fortunately most of the single-equation techniques are easily extendable.

Newton-Based Methods

The multiple equation version of Newton's method is

$$\mathbf{x}_{n+1} = \mathbf{x}_n - \left[\frac{d\mathbf{f}}{d\mathbf{x}} \right]^{-1} \mathbf{f}(\mathbf{x}_n)$$

This is perhaps more easily understood by looking at two equations and two unknowns, in which case

$$\mathbf{x} = \begin{Bmatrix} x \\ y \end{Bmatrix}$$

and

$$\mathbf{f} = \left\{ \begin{array}{l} f(x, y) \\ g(x, y) \end{array} \right\}$$

The analytic approximation step is equivalent to using a Taylor's series expansion through first-order terms:

$$f(x, y) = f(x_n, y_n) + (x - x_n) \left. \frac{\partial f}{\partial x} \right|_{x_n, y_n} + (y - y_n) \left. \frac{\partial f}{\partial y} \right|_{x_n, y_n}$$

$$g(x, y) = g(x_n, y_n) + (x - x_n) \left. \frac{\partial g}{\partial x} \right|_{x_n, y_n} + (y - y_n) \left. \frac{\partial g}{\partial y} \right|_{x_n, y_n}$$

If x_{n+1}, y_{n+1} are at the root, then

$$0 = f(x_n, y_n) + (x_{n+1} - x_n) \left. \frac{\partial f}{\partial x} \right|_{x_n, y_n} + (y_{n+1} - y_n) \left. \frac{\partial f}{\partial y} \right|_{x_n, y_n}$$

$$0 = g(x_n, y_n) + (x_{n+1} - x_n) \left. \frac{\partial g}{\partial x} \right|_{x_n, y_n} + (y_{n+1} - y_n) \left. \frac{\partial g}{\partial y} \right|_{x_n, y_n}$$

This can be rewritten in matrix form as

$$\left\{ \begin{array}{l} 0 \\ 0 \end{array} \right\} = \left\{ \begin{array}{l} f(x_n, y_n) \\ g(x_n, y_n) \end{array} \right\} + \left[\begin{array}{cc} \left. \frac{\partial f}{\partial x} \right|_{x_n, y_n} & \left. \frac{\partial f}{\partial y} \right|_{x_n, y_n} \\ \left. \frac{\partial g}{\partial x} \right|_{x_n, y_n} & \left. \frac{\partial g}{\partial y} \right|_{x_n, y_n} \end{array} \right] \left\{ \begin{array}{l} x_{n+1} - x_n \\ y_{n+1} - y_n \end{array} \right\}$$

which leads to

$$\left\{ \begin{array}{l} x_{n+1} \\ y_{n+1} \end{array} \right\} = \left\{ \begin{array}{l} x_n \\ y_n \end{array} \right\} - \left[\begin{array}{cc} \left. \frac{\partial f}{\partial x} \right|_{x_n, y_n} & \left. \frac{\partial f}{\partial y} \right|_{x_n, y_n} \\ \left. \frac{\partial g}{\partial x} \right|_{x_n, y_n} & \left. \frac{\partial g}{\partial y} \right|_{x_n, y_n} \end{array} \right]^{-1} \left\{ \begin{array}{l} f(x_n, y_n) \\ g(x_n, y_n) \end{array} \right\}$$

This equation follows the general form given earlier, except with fewer variables and equations. Now the slope of the curve is a matrix, so each step will require solving a system of linear equations with one of the techniques discussed earlier in this chapter.

The higher-dimensional Newton's method can be geometrically understood from Fig. 3.7. Each function describes a surface; the equation $0 = f(x, y)$ is simply the intersection of that surface with the horizontal plane. That intersection forms a line, and the roots of the entire system are the intersections of such lines. In Fig. 3.7 two surfaces are shown. Dashed lines indicate the portions of the surface below $z = 0$. To simplify the figure, the two surfaces have been superimposed, but only the positive half of one and the negative half of the other are drawn. Newton's method approximates each surface by a plane, which in turn yields two straight lines in the horizontal plane. The intersection of these lines is easily found. The method converges, because near any root, each surface is approximately a plane.

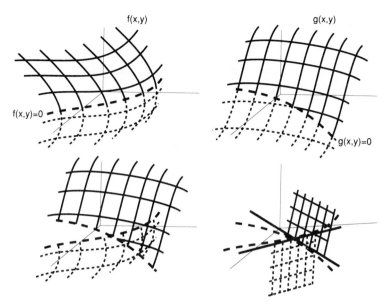

Figure 3.7   Geometric interpretation of Newton's method in two dimensions.

Successive Approximations

The method of successive approximations is also extendable. For two equations it can be written as

$$x_{n+1} = f(x_n, y_n)$$
$$y_{n+1} = g(x_n, y_n)$$

Frequently, faster convergence can be achieved with

$$x_{n+1} = f(x_n, y_n)$$
$$y_{n+1} = g(x_{n+1}, y_n)$$

3.6   OVER/UNDER RELAXATION

Note how in Fig. 3.6, the Jacobi method overshoots the root in each iteration. Similarly, the Gauss-Seidel method, although faster, achieves only 70 percent of the necessary correction during each iteration. This behavior is similar to an underdamped or overdamped single degree of freedom system and typical of iterative methods. Convergence can be accelerated by either overcorrecting or undercorrecting each iteration. Rather than

$$\mathbf{x}^{(2)} \Leftarrow \mathbf{x}^{(1)} + \Delta_{\mathbf{x}}$$

use

$$\mathbf{x}^{(2)} \Leftarrow \mathbf{x}^{(1)} + \omega \Delta_{\mathbf{x}}$$

For example, the Jacobi method would be written as

$$\mathbf{x}^{(2)} \Leftarrow \mathbf{x}^{(1)} + \omega (\mathbf{D}^{-1}(\mathbf{b} - \mathbf{B}\mathbf{x}^{(1)}) - \mathbf{x}^{(1)})$$

$$\Leftarrow (1 - \omega)\mathbf{x}^{(1)} + \omega (\mathbf{D}^{-1}\mathbf{b} - \mathbf{D}^{-1}\mathbf{B}\mathbf{x}^{(1)})$$

Any iterative method can be accelerated in this fashion. Unfortunately, the optimum value of the relaxation parameter ω is not easily determined. However, an approximate value can be determined from the nature of the unrelaxed convergence for the specific combination of algorithm and problem:

$$\begin{array}{llll} & \text{oscillatory convergence} & & 0 < \omega < 1 \\ \text{for} & \text{one-sided convergence} & \text{use} & 1 < \omega \\ & \text{one-sided divergence} & & \omega < 0 \end{array}$$

Example 3.2: Relaxation Applied to Example 3.1. Figure 3.8 shows how Example 3.1 converges for various values of ω.

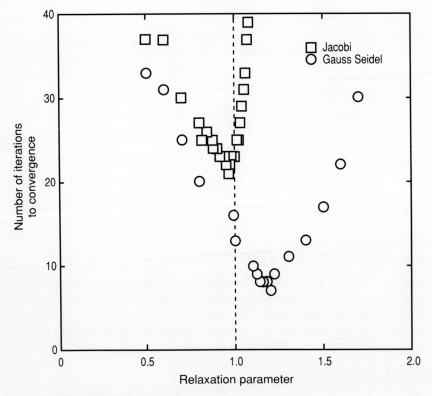

Figure 3.8   Number of iterations as a function of the relaxation parameter.

3.7   SUMMARY OF MATRIX METHODS

Two kinds of matrix solvers have been discussed—direct and iterative. Although different varieties of each can be found, the most common choices in a numerical methods library will be L U (Cholesky) decomposition and Gauss-Seidel iteration. Each method has strengths and weaknesses. Based on algorithm analysis, decomposition is $O(n^3)$ while Gauss-Seidel is $O(n^2)$ per iteration. However, this doesn't allow for problem-specific characteristics such as sparseness, bandedness, and the existence of a very good solution estimate.

The Cholesky decomposition requires a bounded finite number of steps, while Gauss-Seidel is open ended, with the number of iterations dependent on convergence criteria and matrix characteristics. The Cholesky decomposition is sensitive to numerical round-off error, which can build up during the decomposition. Conversely, the Gauss-Seidel method is only sensitive to numerical round-off during one iteration; that is, errors do not propagate from one iteration to another.

The Cholesky decomposition provides a complete solution to the problem. The resulting **L** and **U** matrices can be used for any nonhomogeneous vector **b** (forcing vector). This can save a lot of computer time if the vector **b** is changing throughout the design problem while the "system" (Λ) remains constant. A change in the system will require a completely new decomposition. The Gauss-Seidel method can deal with small changes in both **b** and **A**, because the previous solution will be a good starting point for the iteration. The primary characteristics of these two methods can be summarized as follows:

- Cholesky decomposition
    - Bounded, finite number of steps
    - Sensitive to numerical round-off (ill-conditioned matrix)
    - Easily handles any nonhomogeneous vector **b**
- Gauss-Seidel iteration
    - Open-ended number of steps, may not converge
    - Sensitive only to truncation error
    - Small variations in matrix **A** or nonhomogeneous vector **b** handled easily

Solving matrix problems is one of the most computation-intensive operations in CAD. With interactive programs, it is relatively easy for a user to construct a problem with a very large dimension n that may be beyond the capabilities of the computing resources available. This is particularly true for finite-element problems, the subject of the next chapter.

3.8   ANNOTATED REFERENCES

Coleman, T. F. and Van Loan, C. *Handbook for Matrix Computations*. Philadelphia: SIAM, 1988.

Comprehensive, including a concise introduction to FORTRAN.

Conte, S. D., and deBoor, C. *Elementary Numerical Analysis*. New York: McGraw-Hill, 1977.

Dahlquist, G., Bjorck, A., and Anderson, N. *Numerical Methods*. Englewood Cliffs, N. J.: Prentice-Hall, 1974.

Forsythe, G. E., Malcom, M. A. and Moler, C. B. *Computer Methods for Mathematical Computing*. Englewood Cliffs, N. J.: Prentice-Hall, 1977.

This is a classic book for numerical-methods algorithms, including least square, splines, integration, and matrix decomposition. Contains FORTRAN listings of very good subroutines in each area. The matrix decomposition subroutines (DECOMP and SOLVE) are very useful.

Ketter, R. L., and Prawel, S. P. *Modern Methods of Engineering Computation*. New York: McGraw-Hill, 1980.

Press, W. H., Flannery, B. P., Teukolsky, S.A., and Vetterling, W. T. *Numerical Recipes in C: The Art of Scientific Computing*. New York: Cambridge University Press, 1988.

3.9 PROJECTS

Project 3.1   Fully Stressed Frame

Problem Statement   Determine the cross-sectional properties for a single-bay-beam-and-column frame structure that carries a uniformly distributed load.

Problem Data   The frame configuration is shown in Fig. 3.9. The top corners are welded (so they can carry moment), and the bottom of each column is pinned. The columns and beam have a square cross-section with dimensions $x_1 \times x_1$ and $x_2 \times x_2$ respectively, as shown in the figure.

Analysis   If the design goal is most efficient use of structural material (minimum volume), then constraints on stress level will provide a lower limit on the size of each member. The optimum design can be obtained using optimization techniques discussed in Chapter 6. The rationale behind one design method (fully stressed design) is that the most efficient use of

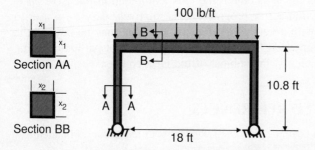

Figure 3.9   Single-bay-beam-and-column frame structure.

material occurs when each member is stressed to its maximum capacity. The critical stress condition leads to a constraint equation for each member, $f_1(x_1, x_2) = 0$ and $f_2(x_1, x_2) = 0$. The fully stressed design occurs at the solution to this system of equations.

The material properties for beam and column should be assumed to be the same.

Comments   This simple set of equations displays a number of solutions. If the volume of the frame is calculated at each solution, one finds (a) a global minimum, (b) a local minimum, (c) a nonoptimal fully stressed design, and (d) a physically meaningless solution.

Optional Exercises   Determine how the solution depends on the loading and on the aspect ratio of the frame.

Additional Information

Burns, S. A., and Locascio, A. "A Monomial Method for Solving Systems of Non-linear Algebraic Equations." *International Journal for Numerical Methods in Engineering*, Vol. 31 (May 1991). pp. 1295–1318.

Burns, S. A., Carr, T. M., and Locascio, A. "Graphical Representation of Design Optimization Processes." *Computer Aided Design*, Vol. 21 (1989). pp. 21–24.

Project 3.2   Truss Design

Problem Statement   Design a pin-jointed truss that can support 5,000 N at a distance of 2.0 m from a supporting wall. The truss can attach to the wall over a distance of 0.6 m.

Number of Nodes		
Node number	x coordinate	y coordinate
:		

Number of Elements			
Element number	First node	Second node	*EA*
:			

Number of Fixed Degrees of Freedom	
First fixed degree of freedom	
:	

Number of Loads	
Degree of freedom	Load
:	

Table 3.2   Truss data format.

Analysis   The analysis of the resulting truss follows directly from the discussion in Sections 3.2 and 3.3. The designer can expect to consider a sequence of solutions and so for efficiency would need both a truss-analysis package and a data format for describing a truss configuration. Develop an analysis package that uses the format in Table 3.2. Note that each line represents a separate line in the data file. Node 1 is assumed to have degrees of freedom 1 and 2; node 2 has 3 and 4, and node N has $2N - 1$ and $2N$.

In your analysis, determine the stress in each bar and check for plastic yielding and buckling.

4

Finite-Element Problems: Solution to Field Equations

4.1 INTRODUCTION

In many cases, the performance or behavior of an engineering system is described by the spatial distribution of a field variable. This field can be determined by solving a partial differential equation. The complete statement of a field problem involves a description of the field equation (the partial differential equation) and the boundary conditions (geometry and loading). Examples of domains that involve field problems include elasticity, heat transfer and thermal conduction, fluid flow, magnetism, and optics. The most common solution technique is the finite-element method.

The finite-element procedure can be described as a way to find an approximate solution to field equations. Analysis begins with an approximation of the region of interest by subdividing it into a number of finite elements that are connected to associated nodes. An interpolation function approximates the distribution of a dependent variable within an element. The shape function interpolates between the values of the dependent variable at the nodes. Then the original problem is replaced by some type of integral statement, and the assumed interpolation functions are substituted into the integral equation, integrated, and combined with the results from the other elements. The net result is a set of algebraic equations to be solved for the dependent variables at each node.

Practical engineering designs are invariably complicated in shape and are often composed of several different materials. Analysis of such systems usually proceeds by breaking the object down into its component parts and analyzing each component. Preserving the physical interrelationships of the elements based on the way that such components are assembled yields an approximate but relatively accurate evaluation of behavior. This is basically how the finite-element method was developed for structural analysis in the 1950s and for many other fields since then.

Suppose we want to analyze the structure shown in Fig. 4.1 for the stresses and displacements throughout the structure. (Note that both stress and displacement are field variables.) The first step in a design process would model this object very crudely as a cantilever beam; however, let us assume that we are further along in the design process and need a more detailed performance prediction. From the basic theory of elasticity, this problem could be formulated as a set of partial differential equations. If we could solve the equations for the given boundary conditions, we would obtain an exact solution to the problem. Books about the advanced theory of stress are filled with specific problems for which closed-form solutions have been determined. In most realistic problems, the geometry is such that a closed-form solution is virtually impossible to find.

As far as engineering design goes, we only want or need a "good" approximate problem and approximate solution. One approximation to the problem replaces the continuous structure with a structure that has a finite number of degrees of freedom. (For example, we could use a lattice of elastic bars, as shown in Fig. 4.2.) If we can specify the right properties for the bars, we can find the displacements of the structure, and these values will be close to the displacements of the original bracket. Once the displacements

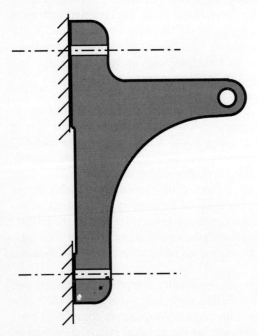

Figure 4.1   Support bracket.

are known, the stresses and strains in the approximate structure can be found easily.

In the finite-element analysis of the support bracket, we use a substitute structure whose parts are pieces of the actual structure. Figure 4.3 illustrates three alternative models for such an approximation. A large variety of shapes are available for these pieces, although three- or four-sided elements are most commonly used in two-dimensional problems. Thus each polygonal area is a flat piece of material, with lines delineating the various areas. The elements are shown slightly reduced in Fig. 4.3a to help distinguish it from Fig. 4.2, in which lines represented truss members. The finer the subdivisions, the more closely that the substitute structure will model the original one. The substitute structure is known as a *finite-element structure* and each area as a *finite element*. *Nodes* are the points where the elements "connect"; the collection of the nodes is the *finite-element mesh*.

A finite element is *not* just a piece of the actual structure. Suppose we were to just pin together a bunch of rectangular plates (at their corners) to make the structure shown in Fig. 4.3a. Clearly, as the structure is loaded, all the load would be carried through the pins, resulting in more distortion at those points. This distortion would lead to gaps appearing between some elements as the element sides begin to curve. These gaps do not occur in a real structure. Thus we have to make sure that the elements do not allow such distortion to happen.

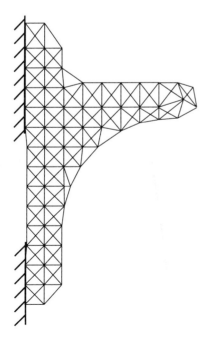

Figure 4.2   Truss approximation of a support bracket.

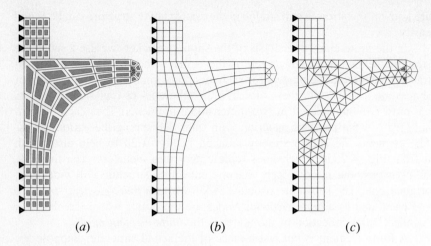

(a) (b) (c)

Figure 4.3   Finite-element approximations of a short beam.

For each element, the force-deflection relation can be written as

$$\mathbf{k\delta} = \mathbf{f}$$

where $\mathbf{k}$ is an $n \times n$ stiffness matrix, $\mathbf{\delta}$ is an n-column of nodal displacements, $\mathbf{f}$ is an n-column of nodal forces, and n is the number of degrees of freedom of the element.

Assembling all the elemental equations yields the structural equation

$$\mathbf{K\delta} = \mathbf{F}$$

where $\mathbf{K}$ is the $N \times N$ global stiffness matrix and $\mathbf{\delta}$ and $\mathbf{F}$ are columns of length N. This equation can be used to solve for all the unknown nodal displacements $\mathbf{\delta}$, using techniques from the previous chapter. Nodal displacements will give us the displacements at any point inside the structure: Interpolation functions calculate the displacements at any point within an element in terms of the nodal displacements of the element. This method of formulation is the *assumed displacement field method*.

Some advantages of the finite-element method include the following:

- Structures of arbitrary geometry can be modeled with elements of various types, sizes, and shapes.

- Structures composed of more than one material can be modeled.

- Arbitrary support conditions and arbitrary loadings can be represented.

- The finite-element model closely resembles the actual structure.

However, the method also has some disadvantages:

- A specific problem generates a specific numerical result. To examine changes in parameters requires going through the whole analysis again.
- Experience and judgment are needed to produce a good model.
- A reasonably powerful computer is required to run realistic problems.
- Pre- and postprocessing of data may be very laborious.

The steady increase in computational horsepower coupled with advances in CAD techniques are helping the designer overcome these disadvantages. A workstation that can support advanced graphics usually has sufficient computation power to support the analysis of realistic problems. Interactive graphics, combined with the appropriate data structures, can solve many of the pre- and postprocessing problems. Techniques developed from artificial-intelligence research and more specifically, expert systems development, may reduce the experience and judgment required to produce a good model. It is important to note that the experience required falls into two areas. The first area concerns the computational aspects of finite-element method (f.e.m.) analysis. Quality of the finite-element mesh is a good example of an aspect of the f.e.m. model that can be improved by CAD programs. The second area concerns engineering judgment about the mechanics of the problem and decisions about which elements and boundary conditions to use. CAD techniques help in this area indirectly, because they free the designer's energy from other aspects to focus more on these problems.

Note that this book will discuss only very introductory concepts of the finite-element method. This chapter cannot hope to provide a comprehensive treatment of either the use or the development of f.e.m. programs; that would require several graduate-level courses. However, the main ideas and the approach are worth knowing, especially now that many finite-element programs are available for use on hardware ranging from PCs to supercomputers.

In the next section, material from the theory of elasticity will be used to introduce structural finite-element analysis. It is important to remember that this technique can be used for any field problem. The finite-element method is central to many thermal and fluid analyses.

After a more detailed discussion of the general process of finite-element analysis, some concepts from the theory of elasticity will be reviewed. Some of the types of interpolation from Chapter 2 will be high lighted, and energy methods for deriving elemental stiffness matrices will be discussed. As an example, we will present the traditional beam element, the 2-D plain stress element, and a 3-D element. Section 4.12, Advanced Topics, will briefly introduce several other concepts. The conclusion will relate this chapter to almost every other chapter in the book.

4.2   GENERAL PROCESS

Fig. 4.4 illustrates models at different stages of the finite-element method. A complete finite-element analysis will usually proceed as follows:

- Geometry definition
- Mesh generation
  - Subdivision into regions
  - Mesh compatibility between regions
- Selection of elements, application to mesh
- Assignment of material properties
- Formation of global stiffness matrix
- Specification of boundary conditions
- Solution of the matrix problem

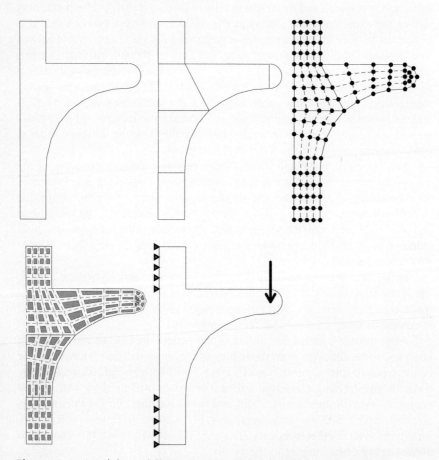

Figure 4.4   Models at different stages of the finite-element method.

Geometry can be either created within the finite-element system using a modeling system, or it can be imported from an existing CAD file. It is important to note that the f.e.m. geometry is almost always an approximation to the actual geometry. For example, details such as fillets may or may not be included in the geometry (compare Figures 4.1 and 4.3). This is an example of a modeling decision made by the designer and based partially on the expected mesh size and on insight as to which regions of the part are critical. (Chapter 9 will discuss the description of geometry in more detail.)

The next step is creating of the mesh, the distribution of the nodes. In many ways, this is the most important stage in the f.e.m. process. The mesh complexity used will determine the size of the global stiffness matrix and the numerical complexity and computing resources required. Given N nodes, the allocation of locations for each will determine the accuracy of the solution.

A wide variety of mesh-generation techniques have been developed. The most common are mapped mesh and Gaussian meshing. Mapped-mesh generation proceeds by identifying regions which are isomorphic to a square or triangle (for 2-D mesh generation). This is equivalent to the tessellation procedure that will be discussed in Chapter 9. Lines of constant parameteric value are used to locate nodes within the mapped mesh. Mapped-mesh generation usually requires the designer to divide the geometry into three- or four-sided subregions, each of which will receive a mapped mesh. Mesh density parameters are used to control the spacing of the nodes. It is important to maintain compatibility between adjoining regions. For example, in Fig. 4.3a, the mesh for the upper tab is not compatible with the mesh for the body of the bracket. An f.e.m. analysis produces more accurate results if the mesh lines are aligned with the stress gradients and contours. In addition, the node density should be higher in regions of higher stress gradient. Neither uniformly distributed nor randomly distributed nodes are desirable. The Gaussian method depends on the solution of a separate problem defined by the model's geometry. The separate problem leads to a solution (a potential function) that can be used to distribute nodes. Many designers use a low-density mesh to quickly produce an estimate of the stress distribution before refining the mesh in specific areas.

It is interesting to note that the mesh and the boundary conditions cannot be separated as cleanly as implied in the previous list. Without consideration of the loading (boundary conditions), the question of a good mesh for a particular geometry is a poorly posed problem. If point loads are to be considered, it is important to generate nodes at those points independent of where the mesh generator would have created them. In the meshes in Fig. 4.3, the meshing is made easier because the support boundary conditions apply to the entire length of both top and bottom tabs. Consider how the mesh would change if the top tab were supported for only two thirds of its length. The best internal distribution of the mesh also depends on the boundary conditions because of the resulting stress distribution. For example, if the upper tab in Fig. 4.3 were not attached to the wall, there would be no need to mesh the upper tab to any great resolution.

Mesh generation is a difficult problem, particularly in three dimensions. Using triangles or tetrahedra can reduce the difficulties considerably by removing most of the mesh compatibility problems. However, most designers who use f.e.m. analysis prefer quadrilateral elements. Although automatic mesh generation for arbitrary geometry is a desirable goal, most existing finite-element programs depend on extensive user experience and judgment for the generation of the mesh. Examples of several meshes can be seen in Chapter 8.

The mesh is distinctly different from the elements that are placed onto that mesh. Obviously the elements must be consistent with the mesh. Four-node elements cannot be used with a mesh developed for three-node elements. However, some elements use mid-side nodes, such as a six-node triangular element with three corner and three mid-side nodes. Mid-side nodes can be created automatically from the original mesh as needed. The most common two-dimensional elements are four-noded quad, eight-noded isoparametric quad, and six-node isoparametric triangles. Three-dimensional analysis uses a wide variety of elements, such as beams, shells, plates, and membranes. Yet another family of elements (gap elements, sliding elements with/without friction) has been developed to model interface conditions. However, it is the designer/analyst who must correctly make the crucial choice of elements. The development of stiffness matrices for specific elements is discussed later in this chapter. Although in most cases the designer is insulated from this aspect of the problem, unusual problems may require the development of custom elements. If custom elements are required, the reader should refer to the extensive f.e.m. literature.

Material properties must be assigned to each element. These material properties are typically Young's modulus and Poisson's ratio, but shell and plate elements and two-dimensional problems, such as those illustrated in Figures 4.1–4.4, treat thickness more like a material property than a geometric one. Interface elements may require a coefficient of friction. It is important to note that a single material property need not be assumed; different regions of mesh may be assigned different material properties. In problems with multiple materials, the treatment of the interface between these materials is one of the most critical modeling decisions.

For each element, the information from the mesh (node coordinates) and material properties are used to calculate a local elemental stiffness matrix. This is transformed into the global coordinate system and combined into a global structural stiffness matrix.

The designer usually thinks of boundary conditions in terms of the geometry of the part; however, the boundary conditions ultimately must be expressed as a set of values for forces or displacement on specific nodes of the mesh. For example, in Fig. 4.3 the upper and lower tabs have been modeled as fixed. The specific nodes that are restrained depend upon the mesh density. The designer will usually divide the object into regions so that the entire edge of a region can have the same boundary condition. Some programs are more successful than others at insulating the engineer from consideration of specific nodal boundary conditions.

Any of the techniques described in the previous chapter can be used to solve the matrix problem. Specific characteristics of f.e.m. problems can be exploited in the solution process. The stiffness matrix is almost always symmetric and diagonally dominant and usually is banded as well. Realistic problems (particularly three-dimensional analyses) can be quite large (several thousand degrees of freedom). This has spurred development of solution techniques that do not require the formation or storage of the entire stiffness matrix. Discussion of these methods is beyond the scope of this book. The interested reader should investigate *skyline storage methods* and *wavefront solution methods*.

While a well-posed finite-element problem consists of geometry, mesh, elements, material properties, and boundary conditions, the solution itself consists of the set of response values at each node. Postprocessing programs use interactive graphics and visualization techniques to present this information to the designer. Several different examples of finite-element results are shown in Color Plates 1 and 6–18.

Most of the remainder of this chapter deals with the formulation of the elemental stiffness matrix and of the global stiffness matrix. It is important to remember the role played by geometry (Chapter 9), data structures (Chapter 10), and user interfaces (Chapter 11) in the implementation of an effective finite element program.

■ **EXERCISE 4.1:** Select a two-dimensional shape and sketch an f.e.m. mesh for that shape. Try to pick a shape from an actual mechanical part; otherwise, refer to textbooks about mechanical components for shapes.

4.3   ELASTICITY THEORY

Referring to Fig. 4.5, consider the stress on a *differential* (not finite) element of thickness t and let F_x and F_y be the body forces per unit volume (caused by gravity, pressure, magnetic field, and so on). The state of stress is a tensor with a spatial variation (a field variable). That is, the stress can vary in x and y. For example, $\partial \sigma_x / \partial x$ is the rate of change of stress σ_x with respect to the variable x. After cancelling terms, equilibrium of forces in the x and y directions is

$$\frac{\partial \sigma_x}{\partial x} + \frac{\partial \tau_{xy}}{\partial y} + F_x = 0$$

$$\frac{\partial \sigma_y}{\partial y} + \frac{\partial \tau_{xy}}{\partial x} + F_y = 0$$

These are the *differential equations of equilibrium*.

Deforming a continuous structure usually does not create any cracks or holes. This means that the displacement field is continuous and single valued, an observation known as the *compatibility condition*.

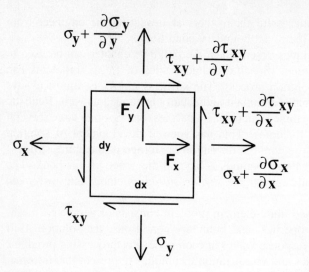

Figure 4.5 A differential element.

Two types of *boundary conditions* can be used in stress analysis. The first is displacement boundary conditions. For example, in the bracket shown in Fig. 4.3, the left wall support is modeled as $\delta_x = 0$ for two portions of the boundary. Stress boundary conditions are the second category. In Fig. 4.3 the normal and shear stress is zero for the remainder of the boundary of the bracket. The contact stress from any load applied to the bracket can be modeled as a load applied to a node. This specified nodal loading is an example of a stress boundary condition. One of these two types of boundary conditions must be specified for all parts of the boundary. When displacements are prescribed, stresses are unknown and will take on values dictated by the solution. Conversely, when stresses are prescribed, displacements are unknown.

If a stress or displacement field satisfies the differential equations of equilibrium, the compatibility conditions at every point, and the boundary conditions at every boundary point, it is a solution. So how does this definition of a solution compare to a solution obtained by finite-element analysis? Finite-element analysis seeks a solution that satisfies the preceding conditions in an *approximate* way. That is, if the assumed displacement-field method is used, the compatibility equation is satisfied within elements. Suitable fields will satisfy interelement compatibility and permit displacement boundary conditions to be met. Although the equilibrium equations and boundary conditions on stress are only approximately satisfied, the solution will improve if more elements are used.

An alternative method based on assumed stress fields can be developed. That alternative would use fields that satisfy equilibrium, and would only approximate compatibility conditions. The reader is referred to a more detailed discussion of the finite-element method for this alternative.

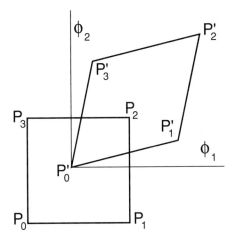

Figure 4.6 Deformed and displaced element.

Next we have to relate stress to strain. Consider the differential element $P_0 P_1 P_2 P_3$, which displaces and deforms to $P_0' P_1' P_2' P_3'$, as shown in Fig. 4.6. The motion is a combination of rigid body motion and distortion. Let u and v represent the displacement of point P_0. Like stress, displacement is a field variable ($u = u(x, y)$, $v = v(x, y)$). Hence the displacements of P_1 and P_3 are not just u and v, but are u and v plus some extra increment based on how u and v vary with position. Here, assuming infinitesimal element size, P_1 moves a distance $u + \partial u/\partial x \, dx$ horizontally and $v + \partial v/\partial x \, dx$ vertically while P_3 moves a distance $u + \partial u/\partial y \, dy$ horizontally and $v + \partial v/\partial y \, dy$ vertically.

The strain in the x direction is just the change in length in the x direction divided by the original length:

$$\epsilon_x = \frac{\partial u}{\partial x}$$

$$\epsilon_y = \frac{\partial v}{\partial y}$$

The shear strain is defined by

$$
\begin{aligned}
\gamma_{xy} &= \phi_1 + \phi_2 \\
&= \frac{(u + \partial u/\partial y \, dy) - u}{dy} + \frac{(v + \partial v/\partial x \, dx) - v}{dx} \\
&= \frac{\partial u}{\partial y} + \frac{\partial v}{\partial x}
\end{aligned}
$$

These three equations are known as the *strain-displacement relations* and can be written as

$$
\left\{ \begin{array}{c} \epsilon_x \\ \epsilon_y \\ \gamma_{xy} \end{array} \right\} =
\begin{bmatrix} \partial/\partial x & 0 \\ 0 & \partial/\partial y \\ \partial/\partial x & \partial/\partial y \end{bmatrix}
\left\{ \begin{array}{c} u \\ v \end{array} \right\}
$$

If we considered a three-dimensional block instead of a rectangular plate, we would find

$$
\begin{Bmatrix} \epsilon_x \\ \epsilon_y \\ \epsilon_z \\ \gamma_{xy} \\ \gamma_{yz} \\ \gamma_{zx} \end{Bmatrix} = \begin{bmatrix} \partial/\partial x & 0 & 0 \\ 0 & \partial/\partial y & 0 \\ 0 & 0 & \partial/\partial z \\ \partial/\partial y & \partial/\partial x & 0 \\ 0 & \partial/\partial z & \partial/\partial y \\ \partial/\partial z & 0 & \partial/\partial x \end{bmatrix} \begin{Bmatrix} u \\ v \\ w \end{Bmatrix}
$$

Three-Dimensional Stress-Strain Relations

In the general three-dimensional case, strains are related to stress and initial strains by

$$
\begin{Bmatrix} \epsilon_x \\ \epsilon_y \\ \epsilon_z \\ \gamma_{xy} \\ \gamma_{yz} \\ \gamma_{zx} \end{Bmatrix} = \mathbf{C} \begin{Bmatrix} \sigma_x \\ \sigma_y \\ \sigma_z \\ \tau_{xy} \\ \tau_{yz} \\ \tau_{zx} \end{Bmatrix} + \begin{Bmatrix} \epsilon_{x0} \\ \epsilon_{y0} \\ \epsilon_{z0} \\ \gamma_{xy0} \\ \gamma_{yz0} \\ \gamma_{zx0} \end{Bmatrix}
$$

where $\mathbf{C}$ is a 6×6 matrix of elastic coefficients.

For an isotropic material

$$
\mathbf{C} = \begin{bmatrix} 1/E & -\nu/E & -\nu/E & 0 & 0 & 0 \\ -\nu/E & 1/E & -\nu/E & 0 & 0 & 0 \\ -\nu/E & -\nu/E & 1/E & 0 & 0 & 0 \\ 0 & 0 & 0 & 1/G & 0 & 0 \\ 0 & 0 & 0 & 0 & 1/G & 0 \\ 0 & 0 & 0 & 0 & 0 & 1/G \end{bmatrix}
$$

If we write "Hookes Law" as

$$
\boldsymbol{\epsilon} = \mathbf{C}\boldsymbol{\sigma} + \boldsymbol{\epsilon}_0
$$

then the inverse equation for stress in terms of strain is

$$
\boldsymbol{\sigma} = \mathbf{E}(\boldsymbol{\epsilon} - \boldsymbol{\epsilon}_0) = \mathbf{E}\boldsymbol{\epsilon} + \boldsymbol{\sigma}_0
$$

where $\mathbf{E} = \mathbf{C}^{-1}$. Note that $\mathbf{E}$ is symmetric and contains at most 21 independent coefficients. For an isotropic material,

$$
\mathbf{E} = \frac{E}{(1 + \nu)(1 - 2\nu)} \begin{bmatrix} 1 - \nu & \nu & \nu & 0 & 0 & 0 \\ \nu & 1 - \nu & \nu & 0 & 0 & 0 \\ \nu & \nu & 1 - \nu & 0 & 0 & 0 \\ 0 & 0 & 0 & (1 - 2\nu)/2 & 0 & 0 \\ 0 & 0 & 0 & 0 & (1 - 2\nu)/2 & 0 \\ 0 & 0 & 0 & 0 & 0 & (1 - 2\nu)/2 \end{bmatrix}
$$

Plane Stress

For the two-dimensional case of plane stress, our equations are required by definition to have

$$\sigma_z = \tau_{yz} = \tau_{zx} = \gamma_{yz} = \gamma_{zx} = 0$$

and we ignore ϵ_z. Thus the resulting stress-strain equation is

$$\left\{ \begin{array}{c} \sigma_x \\ \sigma_y \\ \tau_{xy} \end{array} \right\} = \mathbf{E}_{3\times3} \left\{ \begin{array}{c} \epsilon_x \\ \epsilon_y \\ \gamma_{xy} \end{array} \right\} + \left\{ \begin{array}{c} \sigma_{x0} \\ \sigma_{y0} \\ \tau_{xy0} \end{array} \right\}$$

The stiffness matrix is obtained by discarding rows and columns 3, 5, and 6 from the $\mathbf{C}$ matrix and inverting the resulting 3×3 matrix to obtain

$$\mathbf{E}_{3\times3} = \frac{E}{(1 - \nu^2)} \begin{bmatrix} 1 & \nu & 0 \\ \nu & 1 & 0 \\ 0 & 0 & (1 - \nu)/2 \end{bmatrix}$$

Plane Strain

For the two-dimensional case of plane strain, a necessary requirement is

$$\epsilon_z = \tau_{yz} = \tau_{zx} = \gamma_{yz} = \gamma_{zx} = 0$$

and σ_z is ignored. The appropriate matrix $\mathbf{E}$ is found by discarding rows and columns 3, 5, and 6 from $\mathbf{E}$ to get

$$\mathbf{E}_{3\times3} = \frac{E}{(1 + \nu)(1 - 2\nu)} \begin{bmatrix} 1 - \nu & \nu & 0 \\ \nu & 1 - \nu & 0 \\ 0 & 0 & (1 - 2\nu)/2 \end{bmatrix}$$

Equilibrium

Working with the plane stress case,

$$\sigma_x = \frac{E}{(1 - \nu^2)} (\epsilon_x + \nu\epsilon_y)$$

$$\sigma_y = \frac{E}{(1 - \nu^2)} (\nu\epsilon_x + \epsilon_y)$$

$$\tau_{xy} = \frac{E}{2(1 + \nu)} \gamma_{xy}$$

Finally, assuming $F_x = F_y = 0$ and substituting in the strain-displacement equations yields

$$\frac{\partial^2 u}{\partial x^2} + \frac{\partial^2 u}{\partial y^2} = \frac{1 + \nu}{2} \left(\frac{\partial^2 u}{\partial y^2} - \frac{\partial^2 v}{\partial x \partial y} \right)$$

$$\frac{\partial^2 v}{\partial x^2} + \frac{\partial^2 v}{\partial y^2} = \frac{1 + \nu}{2} \left(\frac{\partial^2 v}{\partial x^2} - \frac{\partial^2 u}{\partial x \partial y} \right)$$

These are the field equations for the displacements u and v. If the distribution of u and v is known, the local stress and strain can be determined.

4.4 INTERPOLATION AND REPRESENTATION OF CURVES

When using the finite-element method based on assumed displacement fields, the displacement of any point within the element is a function of the coordinates of the point within the element and of the nodal displacements. An interpolation scheme can be used to find this displacement.

As discussed in Chapter 2, many interpolation schemes are available. Finite-element methods commonly use a scheme that essentially fits a polynomial through a known set of points. Suppose there is a set of n points with u_i being the known value at position x_i for $i = 1, \ldots, n$. A polynomial of degree $n - 1$ can be defined to fit these points. For example, with two points one could fit a straight line; with three points, a parabola, and so on. As discussed in Section 2.2, the basic Lagrange interpolation formula is given by

$$u = N_1 u_1 + N_2 u_2 + \cdots + N_n u_n$$

where

$$N_1 = \frac{(x - x_2)(x - x_3) \cdots (x - x_n)}{(x_1 - x_2)(x_1 - x_3) \cdots (x_1 - x_n)}$$

$$N_2 = \frac{(x - x_1)(x - x_3) \cdots (x - x_n)}{(x_2 - x_1)(x_2 - x_3) \cdots (x_2 - x_n)}$$

$$\vdots$$

$$N_n = \frac{(x - x_1)(x - x_2) \cdots (x - x_{n-1})}{(x_n - x_1)(x_n - x_2) \cdots (x_n - x_{n-1})}$$

or in a more general form:

$$N_i = \frac{\prod_{j=1, \, j \neq i}^{n} (x - x_j)}{\prod_{j=1, \, j \neq i}^{n} (x_i - x_j)}$$

Note that each N_i is a polynomial of degree $n - 1$ and that $N_i(x_i) = 1$ and $N_i(x_j) = 0$ for $j \neq i$. The above polynomials yield a total polynomial such that the value of u at any x is dependent on all the u_i. The resulting curve may not match exactly the "true" curve being sought. Hence for a finite element approach, the displacements found by interpolation may be slightly different from a solution found theoretically.

To demonstrate how to use this approach for a two-dimensional problem, let us do a simple example.

Example 4.1: Nine-Node Isoparametric Quadrilateral Shape Functions.
Suppose we want to find the displacement u of any point inside the rectangle, given the nodal displacements $u_1, \ldots, u_9$ (as well as $v_1, \ldots, v_9$), Figure 4.7 illustrates this nine-node rectangular element. It includes corner nodes, mid-side nodes, and a mid-element node. An arbitrary location within the element is specified by coordinates x, y, where $x \in [0, 2L_x]$ and $y \in [0, 2L_y]$. The mid-side nodes are assumed to equally divide each side.

Using the interpolation formula yields the following results:

$$u = u_{13} = N_1(x)u_1 + N_2(x)u_2 + N_3(x)u_3$$

along line 1–3

$$u = u_{46} = N_1(x)u_4 + N_2(x)u_5 + N_3(x)u_6$$

along line 4–6

$$u = u_{79} = N_1(x)u_7 + N_2(x)u_8 + N_3(x)u_9$$

along line 7–9, and

$$u = N_1(y)u_{13} + N_2(y)u_{46} + N_3(y)u_{79}$$

along any line parallel to the y-axis, where

$$N_1(s) = \frac{(s - L_s)(s - 2L_s)}{(-L_s)(-2L_s)}$$

$$N_2(s) = \frac{s(s - 2L_s)}{(L_s)(-L_s)} \qquad \text{for } s = x \text{ or } y$$

$$N_3(s) = \frac{s(s - L_s)}{(2L_s)(L_s)}$$

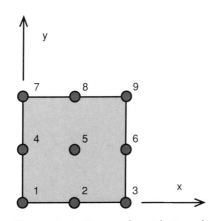

Figure 4.7   Rectangle with 9 nodes.

Combining the preceding equations will give the formula for u,

$$u(x, y) = N_1(x)N_1(y)u_1 + N_2(x)N_1(y)u_2 + N_3(x)N_1(y)u_3 + \cdots$$

or in matrix form:

$$u(x, y) = \{ N_1(y) \quad N_2(y) \quad N_3(y) \} \begin{bmatrix} u_1 & u_2 & u_3 \\ u_4 & u_5 & u_6 \\ u_7 & u_8 & u_9 \end{bmatrix} \begin{Bmatrix} N_1(x) \\ N_2(x) \\ N_3(x) \end{Bmatrix}$$

Similarly, the displacements $v(x, y)$ can be found by replacing the u_i's in the above by v_i's.

The interpolation equations or shape functions $N_i(x)$ and $N_j(y)$ define the general displacement (u, v) of a point in terms of the nodal displacements $u_1, \ldots, u_n$ and the coordinates of the point in question (x, y).

The point to remember about using finite-element methods is that the displacements within an element are governed only by the nodes that describe the element. In other words, a finite-element model of a structure involves a *piecewise* polynomial interpolation. There is no polynomial that defines the displacements of the entire structure.

■ **EXERCISE 4.2:** Derive shape functions for $u(x, y)$ for a four-node quadrilateral element. Use $[0, 2L_x]$, $[0, 2L_y]$.

■ **EXERCISE 4.3:** Derive shape functions for $U(x, y)$ for a six-node triangular element.

■ **EXERCISE 4.4:** Derive displacement functions for $u(x, y)$ for a four-node quadrilateral element assuming that $x \in [-L_x, L_x]$ and $y \in [-L_y, L_y]$.

4.5 ENERGY METHODS

So far the stiffness matrix has been found using considerations of direct physical arguments, in other words, by imposing static equilibrium conditions to find the equation

$$\mathbf{K\delta} = \mathbf{F}$$

This works well when the nodes are the only connections between the elements (as in the truss example in Chapter 3 and the beam example in Section 4.7). Elements more complicated than these two are difficult, if not impossible, to formulate properly with a direct approach; however, an approach based on a minimum potential is more general and more reliable. Recall that the finite-element method is a technique that approximates the equilibrium configuration of the structure under study. Usually designers use a polynomial to describe the approximate displacement field.

Stated simply, the solution method selects the polynomial that simultaneously minimizes the potential energy and approximately satisfies the equilibrium condition.

Total Potential Energy

Let a *system* be an elastic structure plus the loads that act upon it. The system is *conservative* if the work done in deforming the structure to any deformed shape and restoring it back to its original shape is *zero*. The *potential energy* of a system is contained in the elastic deformations and the capacity of the loads to do work.

The *principle of minimum potential energy* states:

> Among all displacement configurations that satisfy internal compatibilities and kinematic boundary conditions, those that also satisfy the equations of equilibrium make the potential energy a stationary value. If the stationary value is a minimum, the equilibrium is stable.

Most simple elastic systems have only one equilibrium, and this position is stable. The principle of minimum potential energy also holds for nonlinear conservative systems that have more than one equilibrium configuration.

Example 4.2: Consider the elastic rod where the only variable given is end displacement δ, and let $\delta = 0$ when the rod is unstretched (as shown in Fig. 4.8). The potential energy is just

$$V = \frac{1}{2}k\delta^2 - P\delta$$

where P is the load applied to the rod. The $P\delta$ term has a negative sign, since the force is doing positive work; thus, the system is losing potential energy. If $\delta = 0$ is the zero-energy state, the *external* work required to move a distance δ is $\frac{1}{2}k\delta^2$ against the spring and $-P\delta$ against the load. The displacement that occurs at static equilibrium makes V stationary with respect to the displacement, in other words:

$$\left.\frac{\partial V}{\partial \delta}\right|_{\delta_{eq}} = 0$$

so that

$$\delta_{eq} = \frac{P}{k}$$

The energy is shown to be a minimum (rather than a maximum or inflection

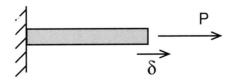

Figure 4.8 Simple elastic rod.

point) by the local curvature of the potential,

$$\left.\frac{\partial^2 V}{\partial \delta^2}\right|_{\delta_{eq}} = k$$

The positive value of the curvature shows that the equilibrium configuration is stable.

Several Degrees of Freedom

Unfortunately, there aren't going to be many one-degree-of-freedom systems that you will need to analyze. Nearly all will have many degrees of freedom (the truss discussed earlier had several degrees of freedom).

An n-degree-of-freedom system is one in which n independent quantities describe the system configuration. These n quantities, also known as *generalized coordinates*, can be displacements, angular rotations, strains, momenta, and so on. Then the potential energy of such an n-degree-of-freedom system can be expressed as $V = V(\delta_1, \delta_2, \ldots, \delta_n)$, where the δ_i are the generalized coordinates. Now,

$$\frac{\partial V}{\partial \boldsymbol{\delta}} = \left\{ \begin{array}{c} \partial V/\partial \delta_1 \\ \vdots \\ \partial V/\partial \delta_n \end{array} \right\}$$

where

$$\boldsymbol{\delta} = \left\{ \begin{array}{c} \delta_1 \\ \vdots \\ \delta_n \end{array} \right\}$$

For a stationary value of the potential energy, $\partial V/\partial \{\delta\} = 0$ is required for *any* set of admissible displacements $\boldsymbol{\delta}$. This can only happen if each coefficient in $\partial V/\partial \boldsymbol{\delta} = 0$ vanishes separately. Thus,

$$\frac{\partial V}{\partial \delta_i} = 0 \qquad i = 1, 2, 3, \ldots, n$$

or

$$\left\{ \begin{array}{c} \partial V/\partial \delta_1 \\ \vdots \\ \partial V/\partial \delta_n \end{array} \right\} = 0$$

The preceding equation defines the equilibrium configuration of the system.

Example 4.3: Consider the two-degree-of-freedom system shown in Fig. 4.9. The object is rigid and weightless, and its external shape is not relevant to this problem. The reference point is only allowed to move in the

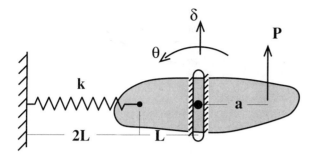

Figure 4.9 Two-degree-of-freedom system.

x direction, but the object can rotate about this pin. Use the generalized coordinates of $\{ \delta \quad \theta \}^{\mathrm{T}}$, the translation of the pin, and the rotation of the object. An external force P can be applied at a specific point as shown. When $\delta = \theta = 0$ the spring of length $2L$ is unstretched.

Thus, finding the equilibrium configuration involves applying the equation found above:

$$\frac{\partial V}{\partial \delta} = 0$$

$$\frac{\partial V}{\partial \theta} = 0$$

In matrix form this reduces to

$$\begin{bmatrix} k & kL \\ kL & kL^2 \end{bmatrix} \begin{Bmatrix} \delta \\ \theta \end{Bmatrix} = \begin{Bmatrix} P \\ Pa \end{Bmatrix}$$

The matrix found is the stiffness matrix, the terms P and Pa can be called the *generalized forces*, and the final results is an equation of the form

$$\mathbf{KD} = \mathbf{R}$$

What we see from all this is that

1. The stiffness matrix of a system that has linear load versus displacement properties is symmetric, in other words, $K_{ij} = K_{ji}$. This is the principle of reciprocity.

2. Each equation $\partial V/\partial \delta_i = 0$ is an equilibrium equation. We could have found our matrix equation by considering the equilibrium of lateral forces and moments about the left end.

3. The product of each generalized displacement and its corresponding generalized force is measured in units of work or energy.

General Expression for Potential Energy

Let's look at a more general three-dimensional case where all six stress components act on a linear elastic material. If we let

$$
\boldsymbol{\sigma} = \begin{Bmatrix} \sigma_x \\ \sigma_y \\ \sigma_z \\ \tau_{xy} \\ \tau_{yz} \\ \tau_{zx} \end{Bmatrix} \quad \text{and} \quad \boldsymbol{\epsilon} = \begin{Bmatrix} \epsilon_x \\ \epsilon_y \\ \epsilon_z \\ \gamma_{xy} \\ \gamma_{yz} \\ \gamma_{zx} \end{Bmatrix}
$$

where the engineering definition for shear strain is

$$
\gamma_{xy} = \frac{\partial v}{\partial x} + \frac{\partial u}{\partial y}
$$

$$
\gamma_{yz} = \frac{\partial w}{\partial y} + \frac{\partial v}{\partial z}
$$

$$
\gamma_{zx} = \frac{\partial u}{\partial z} + \frac{\partial w}{\partial x}
$$

and we let $\boldsymbol{\delta}$ be the vector of displacements in the x, y, and z directions, respectively.

$$
\boldsymbol{\delta} = \begin{Bmatrix} u \\ v \\ w \end{Bmatrix}
$$

From before we have the general stress strain relation

$$
\boldsymbol{\sigma} = \mathbf{E}(\boldsymbol{\epsilon} - \boldsymbol{\epsilon}_0) = \mathbf{E}\boldsymbol{\epsilon} + \boldsymbol{\sigma}_0
$$

where $\mathbf{E}$ is a symmetric matrix of elastic constants. The strain energy per unit volume in the material is

$$
U_0 = \frac{1}{2}\boldsymbol{\epsilon}^{\mathrm{T}}\mathbf{E}\boldsymbol{\epsilon} + \boldsymbol{\epsilon}^{\mathrm{T}}\boldsymbol{\sigma}_0 = \frac{1}{2}\boldsymbol{\epsilon}^{\mathrm{T}}\boldsymbol{\sigma}
$$

as opposed to the one-dimensional case, $U_0 = (1/2)E\epsilon^2 + \sigma_0\epsilon$, so that the incremental strain energy per unit volume due to infinitesimal distortion is given by

$$
\delta U_0 = \frac{1}{2}\delta\boldsymbol{\epsilon}^{\mathrm{T}}\mathbf{E}\boldsymbol{\epsilon} + \frac{1}{2}\boldsymbol{\epsilon}^{\mathrm{T}}\mathbf{E}\delta\boldsymbol{\epsilon} + \delta\boldsymbol{\epsilon}^{\mathrm{T}}\boldsymbol{\sigma}_0
$$

Since $a^{\mathrm{T}} = a$ for a scalar, and $\mathbf{E}$ is symmetric,

$$
\delta U_0 = \boldsymbol{\epsilon}^{\mathrm{T}}\mathbf{E}\delta\boldsymbol{\epsilon} + \boldsymbol{\sigma}_0^{\mathrm{T}}\delta\boldsymbol{\epsilon}
$$

By substituting, simplifying, and then expanding:

$$\delta U_0 = (\mathbf{E}\boldsymbol{\epsilon} + \boldsymbol{\sigma}_0)^\mathrm{T} \delta\boldsymbol{\epsilon}$$

$$\delta U_0 = \boldsymbol{\sigma}^\mathrm{T} \delta\boldsymbol{\epsilon}$$

$$\delta U_0 = \sigma_x \delta\epsilon_x + \sigma_y \delta\epsilon_y + \cdots + \tau_{zx} \delta\gamma_{zx}$$

Observing that for an arbitrary function $V(\mathbf{x})$,

$$\delta V(x_1, \ldots, x_n) = \frac{\partial V}{\partial x_1}\delta x_1 + \cdots + \frac{\partial V}{\partial x_n}\delta x_n$$

it can be seen that for $U_0(\boldsymbol{\epsilon})$

$$\frac{\partial U_0}{\partial \epsilon_x} = \sigma_x, \qquad \frac{\partial U_0}{\partial \epsilon_y} = \sigma_y, \qquad \cdots \qquad \frac{\partial U_0}{\partial \gamma_{zx}} = \tau_{zx}$$

Thus we have

$$\{\partial U_0/\partial\boldsymbol{\epsilon}\} = \left\{ \begin{array}{c} \partial U_0/\partial\epsilon_x \\ \vdots \\ \partial U_0/\partial\gamma_{zx} \end{array} \right\} = \left\{ \begin{array}{c} \sigma_x \\ \vdots \\ \tau_{zx} \end{array} \right\} = \boldsymbol{\sigma} = \mathbf{E}\boldsymbol{\epsilon} + \boldsymbol{\sigma}_0$$

Next, if we define our body forces per unit volume as

$$\mathbf{F} = \left\{ \begin{array}{c} F_x \\ F_y \\ F_z \end{array} \right\}$$

and the surface tractions as

$$\boldsymbol{\phi} = \left\{ \begin{array}{c} \phi_x \\ \phi_y \\ \phi_z \end{array} \right\}$$

we can derive the potential energy for the volume as

$$V = \int_{\mathrm{vol}} U_0 \, dV - \int_{\mathrm{vol}} \mathbf{d}^\mathrm{T}\mathbf{F} \, dV - \int_{\mathrm{surf}} \mathbf{d}^\mathrm{T}\boldsymbol{\phi} \, dS$$

where the first integral represents the work of the internal stresses, the second is the work done (potential lost) by the body forces as they are displaced $\mathbf{d}$, and the third is the work done (potential lost) by the surface forces as they are displaced $\mathbf{d}$. Substituting for U_0 from above

$$V = \int_{\mathrm{vol}} \left(\frac{1}{2}\boldsymbol{\epsilon}^\mathrm{T}\mathbf{E}\boldsymbol{\epsilon} + \boldsymbol{\epsilon}^\mathrm{T}\boldsymbol{\sigma}_0\right) dV - \int_{\mathrm{vol}} \mathbf{d}^\mathrm{T}\mathbf{F} \, dV - \int_{\mathrm{surf}} \mathbf{d}^\mathrm{T}\boldsymbol{\phi} \, dS$$

4.6   USE OF ASSUMED DISPLACEMENT FIELDS

The foundation for linear interpolation holds that a sufficiently small piece of any smooth curve is practically a straight line. Likewise, the physical basis for a finite element is that a sufficiently small piece of any continuum may have a simple state such as constant strain (in larger pieces, a linear strain state might be appropriate). "Joining" these pieces together should yield a reasonable approximation.

The general procedure is very simple. Since displacements are the primary unknowns, the potential energy expression derived in Section 4.5 is a good starting point. First express V in terms of the nodal displacements or degrees of freedom. Then the nodal degrees of freedom or displacements must assume values such that the potential energy V is a minimum. This will provide a set of simultaneous equations to solve for the nodal displacements.

Let the displacements of an arbitrary point within the ith element be given by

$$\mathbf{g} = \begin{Bmatrix} u \\ v \\ w \end{Bmatrix} = \mathbf{Nd}$$

where $\mathbf{d}$ is the vector of generalized coordinates for the element.

Some of the nodal displacements may be physical displacements, others may be strains or rotations. The matrix $\mathbf{N}$ defines the nature of the assumed displacement field, and we will see shortly how it is built.

Strains can be expressed in terms of the nodal displacements δ by applying the normal strain displacement relations to $\mathbf{g}$:

$$\epsilon_x = \frac{\partial u}{\partial x}, \qquad \epsilon_y = \frac{\partial v}{\partial y}, \qquad \dots, \qquad \gamma_{zx} = \frac{\partial u}{\partial z} + \frac{\partial w}{\partial x}.$$

All of these strain relations can be expressed in matrix form as

$$\boldsymbol{\epsilon} = \mathbf{Bd}$$

To shorten the equations that follow, initial strain and body forces will be excluded. These extra terms can be easily developed from the following material and will not interfere with our goal of understanding the general concepts.

The potential energy is now given by

$$V = \int_{\text{vol}} \frac{1}{2} \boldsymbol{\epsilon}^{\mathrm{T}} \mathbf{E} \boldsymbol{\epsilon} - \int_{\text{surf}} \mathbf{d}^{\mathrm{T}} \boldsymbol{\phi} \, dS$$

Next, substituting into the equation for potential energy gives

$$V_i = \int_{\text{vol}} \left(\frac{1}{2} \mathbf{d}^{\mathrm{T}} \mathbf{B}^{\mathrm{T}} \mathbf{E} \mathbf{Bd} \right) dV - \int_{\text{surf}} \mathbf{d}^{\mathrm{T}} \mathbf{N}^{\mathrm{T}} \boldsymbol{\phi} \, dS$$

factoring the nodal displacements

$$V_i = \frac{1}{2}\mathbf{d}^T \left(\int_{\text{vol}} \mathbf{B}^T \mathbf{E} \mathbf{B} \, dV \right) \mathbf{d} - \mathbf{d}^T \int_{\text{surf}} \mathbf{N}^T \boldsymbol{\phi} \, dS$$

The preceding equation is the potential for a single element. Adding this up for all the elements yields the total potential energy for the structure. Thus, given m elements,

$$V = \sum_{i=1}^{m} V_i$$

If there also exist some other external concentrated loads $\mathbf{P}$ on the structure, include them at this stage by writing

$$V = \sum_{i=1}^{m} V_i - \mathbf{D}^T \mathbf{P}$$

where $\mathbf{D}$ is the vector of all nodal displacements. As seen before, each component of each vector $\mathbf{d}$ shows up somewhere in $\mathbf{D}$. Hence, $\mathbf{d}$ in V_i can be replaced by $\mathbf{D}$ by enlarging all the other matrices with the appropriate number of additional rows and columns of zeros. If we enlarge all our matrices to "structure" size, we get

$$V = \frac{1}{2}\mathbf{D}^T \left(\sum_{i=1}^{m} \int_{\text{vol}} \mathbf{B}^T \mathbf{E} \mathbf{B} \, dV \right) \mathbf{D} - \mathbf{D}^T \sum_{i=1}^{m} \int_{\text{surf}} \mathbf{N}^T \boldsymbol{\phi} \, dS - \mathbf{D}^T \mathbf{P}$$

The structure has been replaced now by a finite-element model whose total potential is governed by the nodal displacements $\mathbf{D}$. Thus our static equilibrium condition is given by the particular $\mathbf{D}$ that has to satisfy the equation

$$\frac{\partial V}{\partial \mathbf{D}} = \mathbf{0} \quad \text{or} \quad \frac{\partial V}{\partial D_1} = \frac{\partial V}{\partial D_2} = \quad \cdots \quad = \frac{\partial V}{\partial D_n} = 0$$

Therefore, differentiating the equation for V leads to

$$\frac{\partial V}{\partial \mathbf{D}} = \left(\sum_{i=1}^{m} \int_{\text{vol}} \mathbf{B}^T \mathbf{E} \mathbf{B} \, dV \right) \mathbf{D} - \sum_{i=1}^{m} \int_{\text{surf}} \mathbf{N}^T \boldsymbol{\phi} \, dS - \mathbf{P}$$

or

$$\left(\sum_{i=1}^{m} \int_{\text{vol}} \mathbf{B}^T \mathbf{E} \mathbf{B} \, dV \right) \mathbf{D} = \sum_{i=1}^{m} \int_{\text{surf}} \mathbf{N}^T \boldsymbol{\phi} \, dS + \mathbf{P}$$

The standard formulation is $\mathbf{KD} = \mathbf{R}$, so we can see that each term in the summation on the left is really an elemental stiffness matrix $\mathbf{k}$, where

$$\mathbf{k} = \int_{\text{vol}} \mathbf{B}^T \mathbf{E} \mathbf{B} \, dV$$

The integral on the right-hand side is the array of elemental nodal forces $\mathbf{r}$ caused by surface forces on the element:

$$\mathbf{r} = \int_{\text{surf}} \mathbf{N}^T \boldsymbol{\phi} \, dS$$

Some or all of these terms may be zero. The surface integral in particular is only nonzero for those element boundaries that are also part of a structure boundary subject to externally applied distributed loading.

The force $\mathbf{r}$ is called a *kinematically consistent generalized nodal force*. *Generalized* means that some of the $\mathbf{r}$ components may be things such as moments. These $\mathbf{r}$ terms also satisfy the virtual work equation (i.e., the work done by these forces moving through some generalized displacement is just $\delta \mathbf{d}^T \mathbf{r}$).

Now we return to our basic equation, which we rewrite as

$$\left(\sum_{i=1}^{m} \mathbf{k} \right) \mathbf{D} = \left(\sum_{i=1}^{m} \mathbf{r} \right) + \mathbf{P} \quad \text{or} \quad \mathbf{KD} = \mathbf{R}$$

where we have combined all our elemental stiffness matrices into one. Thus the potential energy for the structure can be rewritten as

$$V = \frac{1}{2} \mathbf{D}^T \mathbf{K} \mathbf{D} - \mathbf{D}^T \mathbf{R}$$

The majority of elements are most conveniently formulated in terms of nodal displacements D_i. Matrices $\mathbf{N}$ and $\mathbf{B}$ can be used to determine the displacements, strains, and stresses at any point of interest in the models.

Example 4.4: Tension/Compression Element.   Consider a one-dimensional, two-force (truss) member with area A and modulus of elasticity E, as shown in Fig. 4.10. Let the bar be on the x-axis, and let the nodal displacements be u_1 and u_2. Then the displacement of any point on the bar,

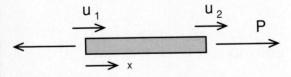

Figure 4.10   One-dimensional element.

assuming a linear relationship along the bar, becomes

$$u = u_1\left(1 - \frac{x}{L}\right) + u_2\left(\frac{x}{L}\right)$$

$$= \left[1 - \frac{x}{L} \quad \frac{x}{L}\right]\left\{\begin{array}{c} u_1 \\ u_2 \end{array}\right\}$$

$$= \mathbf{Nd}$$

Next, the strain is given by

$$\epsilon_x = \frac{\partial u}{\partial x} = \left[-\frac{1}{L} \quad \frac{1}{L}\right]\left\{\begin{array}{c} u_1 \\ u_2 \end{array}\right\}$$

$$\epsilon = \mathbf{Bd}$$

Rather than modify the $\mathbf{E}$ matrix for this special case of uniaxial stress, it is easier to return to the definition of strain energy, where

$$U_0 = \frac{1}{2}E\epsilon_x^2$$

and the single element potential energy is

$$U = \frac{1}{2}\mathbf{d}^T\mathbf{kd}$$

This in turn leads to

$$\mathbf{k} = \int_{vol} \mathbf{B}^T\mathbf{EB}\, dV$$

$$= \int_0^L \mathbf{B}^T E\mathbf{B} A\, dx$$

$$= EA\int_0^L \left[\begin{array}{c} -1/L \\ 1/L \end{array}\right][-1/L \quad 1/L]\, dx$$

$$\mathbf{k} = \frac{AE}{L}\left[\begin{array}{cc} 1 & -1 \\ -1 & 1 \end{array}\right]$$

Then we should formulate the $\mathbf{R}$ vector using our earlier equations. Once we have $\mathbf{R}$, we can solve for $\mathbf{D}$, and with $\mathbf{D}$ we can obtain the element strains and stresses.

■ **EXERCISE 4.5:** Expand Example 4.4 to include the prestrain and body forces in the generalized model force $\mathbf{r}$.

Equilibrium and Compatibility in Using Assumed Displacement Fields

When using assumed displacement fields, consider the following characteristics of equilibrium and compatibility:

- Equilibrium is usually not satisfied within an element.
- Equilibrium is usually not satisfied between elements. Clearly this is the case in the constant strain triangle, when stresses are constant but different in each element.
- Equilibrium of nodal forces and moments is satisfied. A set of nodal equilibrium equations is $\mathbf{R} - \mathbf{KD} = 0$.
- Compatibility is satisfied within elements if the assumed element displacement field is continuous.
- Compatibility may or may not be satisfied between elements.
- Compatibility is enforced at nodes by joining elements there.

Any violations of equilibrium and compatibility tend to vanish as more and more elements are used. Finer meshes will converge to the correct result if

- The displacement field within an element is continuous.
- When the nodal displacements are given values corresponding to a state of constant strain, the displacement field must produce a state of constant strain throughout the element.
- compatibility must exist between elements; in other words, elements must not overlap or separate.

4.7 ONE-DIMENSIONAL SYSTEMS

One-dimensional systems can be modeled by elements that are constructed of shape functions having only a single dimension. The elements can be drawn as a single line, usually with only two nodes. An interior node would be equivalent to a mid-element node for a quadrilateral; there is no equivalent to the mid-side node. The usual finite-element model for a one-dimensional system is a linear string of elements. One-dimensional examples are significantly easier because the nodes can be ordered in a one-to-one correspondence with ordering of the displacements in the vector. We will now look at how to apply the finite-element method to a continuous one-dimensional structure. Consider a one-dimensional system divided into n elements of length h, where $nh = L$, and the lateral motion of the system is defined in terms of the nodal displacements $u_j (j = 1, 2, \ldots, n)$, as shown in Fig. 4.11.

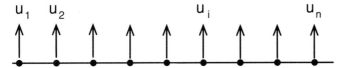

Figure 4.11 One-dimensional system with n nodes.

The displacement of a point inside an element is obtained by means of interpolation functions that are generally low-degree polynomials and are the same for every element. For example, the appropriate shape function for a stretched string is linear (a straight line between the nodes). The mesh in Fig. 4.11 represents a stretched string or a beam, depending upon the variables associated with each node and the elements used.

If we only consider bending in the plane of Fig. 4.11, then Fig. 4.12 shows a typical element. The differential equation for the deflection of the beam $w(x)$ is

$$\frac{d^2}{dx^2}\left(EI\frac{d^2w(x)}{dx^2}\right) = 0, \qquad 0 < x < h$$

Note that this equation assumes no loading other than end conditions. If the beam (element) has uniform cross-section, then this equation can be integrated to obtain

$$w(x) = c_1x^3 + c_2x^2 + c_3x + c_4$$

We can find the constants of integration from the boundary conditions:

$$w(0) = w_1 \qquad \left.\frac{dw}{dx}\right|_{x=0} = \theta_1$$

$$w(h) = w_2 \qquad \left.\frac{dw}{dx}\right|_{x=h} = \theta_2$$

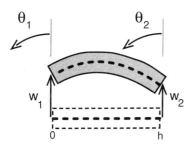

Figure 4.12 A typical one-dimensional beam element.

Thus,

$$w(0) = c_4 = w_1$$

$$\left.\frac{dw}{dx}\right|_{x=0} = c_3 = \theta_1$$

$$w(h) = c_1 h^3 + c_2 h^2 + c_3 h + c_4 = w_2$$

$$\left.\frac{dw}{dx}\right|_{x=h} = 3c_1 h^2 + 2c_2 h + c_3 = \theta_2$$

Solving these equations gives

$$c_1 = \frac{1}{h^3}(2w_1 + h\theta_1 - 2w_2 + h\theta_2)$$

$$c_2 = \frac{1}{h^2}(-3w_1 - 2h\theta_1 + 3w_2 - h\theta_2)$$

$$c_3 = \theta_1$$

$$c_4 = w_1$$

so that, in terms of nodal variables,

$$w(x) = \left[1 - 3\left(\frac{x}{h}\right)^2 + 2\left(\frac{x}{h}\right)^3\right]w_1 + \left[\left(\frac{x}{h}\right) - 2\left(\frac{x}{h}\right)^2 + \left(\frac{x}{h}\right)^3\right]h\theta_1$$

$$+ \left[3\left(\frac{x}{h}\right)^2 - 2\left(\frac{x}{h}\right)^3\right]w_2 + \left[-\left(\frac{x}{h}\right)^2 + \left(\frac{x}{h}\right)^3\right]h\theta_2$$

or

$$w(x) = L_1(x)w_1 + L_2(x)h\theta_1 + L_3(x)w_2 + L_4(x)h\theta_2$$

where $L_i(x)$ are *interpolation* or *shape functions* that describe how to find displacements within the element when given the displacements at the nodes.

The $L_i(x)$ found above are Hermite cubics, which were discussed in Section 2.2. These interpolation functions are not unique, so we can actually choose other functional forms. However, the ones found here are the lowest-degree polynomials possible for this problem. If the displacement vector $\boldsymbol{\delta}$ is defined as $\{\, w_1 \quad h\theta_1 \quad w_2 \quad h\theta_2 \,\}^T$, then the nodal forces are $\{\, f_1 \quad f_2 \quad f_3 \quad f_4 \,\}^T = \{\, F|_{x=0} \quad M|_{x=0} \quad F|_{x=h} \quad M|_{x=h} \,\}^T$. We can relate the bending displacements to the nodal forces f_1, f_2, f_3, f_4 with

$$EI\left.\frac{d^3 w}{dx^3}\right|_{x=0} = f_1, \qquad EI\left.\frac{d^2 w}{dx^2}\right|_{x=0} = f_2,$$

$$EI\left.\frac{d^3 w}{dx^3}\right|_{x=h} = -f_3, \qquad EI\left.\frac{d^2 w}{dx^2}\right|_{x=h} = f_4$$

so that

$$f_1 = \frac{EI}{h^3}(12w_1 + 6h\theta_1 - 12w_2 + 6h\theta_2)$$

$$f_2 = \frac{EI}{h^2}(6w_1 + 4h\theta_1 - 6w_2 + 2h\theta_2)$$

$$f_3 = \frac{EI}{h^3}(-12w_1 - 6h\theta_1 + 12w_2 - 6h\theta_2)$$

$$f_4 = \frac{EI}{h^2}(6w_1 + 2h\theta_1 - 6w_2 + 4h\theta_2)$$

or in matrix form:

$$\mathbf{f} = \begin{Bmatrix} f_1 \\ f_2/h \\ f_3 \\ f_4/h \end{Bmatrix} = \mathbf{k\delta} = \frac{EI}{h^3} \begin{bmatrix} 12 & 6 & -12 & 6 \\ 6 & 4 & -6 & 2 \\ -12 & -6 & 12 & -6 \\ 6 & 2 & -6 & 4 \end{bmatrix} \begin{Bmatrix} w_1 \\ h\theta_1 \\ w_2 \\ h\theta_2 \end{Bmatrix}$$

This is the elemental stiffness matrix for a beam element. The assembly process for the global stiffness matrix proceeds exactly as it did in the truss problem discussed in Section 3.3. We would look at the nodal force equations and combine all the stiffness matrices into a system stiffness matrix that relates the applied loads to the displacements at all nodes.

■ **EXERCISE 4.6:** Consider a beam element with a uniformly distributed external load of constant value p. Determine the contribution to the kinematically consistent generalized nodal force.

■ **EXERCISE 4.7:** Repeat the previous exercise for a distributed external load that varies linearly from p_0 to p_1.

4.8 TWO-DIMENSIONAL ELEMENTS

The Plane Constant-Strain Triangle

The plane constant-strain triangle was used in early finite-element analyses, but now there are better elements available. Because the constant-strain triangle is known to be a poor element, it is seldom used. However, it does provide the lowest complexity of any two-dimensional element and is highly useful here for discussion purposes. It should be mentioned that the generally accepted substitute for this element is the six-noded isoparametric triangle, obtained by including mid-side nodes.

So how do we find the elemental stiffness matrix? First we need to find the general displacements u and v in terms of the nodal displacements u_1, u_2, u_3, v_1, v_2, and v_3. Consider a plane triangle having six degrees of freedom, as shown in Fig. 4.13.

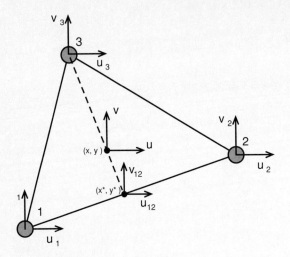

Figure 4.13 Plane triangle.

If we use linear interpolation, along the line 1–2 we have

$$u_{12} = \frac{1}{2}\left(\frac{x^* - x_2}{x_1 - x_2} + \frac{y^* - y_2}{y_1 - y_2}\right)u_1 + \frac{1}{2}\left(\frac{x^* - x_1}{x_2 - x_1} + \frac{y^* - y_1}{y_2 - y_1}\right)u_2$$

Then along the line from (x^*, y^*) to (x_3, y_3), we have

$$u = \frac{1}{2}\left(\frac{x - x_3}{x^* - x_3} + \frac{y - y_3}{y^* - y_3}\right)u_{12} + \frac{1}{2}\left(\frac{x - x^*}{x_3 - x^*} + \frac{y - y^*}{y_3 - y^*}\right)u_3$$

but we also have the slope conditions:

$$\frac{y^* - y_1}{x^* - x_1} = \frac{y_2 - y_1}{x_2 - x_1} \quad \text{and} \quad \frac{y - y_3}{x - x_3} = \frac{y^* - y_3}{x^* - x_3}$$

Solving these equations for u in terms of u_1, u_2 and u_3, and x and y results in

$$u = \frac{p_1(x, y)u_1 + p_2(x, y)u_2 + p_3(x, y)u_3}{\Delta}$$

where

$$p_1(x, y) = \left(x_2 y_3 - x_3 y_2 + x(y_2 - y_3) + y(x_3 - x_2)\right)$$
$$p_2(x, y) = \left(x_3 y_1 - x_1 y_3 + x(y_3 - y_1) + y(x_1 - x_3)\right)$$
$$p_3(x, y) = \left(x_1 y_2 - x_2 y_1 + x(y_1 - y_2) + y(x_2 - x_1)\right)$$
$$\Delta = \left(x_2 y_3 - x_1 y_3 - x_3 y_2 + x_1 y_2 + x_3 y_1 - x_2 y_1\right)$$

A similar expression for v is obtained when u_1, u_2 and u_3 is replaced by v_1, v_2, and v_3. Thus, the equation $\mathbf{g} = \mathbf{Nd}$ can be written as

$$\mathbf{g} = \left\{ \begin{array}{c} u \\ v \end{array} \right\} = \frac{1}{\Delta} \left[\begin{array}{cccccc} p_1(x,y) & p_2(x,y) & p_3(x,y) & 0 & 0 & 0 \\ 0 & 0 & 0 & p_1(x,y) & p_2(x,y) & p_3(x,y) \end{array} \right] \left\{ \begin{array}{c} u_1 \\ u_2 \\ u_3 \\ v_1 \\ v_2 \\ v_3 \end{array} \right\}$$

Next we can express the strains as

$$\boldsymbol{\epsilon} = \left\{ \begin{array}{c} \epsilon_x \\ \epsilon_y \\ \gamma_{xy} \end{array} \right\} = \mathbf{Bd}$$

Since $\epsilon_x = \dfrac{\partial u}{\partial x}$, $\epsilon_y = \dfrac{\partial v}{\partial y}$, and $\gamma_{xy} = \dfrac{\partial u}{\partial y} + \dfrac{\partial v}{\partial x}$, this means that

$$\boldsymbol{\epsilon} = \left[\begin{array}{cc} \partial/\partial x & 0 \\ 0 & \partial/\partial y \\ \partial/\partial y & \partial/\partial x \end{array} \right] \left\{ \begin{array}{c} u \\ v \end{array} \right\} = \left[\begin{array}{cc} \partial/\partial x & 0 \\ 0 & \partial/\partial y \\ \partial/\partial y & \partial/\partial x \end{array} \right] \mathbf{Nd}$$

Therefore,

$$\mathbf{B} = \left[\begin{array}{cc} \partial/\partial x & 0 \\ 0 & \partial/\partial y \\ \partial/\partial y & \partial/\partial x \end{array} \right] \mathbf{N}$$

$$\mathbf{B} = \frac{1}{\Delta} \left[\begin{array}{cccccc} y_2 - y_3 & y_3 - y_1 & y_1 - y_2 & 0 & 0 & 0 \\ 0 & 0 & 0 & x_3 - x_2 & x_1 - x_3 & x_2 - x_1 \\ x_3 - x_2 & x_1 - x_3 & x_2 - x_1 & y_2 - y_3 & y_3 - y_1 & y_1 - y_2 \end{array} \right]$$

Clearly $\mathbf{B}$ is not a function of x or y, so the integral in the element stiffness matrix is trivial:

$$\mathbf{k} = \int_{\text{vol}} \mathbf{B}_{6\times3}^{\mathrm{T}} \mathbf{E}_{3\times3} \mathbf{B}_{3\times6} \, dV = \mathbf{B}^{\mathrm{T}} \mathbf{E} \mathbf{B} t A$$

where t is the element thickness and A the element area.

Now, we have several choices for $\mathbf{E}$ for a linear isotropic material. For plane stress, there is

$$\mathbf{E} = \frac{E}{1 - \nu^2} \left[\begin{array}{ccc} 1 & \nu & 0 \\ \nu & 1 & 0 \\ 0 & 0 & (1-\nu)/2 \end{array} \right]$$

and for plane strain:

$$\mathbf{E} = \frac{E}{(1 + \nu)(1 - 2\nu)} \begin{bmatrix} 1 - \nu & \nu & 0 \\ \nu & 1 - \nu & 0 \\ 0 & 0 & (1 - 2\nu)/2 \end{bmatrix}$$

Multiplying the $\mathbf{B}$ and $\mathbf{E}$ matrices together will give the stiffness matrix for this element. This element is referred to as a constant-strain element, because the assumed shape function yields a strain independent of location within the element (see the preceding equation for ϵ).

We could also include variable thickness by interpolating the nodal values of thickness. Specifically, we use the same shape functions (p_1, p_2, p_3, Δ), with t replacing u, and t_1, t_2, and t_3 replacing u_1, u_2, and u_3, respectively. Finally, when we find $\mathbf{k}$ we will have to integrate this linear function of x and y over the volume.

Rectangular Element

The four-node quadrilateral element is commonly used. Meshes for quadrilaterals are easily generated by mapped mesh algorithms. The shape functions of this element have much in common with the bilinear patch discussed in Section 9.6. The element shown in Fig. 4.14 has eight degrees of freedom. With a technique similar to that used for the triangular element, we find that

$$u = \frac{1}{4bc}\big((b - x)(c - y)u_1 + (b + x)(c - y)u_2 + (b + x)(c + y)u_3 \\ + (b - x)(c + y)u_4\big)$$

There is a similar result for v; therefore, we can write general displacement as

$$\left\{ \begin{array}{c} u \\ v \end{array} \right\} = \frac{1}{4bc} \begin{bmatrix} (b - x)(c - y) & 0 \\ (b + x)(c - y) & 0 \\ (b + x)(c + y) & 0 \\ (b - x)(c + y) & 0 \\ 0 & (b - x)(c - y) \\ 0 & (b + x)(c - y) \\ 0 & (b + x)(c + y) \\ 0 & (b - x)(c + y) \end{bmatrix}^{\mathrm{T}} \left\{ \begin{array}{c} u_1 \\ u_2 \\ u_3 \\ u_4 \\ v_1 \\ v_2 \\ v_3 \\ v_4 \end{array} \right\} = \mathbf{Nd}$$

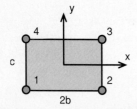

Figure 4.14 Four-noded quadrilateral element.

Note that for convenience, $\mathbf{N}$ has been printed (and labeled) transposed. Then we just use

$$\mathbf{B} = \begin{bmatrix} \partial/\partial x & 0 \\ 0 & \partial/\partial y \\ \partial/\partial y & \partial/\partial x \end{bmatrix} \mathbf{N}$$

to find $\mathbf{B}$ and then $\mathbf{k}$.

Notice that the elements of the $\mathbf{N}$ matrix are simple polynomials whose values are one at one node and zero at all the other nodes. If we had used different types of interpolation functions, we can match the values and slopes specified at each node.

4.9 THREE-DIMENSIONAL ELEMENTS

Three-dimensional elements are a straightforward extension of the previous material. Because the algebra does get more complicated, no specific element will be developed. Readers should refer instead to the texts mentioned in the Annotated References.

Typically, the CAD system designer will integrate existing f.e.m. software instead of developing these elements. Although designers will never be concerned with element formulation, they must select which elements to use.

The 3-D elements can be understood by comparison to the 2-D elements. The equivalent to the three-node constant-strain triangle is the four-node constant-strain tetrahedron. Although this element is easy to derive, it has all of the disadvantages of the constant-strain triangle. The four-node rectangle is equivalent to the eight-node "brick." Similarly isoparametric elements with mid-side nodes can also be used.

Two-dimensional elements are usually either triangles or quadrilaterals. Quadrilaterals are usually preferred, but most two-dimensional problems require some triangles to maintain mesh consistency between regions with different mesh densities. Three-dimensional meshing can use a wider range of elements to maintain consistency. Most programs will provide wedge elements, as shown in Fig. 4.15.

Elements with mid-side nodes have been mentioned several times. These elements use higher-order shape functions and so provide an increase in accuracy, just as using additional, smaller elements could. In addition, the mid-side nodes also allow the elements to better represent the geometry. The mid-side nodes need not be on a straight line between the corner nodes. The mid-side node should be located to best represent the geometry, as shown in Fig. 4.16.

■ **EXERCISE 4.8:** Beginning with a cube with six sides and eight nodes, draw all possible shapes that can be obtained by sequentially eliminating one, two, three, and four nodes. For example, more than one shape can be obtained

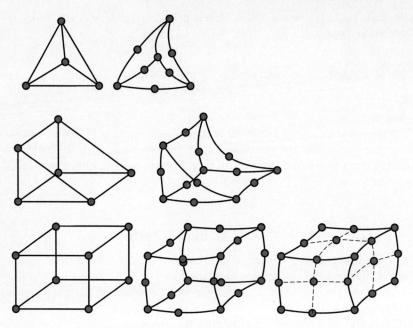

Figure 4.15 Three-dimensional elements.

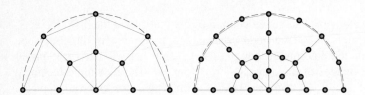

Figure 4.16 Mid-side nodes allow better fit to object geometry.

by eliminating two nodes that share a face and an edge, two nodes that share only a face, and two nodes that do not share a face. The resulting shapes are different, because they have a different number of faces. For the purposes of this exercise, all shapes obtained by deleting one corner of the cube are equivalent, independent of which corner is deleted.

4.10 FINITE-DIFFERENCE METHOD

The finite-difference method is a very common alternative for solving field problems in the domains of thermal conduction or fluid flow. This method is very similar to the finite-element method and leads to a matrix problem:

$$\mathbf{KD} = \mathbf{R}$$

Because it is often much easier to implement than the finite-element method, this method is significant to CAD. The finite-difference method is an attractive alternative for solving field problems for which a package is not available.

The method proceeds as follows: First, mesh the domain of interest (geometry) with a distribution of discrete points; then, at each discrete point replace the partial derivatives in the governing equation with finite difference operators, and last, collect the individual equations into a system of equations.

Describing the finite-difference method in a generalized notation is difficult and would provide little insight that could not be gained from a specific example. We will therefore discuss the method in terms of the following specific example.

Example 4.5: Thermal Distribution by Finite-Difference Analysis. Consider heat conduction in a two-dimensional rectangular domain with no internal heat sources and specified temperature boundary conditions (see Fig. 4.17). The temperature distribution is described by the Poisson equation

$$\nabla^2 T = 0$$

The domain is meshed with a uniformly spaced Cartesian grid of $N \times M$ points with temperatures T_i $(i = 1, \dots, N \times M)$. The finite-difference

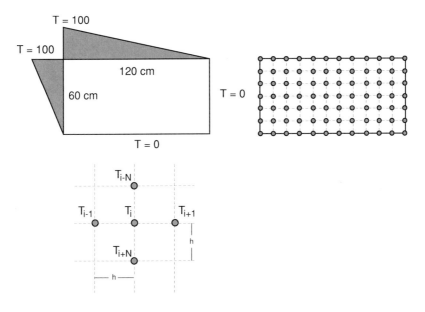

Figure 4.17   Finite-difference model for thermal distribution.

approximation for $\nabla^2 T = 0$ is

$$\frac{T_{i-1} - 2T_i + T_{i+1}}{h^2} + \frac{T_{i-N} - 2T_i + T_{i+N}}{h^2} = 0$$

which can be rewritten as

$$\frac{1}{h^2}(T_{i-N} + T_{i-1} - 4T_i + T_{i+1} + T_{i+N}) = 0$$

$$\text{for } i = 1, \ldots, N \times M$$

Each value of i leads to a row in the matrix $\mathbf{K}$. Those points adjacent to the boundary will require a specialized version of this equation that uses a specified value for temperature. These terms will be transferred to the right side of the equation, forming the load vector $\mathbf{R}$.

The preceding example shows that the finite-difference operator is most easily applied if the spacing of the discrete points is uniform and Cartesian. However, operators are usually published for nonuniform spacing (unequal legs of the operator) and for non-Cartesian grids (most commonly polar). The derivation of finite-difference operators (often called "molecules") was discussed in Section 2.5. A variety of these "molecules" has been published (just as a variety of finite-element stiffness matrices has been published). In addition to the specific operators required, key aspects of the finite-difference method are the treatment of boundary conditions and the bookkeeping for determining the neighbors of specific discrete points.

When considering ways to solve the resulting matrix problem, think of the system matrix as diagonally dominant and extremely sparse. Iterative techniques and relaxation methods are often used in finite-difference problems. Because the same "molecule" is applied to almost all nodes, there are very few distinctly different entries in the system matrix. Techniques have been developed that avoid actually forming the system matrix.

■ **EXERCISE 4.9:** Solve Example 4.5 for the temperature distribution.

■ **EXERCISE 4.10:** Extend Example 4.5 to include thermal insulation along the right-hand side. What is the appropriate formulation for the discretized version of the governing differential equation?

■ **EXERCISE 4.11:** Modify the boundary conditions in Example 4.5 to represent the specified linear temperature along the left side, thermal radiation along the top, thermal convection along the right side, and insulation along the bottom.

■ **EXERCISE 4.12:** Although finite-difference operators can be derived as described in Chapter 2, they are generally taken from a reference book. Determine the following finite difference operators:

1. ∇^2 in Cartesian frame with leg lengths h_1, h_2, h_3, h_4
2. ∇^2 in a cylindrical frame with leg lengths $\pm h_1, \pm h_2$
3. ∇^4 in a Cartesian frame with equal leg lengths
4. ∇^4 in a cylindrical frame

4.11 BOUNDARY-INTEGRAL METHOD

Besides finite-element and finite-difference methods, the only other technique used to solve field problems is the boundary-integral or boundary-element method. Although discussing this method goes beyond the scope of a CAD book, the technique's basic approach can be summarized and some strengths and weaknesses noted.

Any field equation with a simplified domain and boundary conditions has a specific solution. The Green's function for the equation is an example of a specific solution, analogous to the step response and the impulse response of a dynamic system. For stress analysis, this might be the stress field resulting from a point load applied to an infinite domain. The response to a more complicated loading with a more complicated geometric domain can be obtained by the appropriate superposition of these characteristic functions. The *boundary-integral method* finds the field distribution by determining the correct superposition of these functions.

The technique earns its name because only the boundary of the domain is used. This characteristic is important because it means that the mesh-generation step only needs to address the boundary (not the interior), which significantly simplifies the mesh-generation task. The resulting numerical problem is appropriately simpler. The stiffness matrix is substantially smaller but is usually completely filled (no nonzero entries). The solution is only the appropriate constants for the superposition of the characteristic functions. This highly complex function must be evaluated (at moderate cost) for every point at which the field variable is desired. If only the values along the boundary are of interest, some computer time can still be saved. But if the entire field is required to produce a color-shaded stress picture, the computational effort needed is as great or greater than that required by the finite-element method.

From the viewpoint of the CAD designer, the boundary-integral method differs little from the finite-element and finite-difference methods. Each method has unique data structure requirements, but all use the same class of user interfaces and data interfaces.

4.12   ADVANCED TOPICS

The finite-element methods presented in this chapter can be used to address the majority of design problems, which also can be classified as linear static problems. Fortunately, the technique can be modified to deal with more difficult problems (nonlinear and/or dynamic).

For example, dynamic systems can be modeled by partial differential equations that include derivatives with respect to time. Such systems can be either periodic (such as vibrations) or simply transient (such as the mold temperature in injection molding and the deformation that occurs during forging). The finite-element technique leads to a system of ordinary differential equations instead of a system of algebraic equations. If these equations are linear, the appropriate numerical technique is eigenvalue/eigenvector extraction to determine the natural frequencies and mode shapes. The general form for this problem is

$$\mathbf{M\ddot{D}} + \mathbf{B\dot{D}} + \mathbf{KD} = \mathbf{R}(t)$$

In addition to the stiffness matrix $\mathbf{K}$, the finite-element formulation leads to a mass matrix $\mathbf{M}$, and possibly a damping matrix $\mathbf{B}$. If the differential equations are nonlinear, the appropriate technique is numerical integration as developed in Chapter 5.

A nonlinear static problem usually arises from either material or interface nonlinearity. The stress-strain relationship for materials is not linear, particularly as yield is approached. This is important, because the objective of many design analyses is to determine failure loads or safety factors.

The best example of interface nonlinearity is an unbonded contact face. The stiffness in compression is governed by the material properties, but the stiffness to open the interface is effectively zero. Sliding contact, with or without friction, is another case of interface nonlinearity.

The most important aspect of nonlinear problems is that the principle of superposition cannot be used; thus, loading cannot be considered independently, and the resulting stress states cannot be superimposed.

Nonlinear problems can be solved by techniques similar to those presented in Section 3.6, although further detail is beyond the scope of this book. However, a typical nonlinear problem will be a series of linear problems. It should be clear that a nonlinear problem with a large number of degrees of freedom is extremely demanding on computing resources. Linear f.e.m. codes in two or three dimensions are not difficult to develop, if a limited repertoire of elements is acceptable. While many designers may eventually need to use a nonlinear f.e.m. code, CAD system designers will probably never have to develop such a package.

The accuracy of the solution in a finite-element problem depends on the size of elements chosen (the mesh density) and on the accuracy of the element chosen (order of the element). A typical procedure uses a relatively coarse mesh and then, based on the predicted stress distribution, increases the mesh density in areas of high stress gradient. This process, referred to as *h-refinement*, can be continued until the stress distribution is no longer improved (*h-convergence*). An alternate approach uses a relatively coarse mesh and then proceeds to use elements of increasingly higher-order interpolation functions. This process, referred to as *p-refinement*, leads to *p-convergence*. An adequate development of the higher-order elements required by the *p-method* is beyond the scope of this book. The choice between p- and h-methods has been and will probably continue to be hotly debated, although most finite-element analyses at this point are based on the *h-method*. Interestingly, there is little debate between finite-element and finite-difference users.

4.13   SUMMARY

The finite-element method as presented in this chapter is a technique for determining the distribution of a field quantity governed by a partial differential equation. The problem's components include a geometry that delimits the domain, a distribution of nodes (the mesh), a set of elements, and a set of boundary conditions.

As presented, the method is fundamentally a numerical method. However, the discussions in this chapter highlight the importance of CAD techniques in the efficient use of finite-element methods. In the design process, f.e.m. analysis is a series of operations rather than a single one-shot analysis. The volume of data generated demands good visualization techniques. Finite-element results cannot be interpreted from pages consisting of columns of numbers. Based on the results of previous analyses, the designer may need to either refine the accuracy of the model or change its design. Interactive graphics are vital to making these changes, and efficient data structures are vital to maintaining the relationships between geometry, mesh, elements, and so on, to minimize the amount of computation at each step. The computations required for finite-element problems are too extensive to allow recomputation of known data.

4.14   REFERENCES

Bathe, K. J. and Wilson, E. *Numerical Methods in Finite Element Analysis*. Englewood Cliffs, N.J.: Prentice-Hall, 1976.

Bathe, K. J. *Finite Element Procedures in Engineering Analysis*. Englewood Cliffs, N.J.: Prentice-Hall, 1982.

Brebbia, C. A. *Finite Element Systems—A Handbook*. 2d ed. New York: Springer-Verlag, 1982.

Cook, R. D., Malkus, D. S., and Plesha, M. E. *Concepts and Applications of Finite Element Analysis*. 3d ed. New York: Wiley, 1989.

Desai, C. S. and Abel, J. F. *Introduction to the Finite Element Method*. New York: Van Nostrand Reinhold, 1972.

Gallagher, R. H. *Finite Element Analysis: Fundamentals*. Englewood Cliffs, N.J.: Prentice-Hall, 1975.

Grandin, H., Jr. *Fundamentals of the Finite Element Method*. New York: Macmillan, 1986.

Huebner, K. H. and Thornton, E. A. *The Finite Element Method for Engineers*. 2d ed. New York: Wiley, 1982.

Hughes, T. J. R. *The Finite Element Method, Linear Static and Dynamic Finite Element Analysis*.Englwood Cliffs, N.J.: Prentice-Hall, 1987.

Ketter, R. L., and Prawel, S. P. *Modern Methods of Engineering Computation*. New York: McGraw-Hill, 1980.

Reddy, J. N. *An Introduction to the Finite Element Method*. New York: McGraw-Hill, 1984.

Rockey, K. C., Evans, H. R., Griffiths, D. W., and Nethercot, D. A. *The Finite Element Method—A Basic Introduction*. 2d ed. New York: Wiley, 1983.

Stasa, F. L. *Applied Finite Element Analysis for Engineers*. New York: Holt, Rinehart & Winston, 1985.

Zienkiewicz, O. C. *The Finite Element Method*. 3d ed. New York: McGraw-Hill, 1977.

4.15   PROJECTS

Project 4.1   Sail Shape

Problem Statement   Determine the loaded shape for a triangular mainsail.

Problem Data   The sail dimensions can be taken from Fig. 4.18. Assume a uniform pressure loading of 15 N/m^2.

Analysis   Many engineering analyses reduce to the solution of the Poisson equation over a two-dimensional domain. This includes the torsion of irregular cross-sections, temperature distributions in heat conduction problems, and membrane deflection.

$$\nabla^2\phi = p(x, y)$$

We will give the elemental stiffness matrix for a triangular element that can be used in these problems. Except for beam and truss problems, the two-dimensional Poisson problem is all that most engineers would attempt with a home-grown finite element program.

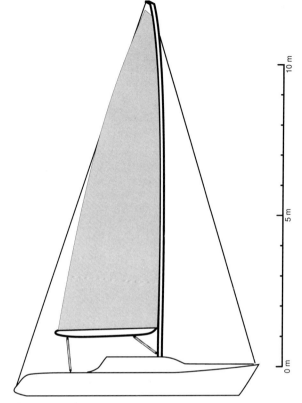

10 m

5 m

0 m

Figure 4.18   Sailplan for a competition sloop.

If the three corners of the element are designated $x_1, y_1, x_2, y_2, x_3, y_3$ and

$$x_\xi = x_2 - x_1 \qquad y_\xi = y_2 - y_1$$
$$x_\eta = x_3 - x_1 \qquad y_\eta = y_3 - y_1$$
$$J = x_\xi y_\eta - x_\eta y_\xi$$

$$N_{i,x} = \begin{cases} -(y_\eta - y_\xi) \\ y_\eta \\ -y_\xi \end{cases} \qquad N_{i,y} = \begin{cases} x_\eta - x_\xi & i = 1; \\ -x_\eta & i = 2; \\ x_\xi & i = 3. \end{cases}$$

Then the entries in the element stiffness matrix can be given by

$$k_{ij} = \frac{\alpha}{J}\left(N_{i,x}N_{j,x} + N_{i,y}N_{j,y}\right)$$

where α represents the relevant element material property.

Comments   The membrane analysis is an extremely simplistic approach to sail design. Most sails are not cut flat but are cut and then sewn to a desired shape. Although the sail is tensioned, it tends to deform under load instead of stretching as in membrane analysis. For example, loading the sail will lift the boom and deform the mast, significantly changing the shape of the sail. Furthermore, the loading is not uniform and is actually a function of the deformed shape. Therefore sail design is a coupled stress-analysis fluid-flow problem. However, this project is a very good introduction to the finite-element method.

Optional Exercises   Determine the stress state at points in the sail and the directions of principal stress across the sail. This information is useful for determining how to piece together the sail. A woven material works best if the threads (weave and warp) are aligned with the loads.

Determine the distributed loading along the boom and the mast, which is necessary for designing the cross-sectional properties (stiffness) for both.

Include the effects of sail battens (stiffening strips that are typically horizontal, sometimes running the full chord width).

Project 4.2   Sailboat Rigging Plan

Problem Statement   Design a stay system for the mainmast of a sloop-rigged yacht.

Problem Data   A scaled plan of the deck of the hull is shown in Fig. 4.19. The proposed mainmast is 11.8 m, and it has cross-sectional properties EI. Plan for a distributed lateral loading on the mainmast of 40 N/m.

Analysis   Although the mainmast can be expected to flex under load, it might be sufficiently stiff to be considered rigid in comparison to the stays.

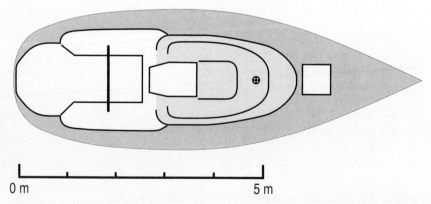

0 m   5 m

Figure 4.19   Deck plan for a yacht.

The hull will provide very little rotational stiffness at the base of the mast, so this end should be modeled as a hinge joint. The rigging will usually be a statically indeterminate system, so it cannot be analyzed by a free-body diagram; however, the rigging can be analyzed by a version of the truss system.

Comments   Typically, the rigging will consist of the forestay, backstay, and sidestays. The sidestays will utilize one or more spreaders. Several stays may be used, some going to the top of the mast and some going to an intermediate location. On an actual yacht, the attachments cannot be arbitrarily located on the deck because of hull strength considerations. For this project, consider that full-strength attachments can be made at any location. The design will consist of specifications for stay material, diameter, and attachment coordinates.

Optional Exercises   In a sloop-rigged vessel, the forestay also carries the loading of the foresail. Now include the effect of an additional load uniformly distributed along the forestay.

Pre-tension allows a cable to effectively carry some compression before going slack. Include pre-tension in your analysis and specify the design values for pre-tension.

Project 4.3   Cantilever Beam

Problem Statement   Identify the reinforcement needed for a cantilever beam under nonuniform loading.

Problem Data   The 10-m steel cantilever beam is shown in Fig. 4.20. The loading is a tip moment of 10^4 N·m and a distributed load of $W(x) = 10^2 x$ N/m. The original beam is an I-beam that is 10 cm deep, 6 cm wide, and 2 cm thick.

The I-beam can be replaced by one with different dimensions (8 cm deep, 6 cm wide, and 1 cm thick) and then reinforced with additional

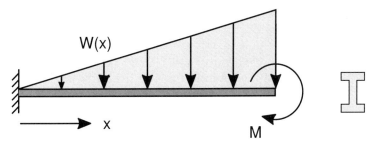

Figure 4.20   Cantilever beam loading.

1-cm-thick plates on top and bottom. Assume that the plates are securely bonded to the I-beam and that each plate i extends from the root to some point x_i along the beam. How many plates, and of what length, should be added to produce a beam of equivalent strength and tip deflection under the specified loading?

Analysis   There are two alternatives to handle the nonuniform transverse loading. The best one uses numerical quadrature to integrate the transverse load term for each individual element. This process would determine the "work equivalent" loading. The load vector for each element can be determined from the shape functions and from the applied load at each quadrature point (η_i) as below. The quadrature points are defined within a normalized element of length [0, 1].

$$\eta_1 = 0.1127 \qquad \eta_2 = 0.5 \qquad \eta_3 = 0.8873$$

$$N_1(\eta) = 2(\eta - 1)^2 \left(\eta + \frac{1}{2} \right)$$

$$N_2(\eta) = \eta(\eta - 1)^2$$

$$N_3(\eta) = 2 \left(\frac{3}{2} - \eta \right) \eta^2$$

$$N_4(\eta) = \eta^2(\eta - 1)$$

$$\begin{Bmatrix} f_1 \\ f_2 \\ f_3 \\ f_4 \end{Bmatrix} = \frac{1}{2} \begin{bmatrix} dx & 0 & 0 & 0 \\ 0 & dx^2 & 0 & 0 \\ 0 & 0 & dx & 0 \\ 0 & 0 & 0 & dx^2 \end{bmatrix} \begin{bmatrix} N_1(\eta_1) & N_1(\eta_2) & N_1(\eta_3) \\ N_2(\eta_1) & N_2(\eta_2) & N_2(\eta_3) \\ N_3(\eta_1) & N_3(\eta_2) & N_3(\eta_3) \\ N_4(\eta_1) & N_4(\eta_2) & N_4(\eta_3) \end{bmatrix} \begin{Bmatrix} 5/9W(x|_{\eta_1}) \\ 8/9W(x|_{\eta_2}) \\ 5/9W(x|_{\eta_3}) \end{Bmatrix}$$

This formula can also be written in a form more amenable to computation:

$$f_i = d_i \frac{1}{2} \sum_{k=1}^{3} N_i(\eta_k) w_k W(x|_{\eta_k})$$

where

$$d_i = \begin{cases} dL, & \text{if } i = 1, 3 \\ dL^2, & \text{if } i = 2, 4 \end{cases}$$

$$w_1 = \frac{5}{9} \qquad w_2 = \frac{8}{9} \qquad w_3 = \frac{5}{9}$$

A more simplistic approach is to approximate the load using point loads at the nodes of the element. These point loads for each element would have to equal the net distributed force on the element.

$$f_1 = f_3 = \frac{1}{2} \int_0^{dL} W(x)\,dx \qquad f_2 = f_4 = 0$$

Comments   Determine the distribution of displacement and examine the relationship between the number of elements and accuracy. Use a file-based interface to define the model and loading conditions. You may wish to use a general-purpose format that reads individual nodal locations. Alternatively, you may wish to use a special-purpose format that simply specifies total beam length and number of elements desired, then calculates individual nodal locations and element dimensions internally. Although the latter might be easier to write, the former can be used to study the effects of nonuniform distribution of nodes.

Because the gradients will be increasing from the tip to the root of the beam, for n elements, the best results are obtained if the nodes are biased toward the root. Examine the solution's consistency with the assumptions of the governing equations.

For comparison purposes, the exact solution for the uniform beam is

$$u(x) = \frac{1}{EI} \frac{5}{6} \left(x^5 - 1000x^3 + 26,000x^2\right)$$

Optional Exercises   Determine the distributions of slope, shear, and moment. Examine these solutions for consistency with the assumptions of the governing equations. Select a specific number of nodes (e.g., $n = 10$), and compare the loading vectors for "work equivalent loading" and "lumped nodal loading."

Project 4.4   Bicycle Rim

Problem Statement   Design the spoke supports for a bicycle wheel. Select a spoke diameter and spoke spacing such that the deflection under load is less than a specified amount.

Problem Data   The bicycle rim shown in Fig. 4.21a can be modeled as a beam on an elastic foundation as shown in Figure 4.21b. For an extruded aluminum alloy, the EI for the rim ranges from 43–172 Nm^2. For steel spokes, k typically ranges from 20–80 MPa. A typical tire diameter is 670 mm.

Analysis   The analytical solution for a beam on elastic foundation problem involves the term β, which is the inverse of the characteristic length.

$$\beta = \left(\frac{k_f}{4EI}\right)^{1/4}$$

This equation can be used to determine if the spoke spacing is sufficiently small to justify the assumption of a continuous elastic foundation.

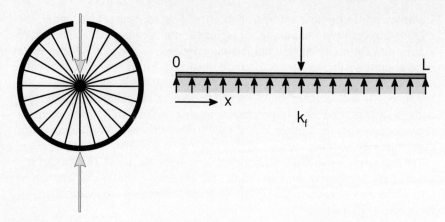

Figure 4.21   A bicycle rim modeled as a beam on an elastic foundation.

In addition to the beam element presented previously, an elastic foundation element must be determined. This can be determined as

$$[k_f^e] = \int_l \begin{Bmatrix} N_1 \\ N_2 \\ N_3 \\ N_4 \end{Bmatrix} k \{ N_1 \quad N_2 \quad N_3 \quad N_4 \} \, dx$$

or

$$[k_f^e] = k \begin{bmatrix} \int N_1 N_1 \, dx & \int N_1 N_2 \, dx & \int N_1 N_3 \, dx & \int N_1 N_4 \, dx \\ \int N_2 N_1 \, dx & \int N_2 N_2 \, dx & \int N_2 N_3 \, dx & \int N_2 N_4 \, dx \\ \int N_3 N_1 \, dx & \int N_3 N_2 \, dx & \int N_3 N_3 \, dx & \int N_3 N_4 \, dx \\ \int N_4 N_1 \, dx & \int N_4 N_2 \, dx & \int N_4 N_3 \, dx & \int N_4 N_4 \, dx \end{bmatrix}$$

The entries in the element matrix can be determined from

$$k_{ij} = d_i d_j k_f \frac{dL}{2} \sum_{k=1}^{3} N_i(\eta_k) N_j(\eta_k) w_k$$

where

$$d_i = \begin{cases} 1, & \text{if } i = 1, 3 \\ dL, & \text{if } i = 2, 4 \end{cases}$$

$$w_1 = \frac{5}{9} \qquad w_2 = \frac{8}{9} \qquad w_3 = \frac{5}{9}$$

The boundary conditions for this problem are periodic; $u(0) = u(L)$. Furthermore, because of symmetry, $u_x(L/2) = 0$ and $u_x(0) = u_x(L) = 0$. For efficiency, the problem can be solved by only considering $0 < x < L/2$.

Project 4.5   Bracket Analysis

Problem Statement   It is beyond the scope of a CAD course to develop a general-purpose two-dimensional finite-element package (let alone a three-dimensional package). If you can obtain access to a general-purpose f.e.m. program, perform a plane-stress analysis of the bracket shown in Fig. 4.1. Determine if the radius of the curve on the lower side can be reduced, and if so, by how much.

Comments   Look at the distribution of the nodes generated by the finite-element program, and note how mesh density affects the results. Determine whether biasing the mesh density to one side improves the results.

C H A P T E R

5
Simulation

5.1 INTRODUCTION

As discussed previously, simulation of dynamic systems is one of the three analytical *raisons d'être* of computer-aided design. The success of most large technological systems is due to their designers' ability to simulate responses without extensive laboratory testing of the entire assembled system. Although current simulation techniques are well developed, they are not usually well integrated with CAD systems. This chapter will begin with a review of the numerical methods appropriate to the integration of ordinary differential equations (a single equation and then multiple equations). From a numerical perspective, simulation is simply an extrapolation process. Then the discussion will briefly touch on simulation languages and address their integration with general-purpose CAD programs. Section 5.12 will explore the types of data and data structures necessary to support simulation. Animation, the combination of simulation and computer graphics, is the subject of Sections 5.13 and 5.14. Finally, Section 5.15 will discuss how model changes in simulation relate to those in variational geometry. The subjects of these latter sections will overlap with other topics such as graphics, data structures, geometry, and user interface.

The generic term "simulation" is often applied more broadly than "dynamic response," encompassing almost any computer model of a physical system or process. "Simulation," as presented here, is limited to dynamic systems described by ordinary differential equations (continuous-time systems with a finite number of degrees of freedom). The simulation of discrete-time systems described by difference equations will not be addressed here. However, in data structures, graphics, and user interfaces, there is essentially no distinction between continuous or discrete systems.

Development of a simulation begins with a detailed modeling phase that is beyond the scope of this book. During modeling, the engineer must determine variables to represent the state of the system, such as its configuration and energy content. This is frequently accomplished by developing a lumped parameter approximation to the system. The interactions between parts of the system (such as forces) are represented as functions of the state of the system. These functions may come from well-known relationships for simple components such as springs and dampers, or they may come from more detailed analyses, such as the forces generated within a fluid film bearing or a magnetic bearing. The modeling process also assigns names to parameter values that represent the constitutive relations between state variables and forces (e.g., labeling of effective spring stiffnesses, etc.). A conservation law such as $\sum F = m\ddot{x}$ is used to determine the differential equations, and the constitutive relations are used to eliminate the forces.

The result of the modeling phase will be a list of *state variables* $\mathbf{x}$ and a procedure to determine the rate of change of these at any arbitrary point in time:

$$\frac{d\mathbf{x}}{dt}\bigg|_{t_0} = \mathbf{f}(\mathbf{x}|_{t_0})$$

A properly posed problem will include initial conditions $\mathbf{x}(t_0)$ and an upper limit on time $t_0 < t < t_f$. The *solution* will consist of a set of values, $(\mathbf{x}_0, t_0), (\mathbf{x}_1, t_1), \ldots, (\mathbf{x}_f, t_f)$, which may or may not be equally spaced and may fall on certain prespecified key times $t_0 < t_a, t_b, t_c < t_f$.

Note that no simulation program or language is capable of determining the global response of realistic physical systems yet; they can only calculate the specific response flowing from given initial conditions for a single set of physical parameters. For example, the specific response of a sinusoidally forced, single-degree-of-freedom, mass-spring system with a hardening spring can be found to be periodic with a specific amplitude. However, there is much about the behavior of this system, such as the jump/drop phenomenon and possible multiple solutions (nonunique), that cannot be found from a single specific response. The multiple solutions illustrate dependence on initial conditions; the jump/drop phenomenon, on system parameters (excitation frequency and hardening coefficient).

The reader will encounter the use of simulation to determine the response of linear systems. In general this is inefficient, because the response is obtained faster by evaluating the homogeneous and particular solutions. In this spirit, most of the examples in this chapter deal with nonlinear equations. Examples for which an analytical solution exists are included only to allow a comparison between numerical and analytical results.

The simulation problem can be stated as

Given: $\mathbf{x}(t_0)$, $\dfrac{d}{dt}\mathbf{x} = \mathbf{f}(\mathbf{x}, t)$

Determine: $\mathbf{x}(t_0 + \Delta t)$

Figure 5.1 shows the algorithm used in the integration process. The main procedure repetitively executes the preceding problem, developing a sequence of values for $\mathbf{x}(t)$. For each time step, the time step integrator receives

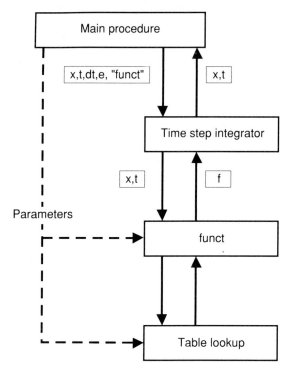

Figure 5.1   A flowchart for an integration program.

the current state **x**, time t, time step Δt, acceptable error e, and name of the subroutine that contains the differential equations funct. It determines $\mathbf{x}(t + \Delta t)$ and also usually increments t.

Naming the differential equations allows multiple sets of equations to exist in the same program. This would be impossible if the integrator could call only one particular predetermined procedure.

In most realistic problems, some aspects of the differential equations cannot be written in analytic form but instead require functions that only exist in tabular form. Usually these are complex constitutive relationships that have been measured but are not derived from fundamental principles. This can reflect either a lack of knowledge or a need for efficiency. The funct procedure will often require table lookup and interpolation procedures. Examples of these constitutive relationships include torque as a function of speed for motors and engines, viscosity as a function of temperature and/or pressure, growth rate as a function of temperature, and lift as a function of angle of attack. In terms of program architecture, these tables should not be coded into the simulation but should reside as data files independent of the program. When implementing an integration program, it is important to note that the values of constants (the physical parameters) must pass through to the function evaluation procedure. However, these values should not (and in most cases cannot) pass through the integrator.

Before considering multiple-degree-of-freedom systems, we will develop the numerical algorithms for a single-degree-of-freedom system.

5.2 EULER'S METHOD

The discussion begins with *Euler's method*, because it is the simplest algorithm and demonstrates extrapolation, error estimation, the importance of time step, and stability. The reader is cautioned, however, that the technique is unstable unless very small time steps are used; therefore, Euler's method is seldom used in practice.

At the point x_0, t_0, straight-line extrapolation is used over the interval Δt to determine x_1:

$$x_1 = x_0 + f(x_0, t_0)\Delta t$$

This is yet another application of analytic approximation as discussed in Chapter 2. In the larger scheme of things, this is a first-order Runge-Kutta equation and is equivalent to retaining the first term of a Taylor's series expansion of the solution:

$$x(t_1) = x(t_0 + \Delta t) = x(t_0) + \frac{dx}{dt}\bigg|_{t_0}\Delta t + \frac{1}{2}\frac{d^2x}{dt^2}\bigg|_{t_0}\Delta t^2 + \cdots$$

Of course, unless the actual solution is a straight line, the integrator will produce an error. Note that the next term in the series is an estimate of the error:

$$\epsilon \approx \frac{1}{2}\frac{d^2x}{dt^2}\Delta t^2$$

With repetitive application, the response may drift away from the true solution—Euler's method is notorious for this. The error depends on the time step Δt. Depending on the differential equation, if given sufficiently large time steps, the predicted solution will diverge.

Example 5.1: Euler Integration. Consider the following equation, which represents a lightly damped mass spring system starting from rest with an applied force.

$$\ddot{x} + 0.1\dot{x} + x = 2.0$$

$$x(0) = \dot{x}(0) = 0.0$$

The response will be a decaying sinusoid, converging to $x = 2.0$. First, the problem is converted to first-order form:

$$\begin{Bmatrix}\dot{x}_1\\\dot{x}_2\end{Bmatrix} = \begin{Bmatrix}x_2\\-0.1x_2 - x_1 + 2.0\end{Bmatrix}$$

t	Euler's		Exact	
	x	$\dot{x}$	x	$\dot{x}$
0.1	0.000	0.20	0.010	0.20
0.2	0.020	0.40	0.039	0.39
0.3	0.060	0.59	0.088	0.58
0.4	0.119	0.78	0.155	0.76
0.5	0.197	0.96	0.239	0.93
0.6	0.293	1.13	0.340	1.09
0.7	0.406	1.29	0.456	1.24
0.8	0.535	1.44	0.587	1.37
0.9	0.679	1.57	0.730	1.49
1.0	0.836	1.69	0.884	1.59

Table 5.1   Responses from Example 5.1.

where

$$\begin{Bmatrix} x_1(0) \\ x_2(0) \end{Bmatrix} = \begin{Bmatrix} 0 \\ 0 \end{Bmatrix}$$

Using an Euler's integrator with $\Delta t = 0.1$ s, the solution in Table 5.1 is obtained. The period for this system is $T = 2\pi$ sec so the time step is $\Delta t = 0.016T$. Table 5.1 compares the responses obtained with Euler's method to the exact values; Fig. 5.2 plots the Euler responses for several values of Δt. The solution with $\Delta t = 0.01$ s is very close to the analytical solution. The stability boundary is seen to be close to $\Delta t = 0.1$.

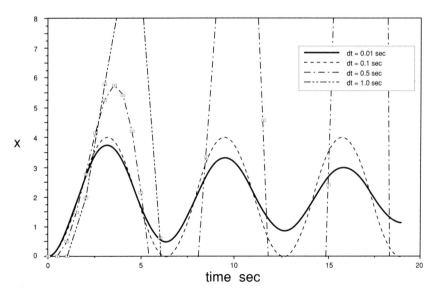

Figure 5.2   A plot of time responses using Euler's integration scheme.

The accuracy of the solution can be improved by either reducing the step size or using a higher-order approximation by including an additional term from the series expansion. The second-order term could be evaluated as

$$\frac{d^2x}{dt^2} = \frac{d}{dt}\frac{dx}{dt} = \frac{d}{dt}f = \frac{\partial f}{\partial t} + \frac{\partial f}{\partial x}\frac{dx}{dt}$$

In most cases it is not possible to actually evaluate the second-order term in the series, because f cannot be differentiated symbolically. However, this piece of information can be replaced with an evaluation of the derivative at a second point.

The *Modified Euler's technique* uses a midpoint slope to effectively estimate a curvature and more accurately predict the final value of x. Note that the curvature is not actually calculated and that a straight-line extrapolation is still the final step.

As shown in Fig. 5.3, the slope $f(x_0, t_0)$ is used to extrapolate halfway through the interval to $\hat{t} = t_0 + \frac{1}{2}\Delta t$:

$$\hat{x} = x_0 + \frac{1}{2}f(x_0, t_0)\,\Delta t$$

Note that although this point does not lie on the solution curve, it does provide information about how the slope is changing. The slope at point $\hat{x}$

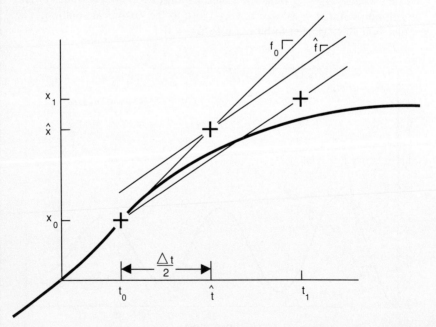

Figure 5.3   Modified Euler's integration.

is evaluated:

$$\hat{f} = f\left(\hat{x}, t_0 + \frac{1}{2}\Delta t\right)$$

To extrapolate from (t_0, x_0) to (t_1, x_1),

$$x_1 = x_0 + f\left(\hat{x}, t_0 + \frac{1}{2}\Delta t\right)\Delta t$$

Combining all steps,

$$x_1 = x_0 + f\left(x_0 + \frac{1}{2}f(x_0, t_0)\Delta t, t_0 + \frac{1}{2}\Delta t\right)\Delta t$$

The *Improved Euler's algorithm*, as shown in Fig. 5.4, is an alternative way of obtaining an improved effective slope. The slope $f(x_0, t_0)$ is used to extrapolate over the entire step to $t_0 + \Delta t$:

$$\hat{x} = x_0 + f(x_0, t_0)\Delta t$$

Then the slope at point $\hat{x}$ is evaluated:

$$\hat{f} = f(\hat{x}, t_0 + \Delta t)$$

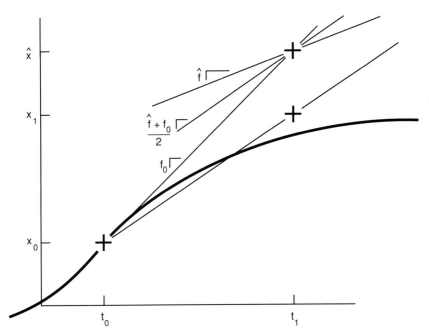

Figure 5.4 Improved Euler's integration.

Next the average of these two slopes (f and $\hat{f}$) is used for straight-line extrapolation from (t_0, x_0) to (t_1, x_1):

$$f_{\text{avg}} = \frac{1}{2}(f_0 + \hat{f}_1) = \frac{1}{2}\big(f(t_0, x_0) + f(t_1, \hat{x}_1)\big)$$

$$x_1 = x_0 + \frac{1}{2}(f_0 + \hat{f}_1)\Delta t$$

Combining all steps,

$$x_1 = x_0 + \frac{1}{2}\big(f(x_0, t_0) + f(x_0 + f(x_0, t_0)\Delta t, t_0 + \Delta t)\big)\Delta t$$

5.3 GENERAL SECOND-ORDER RUNGE-KUTTA METHOD

Both of the modifications to Euler's method are second-order Runge-Kutta integrators. In other words, these modifications are accurate through a second-order truncation of the Taylor's series of the solution without requiring an evaluation of $\partial f/\partial x$ or $d^2 x/dt^2$. Instead an intermediate evaluation of f is used. Of course there is nothing magical about the points $\Delta t/2$ or Δt. In this section we will generalize the method to use other intermediate evaluation locations.

An entire family of integrators can be developed that are all second-order accurate. The general procedure is to extrapolate to an arbitrary intermediate point $c\Delta t$, and use a weighted average of initial and intermediate slopes to extrapolate over the entire step:

$$f_0 = f(x_0, t_0)$$
$$\hat{t} = t_0 + c\Delta t$$
$$\hat{x} = x_0 + cf_0\Delta t$$
$$\hat{f} = f(\hat{x}, \hat{t})$$
$$x_1 = x_0 + (af_0 + b\hat{f})\Delta t$$

Certain combinations of a, b, and c provide second-order accuracy. Expanding $\hat{f}$ in the previous equation as a series,

$$x_1 = x_0 + \left(af_0 + bf_0 + bc\frac{\partial f}{\partial t}\Delta t + bc\frac{\partial f}{\partial x}f_0\Delta t + O(\Delta t^2)\right)\Delta t$$

and collecting terms of like order gives

$$x_1 = x_0 + (a+b)f_0\,\Delta t + \left(bc\frac{\partial f}{\partial t} + bc\frac{\partial f}{\partial x}f_0\right)\Delta t^2 + O(\Delta t^3)$$

The Taylor series is known to be

$$x_1 = x_0 + f_0\,\Delta t + \frac{1}{2}\left(\frac{\partial f}{\partial t} + \frac{\partial f}{\partial x}\,f_0\right)\Delta t^2 + O(\Delta t^3)$$

So for second-order accuracy, term-by-term comparison shows that

$$a + b = 1$$

$$bc = \frac{1}{2}$$

The three parameters a, b, and c are related by the two constraints in the preceding equation, so an entire family of second-order integrators exists. Selecting b as the free parameter, the constants a and c are given by

$$a = 1 - b$$

$$c = \frac{1}{2b}$$

Therefore the general second-order Runge-Kutta method is

$$x_1 = x_0 + \left((1 - b)f_0 + bf\left(x_0 + f_0\frac{\Delta t}{2b}, t_0 + \frac{\Delta t}{2b}\right)\right)\Delta t$$

$$\text{Note:} \quad b = \begin{cases} 1, & \text{if modified Euler's method} \\ \frac{1}{2}, & \text{if improved Euler's method} \end{cases}$$

Of course, the student should remember that different values of b will not produce the same results. However, the difference will be on the order of Δt^3.

Second-order R-K integrators are quite easy to code and are probably the logical choice if a library routine is not available. Unfortunately, second-order integrators generally are not accurate enough for realistic problems.

■ **EXERCISE 5.1:** Consider the differential equation

$$\frac{d}{dt}x = -3x, \, x(0) = 5.0$$

Determine $x(t)$ using the following techniques:

1. Euler's method
2. Improved Euler's method
3. Modified Euler's method
4. A second-order R-K procedure other than methods (2) or (3)

Use a variety of time steps for each method. Determine the relative error at each point in time. Show how the four techniques compare and show how the relative error depends upon the time step for each method.

5.4 FOURTH-ORDER RUNGE-KUTTA METHOD

A family of integrators exists that is accurate through the first four terms
of a Taylor series expansion. This family requires four function evaluations,
one at the start and three at points intermediate to the time step. A weighted
average of these four slopes is used to extrapolate to $x(t_f)$. This family is
referred to colloquially as the "RK-4" integrators.

One form of the fourth-order Runge-Kutta integration first uses the initial slope to extrapolate to the midpoint; next uses the slope at midpoint
to extrapolate from start to midpoint; then uses the corrected slope at midpoint to extrapolate to the full step; and finally, uses a weighted average of
preceding four slopes to extrapolate to the full step (see Fig. 5.5).

$$k_1 = f(x_0, t_0)$$

$$k_2 = f\left(x_0 + k_1\frac{\Delta t}{2}, t_0 + \frac{\Delta t}{2}\right)$$

$$k_3 = f\left(x_0 + k_2\frac{\Delta t}{2}, t_0 + \frac{\Delta t}{2}\right)$$

$$k_4 = f(x_0 + k_3\Delta t, t_0 + \Delta t)$$

$$x_1 = x_0 + \frac{1}{6}(k_1 + 2k_2 + 2k_3 + k_4)\Delta t$$

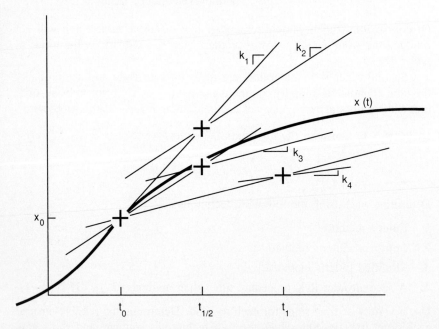

Figure 5.5   Fourth-order Runge-Kutta integration.

The weighted sum is an approximation to the first derivative; it is also equivalent to a Taylor series approximation through the fourth order. Note that four function evaluations are required.

Example 5.2: Fourth-Order Runge-Kutta Integration. Consider the following problem:

$$\frac{dx}{dt} = -x \qquad t_0 = 0 \qquad x(t_0) = 1$$

Analytically, it is easily shown that the solution is $x = e^{-t}$. The fourth-order R-K integration, for arbitrary Δt, proceeds as follows:

$$k_1 = f_0 = -1$$

$$k_2 = f\left(x_0 - \frac{1}{2}\Delta t, t_0 + \frac{1}{2}\Delta t\right) = -1 + \frac{1}{2}\Delta t$$

$$k_3 = f\left(x_0 + \left(-1 + \frac{1}{2}\Delta t\right)\frac{1}{2}\Delta t, t_0 + \frac{1}{2}\Delta t\right) = -1 + \frac{1}{2}\Delta t - \frac{\Delta t^2}{4}$$

$$k_4 = -1 + \Delta t - \frac{1}{2}\Delta t^2 + \frac{\Delta t^3}{4}$$

$$x(t) = 1 - \Delta t + \frac{1}{2}\Delta t^2 - \frac{1}{6}\Delta t^3 + \frac{1}{24}\Delta t^4$$

which are the first five terms of the series expansion for the proper solution.

■ **EXERCISE 5.2:** Most numerical methods libraries contain fourth-order R-K integrators. Repeat Example 5.1 using such an integrator. *Note:* If variable time step is available, make sure to turn off this option (see Section 5.7). The analytical solution is

$$x(t) = 2 + 2e^{-0.5t}\left(-\cos at - \frac{.05}{a}\sin at\right)$$

where $a = \sqrt{0.9975}$. Study how the error is dependent on the time step. What is the largest Δt possible for stable integration?

Note that in terms of computational effort, a fourth-order R-K using time step Δt is equivalent to an Euler's method using time step $\Delta t/4$. How does the error compare in each case? It may be useful to plot error versus Δt for each algorithm.

5.5 MULTIPLE COUPLED FIRST-ORDER EQUATIONS

Very few interesting engineering problems can be studied with a single first-order equation. Rather, for most real problems there are several state variables $x_1, \ldots, x_n$, and the derivative of each is a function of possibly all of them, $\dot{x}_i = f(x_1, \ldots, x_n)$. This is handled simply by considering x

as a column vector $\mathbf{x}$ and generalizing any of the previous techniques. The vector equation

$$\frac{d}{dt}\mathbf{x} = \mathbf{f}(\mathbf{x}, t)$$

represents

$$\dot{x}_1 = f_1(x_1, x_2, \ldots, t)$$
$$\dot{x}_2 = f_2(x_1, x_2, \ldots, t)$$
$$\vdots$$
$$\dot{x}_n = f_n(x_1, x_2, \ldots, t)$$

The fourth-order R-K method proceeds in parallel as follows:

$$\mathbf{x}_1 = \mathbf{x}_0 + \frac{1}{6}(\mathbf{k}_1 + 2\mathbf{k}_2 + 2\mathbf{k}_3 + \mathbf{k}_4)\Delta t$$

where

$$\mathbf{k}_1 = \mathbf{f}(\mathbf{x}_0, t_0)$$
$$\mathbf{k}_2 = \mathbf{f}\left(\mathbf{x}_0 + \mathbf{k}_1\frac{\Delta t}{2}, t_0 + \frac{\Delta t}{2}\right)$$
$$\mathbf{k}_3 = \mathbf{f}\left(\mathbf{x}_0 + \mathbf{k}_2\frac{\Delta t}{2}, t_0 + \frac{\Delta t}{2}\right)$$
$$\mathbf{k}_4 = \mathbf{f}(\mathbf{x}_0 + \mathbf{k}_3\Delta t, t_0 + \Delta t)$$

Usually in numerical implementations, the ordering of the equations is ignored, and $x_1(t_1)$ and $x_2(t_1)$ are not used in calculating $x_3(t_1)$. That is, $x_3(t_1)$ is calculated using only information from $\mathbf{x}|_{t<t_1}$.

Example 5.3: Integration of a System with More Than One Mode.
Consider a second-order system

$$\ddot{x} - x = 0$$

with initial conditions

$$x_0 = 5 \qquad \dot{x}_0 = -5$$

The analytical solution can be shown to be

$$x(t) = 5e^{-t}$$

The results using an fourth-order R-K integrator are shown in Fig. 5.6. What has gone wrong? A linear stability analysis reveals the problem. The homogeneous solution is

$$x = C_1 e^t + C_2 e^{-t}$$

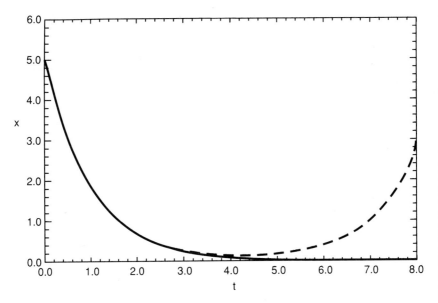

Figure 5.6   Analytical and numerical responses.

where

$$C_1 = \frac{x_0 + \dot{x}_0}{2} \qquad C_2 = \frac{x_0 - \dot{x}_0}{2}$$

The system has two modes—one stable and one unstable. The initial conditions specified above excited only the stable mode. However, the "noise" generated by numerical integration (the numerical errors) excited both modes, so the numerical response was unstable.

Interpreting the stability of a system from numerical results is difficult. In most cases, an unstable numerical result means that the physical system is unstable. In such a case the response is accurately predicted, because in the physical system any naturally occurring small perturbations in the initial conditions will excite the unstable mode.

It is important to note that the prediction of the unstable response is accurate qualitatively but not quantitatively. Because the system is unstable, the actual values of the exponentially growing response at a specific time cannot be predicted. A corollary holds that a stable system cannot be extrapolated backward in time, because in the negative time direction the system is unstable.

Numerical stability and convergence have been major concerns for simulation programs. Because of the repeated approximations in the extrapolation algorithm, the solution is always in error. In fact, the simulation can be viewed as attempting to track the true solution but being disturbed every time step. In terms of mechanical systems, this is analogous to a low level of noise and external excitation. If the physical system represented in the equations can reject this noise (i.e., it is stable), then its simulation should also be stable and should produce a reasonable approximation to the solution.

To produce convergence, the integration algorithm requires some additional damping. The response generated by the simulation is therefore artificially damped and subject to continual noise. In most cases this is unimportant. However, there are two situations in which this matters: (1) accurately predicting the response at some specific time, and (2) predicting the stability boundary of a system. It is very difficult to separate slow integrator instability from slow system instability. Consider the following possible combinations:

	integrator	
	stable	**unstable**
stable	**I**	**II**
unstable	**III**	**IV**

system (labels rows: stable, unstable)

Obviously, Case I is well behaved and Case IV should be avoided. Unfortunately, Case II is difficult to distinguish from Case III.

Given sufficiently large time steps, all integrators will display instability. Unless the integrator provides an internal time-step adjustment, the engineer must specify the time step. Furthermore, even if a variable time-step integrator is used, the engineer should know the approximate value of the time step, because it determines the number of integration steps, the amount of computer cycles required, and the turnaround time for the simulation. Example 5.1 illustrates that the absolute value of the time step is not meaningful; rather, the time step is interpreted relative to a natural period or time constant of the system. For systems with many degrees of freedom, modes, and natural frequencies, the fastest time constant or period will drive the time step. This time constant can be very small compared to the dominant mode of interest, making simulation very expensive. Since the high-frequency modes drive the time step, such systems are sometimes referred to as stiff systems. The reader is referred to literature specializing in techniques for integrating stiff systems.

5.6 SECOND-ORDER EQUATIONS

Most physical systems are fundamentally second order (thermal problems are a notable exception). The most common dynamic equation is probably

$$\ddot{x} = f(x, \dot{x}, t) \qquad x(t_0) = x_0 \qquad \dot{x}(t_0) = v_0$$

It is possible to develop integration schemes that are specifically tailored to handle second-order equations. However, in practice these are not used, probably because of the difficulties involved in generalizing to multiple simultaneous equations and mixing first-order and second-order equations within the same system.

The universal solution is to convert all second-order (and higher) equations to a set of first-order equations. In the case of a second order set, let

$$x_1 = x \qquad x_2 = \dot{x}$$

then

$$\dot{x}_1 = x_2$$
$$\dot{x}_2 = f(x_1, x_2, t)$$

It is important to reconsider the comment in the previous section regarding the order of the equations. The same results are obtained independent of the order in which x_1 and x_2 are calculated. Thus the special relationship between x_1 and x_2 (i.e., $x_1 = \int x_2 \, dt$) is ignored and $\dot{x}_1 = x_2$ is treated as any other differential equation. The variable x_1 is treated as a function of all other state variables, and as a result, position will appear to lag slightly behind velocity. This can be seen in the response values listed in Table 5.1.

Linear second-order equations occur so often that special techniques are frequently proposed. For a linear system ($a\ddot{x} + b\dot{x} + cx = f(t)$) the impulse response $h(t)$ can be obtained analytically and used in a convolution integral:

$$x(t) = \int_{-\infty}^{t} h(t - \tau) f(\tau) \, d\tau$$

where $f(\tau)$ is the external forcing function. This changes the problem to integration in the quadrature form. Note that each time step requires a full quadrature integration.

Another alternative approximates $f(t)$ by a very simple function over intervals $t_i \rightarrow t_{i+1}$ (usually a straight line). The ramp response for a linear system can be obtained analytically and the initial conditions used to match the final conditions of the previous step. The response is then known analytically as a sequence of functions patched together with matching boundary conditions. However interesting these (and other specialized techniques) may be, generally it is easier to simply integrate the original differential equation (even if it is linear).

5.7   ERROR ESTIMATES

In any particular integration scheme, the error estimate is often difficult to derive. However, a well-documented library subroutine will provide information on the error estimate. A common technique uses the error estimate to adjust the step size Δt to maintain a desired level of accuracy. In a general program, this leads to some difficulties in programming, because the overall program for plotting and other graphic functions is probably expecting the response to come out at evenly spaced intervals, although the physics of the problem may demand variably spaced intervals to maintain accuracy.

To understand how error estimates are obtained, consider a first-order R-K algorithm (Euler's):

$$x_1 = x_0 + f_0 \Delta t$$

The truncation error can be approximated by the second-order term of the expansion:

$$e_T \approx \frac{x''(\xi)}{2} \Delta t^2, \qquad \xi = [t_0, t_1]$$

This can be rewritten as

$$e_T \approx \frac{\Delta t^2}{2} \frac{d}{dt} f|_\xi$$

Expanding f in a Taylor series,

$$f_1 = f_0 + \left(\frac{df}{dt}\right)\Delta t + O(\Delta t^2)$$

which can be truncated and rearranged to give

$$\frac{df}{dt} \approx \frac{f_1 - f_0}{\Delta t}$$

therefore,

$$e_T \approx \frac{f_1 - f_0}{2} \Delta t$$

It is possible to estimate the truncation error at the cost of an additional function evaluation (f_1). Remember that $f_1 = f(x_1, t_1)$ normally would not be evaluated for a single Euler's step; instead, f_1 would be used to step from t_1 to t_2. In fact, it would be more tempting to use the additional function evaluation in a second-order R-K method than to estimate the error. A commonly suggested error criteria for a fourth-order R-K method is

$$\left|\frac{k_2 - k_3}{k_1 - k_2}\right| < 0.05$$

Adaptive step size proceeds as follows: Let e_0 denote the desired accuracy. On any step where $e_t > e_0$, the step is rejected, Δt is halved, and the integration is restarted. If, on the other hand, $e_t \ll e_0$, the next time step can be doubled.

```
do until t>t_final

    x_old = x

    call integrate(t, dt, x, et)

    if (et>e0)

        t = t - dt

        x = x_old

        dt = dt/2

    else if (et<0.2 e0)

        dt = 2 dt

    endif

enddo
```

Note that integration subroutines usually update the time and state variables, which explains why the rejected time step et > e0 requires stepping back. Most library subroutines use an internal error estimator and a strategy similar to the preceding program to adjust an internal time step to maintain the level of accuracy requested by the user.

■ **EXERCISE 5.3:** Consider a mass spring system with a highly nonlinear spring $F_s = x^{-3}$. This is a reasonable approximation to the extreme hardening of resistance (or stiffness) of a thin fluid film as found in a fluid film bearing. Without an external load, the film simply pushes the mass away (x increases without bound). An external load of -10 is assumed and initial conditions of $x_0 = 5, \dot{x}_0 = -30$. Thus the differential equation is

$$\ddot{x} - \frac{1}{x^3} = -10$$

Note that the resistance approaches infinity as x approaches zero. This means that theoretically the displacement x must remain positive. Using a fixed time-step integration scheme, study how the response depends upon the choice of time step. Using a variable time-step integrator (probably taken from a library) study how the time step changes through the integration.

5.8 PREDICTOR-CORRECTOR TECHNIQUES

One clear disadvantage of the R-K family of integrators is that the response at preceding time steps is not used to better estimate the future response. Thinking in terms of extrapolation, it should be clear that higher-order extrapolation is possible by using previous points rather than intermediate points.

Let us begin by considering a second-order predictor-corrector. The slope at x_0, t_0 is used for straight-line extrapolation from x_{-1}, t_{-1}:

$$x_1^{(0)} = x_{-1} + 2\Delta t\, f_0$$

The superscript $^{(0)}$ indicates that this is a zeroth iterate estimate for x_1. The preceeding equation can be derived also from a two-point centered formula for the first derivative:

$$\frac{d}{dt} x \bigg|_0 = \frac{x_1 - x_{-1}}{2\Delta t}$$

The issue is how to improve this estimate for x_1. One approach calculates the slope at the end points:

$$f_1^{(0)} = f(x_1^{(0)}, t_1)$$

Then, averaging with f_0, and extrapolating from t_0,

$$x_1^{(1)} = x_0 + \frac{1}{2}(f_0 + f_1^{(0)})\,\Delta t$$

At this point the algorithm is similar to the Improved Euler's method; however, it is different. As an exercise, consider the general second-order Runge-Kutta using $c = -1.0$. It is tempting to continue to iterate on this scheme, finding $f_1^{(1)}$ and $x_1^{(2)}$, and so on. The iteration could continue until

$$\left| x_1^{(i+1)} - x_1^{(i)} \right| < \epsilon$$

Two questions are relevant here:

- Will it converge?
- Will it converge to the true value of x_1?

So long as

$$\Delta t < \frac{2}{f_x}$$

it can be shown that the algorithm converges to within a truncation error. Furthermore, the truncation errors are easily estimated in this case. The predictor is second-order accurate, coming from an estimate for the derivative.

The truncation error for the predictor is

$$e_{Tp} = \frac{h^3}{3} x'''(\xi), \qquad \xi \in [t_{-1}, t_1]$$

The corrector comes from a second-order approximation to $\int_0^1 f \, dt$, and the truncation error for the corrector is

$$e_{Tc} = \frac{h^3}{12} x'''(\xi), \qquad \xi \in [t_{-1}, t_1]$$

Once again, the errors can be approximated. Let the true value of x_1 be denoted by $\hat{x}$. Then

$$\hat{x} = x_1^{(0)} + \frac{h^3}{3} x'''(\xi)$$

$$\hat{x} = x_1^{(i)} + \frac{h^3}{12} x'''(\eta)$$

Using magnitudes and assuming $\xi = \eta$,

$$\frac{5h^3}{12} x''' = x_1^{(i)} - x_1^{(0)}$$

Therefore,

$$e_{Tc} = \frac{1}{5}(x_1^{(i)} - x_1^{(0)})$$

It is easy to calculate e_{Tc} for each iteration, and after comparing to desired error e_0, to decide whether to half or double the step size. The usual procedure allows for two iterations. If $e_{Tc} < e_0$ within the first iteration, double the time step for the next integration step. If after the second iteration, $e_{Tc} \not< e_0$, halve the time step and repeat from t_0.

Figure 5.7 shows a higher-order predictor corrector scheme. A quadratic curve is fit through points f_{-2}, f_{-1}, and f_0; then, the area under this curve from t_{-3} to t_1 is used to generate x_{1p}. The estimated values for the new state generate an estimated slope f_{1p}, which is used to form a second quadratic curve based on f_{-1}, f_0, f_{1p}. The area under the second curve from t_{-1} to t_1 is used to generate x_{1c}.

As with the second-order R-K methods, second-order predictor correctors usually are not used for actual problems. Rather, a fourth-order version is typically used. An integration formula over four panel widths, fourth-order accurate, is

$$x_2 - x_{-2} = \int_{-2}^{2} f(t) \, dt = \frac{4}{3} \Delta t (2f_{-1} - f_0 + 2f_1) + \frac{14}{45} \Delta t^5 f'''(\xi)$$

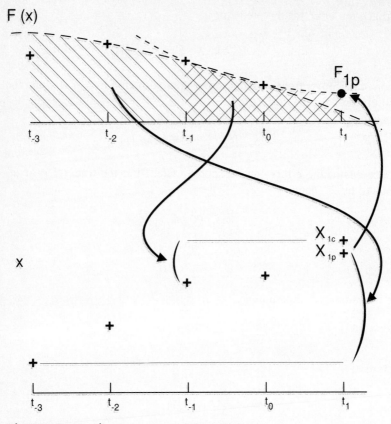

Figure 5.7 Predictor corrector integration.

Shifting the indexing so that the highest term for x is subscripted by one:

$$x_1 - x_{-3} = \frac{4}{3}\Delta t (2f_{-2} - f_{-1} + 2f_0)$$

Alternatively, a formula over five panel widths, fourth-order accurate is

$$x_1 - x_{-4} = \frac{5}{24}\Delta t (11f_{-3} + f_{-2} + f_{-1} + 11f_0) + \frac{95}{144}\Delta t^5 f'''(\xi)$$

Either of these is a usable fourth-order predictor. Any fourth-order accurate integration formula that does not use the highest end of the interval is a legitimate candidate. Specifically, note that neither equation above uses f_1.

The matching fourth-order corrector is chosen from a fourth-order integration formula that does use the upper end of the interval. For instance, Simpson's integration formula is

$$x_1 - x_{-1} = \frac{1}{3}\Delta t (f_{-1} + 4f_0 + f_1)$$

Although in one sense all fourth-order methods are equivalent, some are more commonly used than others. The following is the predictor and corrector for the Adams-Moulton method:

$$x_1 = x_0 + \frac{\Delta t}{24}(55f_0 - 59f_{-1} + 37f_{-2} - 9f_{-3}) + \frac{251}{720}\Delta t^5\, x'''(\xi)$$

$$x_1 = x_0 + \frac{\Delta t}{24}(9f_1 + 19f_0 - 5x_{-1} + x_{-2}) - \frac{19}{720}\Delta t^5\, x'''(\eta)$$

The estimation of the error can be shown to be

$$e_{Tc} = -\frac{29}{720}\left(x_1^{(0)} - x_1^{(1)} + \frac{\Delta t}{24}(9f_1 - 36f_0 + 59f_{-1} - 37f_{-2} + 9f_{-3} - 5x_{-1} + x_{-2})\right)$$

5.9   COMPARISON OF METHODS

The Runge-Kutta and Predictor-Corrector integration schemes both have strengths and weaknesses, which can be summarized as follows:

Runge-Kutta

- Self starting—needs no previous information
- Expensive—requires several function evaluations per time step
- Easy to change the step size
- Difficult to estimate the truncation error

Predictor-Corrector

- Difficult to start—requires several equally spaced previous values
- Fast—uses prior information instead of repeated function evaluations
- Difficult to change step size because of starting problems
- Easy to estimate truncation error

The two methods are complementary: The strengths of the Runge-Kutta method, its self-starting characteristic and its easily changed step size, are the weaknesses of the Predictor-Corrector method. Similarly, the strengths of the Predictor-Corrector method, namely, its speed and its accurate error estimate, are the weaknesses of the Runge-Kutta method. A common practice is to start with R-K, then switch to Predictor-Corrector. As the simulation proceeds, if estimated error exceeds its bounds, then halve the time step and restart with the R-K method.

5.10   TWO-POINT BOUNDARY-VALUE PROBLEMS

One-dimensional field problems such as thermal conduction lead to a differential equation with boundary conditions instead of initial conditions. In spirit, such an ordinary differential equation is more like a partial differential equation (Chapter 4) than the dynamic problems of the preceding sections. Boundary conditions are usually associated with field problems; initial conditions, with simulation problems. The bending of a beam with a nonuniform cross-section under distributed loading $p(x)$ is described by

$$\frac{d^2}{dx^2}\left(EI\,\frac{d^2y}{dx^2}\right) = p(x)$$

For an easier example, consider the second-order problem, using the notation of $x(t)$ rather than $y(x)$

$$x'' = x^2 \qquad x(0) = 1 \qquad x(1) = 1$$

Given $x(0)$ and $x'(0)$, the response $x(t)$ can be easily calculated by integration. An effective technique considers the nonlinear root-finding problem:

$$\text{What is} \quad x'(0) \quad \text{such that} \quad x(1) = 1$$

This technique proceeds by choosing two values for $x'(0)$ and integrating to obtain $x(1)$

$$x'(0) = -1 \quad \rightarrow \quad x(1) = 0.2782$$
$$x'(0) = 0 \quad \rightarrow \quad x(1) = 1.5995$$

A secant approach to the root-finding problem yields the next estimate:

$$x'(0) = -0.4537 \quad \rightarrow \quad x(1) = 0.97$$

This method converges very rapidly. Figure 5.8 shows the actual responses

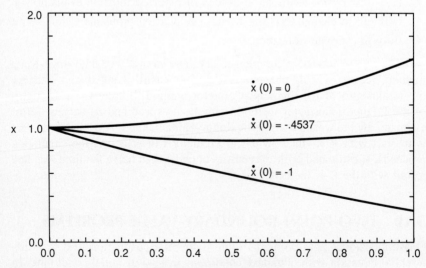

Figure 5.8   The response for three different initial conditions $\dot{x}(0)$.

from the first three guesses at the value of $x'(0)$. Figure 5.9 illustrates $x(1)$ as a function of $x'(0)$.

An alternative approach using the technique discussed in Section 4.10 takes the finite difference operator for the second derivative and discretizes the continuous variable x:

$$x_i'' = x_i^2 \qquad i \in [0, \ldots, n]$$

$$x_i'' = \frac{-x_{i-1} + 2x_i - x_{i+1}}{\delta t^2}$$

This leads to a system of simultaneous nonlinear equations that can be written as the matrix equation

$$\mathbf{A} \begin{Bmatrix} x_1 \\ \vdots \\ x_n \end{Bmatrix} = \begin{Bmatrix} f_1(t_1) \\ \vdots \\ f_n(t_n) \end{Bmatrix}$$

Any of the methods from Chapter 3 can be used to solve the matrix problem. An important issue is whether $\mathbf{f}$ depends upon $\mathbf{x}$. If the forcing vector is independent of $\mathbf{x}$, then $\mathbf{x}$ can be found in a straightforward fashion. However, if $\mathbf{f}$ depends upon $\mathbf{x}$, the problem can be attacked by an iterative scheme

$$\mathbf{A}\mathbf{x}^{(2)} = \mathbf{f}^{(1)}$$

$$\mathbf{A}\mathbf{x}^{(3)} = \mathbf{f}^{(2)}$$

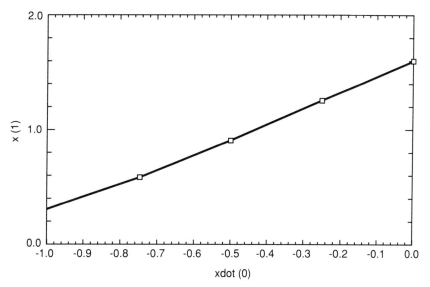

Figure 5.9 A plot of $x|_1$ as a function of initial condition.

A decomposition method for solution is particularly efficient because the matrix $\mathbf{A}$ remains the same for each iteration.

■ **EXERCISE 5.4:** Determine the response $x(t)$ given the following:

$$\ddot{x} + 0.01\dot{x} + x = 0$$
$$\dot{x}(0) = 0.0 \qquad x(0) = 1.0 \qquad 0 < t < 120$$

Using different R-K schemes and different time steps, note the qualitative and quantitative differences.

■ **EXERCISE 5.5:** Using second- and fourth-order R-K schemes, determine the response $x(t)$ for $0 < t < 300$ for

$$\ddot{x} + 0.03\dot{x} + x = 1.0\cos t$$

Compare the response for the time period $290 < t < 300$. This exercise shows how periodic forced response can depend upon the integrator and time step used. Initial conditions can be arbitrary because the response caused by initial conditions should have died out.

5.11   INTEGRATION WITH CAD PACKAGES

The previous sections have discussed the numerical aspects of the integration of differential equations. From a broader perspective, a simulation can consist of state variables (names), initial conditions, differential equations, parameter values, excitations (disturbances and/or forcing functions), and integrator parameters. Design uses simulations as prototypes, so it is important to be able to create and edit simulations quickly for parameter studies. As a result, all of the advantages commonly attributed to finite-element pre- and postprocessors also accrue to an interactive system dynamics package. Simulation programs are not as widely available as finite-element programs, so many (if not most) simulations are custom programs. Unfortunately, when required to develop a new simulation program for every new system, an engineer may spend as much time in development as is eventually saved by using the completed software. Ideally, an engineer would prefer not only to use an existing software package to develop the model of the system, but also to be able to tailor the package to fit the system's particular needs. An existing package should take advantage of interactive graphics for input and output, because interactive graphics is efficient and provides clarity of intent for the user. The software must also be able to interact with a wide variety of analytical processes (e.g., f.e.m, kinematics, dynamics).

A general-purpose program can best be considered by looking at examples of simulation programs that have been developed to meet specific needs. Such examples also will highlight specific interactive techniques.

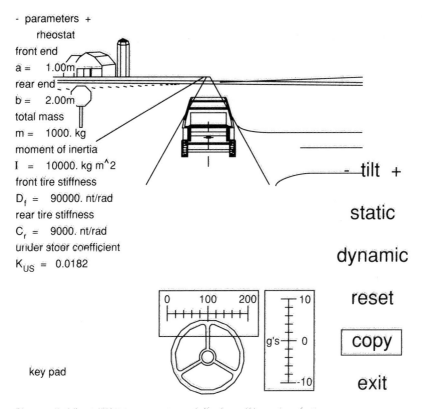

Cornell School of Mechanical and Aerospace Engineering, Vehicle Simulation Program

- parameters +
    rheostat
front end
a =   1.00m
rear end
b =   2.00m
total mass
m =   1000. kg
moment of inertia
I = 10000. kg m^2
front tire stiffness
D_f =   90000. nt/rad
rear tire stiffness
C_r =   9000. nt/rad
under steer coefficient
K_{US} = 0.0182

key pad

0   100   200
g's
10
0
-10

–tilt +

static

dynamic

reset

copy

exit

Figure 5.10   VDYN, an automobile handling simulation.

The first example is a vehicle simulation in which a nonlinear two-wheel model of the car describes the motion. (This problem is posed in more detail in Project 5.2.) Figure 5.10 shows a screen image from this program. It is important to note that this program was developed for a vector display. User interaction during the simulation consists of setting the steering wheel angle and velocity. In addition, the user may vary any of the vehicle's physical parameters (e.g., tire stiffness, mass, wheelbase, etc.), with feedback given graphically on the screen. The user interface includes two menus. The right one is used for program control, and the left menu sets physical parameters. The menus actually overlay portions of the display of the surrounding terrain. Once parameters are set, the new design may be tested for handling characteristics; for example, the designer may take a "test drive" around a simulated course.

The wind-excited dynamic sculpture, as shown in Fig. 5.11, is a two-degree-of-freedom nutation-precision rotational system, with nonlinear

Figure 5.11 Wind-excited dynamic sculpture.

equations of motion. The sculpture consists of two parts: (a) the base and supporting pole, and (b) the "tuning fork" and paddles. The two parts are connected by a joint that allows rotation about two axes, one vertical and one horizontal. The vertical axis always remains vertical; rotation about this axis also rotates the horizontal axis. The twin lower arms swing on either side of the support pole. The square paddles are fixed 90° to the circular paddle. As designed, the center of gravity of the "tuning fork" and paddles lies below the joint, so the equilibrium position is in the vertical position (circle up, squares down). By exerting pressure on the circular paddle, wind excitation will cause the assembly to tip (as shown in Fig. 5.11), and, by pressure on the square paddles, to spin. Simulation is useful to determine sizes that will produce "interesting" motion.

Note that these simulations are useful less from their ability to simulate a particular response, than from their assistance in visualizing the response and in setting the physical parameters and excitations.

5.12   DATA STRUCTURES

It should be clear by now that a simulation program requires a variety of data structures. A detailed discussion requires concepts that will be developed in Chapter 10; however, certain aspects of data structures can be discussed now. Some data structures are quite simple. Usually values for state variables, and sometimes parameters, are stored in arrays. Note that the names of variables and parameters should also be stored, which implies a linkage to the ordering of the value arrays. Names are also important for postprocessing (graphing). In a simulation with 25 degrees of freedom, it is unacceptable to require the user to remember that $x(21)$ is, for example, the position of the horizontal stabilizer.

Graphical representations of the system and its environs require data structures which usually are easily obtained from geometry and graphics packages. Data structures are also required for the user interface (pseudo instrument panels, etc.). Finally, different data structures are required for the analytical models of the system. At the most crude level, structures for models can be no more than the FORTRAN or C source code within the funct procedure. However, any alterations beyond simple changes in parameter values would require editing and program compilation. Fortunately, a wide variety of system specifications have been developed. Most of these are graph based and can serve as the basis for a data structure.

Equations of motion can be stored as ASCII text files and read rather than compiled. This depends upon parsing, which is discussed in Chapter 11, and the creating of a parse graph. Although this is perhaps the most difficult data structure to develop, it is also the most general. Examples of this approach are Macsyma, Mathematica, MathCAD, and other engineering spreadsheet programs. The equation parsing approach will usually require pen-and-paper work by the designer to derive the new equations of motion for a new system.

The parsing approach has allowed for definitions of an entire class of simulation languages known as the CSSL (Continuous System Simulation Language). The following program is an example of a simulation written in one such language, ACSL (Advanced Continuous Simulation Language):

```
TITLE PILOT EJECTION STUDY. ITERATED
SOLUTION
INTGER SW
PARAM H=0.,VA=100.
CONTRL FINTI=2.,DELT=0.1
CONST
M=150.,G=9.8,CD=1.,S=1.2,Y1=1.5,THETD=15.,VE=15.
PARAM SW=1
AFGEN DNSTY=0.,2.917E-2,  300.,2.832E-2,  600.,2.750E-2,...
             1200.,2.598E-2, 1800.,2.438E-2, 3000.,2.154E-2,...
             4500.,1.837E-2, 6000.,1.555E-2, 9000.,1.093E-2,...
             12000.,0.720E-2,15000.,0.447E-2,18000.,0.275E-2
INTEG MILNE
NOSORT
      GO TO (1,2),SW
    1 SW=2
      THETE=.01745*THETD
      VX=VA-VE*SIN(THETE)
      VY=VE*COS(THETE)
      V0=SQRT(VX*VX+VY*VY)
      THETA0=ATAN(VY/VX)
    2 CONTINUE
SORT
FINISH X=-10.
```

Several structural approaches to system dynamics have been developed that provide automated derivation of the governing differential equations. These methods use fundamental components (usually a limited number), which are connected in a graph or network structure. Equations are derived by enforcing continuity (conservation at a node in the network) and/or compatibility (conservation around a loop in the network). Examples of these structures include block diagrams, signal flow graphs, electrical-circuit analogs, and bond graphs. The reader should refer to system-dynamics texts for particulars. It is sufficient for our purposes here to note that the description of a dynamic system can be formalized.

Interestingly, all of the data structures mentioned are graph based, depending on quantities attached to edges or nodes in a network. As shown in Chapter 7, the graphics structures as well as the user interface structure can be graph based. Thus, the techniques from these areas also can be used to develop dynamic-system data structures.

Figure 5.12 shows the unified data structure required, including a physical model, a geometric model, a parameters list, and the logical connections between each model. The loop shows points where the database is accessed during the design process. A typical design session proceeds as follows: The designer initiates the process by selecting an initial set of parameter values, with visual feedback showing the pictorial consequences of each. Then, simulation begins with the equations of motion reformulated with new parameter values. The equations are solved and the system response displayed. The simulation may require direct user interaction or control. After completing the simulation, the user may change the system parameters by selecting either picture components or items from a list (since some users may feel more comfortable with a list, all options should be available).

The sets of correspondences between physical and geometric models are crucial to the integration of a complete system model. Physical response (output variables) must be connected with the pictorial representation; in

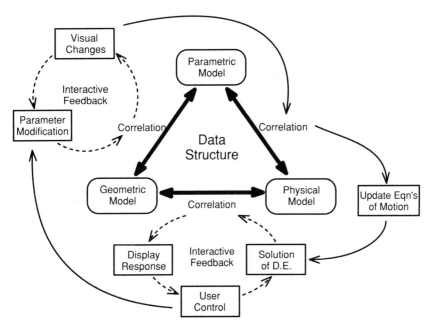

Figure 5.12   A unified data structure for simulation.

addition, correlations are needed to describe the relationship of picture components to dynamic system parameters. Most importantly, an internal correspondence of picture components with one another is necessary to prevent voids or overlaps and maintain consistency.

The sculpture in Figure 5.11 demonstrates this difficulty. Consider the upper circular area and the neck; each one is considered an individual component. However, when the neck is elongated, the center of the circle must change accordingly; likewise, changing the radius of the circle requires recalculating its center if the neck length is to remain constant. Of course, the user may wish to define the system so that elongation of the neck changes the radius instead of the center of the circle. The same problem is faced with the lower paddles and their associated arms. Looking ahead to Section 5.15, Figure 5.14 shows different generic variations of the wind-excited sculpture.

In most cases, the object changes required can be achieved by straightforward applications of geometric transformations such as translation and scale. However, an engineer trying to create a specific instantiation of a generic system by using only geometric transformations will quickly realize the advantages of a system that can represent generic objects through variational geometry (see Section 5.15).

The next logical step may be automatic generation of the equations of motion; however, this is difficult to do in a generic system. If the system were purely mechanical, an engineer could take a structural-dynamics finite-element approach, using a solid geometric modeler and automatic mesh generator. But if there are nonlinear interaction forces, or if the system is not purely elasto-mechanical (i.e., the electrical, fluid, thermal, or magnetic domains are involved), then those equations need to be entered algebraically. A very attractive approach would use the bond-graph technique to "draw in the circuit" for the dynamic system. It is beyond the scope of this book to discuss bond-graph theory, but the theory does provide a highly structured, graphical method to describe the topology of a dynamic system. If a system is described in a bond-graph database, the governing differential equations may be generated automatically.

General-purpose parsing programs are needed to handle the constraints in variational geometry and the equations of motion. Although these equations can be programmed in a high-level language, that approach requires a compile-and-link step every time the system equations are changed in form. A general-purpose parsing capability allows the equations to be changed as necessary during execution, without recompilation or linking.

5.13   ANIMATION: THE GRAPHIC DISPLAY OF OUTPUT VARIABLES

All dynamic motion can be displayed using either of two techniques: rigid-body matrix transformation or object deformation. Matrix transformations (with a hierarchical display list) can selectively transform system components through rotation and/or translation matrix operations. Also, as discussed in

Chapter 7, matrix transforms can be done in hardware, greatly enhancing update rates. The vehicle and wind-excited sculpture of Figures 5.10 and 5.11 illustrate the use of matrix transformations. In these cases rigid-body translation or rotation was the desired response, hence obviating the need for deformation.

Deforming a body implies nonuniformly displacing its points to create the required shape. This technique is used to show vibrational modes in finite-element programs. Deformation requires the lines connecting picture elements to rubberband along with the deformation, which is not possible with matrix transforms. Therefore rubberbanding must be done through software in the host computer. In almost all simulations, it is impractical to apply individual rigid-body matrix operations to each location in the system, which is an essential advantage that lumped parameter systems have over continuous systems. In general, simulation is limited to lumped parameter systems. Although the time response of elastic systems is important, a detailed discussion of this topic is beyond the scope of this book.

Unfortunately, deformation's greatest drawback is the time required to redraw the system during each timestep. In complex pictures of several hundred points the intended effect of dynamic motion begins to disappear, because the slow updating process causes jerky motion in the picture. This problem is solved by resorting to film stripping. If the motion is periodic, the sequence may be broken into frames (18 is usually satisfactory). Each is precalculated, stored, and then cyclically redisplayed as a "movie" of the motion. Unfortunately, filmstripping is only practical for steady-state periodic motion; with transient response only matrix transforms are acceptable.

5.14   HUMAN FACTORS RELATING TO ANIMATION

Nonvisual quantities are common in systems, and some scheme should be adopted to display these quantities to user satisfaction, while minimizing the confusion associated with numeric displays. Color or arrows are good alternatives: For instance, in the vehicle dynamics program, forward velocity and radial acceleration are shown with lengthening arrows. Also, simulated gauges are used to give more accurate numerical magnitudes. Indicators are also useful for random-response studies, where the response RMS is the quantity of interest. Color raster displays have an unlimited potential for the display of nonvisual quantities; finite-element postprocessors now use this capability for display of stress-strain fields.

5.15   VARIATIONAL GEOMETRY:
SETTING PARAMETERS

Producing efficient, natural program interaction requires the consideration of human factors. Cursor selection of a picture component for modification is an example of natural user interaction. However, determining what constitutes natural interaction becomes less clear when numeric input is required.

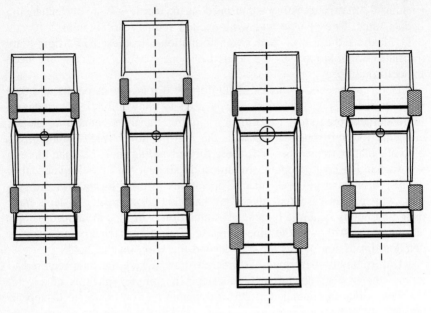

Figure 5.13 A collage of various vehicles.

Aside from the terminal keyboard, a tablet or mouse can be used for numerical input via software keypads and rheostats. These two evaluators form a complimentary set: Keypads are better for setting up initial values; rheostats, for perturbations away from the present value. Using a tablet and pen or mouse for this interaction is preferred, because then a user need not redirect attention from the scope to the console. Users should rely exclusively on rheostats to control forcing functions during simulation. For instance, the program associated with the system in Figure 5.11 allows the user to vary the wind speed, direction, and gusting separately with rheostats; the vehicle dynamics program uses a polar rheostat to vary the angle of steer and a position rheostat for velocity control. Because of the wide variety of possible user controls in a system, the development of realistic user input devices is important if authenticity is desired.

Parameter changes may be made highly interactive if user actions are directed to the picture; in other words, the user points to the component that she wishes to change. When a parameter varies, the picture immediately reflects it and provides a numerical output as well. Figures 5.13 and 5.14 show how the pictorial representation of a system can be varied to reflect changes in parameters. As discussed in Section 5.12, the wind-excited sculpture system demonstrates the difficulties faced in obtaining correspondence between physical parameters and visual aspects of the system. It is rather easy to change the radius of the circular upper surface; tracing the corresponding changes in area, weight, and location of the center of gravity

Figure 5.14 A collage of various wind sculptures.

are also straightforward. However, the damping at the mounting bearing is not readily determined from the figure, and there exists no specific "portion" of the picture to point at to select damping for modification. Generally, systems will have some parameters that are easily obtained from the display, and others that must be taken from a list or menu.

A system with desirable human factors provides both methods of parameter selection (selection from the picture or from a list). Even if there is a natural way to select the parameter from the picture, the simultaneous availability of a corresponding list item (as in VDYN) helps untrained users. After parameter selection, the types of valuators used to set the parameter can be either keypads or rheostats, as previously discussed. Some parameters, such as sizes, positions, and force locations, can even be set by using the picture. The only difficulties arise from providing easy use of each method in the same program, without confusing the user.

5.16 CONCLUSION

The numerical methods for simulation have been presented. But to fully exploit its potential, a computer graphics program must be used and made interactive. The complete simulation package needs to be interactive at all levels, including the geometric modeler, a physical model parser, the establishment of logical connections between response variables, system parameters and pictorial representation, and finally, the actual simulation. The more interactive the system, the easier that users will learn the program's features, the quicker they will make design changes, and the sooner they will be able to complete a design phase. Human factors are as important in program structure as the hidden internal programming, numerical methods, and database structure are. Thus, dynamic systems will require selective picture modification with feedback, plus actual response cues (lengths, displacements), and virtual response cues (lists, velocity arrows, etc.), to enhance communication between user and machine. The rapid turnaround improves productivity and the user also attains key insight into the problem. As a result, the user becomes a more integral part of the overall design process by providing the brains to support the computer's brawn.

5.17 ANNOTATED REFERENCES

Aburdene, M. F. *Computer Simulation of Dynamic Systems*. Dubuque, Ia: William C. Brown, 1988.

An applied book with many cases in discrete- and continuous-time-simulation languages.

ACSL Manual. Concord, Mass.: Mitchell and Gauthier Associates, 1981.

Auslander, D. M., Takahashi, Y., and Rabins, M. J. *Introducing Systems and Control*. New York: McGraw-Hill, 1974.

Broad introduction.

Cannon, R. H., Jr. *Dynamics of Physical Systems*. New York: McGraw-Hill, 1967.

Broad introduction.

Chu, Y. *Digital Simulation of Continuous Systems*. New York: McGraw-Hill, 1969.

Chiefly simulation languages.

Close, C. M. and Frederick, D. K. *Modelling and Analysis of Dynamic Systems*. Boston: Houghton Mifflin, 1978.

Broad introduction.

CSSL-IV Continuous System Simulation Language Reference Manual. SS20-8040-1-01. Chatsworth, Calif.: Simulation Services, 1984.

Forsythe, G. E., Malcom, M. A. and Moler, C. B. *Computer Methods for Mathematical Computing*. Englewood Cliffs, N. J.: Prentice Hall, 1977.

This is a classic book for numerical methods algorithms, including least squares, splines, integration, and matrix decomposition. Contains FORTRAN listings of very good subroutines in each area.

Karnopp, D. C. and Rosenberg, R. *System Dynamics: A Unified Approach*. New York: Wiley, 1975.

Korn, G. A. and Wait, J. V. *Digital Continuous-System Simulation*. Englewood Cliffs, N.J.: Prentice-Hall, 1978.

Applied, including FORTRAN and CSSL-type language.

Luenberger, D. G. *Introduction to Dynamic Systems*. New York: Wiley, 1979.
Broad Introduction.

Press, W. H., Flannery, B. P., Teukolsky, S. A., Vetterling, W. T. *Numerical Recipes in C: The Art of Scientific Computing*. New York: Cambridge University Press, 1988.

Rieder, W. G. and Busby, H. R. *Introductory Engineering Modeling Emphasizing Differential Models and Computer Simulations*. New York: Wiley, 1986.
General introduction, treating both ordinary differential equations and partial differential equations.

Rosenberg, R. *ENPORT*. Lansing, Mich.: Rosencode.

Shearer, J. L. and Kulakowski, B. T. *Dynamic Modeling and Control of Engineering Systems*. New York: Macmillan, 1990.
Broad introduction.

"Simulation Software Catalog," *Simulation*, Vol. 51, No. 4, (1988) p. 36.
Comprehensive survey of (then) available programs, comparison of characteristics and brief abstract of each.

Shaw, Manesh J. *Engineering Simulation: Tools and Applications using the IBM PC Family*. Englewood Cliffs, N.J.: Prentice-Hall, 1988.
Contains many good examples and problems. Describes simulation in the context of PCESP, a subset of DSL/VS.

Shaw, M. *Engineering Simulation using Small Scientific Computers*. Englewood Cliffs, N. J.: Prentice Hall, 1976.
Contains good examples and problems. Describes simulation in the context of DSL/VS language.

Speckhart, F. and Green, W. *A Guide to Using CSMP*. Englewood Cliffs, N. J.: Prentice-Hall, 1976.
Focuses entirely on one simulation language, CSMP.

Thoma, Jean U. *Simulation by Bondgraphs: Introduction to a graphical method*. New York: Springer-Verlag, 1990.

5.18   PROJECTS

Project 5.1   A Simulation of Sailing

Problem Statement   The first part of this project is to simulate the response of a 5.5-m yacht; the second, to design an interactive graphical program to help run the simulation. Figure 5.15 shows the data flow between the two programs. Requirements for this basic project include developing the simulation program that determines dynamic response and creating minimal graphics display and user interface. The programs should communicate by standard techniques for the local operating system.

(A more extended project, drawing on material from Chapters 7 and 11, would include a complete user-interface program. One possibility is a

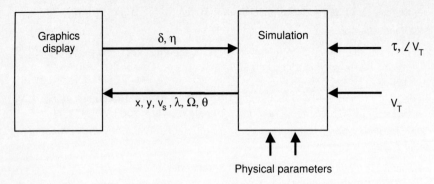

Figure 5.15 Suggested simulation program structure.

regatta with several boats. This would require a third program, a master race-manager to synchronize simulations and distribute information.)

In the graphics program, all aspects of the program are at the designer's discretion except that the user must be able to interactively vary rudder angle η and sheeting angle δ. Major considerations for assessment are aesthetics and human factors. The dynamic quantities are

V_T	True wind velocity
τ	Angle of true wind
δ	Sheeting angle
η	Rudder angle
x, y	Cartesian coordinates of yacht
V_s	Forward velocity of yacht
λ	Heading angle of yacht
Ω	Yaw rate of yacht ($\dot{\lambda}$)
θ	Heel angle

Problem Data The following parameters are intended to represent a typical 5.5-m yacht. Refer to Figures 5.16 and 5.17 for additional information.

LWL	26 ft	Length at water line
m	4,480 lb_m	Mass
I	645,120 $lb_m ft^2$	Directional moment of inertia
J		Roll moment of inertia
S_A	300 ft^2	Sail area
R_A	4 ft^2	Rudder area
d_1	10.5 ft	Rudder moment arm
d_2	+6% LWL	Sail center of pressure

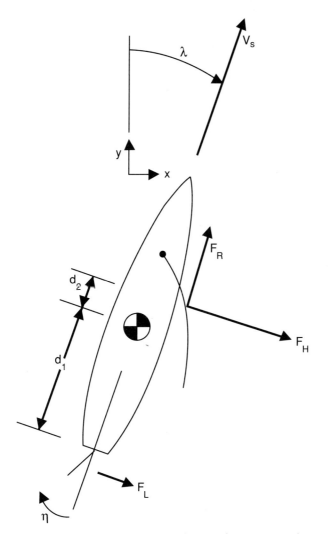

Figure 5.16 Notation for yacht simulation: yaw degree of freedom.

| d_3 | 71% LWL | Sail center of pressure |
| d_4 | 41% LWL | Keel moment arm |

Analysis The following simplifying assumptions have been made:

- Neglect any affects of path curvature, Coriolis acceleration, and centrifugal forces.
- Neglect dependence of d_2 and d_3 upon δ.
- Neglect keel sideslip and assume that the keel provides sufficient side

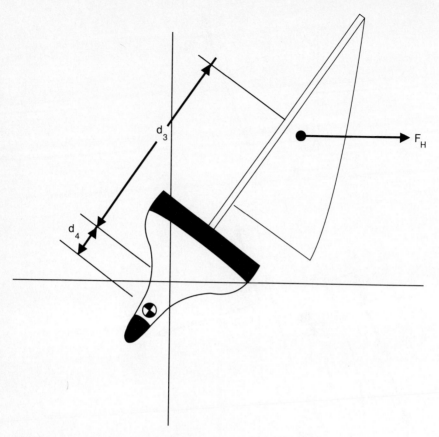

Figure 5.17 Notation for yacht simulation: heel angle
and roll degree of freedom.

force to balance F_H (the lateral sail force). This means that the hull will
have zero angle of attack relative to the water.

• Neglect drag caused by the rudder.

The sail force (F_R, F_H) can be determined using the relationships from
Project 6.1, which also discusses the mechanics of sailing and sail forces in
more detail. Note that in this project λ is the course angle relative to North,
and τ is the wind angle relative to North. The heading angle relative to the
wind is still γ. Similarly, the drag force F_{HD} is given by relationships from
Project 6.1. However, these must be modified to reflect the affect of heel
angle θ:

$$F_{HD}^* = F_{HD} + \left(0.0105\frac{F_H^2}{V_s^2} + 0.0018F_H V_s^2\right)\sec^2(\theta)$$

and

$$F_R^* = F_R(1 - \sin^2 \theta \cos \epsilon)$$

where

$$\epsilon = \tan^{-1}\left(\frac{\text{drag}}{\text{lift}}\right)$$

The hydrodynamics of the rudder is modeled by

$$F_L = 0.97C_s V_s^2 R_A$$

where

$$C_s = \begin{cases} \dfrac{\eta}{40°}, & \text{if } \eta \le 40° \\[2mm] \dfrac{60° - \eta}{20°}, & \text{if } 40° \le \eta \le 60° \\[2mm] 0, & \text{if } 60° \le \eta \end{cases}$$

In the forward direction,

$$m\dot{V}_s = F_R^* - F_{HD}^*$$

About the yaw axis:

$$I\ddot{\lambda} = F_H d_2 - F_L d_1$$

About the roll axis:

$$I\ddot{\theta} = F_H^* d_3 \cos \theta - mg d_4 \sin \theta$$

However, in the interest of simplicity, this project will assume that the yacht responds instantly in roll. Therefore, θ and θ will not be state variables. Instead, the roll angle θ will be determined using an equation given by Kay:

$$F_H = (157.0\,\theta - 1.18\theta^2)\cos\theta$$

Due to the assumption neglecting keel sideslip, the equation for summation of lateral forces is not needed.

Comments   In developing the simulation, it is important to watch the signs of all quantities very carefully, particularly considering what happens when certain quantities are negative. The performance should be different from that found in the optimization Project 6.1. The optimum should have shifted in this project due to heel effects. Consider carefully the time step that the simulation should be using and what might be done to correct any potential problems with the yaw equation.

The project requires material from Chapter 7, Graphics, and Chapter 11, User Interfaces. Comments about these topics are included here for completeness. In designing the graphics program, consider the following:

- The yacht can be represented by two geometric objects, the hull and the sail.
- The simulation will include the heeling angle.
- The wind velocity and direction will be changing and that information should be available to the helmsman.
- Other yachts will be in competition; knowledge of their positions will be available, and the helmsman may wish to know those positions.

Project 5.2   Design of a Railroad Classification Yard

Problem Statement   Determine the profile of a gravity-driven railroad classification yard and the appropriate location of retarder devices. You must also determine the maximum processing rate for your design in cars per minute. How soon can the easy-rolling car be released after the hard-rolling car?

Problem Background   Railroad yards serve as sorting and classification systems where arriving trains are disassembled and departing trains are assembled. Although the cars can be moved using switching engines, sufficient volume can justify the construction and use of a gravity-driven system. The yard can be visualized as a binary tree where cars are individually fed in the root and switched to the correct leaf (see Fig. 5.18). The root is at a higher elevation than the leaves, and the tracks run downhill. Gravity is used to accelerate and drive the cars. Because the acceleration hill is often

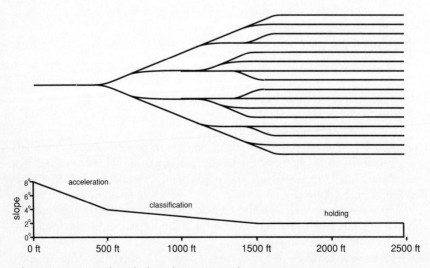

Figure 5.18   Railroad classification yard.

artificial, these railroad yards are called "hump yards" in the industry. The car ID is sensed remotely, and then the switches are set by computer based on a destination designated by a database. When operating, the yard contains a steady sequence of cars being released individually and entering the tree (the classification tracks) and working their way to the leaves (the holding tracks). Upon arrival at the leaves, the cars must couple securely to the line of cars already in the holding tracks. Unfortunately, some cars will roll faster than others, so the spacing cannot be controlled simply by timing each car's release. Retarders are placed at chosen locations to help control car velocity.

The procedures for the grade profile's design are based on a worst-case design philosophy. The assumption here is that if a design can satisfactorily handle a worst-case situation, it can certainly handle less severe situations, which occur much more frequently. Although a worst-case situation may occur relatively infrequently, the consequences of, for instance, overspeed impacts between cars or overrun switches are severe from an operational and cost standpoint.

The worst-case situation occurs when a hard-rolling car is followed by an easy-rolling car, which in turn is followed by another hard-rolling car (HEH). The grade must be designed (perhaps with a small amount of retardation) so that the hard-rolling cars observe all speed constraints at various points between the hump and the tangent point. Such a design results in the easy-rolling car quickly catching the hard-rolling car, unless a large amount of retardation is applied to the easy-rolling car. In some cases, the easy-rolling car is retarded so much that a second catch-up problem can occur when a second (unretarded) hard-rolling car is following the easy-rolling car. In this situation, if too much retardation is given to the second car, it may not enter the classification tracks with sufficient velocity for proper coupling. The objective of this project is to design the hump yard so that the hard-rolling car is delivered to the clearance point (or to some other point specified by the user) with a specified velocity, while meeting all speed and headway constraints for an HEH group of cars.

Problem Data

0.0 mph	Release velocity
200 tons	Car mass
40 ft	Minimum allowable headway
15 mph	Maximum speed
1.0–3.0 mph	Coupling speed range

Resistance Coefficients

| R_1 | 3000 lb | Easy-rolling |
| R_2 | 2000 lb/mph | Easy-rolling |

R_1	7000 lb	Hard-rolling
R_2	3000 lb/mph	Hard-rolling
	−4 mph	Retarder effect
	13 mph	Retarder set-point

The retarder will reduce the car velocity by 4 mph. It will take effect when the car's velocity exceeds 13 mph. Consider the retarder as having no length.

Retarders must be located so as to satisfy the constraints of headway, speed limit, and coupling velocity window. Obviously, the fewer retarders used, the better. The acceleration hump must be artificially constructed, so lower is better.

Analysis   The velocity of each car is determined by the following equation:

$$\dot{V} = \frac{1}{m}(mg\theta - R_1 - R_2V)$$

where

V = car velocity

θ = local slope

g = gravitational acceleration constant

m = car mass

R_1 = sum of all static rolling-resistance terms

R_2 = sum of all velocity-dependent rolling-resistance terms

Additional Information

Cracker, William F., and Wong, Peter J. "New Technology in the Design, Measurement, and Control of Railroad Yards," ASME Winter Annual Meeting, 1978.

Wong, P. J., Elliot, C. V., Kiang, R. L., Sakasito, M., and Stock, W. A. "Railroad Classification Yard Technology—Design Methodology Study," Report to U.S. Department of Transportation, Contract No. DOT-TSC-1337, Stanford Research Institute, 1978.

Project 5.3   Ejection Seat Alignment

Problem Statement   Determine the required ejection velocity and the angle of the guide rails for the ejection seat of a jet aircraft. The pilot and seat must clear the aircraft's vertical stabilizer.

Theory   Ejection can be divided into two phases. During the first phase the pilot and seat are accelerated out of the aircraft guided by a set of rails. During the second phase, the pilot and seat are decelerated by air drag and accelerated by gravity. For this project, assume that the powered phase is completed before the seat clears the guide rails. Therefore the initial conditions for the second phase are the ejection velocity and the angle of ejection from the aircraft. The pilot and seat follow a curved trajectory up and to the rear. Although the seat will tumble, a first approximation treats the pilot and seat as a point mass. The equations of motion can be formulated in two alternative inertial reference frames.

First, in an inertial reference fixed in the ground, ξ, η, the equations of motion are

$$\rho = f(h)$$

$$F_d = \frac{1}{2}\rho C_d S V^2$$

$$V = \sqrt{v_\xi^2 + v_\eta^2}$$

$$v_{\xi 0} = v_a - v_e \sin\theta_e$$

$$v_{\eta 0} = v_e \cos\theta_e$$

$$\theta = \tan^{-1}\left(\frac{v_\eta}{v_\xi}\right)$$

$$m\dot{v}_\eta = -F_d \sin\theta - mg$$

$$m\dot{v}_\xi = -F_d \cos\theta$$

$$\dot{\xi} = v_\xi$$

$$\dot{\eta} = v_\eta$$

The coordinates of the seat relative to the aircraft x, y, can be found from

$$x = v_a t - \xi$$

$$y = \eta$$

Alternatively, in an inertial reference frame fixed in the constant velocity aircraft, x, y, the equations of motion are

$$v_0 = \sqrt{(v_a - v_e \sin\theta_e)^2 + v_e \cos\theta_e}$$

$$\theta_0 = \tan^{-1}\frac{v_e \cos\theta_e}{v_a - v_e \sin\theta_e}$$

$$m\dot{v} = -F_d - g\sin\theta$$

$$\dot{\theta} = -\frac{g\cos\theta}{v}$$

$$\dot{x} = v\cos\theta - v_a$$

$$\dot{y} = v\sin\theta$$

Obviously, an extremely high value of v_e will clear the tail. However, this will impose high acceleration during the first phase. Therefore lower values for v_e are preferable. Similarly, vertical guide rails ($\theta_e = 0$) will clear

h (in m)	ρ (in kg/m^3)	h (in m)	ρ (in kg/m^3)
0	2.917×10^{-2}	4,500	$1,837 \times 10^{-2}$
300	$2,832 \times 10^{-2}$	6,000	1.555×10^{-2}
600	2.750×10^{-2}	9,000	1.093×10^{-2}
1,200	2.598×10^{-2}	12,000	0.620×10^{-2}
1,800	2.438×10^{-2}	15,000	0.447×10^{-2}
3,000	2.154×10^{-2}	18,000	0.275×10^{-2}

Table 5.2 Atmospheric density versus altitude.

the tail better than guide rails inclined to the rear. However, vertical guide rails increase the possibility of bind-up caused by aerodynamic forces when the ejection seat exits the guide rails. They also increase the deceleration forces in the high-speed airstream.

Once values have been selected for v_e, θ_e, it is important to know the operating envelope for safe ejection. This can be described in terms of a region in a h versus v_a space.

Problem Data

m	150	kg	Mass
C_d	1.0		Drag coefficient
S	1.2	m^2	Cross-sectional area
y_1	1.5	m	Corner of vertical stabilizer
x_1	-10	m	Corner of vertical stabilizer
h		m	Altitude
ρ		kg/m^3	Air density
v_a	100	m/sec	Aircraft velocity
θ_e	15°		Angle of ejection seat rails
v_e	15	m/sec	Ejection velocity

Table 5.2 lists specific values for ρ and h.

Project 5.4   Shell-and-Tube Heat Exchanger

Problem Statement   The shell-and-tube heat exchanger shown schematically in Fig. 5.19 uses saturated steam to heat a stream of ethylene glycol. Determine the temperature to which the glycol is heated.

Problem Data

D	1.032 in	Tube diameter
L	23.56 ft	Effective tube length

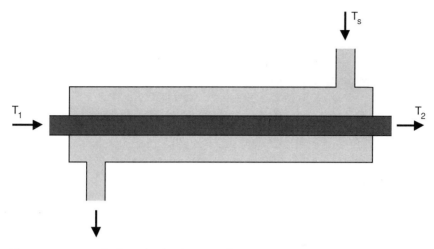

Figure 5.19   A shell-and-tube heat exchanger.

$\dot{m}$	45,000 lbₘ/hr	Flow rate of the glycol
T_1	0 °F	Inlet glycol temperature
T_s	250 °F	Steam temperature

Properties of the glycol

c	Btu/(lbₘ °F)	Specific heat
k	0.153 Btu/(hr · ft °F)	Thermal conductivity
μ	see Table 5.3	Viscosity

The specific heat of glycol can be approximated by

$$c = 0.53 + 6.5 \times 10^{-4}T$$

The film coefficient for convective heat transfer (h) is

$$h = \frac{0.023k}{D}\left(\frac{4\dot{m}}{\pi D\mu}\right)^{0.8}\left(\frac{\mu c}{k}\right)^{0.4}$$

T (°F)	μ(lbₘ/ft/hr)
0	242.
50	82.1
100	30.5
150	12.6
200	5.57

Table 5.3   Viscosity of ethylene glycol.

Analysis   Within a small element of the tube (length dx), the heat transfer from the steam equals the energy convectively removed within the glycol:

$$h(T_s - T)\pi D\,dx = \dot{m}c\,dT$$

This can be reduced to a nonlinear ordinary differential equation for $T(x)$, with $T|_0 = T_1$ specified and $T|_{23.56} = T_2$ to be determined.

Comments   The major decisions in this project relate to the choice of integrator and the step size. A complete report would include plots of $T(x)$, $\mu(x)$, and $h(x)$.

Optional Exercises   What diameter and tube length should be chosen to produce $T_2 = 150°F$?
   Compare the exchanger in this project with two alternative designs, both consisting of two pipes of the same length but half the cross-sectional area. The first has these two pipes in parallel, and the second has these two pipes in series.

Project 5.5   A Simulation of Automobile Handling

Problem Statement   This project will use an automobile handling simulation to illustrate interactive program control, dynamic system simulation, and low-level graphics output. The objective is to determine the maximum velocity with which a specified car can successfully negotiate a sequence of turns. The user determines the sequence of the steering angle input.

Theory   A two-degree-of-freedom model is the simplest model capable of simulating the handling dynamics of a vehicle.[1] The longitudinal velocity is assumed to remain constant, and suspension mechanics are ignored (i.e., there is no roll degree of freedom.) Figure 5.20 illustrates the associated free-body diagram. Summing the lateral forces and summing the moments about the vertical axis through the center of gravity yields two dynamic equations:

$$m\dot{v} + F_f(\alpha_f) + F_r(\alpha_r) = 0$$
$$I\dot{r} + aF_f(\alpha_f) - bF_r(\alpha_r) = 0$$

These determine the lateral velocity v and the yaw rate r.
   The rubber tires generate side forces (F_f, F_r), which can be determined as functions of the slip angle for each tire. These data are usually determined experimentally, much as the lift versus angle of attack is determined for a

---

[1]J. R. Ellis, *Vehicle Dynamics,* London: London Business Books Ltd.; and J. Y. Wong, *Theory of Ground Vehicles,* New York: Wiley, 1978.

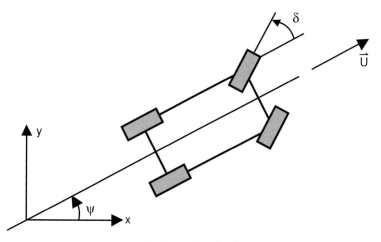

Figure 5.20   An automobile free-body diagram.

wing in a wind tunnel. The slip angle for each tire is given by

$$\alpha_f = \frac{(v + ar)}{U} - \delta$$

$$\alpha_r = \frac{(v - br)}{U}$$

The position in the global coordinate system is found by integrating the velocities in the global coordinate system:

$$\dot{\psi} = r$$
$$\dot{x} = U \cos \psi - v \sin \psi$$
$$\dot{y} = U \sin \psi + v \cos \psi$$

The variables as shown in Fig. 5.20 are

x, y	Global coordinates
ψ	Heading angle
U	Forward velocity
v	Lateral velocity
r	Yaw rate
δ	Steer angle
α	Tire slip angle
$F(\alpha)$	Tire cornering force

Problem Data   Typical parameter values for a sports car are:

M	1000 kg	Mass
I	1000 kg m^2	Yaw moment of inertia

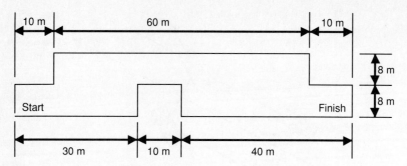

Figure 5.21   A course layout.

a	1.0 m	Distance from the center of gravity to front axle
b	1.4 m	Distance from the center of gravity to rear axle

Nonlinear tire forces.

α (rad)	$F(\alpha)$ (kN)
0.0	0.0
0.2	78.0
0.4	143.0
0.5	168.0
0.6	186.0
0.7	197.0
0.8	200.0
0.9	195.0
1.0	182.0

The race car must remain at all times within the course shown in Fig. 5.21 (all lengths are given in meters).

Comments   A well-planned program will interactively query for the forward velocity before starting a simulation and read parameter values from a disk file. The program will interactively read the steer angle at each time step. The designer must choose either table lookup and interpolation or least-square fit to represent the nonlinear tire forces.

This project can use several kinds of graphics. One approach is a character array (possibly 80 × 16) that contains the track and the generated trajectory. In addition to being displayed on the terminal, this could be printed after each run and included in the report. Alternatively, a graphics package could be provided to plot symbols on the alphanumeric terminals. You can draw the track and then draw points along the path of the car as the simulation proceeds.

The material in Chapter 7, Graphics, and Chapter 11, User Interfaces, is useful for more advanced versions of this project.

C H A P T E R

6
Optimization

6.1 INTRODUCTION

Design has been described as the generation of alternatives and the selection of a specific instantiation. Usually the chosen design is considered better or more desirable in some sense. Optimization is a formalized process of selecting alternatives to consider and choosing between them to achieve a "best" design. It should be noted that all optimization programs are basically iterative, continuing to consider new designs until some convergence criteria is satisfied.

Optimization as a formal method applies only to design improvement within the limitations of a specific design concept. For instance, a prime mover for a vehicle may consist of a reciprocating internal combustion engine, a turbine engine, a battery-electric system, or a fuel-cell electric system. A bearing may be a rolling-element bearing, a journal bearing, or a sliding bearing. A bridge may be a suspension, truss, or beam-and-post bridge. Optimization is not intended to choose between concept alternatives such as these; rather, optimization is used to select the best internal combustion engine, the best battery-electric system, the best journal bearing, or the best suspension bridge. Furthermore, the method can only be applied if the design concept has been parameterized. The design concept consists of a set of possible designs, all with the same concept. A finite set of design values is sufficient to distinguish among designs of the same concept. For example, a journal bearing can be described by the radius, length, clearance, fluid viscosity, and inlet and outlet conditions.

A designer can achieve optimization by searching through a possibly infinite number of designs within a particular parameter space. The formalized optimization process has the advantage of producing a series of instantiations, each one better than its predecessor. It is critical to note that optimization depends upon the existence of an accepted method of analysis to predict design performance. This predicted performance is the basis for a determination of "better."

This chapter begins with a review of the numerical methods available for unconstrained and constrained optimization. The architecture and components of an optimal design system are discussed, including applications of concepts from artificial intelligence and database management.

The variables in the problem can be divided into three categories: parameters, design variables, and performance variables. Parameters are preassigned and are considered invariant during the optimization process. Of course, in practice a parameter study will involve studying several proposed values for these "fixed" quantities, and the objective function depends upon the values chosen. Nevertheless, these parameters are not considered as changeable by the optimization process. It is unfortunate that optimization is often described as a search through parameter space. This is incorrect because parameter values in this text are considered as "fixed."

The design variables are the unknown quantities that are to be determined by the optimization process. When viewed as a vector, these variables span the design space. Because design space need not be three dimensional, it can be difficult to visualize. However, in the journal bearing example mentioned previously, if fluid viscosity is considered as a (fixed) parameter, then the parameterization and design space will look like Fig. 6.1.

Performance variables are functions of the design variables and are used in some sense as measures of performance, contributing to either the objective function or to the constraint functions. A very simple example is a hollow cylinder parameterized by an inner and outer radius. The thickness is a performance variable, in this case, an explicit function of the design variables. The stress in the cylinder is another performance variable. This example illustrates that performance variables may seem to be either alternatives to the design variables or the results of some analytical prediction of behavior. In theory, they can be eliminated algebraically in favor of the design variables; in practice, this usually is not possible.

The functions involved consist of the objective function and all applicable constraints. In almost all cases, these functions do not exist analytically but only as the result of a procedure (that may involve quite extensive numerical calculations).

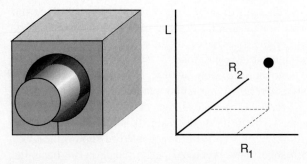

Figure 6.1   Design variables define design space.

Design constraints limit the feasible solutions. These constraints can apply to design variables directly or contribute to the need for a performance variable. For example: a truss might be required to fit within a specific geometric envelope; the thickness of a hollow cylinder must be less than the outer radius and the maximum stress less than the buckling stress; the flux density in a magnetic field may be required to be less than some saturation level; and the flutter velocity for a wing must be greater than the expected operating regime. Finally, design variables may be limited to discrete values within a range. Typically, a rod diameter may be limited to $1''$, $1.5''$, $2''$, $2.5''$, and so on. The number of teeth on a gear, the number of bays in a truss, or the number of bolts in a fastener must be integer values. A special subset of the constraints are upper and lower bounds for the design variables.

The problem can be stated as

$$\text{minimize } E \qquad \text{where } E = f(\mathbf{D})$$

subject to

$$g_i(\mathbf{D}) = 0, \qquad i = 1, \ldots, N_e$$
$$g_i(\mathbf{D}) \leq 0, \qquad i = N_e + 1, \ldots, N$$
$$\mathbf{D} \in R^n$$
$$\mathbf{l} \leq \mathbf{D} \leq \mathbf{u}$$

where the design vector $\mathbf{D}$ also includes the performance variables. Note that there is no loss of generality in posing the problem as minimization rather than maximization.

In general, determining the proper objective function E is the most important decision that the engineer will make. Because few problems have a single merit criterion, the engineer will have to choose between criteria or formulate one that is a composite of several merit functions with weighting factors applied. The latter process can be viewed as the formulation of a *composite objective function*. If one objective function decreases while another increases, the method becomes the *method of competing objective functions*. Alternatively, the engineer may decide to use certain merit criteria as constraints. For example, instead of minimizing weight and stress in a beam, the engineer may minimize the weight and enforce the constraint that stress not exceed the yield value. Determining the formulation of the objective function, the selection criteria, and the weighting factors is often a judgment call. The key point here is that the formal method of optimization requires a single scalar value that measures the merit of the entire design.

The nature of the objective function significantly affects the behavior of the optimization process. Usually optimization techniques assume that the objective function and constraints (E, g_i, $i = 1, \ldots, n$) are twice differentiable. Other typical assumptions include unimodality and convexity of the objective function. Unimodality simply means that only one minimum exists; convexity for a minimization problem means that the curvature is always positive. These characteristics are shown in Fig. 6.2.

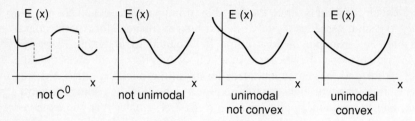

Figure 6.2 Objective functions can be characterized by
continuity, modality, and convexity.

Unfortunately, realistic engineering problems are not so well behaved.
The functions may be only C^0 or often not even continuous as alternate
branches in an analysis scheme are exercised due to yielding, buckling, and
so forth.

6.2   LINE-SEARCH ALGORITHMS AND SINGLE-VARIABLE OPTIMIZATION

The optimization process can be posed as a root-finding problem (a calculus
review follows later in this section), but most optimization algorithms are
based on what are called direct-search methods. The direct-search method
works from a current design variable vector $\mathbf{D}_k$, that probably is not the
optimal. Then the method attempts iteratively to improve this initial estimate
by performing local mathematical tests, based on information limited to a
small region in design space around the current design. Thus, using only
this local information, the process chooses a strategy that ensures a move to
a new design $\mathbf{D}_{k+1}$ that costs less than the preceding estimate $\mathbf{D}_k$.

In many direct-search algorithms, the new estimate $\mathbf{D}_{k+1}$ is determined
from $\mathbf{D}_k$ by

$$\mathbf{D}_{k+1} = \mathbf{D}_k + \lambda_k^* \mathbf{u}_k$$

where $\mathbf{u}_k$ denotes the search direction obtained by one of the search strategies
and λ_k^*, the step length along $\mathbf{u}_k$ that needs to be moved to obtain the new
iterate $\mathbf{D}_{k+1}$.

The line-search algorithm determines a value for λ_k^* by minimizing a
descent function along the search direction for the current iteration. Hence,
the following subproblem needs to be solved at any iteration step:

$$\min F(\lambda) = F(\mathbf{D}_k + \lambda \mathbf{u}_k), \qquad 0 < \lambda < \infty$$

where F is the descent function. This descent function F is determined
from the objective function and the constraints, depending on the underlying mathematical technique used to solve the constrained problem posed in

Section 2.1. In the simplest case of unconstrained minimization, the descent function is the same as the objective function

$$\min E = E(x), \qquad x_l \le x \le x_u$$

Note that for the remainder of Section 6.2, x will denote the design variable in a one-dimensional problem. However, in subsequent sections the notation of $\mathbf{D}$ and λ will be used.

A fundamental measure of an optimization algorithm is the change in objective function at each iteration. If convergence is to be assured, the step length must produce a "sufficient decrease" in the objective function $E(\mathbf{D})$ (Gill,Murray, and Wright, 1981). This sufficient decrease may be measured by sets of conditions on λ_k. Alternatively, these conditions could be used as stopping criteria for some of the line search methods mentioned later in this section and in Section 6.3.

Solving of the one-dimensional optimization problem deserves careful attention. Because multi-degree-of-freedom optimization usually reduces to a series of single-dimension optimizations, which are called line searches, it is important to have efficient line-search algorithms. A line-search algorithm may require the problem functions to be evaluated many times in order to determine the step length. Since evaluating problem functions may require a lot of expensive computer time, it is crucial to implement an efficient line search algorithm within the optimization programs. The number of function evaluations per iteration, when gradients are computed by finite differences, is one measure of line-search efficiency.

There are three types of methods used to attack the line-search problem:

1. Straightforward calculus using root-finding techniques (this requires explicit derivatives)

2. Analytical approximation, where $E(x)$ is replaced by a low-order polynomial that is minimized

3. Search methods that use only function evaluations, such as Fibonacci or golden section search.

The first two methods are discussed in the rest of this section. Search methods are discussed in Section 6.3.

Calculus Review

Using calculus, a minimum of a function can be defined analytically as the point with zero slope. The optimization problem can therefore be treated as a root-finding problem. So if $E(x)$ exists analytically, and $\partial E / \partial x$ can be easily evaluated, an efficient approach would use Newton's method to solve $\partial E / \partial x = 0$. This can be written as

$$\hat{x} = x - \frac{\partial E / \partial x}{\partial^2 E / \partial x^2}$$

Note that this formulation uses the second derivative of the objective function $\partial^2 E / \partial x^2$. Usually an analytical second derivative is unavailable, but it is possible to use the secant method and two gradient evaluations at x_a, x_b to find x such that $\partial E / \partial x = 0$. An iterative approach can be built on

$$\hat{x} = x_a - \frac{\partial E}{\partial x}\bigg|_{x_a} \left(\frac{(x_b - x_a)}{(\partial E / \partial x)|_{x_b} - (\partial E / \partial x)|_{x_a}} \right)$$

The calculus of a function of several variables will be discussed in Section 6.4.

Analytical Approximation

The general method of analytical approximation introduced in Chapter 2 is also useful in line-search problems. The function with an unknown minimum is replaced by a simpler function whose minimum can be located analytically. Two possibilities for approximating functions are quadratic and cubic polynomials.

It can be easily shown that the extreme value of a quadratic

$$p(x) = a_0 + a_1 x + a_2 x^2$$

occurs at

$$x_{min} = \frac{-a_1}{2a_2}$$

Given three function evaluations, the quadratic coefficients a_0, a_1, a_2 can be determined. If the trial points x_1, x_2, x_3 are equally spaced (spacing s), as shown in Fig 6.3, then a_0, a_1, a_2 are easily found in terms of E_1, E_2, E_3 and

$$x_{min} = x_2 + s \frac{E_1 - E_3}{2(E_3 - 2E_2 + E_1)}$$

If the three points are unequally spaced, the appropriate formula is

$$x_{min} = \frac{1}{2} \frac{(x_2^2 - x_3^2)E_1 + (x_3^2 - x_1^2)E_2 + (x_1^2 - x_2^2)E_3}{(x_2 - x_3)E_1 + (x_3 - x_1)E_2 + (x_1 - x_2)E_3}$$

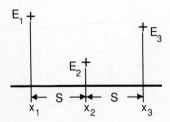

Figure 6.3   Three-Point evaluation for quadratic fit.
Note: If $E_2 < E_3$ and $E_2 < E_1$, the minimum
can be localized to within three values.

Given four function evaluations, the cubic coefficients can be determined as shown in Section 2.2. For a general cubic,

$$p(x) = a_0 + a_1 x + a_2 x^2 + a_3 x^3$$

it can be shown that the extrema will occur at

$$x_{min} = \frac{-a_2 \pm \sqrt{a_2^2 - 3a_1 a_3}}{3a_3}$$

It is important to note that either there are two roots to choose between, or there may be no minimum. That is, the extremum may be a maximum, or a saddle.

The quadratic presents fewer problems than the cubic, but possible discontinuities in the objective function may make a quadratic polynomial a poor approximation. In general the quadratic will approximate the function best if the evaluation points bracket the minimum. Also note that the value of the midpoint is not sufficient to limit the location of the minimum, other than in the range (E_1, E_3).

■ **EXERCISE 6.1:** If analytical expressions for derivatives are available, then they can help develope other approximations. Derive an analytical approximation, assuming that $E(x_0)$ and $\partial E / \partial x(x_0)$ can be calculated explicitly.

■ **EXERCISE 6.2:** In the extremely rare case that an analytical expression for $\partial^2 E / \partial x^2$ is available, derive a quadratic analytic approximation.

Method of Davies, Swann, and Campey

This Davies, Swann, and Campey technique can be used to produce a set of three equally spaced points that spans the minimum. A quadratic approximation can then be determined and used as discussed in the preceding subsection. As illustrated in Fig. 6.4, the method starts at x_0:

1. Evaluate the objective function in steps of $\delta x, 2\delta x, 4\delta x, 8\delta x, \ldots$ until an increase in the function is detected.

2. Assume the minimum is within the last three points.

3. Add a point at the center of last interval (this results in four equally spaced points that span the minimum).

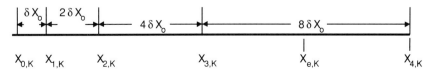

Figure 6.4 Method of Davies, Swann, and Campey.

4. Select the minimum of the two center points; keep the point to its left and right, and discard the outermost point (this results in three equally spaced points which span the minimum).

5. Determine x_{min} by quadratic approximation $x_{min} = -a_1/2a_2$.

6. Use the predicted minimum as the new starting point, reducing δx by a factor k.

For completeness, the algorithm must be modified to handle starting problems. If the objective function is increasing on the first interval $E_{1,k} > E_{0,k}$, reverse direction and use $-\delta x$. If the objective function is also increasing in the first interval after reversing direction, the method has produced three equally spaced points. The search iteration can be terminated when the interval between δx_k is less than some ϵ.

Let $x_{n,k}$ denote the nth step in the kth iteration:

$$x_{n,k} = x_{n-1,k} + 2^{n-1}\delta x_k$$

This produces a sequence of evaluations of the objective function $E_{0,k}, E_{1,k}, E_{2,k}, \ldots, E_{n,k}$. The midpoint of the last step is

$$x_{e,k} = x_{n,k} - 2^{n-2}\delta x_k$$

The four spanning points are $x_{n-2,k}, x_{n-1,k}, x_{e,k}, x_{n,k}$. And, if

$$E_{e,k} \geq E_{n-1,k}$$

then

$$x_{0,k+1} = x_{min} = x_{n-1,k} + \frac{2^{n-2}\delta x_k(E_{n-2,k} - E_{e,k})}{2(E_{e,k} - 2E_{n-1,k} + E_{n-2,k})}$$

or, if

$$E_{e,k} \leq E_{n-1,k}$$

then

$$x_{0,k+1} = x_{min} = x_{e,k} + \frac{2^{n-2}\delta x_k(E_{n-1,k} - E_{n,k})}{2(E_{n,k} - 2E_{e,k} + E_{n-1,k})}$$

A variety of methods are reasonable for reducing the step size

$$\delta x_k = \delta x_0 10^{-k}$$

$$\delta x_k = (\delta x_0)^{1/k}$$

$$\delta x_k = \frac{\delta x_0}{2^k}$$

Convergence can be determined from the active step size δ_k or the amount of reduction in the objective function.

6.3   SEARCH TECHNIQUES

Of the three kinds of methods listed in the previous section, the most straight-forward approach to optimization is to search the entire range of the design variable $[x_l, x_u]$. Evaluating the objective function on uniform spaced intervals of s can locate the minimum to an accuracy of two intervals, $2s$. Of course, this approach is extremely inefficient, requiring $N - 1$ evaluations within the initial interval to reduce that interval by $2/N$ times the initial interval. The efficiency of an algorithm depends on the location of the relatively expensive evaluations of the objective function. The best alternative would repetitively place two evaluations within the interval (x_L, x_U), thus creating three subintervals and reducing the range to two of these three. Any algorithm using more than two evaluations inside the interval for each iteration will be less efficient.

Dichotomous Search

Dichotomous search, also called interval halving or binary chop, uses two evaluations and reduces the range by a factor of two. As shown in Fig. 6.5 the midpoint of the range of interest is

$$x_{1/2} = \frac{x_u - x_l}{2}$$

The objective function is evaluated at $x_a = x_{1/2} - \epsilon$ and $x_b = x_{1/2} + \epsilon$. The range of interest is reduced to a subrange, $x_l \leq x \leq x_{1/2}$, or $x_{1/2} \leq x \leq x_u$ depending on whether $E(x_{1/2} - \epsilon)$ or $E(x_{1/2} + \epsilon)$ is less. Note that the resulting subrange is not precisely $x_l \leq x \leq x_b$ or $x_a \leq x \leq x_u$, but is ϵ larger.

   This process is too inefficient; it requires two function evaluations to reduce the range by a factor of two (25 percent per evaluation). Spreading the two evaluations further apart can increase efficiency. Thus, choosing x_a and x_b logically becomes the issue.

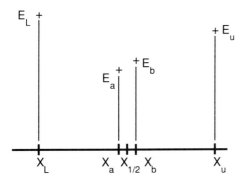

Figure 6.5   Two central evaluations to reduce the range of minimum.

Golden Section Search

The basis of the golden section search is to require only a single function evaluation to eliminate a portion of the interval of the design variable. This means that either x_a or x_b (and therefore E_a or E_b) must be left over from the previous larger interval. If the interval of the design variable is $I = x_l - x_u$ then the inserted points can be determined by

$$x_b = x_l + kI$$
$$x_a = x_u - kI$$

If $E_b < E_a$, then the minimum must lie within the range of (x_a, x_u). On the next iteration (see also Fig. 6.6):

$$I_1 = kI_0$$
$$x_{l,1} = x_{a,0}$$
$$x_{b,1} = x_{l,1} + kI_1$$
$$x_{a,1} = x_{u,0} - kI_1$$
$$x_{u,1} = x_{u,0}$$

The most efficient use of information, requiring only one function evaluation per cycle, occurs if

$$x_{a,1} = x_{b,0}$$

This is true if $k = 0.618033989 \cdots$, the golden ratio, which is a root of the equation $k^2 + k - 1 = 0$. Therefore, on the ith interval

$$I_{i+1} = kI$$
$$x_{b,i} = x_{l,i} + kI_i$$
$$x_{a,i} = x_{u,i} - kI_i$$

Note that the interval is reduced by a factor of $1 - k$ (approximately 39 percent) during each iteration which is better than interval halving. If the convergence criterion requires iteration until $I_i \leq \epsilon$, it is easy to predict how many iterations will be needed.

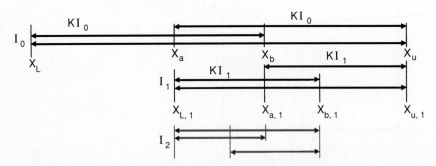

Figure 6.6 Successive intervals for the golden section search.

I_i	x_l	x_a	x_b	x_u
14.00	−5.00	0.35	3.65	9.00
8.65	−5.00	−1.70	0.35	3.65
5.35	−1.70	0.35	1.61	3.65
3.30	0.35	1.61	2.39	3.65
2.04	0.35	1.13	1.61	2.39
1.26	0.35	0.83	1.13	1.61
0.78	0.83	1.13	1.31	1.61
0.48	0.83	1.01	1.13	1.31
0.30	0.83	0.94	1.01	1.13
0.18	0.94	1.01	1.06	1.13
0.11	0.94	0.99	1.01	1.06
0.07	0.94	0.97	0.99	1.01

Table 6.1   Iteration values for Example 6.1.

Example 6.1: Golden Section Search. Consider the function $E = (x-1)^2$ over the range $(-5, 9)$. The minimum can be found to an accuracy of $\epsilon = 0.1$ with 11 iterations, as shown in Table 6.1.

Figure 6.7 shows how the search process converges. Observe that either x_a or x_b serves as the outer limit for the next iteration. Also, note that one end of the interval may remain fixed for several iterations.

Fibonacci Search

A slightly more efficient algorithm can be based on the Fibonacci series:

$$1, 1, 2, 3, 5, 8, 13, 21, 34, 55, 89, 144, \ldots$$

This series is used to give a varying value for k as the search iterates. However, each iteration will reuse one of the interior points from the previous

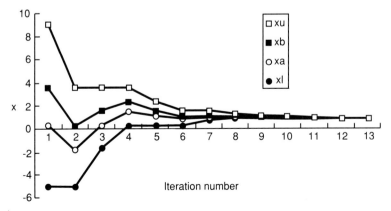

Figure 6.7   Golden section search iterations for $E = (x - 1)^2$.

larger interval. The k value is calculated by F_i/F_{i-1} where F_i represents the ith Fibonacci number. Specifically, if the best estimate of the optimum is required in 11 iterations, the first value for k will be

$$k_1 = \frac{F_{11}}{F_{12}}$$

Further values for k will be

$$k_2 = \frac{F_{10}}{F_{11}}, \qquad k_3 = \frac{F_9}{F_{10}}, \qquad k_4 = \frac{F_8}{F_9}, \qquad \dots$$

Because $x_a = x_b$, ($k = 0.5$) in the last iteration, no function evaluation is needed in the last iteration. Therefore the Fibonacci method effectively uses 10 function evaluations to produce a final interval of $\frac{1}{144}I_1$ or $0.0069I_1$, as opposed to the $0.6180^{10}I_1$ or $0.0081I_1$ obtained for 10 function evaluations with the golden section search. However, this apparent advantage is only marginal, because the golden section search is easily continued for more iterations whereas the Fibonacci search must be restarted for further accuracy.

6.4 OPTIMIZATION IN MORE THAN ONE DIMENSION

Design variables define design space; the objective variable adds one additional dimension. The objective function is a "surface" of dimension N embedded in a space of dimension $N + 1$. If one can visualize geometry in more than three dimensions, it is a small step to conceive of optimization in $N + 1$ dimensions. Since this is difficult to represent in print, the techniques presented in this section will be illustrated in only two dimensions, with the objective function serving as the third dimension. In this case, the objective function can be visualized as a surface. This surface could be drawn in perspective views; however, it is more typical to present the surface in a contour plot similar to a topographic map, as illustrated in Fig. 6.8. The optimization process has been compared to mountain climbing in a dense fog without a topographic map. The climber can determine the local altitude with an altimeter and and look around to determine downhill and uphill directions, but obviously cannot scan the topology for the peak or identify local ridges and canyons that may make certain paths difficult.

Optimization for mechanical design problems can vary greatly in the number of degrees of freedom. Many design problems can be parameterized to a few variables, and in optimization, limited to a space of less than ten dimensions. In fact, the reduction to a design space with few dimensions is one of the primary reasons for design parameterization. However, other problems may have many degrees of freedom. Structural problems (such

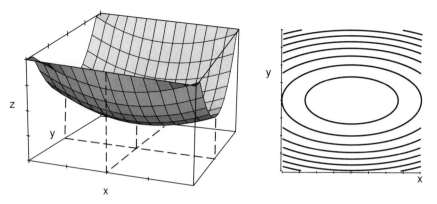

Figure 6.8   Surface and contour plot visualization for
$E(x, y) = 4 + (2x + 2)^2 + (y + 2)^2$.

as truss problems) with many structural members, all of which can have different cross-sectional properties, and the different locations of joints that can move independently, can easily lead to problems with 300–400, or even several thousand dimensions. As engineered materials (such as composites) become more widespread, these problems will become more common. In certain composites, the material properties can be varied tremendously from location to location. This can lead to an optimization problem based on a finite-element analysis where literally each element's properties are distinct degrees of freedom.

Multiple-degree-of-freedom problems are less likely to have explicit derivatives available and so straightforward calculus does not provide an efficient approach. This leaves two optimization methods:

1.   Gradient techniques based on analytical approximation

2.   Pure search techniques (pattern based)

This book will not discuss the pure search techniques that can be built on patterns of various kinds. To evaluate the full pattern usually requires as many evaluations as are needed to approximate the gradient; thus, there is no efficiency advantage in these pattern-based search techniques. To understand this shortcoming, consider how the one-dimensional search proceeded and the enormity of hyperspace. The function evaluations in a one-dimensional search were used to rule out certain regions, rather than to localize the minimum to within a certain region. Given a unit cube in 10 dimensions (R^{10}), suppose that some search algorithm has eliminated the lower half of all ten variables. However, the volume eliminated is only 0.5^{10} or $\frac{1}{1024}$. Approximately 99.9 percent of the design space still remains to be searched.

Calculus Review

Before proceeding, it is useful to review the notation for calculus of several variables and some concepts from analytical geometry. A scalar function of a vector variable can be written as $E = E(\mathbf{D})$. This can be expanded in a Taylor series as

$$E(\mathbf{D} + \boldsymbol{\delta}) = E(\mathbf{D}) + \mathbf{g}^T\boldsymbol{\delta} + \frac{1}{2}\boldsymbol{\delta}^T(\mathbf{H})\boldsymbol{\delta} + \cdots$$

The gradient $\mathbf{g}$ is the Jacobian vector:

$$\mathbf{g} = \nabla E = \frac{\partial E}{\partial \mathbf{x}} = \begin{Bmatrix} \partial E/\partial x_1 \\ \partial E/\partial x_2 \\ \partial E/\partial x_3 \\ \vdots \\ \partial E/\partial x_n \end{Bmatrix}$$

The second derivative is the Hessian Matrix $\mathbf{H}$:

$$\mathbf{H} = \left[\frac{\partial^2 E}{\partial \mathbf{x}^2}\right] = \begin{bmatrix} \partial^2 E/\partial x_1^2 & \partial^2 E/\partial x_1\partial x_2 & \cdots & \partial^2 E/\partial x_1\partial x_n \\ \partial^2 E/\partial x_2\partial x_1 & \partial^2 E/\partial x_2\partial x_2 & \cdots & \partial^2 E/\partial x_2\partial x_n \\ \vdots & \vdots & \ddots & \vdots \\ \partial^2 E/\partial x_n\partial x_1 & \partial^2 E/\partial x_n\partial x_2 & \cdots & \partial^2 E/\partial x_n^2 \end{bmatrix}$$

A local minimum occurs if $\mathbf{g} = \mathbf{0}$ and $\mathbf{H}$ is positive definite (all eigenvalues are greater than zero).

Example 6.2: As an example that can be treated analytically, consider the function

$$E = 4x^2 + y^2 + 2x^4 + 3x^2y^2$$

The gradient is

$$\mathbf{g} = \nabla E = \begin{Bmatrix} \partial E/\partial x \\ \partial E/\partial y \end{Bmatrix} = \begin{Bmatrix} 8x + 8x^3 + 6xy^2 \\ 2y + 6x^2y \end{Bmatrix}$$

and the Hessian is

$$\mathbf{H} = \begin{bmatrix} 8 + 24x^2 + 6y^2 & 12xy \\ 12xy & 2 + 6x^2 \end{bmatrix}$$

Note that $\mathbf{g}$ and $\mathbf{H}$ depend upon the location (x, y). For instance, at $\mathbf{D}_o = \begin{Bmatrix} 0 \\ 0 \end{Bmatrix}$:

$$E_0 = 4$$

$$\mathbf{g}_o = \begin{Bmatrix} 0 \\ 0 \end{Bmatrix}$$

$$\mathbf{H}_o = \begin{bmatrix} 8 & 0 \\ 0 & 2 \end{bmatrix}$$

Choice of Search Direction

The line-search approach will use a given technique to determine a desired direction and then minimize in that single direction (in a one-dimensional problem). Various methods are used to determine the direction for this search; however, the simplest is *one at a time*. This method will cycle through the design variables, sequentially minimizing $E(\vec{D})$ with respect to D_i. Figure 6.9 shows this as a series of line searches, each aligned with the basis vectors for the design space. Unfortunately, such a search tends to follow a zigzag path, and convergence is not fast. The rate of convergence and zigzag nature of the search depends greatly on the accuracy of the line search.

All minima, viewed closely enough, have the form of an elliptical bowl described by the second-order terms in the Taylor series expansion about the minimum. The "one at a time" approach will zigzag unless the principal axes of the ellipse coincide with the design variables. This method can yield false results on a long narrow valley at a 45° angle to the axes.

The "one at a time" method can be written as

$$\mathbf{u}_1 = \lambda \begin{Bmatrix} 1 \\ 0 \\ 0 \\ 0 \\ \vdots \\ 0 \end{Bmatrix} \qquad \mathbf{u}_2 = \lambda \begin{Bmatrix} 0 \\ 1 \\ 0 \\ 0 \\ \vdots \\ 0 \end{Bmatrix} \qquad \cdots \qquad \mathbf{u}_n = \lambda \begin{Bmatrix} 0 \\ 0 \\ 0 \\ 0 \\ \vdots \\ 1 \end{Bmatrix}$$

Note that this approach uses successive directions that are in some sense normal to the preceding search. Also, the process probably will not reach the minimum in one cycle through all the design dimensions, so an outer loop must be crafted.

The *steepest-descent approach* uses the direction information that is contained in the gradient of the objective function. Expanding the objective function in a Taylor series,

$$E(\mathbf{D} + \boldsymbol{\delta}) = E(\mathbf{D}) + \mathbf{g}^{\mathsf{T}}\boldsymbol{\delta} + \frac{1}{2}\boldsymbol{\delta}^{\mathsf{T}}\mathbf{H}\boldsymbol{\delta} + \cdots$$

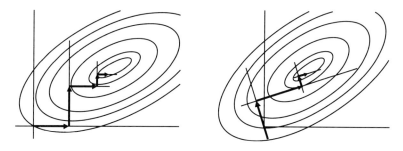

Figure 6.9 "One at a time" and steepest-descent line searches.

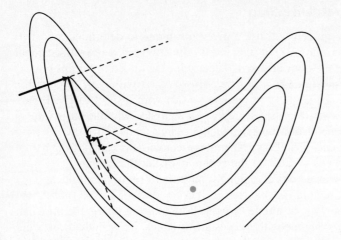

Figure 6.10   Steepest-descent line searches may converge slowly.

The gradient is normal to a unit vector along a level curve (a curve of equal altitude):

$$0 = \left\{ \frac{\partial E}{\partial x} \right\}^{\mathrm{T}} \left\{ \begin{array}{c} \partial x_1/\partial s \\ \partial x_2/\partial s \\ \vdots \\ \partial x_n/\partial s \end{array} \right\} = \mathbf{g} \cdot \frac{\partial \mathbf{x}}{\partial s}$$

where the vector $\partial \mathbf{x}/\partial s$ gives the direction cosines of the level curve. Specifically, $\mathbf{g}$ is the direction of steepest ascent, and $-\mathbf{g}$ is the direction of steepest descent. A unit vector in direction of steepest descent therefore is

$$\mathbf{u} = \frac{-\mathbf{g}}{|\mathbf{g}|}$$

Successive iterations of the method of steepest descent, as shown in Fig. 6.9, are orthogonal to the immediately preceding search. This orthogonality can slow the convergence rate, since this approach does not use information from the previous iteration to accelerate the convergence. Thus, it is not recommended for general use if more sophisticated techniques are available. Figure 6.10 shows how a curving valley can slow this method by shifting the principal axes of the local Hessian.

Example 6.3: Continuing with the function used in Example 6.2, a plot of the objective function is shown in Fig. 6.11. At point A,

$$\mathbf{D}_A = \left\{ \begin{array}{c} 1 \\ 1 \end{array} \right\} \qquad E_A = 14, \qquad \mathbf{g}_A = \left\{ \begin{array}{c} 22 \\ 8 \end{array} \right\}$$

Note that $-\mathbf{g}$ does not point toward the minimum at $\left\{ \begin{array}{c} 0 \\ 0 \end{array} \right\}$. Searching along

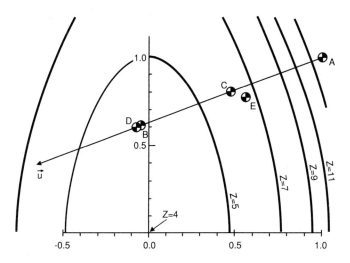

Figure 6.11   The direction of steepest-descent for
$F(x, y) = 4x^2 + y^2 + 2x^4 + 3x^2y^2$.

the steepest descent direction $\mathbf{u}$, the line-search minimum is at $\lambda = 1.1108$,
giving $\mathbf{D}_B = \left\{ \begin{array}{c} -0.0440 \\ 0.6204 \end{array} \right\}$.

   A modification to correct the orientation of the line search produces the
conjugate gradient algorithms. A conjugate direction algorithm, used for
minimizing a strictly convex quadratic function with exact line search, is
finite (bounded in time) and attains the minimum of E in no more than n
iterations. An unconstrained optimization method is a conjugate-direction
algorithm, if the search directions $\mathbf{u}_k$ are conjugate with respect to a matrix
$\mathbf{B}$, when minimizing a *quadratic function* of the kind

$$E(\mathbf{x}) = \frac{1}{2}\mathbf{x}^T\mathbf{B}\mathbf{x} + \mathbf{C}^T\mathbf{x}$$

The search is in conjugate directions if

$$\mathbf{u}_j^T\mathbf{B}\mathbf{u}_i = 0 \quad \text{for } i = 0, 1, \ldots, n-1, \ j = 0, 1, \ldots, n-1, i \neq j$$

   The matrix $\mathbf{B}$ is usually the Hessian or an approximation to it. However,
the use of constraints and a descent function can lead to algorithms where
$\mathbf{B}$ is not the Hessian of the objective function.
   The most common method for generating conjugate directions is to
ensure that successive search directions are perpendicular to all preceding
directions. In this method, the *conjugate-gradient method*, search directions
are generated as follows:

$$\mathbf{u}_0 = -\mathbf{g}_0$$

$$\mathbf{u}_k = -\mathbf{g}_k + \frac{\|\mathbf{g}_k\|^2}{\|\mathbf{g}_k - 1\|^2}\mathbf{u}_{k-1} \quad \text{for } k = 1, 2, \ldots$$

The conjugate-direction methods are generally considered inferior to the quasi-Newton methods described later in this section. However, these methods have one advantage: They do not require the storage of matrices to compute the search direction $\mathbf{u}_k$. Hence, the conjugate gradient methods can be implemented to solve large problems with hundreds or thousands of design variables.

Analytical Approximation for Line Search in N Dimensions

Optimization in N dimensions consists of a series of problems, each based on a change in design variables $\boldsymbol{\delta} = \lambda\mathbf{u}$, that searches for a minimum value of λ in one direction. Each line search, if implemented as described previously, is itself an iteration; therefore, the potential exists for a double-nested iteration. However, because of the overall iterative nature of optimization, there is no reason to pursue the line search to high accuracy. This usually means that only one analytical approximation is used for a particular direction before another line search is begun.

A variety of analytical functions can be used as a basis for approximation. One possibility is the quadratic analytical approximation. As discussed in Section 6.2, any of several combinations of the objective function values, slopes, and curvatures can generate such an approximation.

The curvature of the objective function can be exploited (if H is known or approximated) to proceed immediately to the minimum of a quadratic analytical approximation without additional function evaluations. This method is analogous to fitting a quadratic curve to a value, slope, and curvature at a point, using

$$\boldsymbol{\delta} = -\lambda\frac{\mathbf{g}}{|\mathbf{g}|}$$

Then the change along the search direction can be written as

$$E(\mathbf{D} + \boldsymbol{\delta}) = E(\mathbf{D}) - \lambda|\mathbf{g}| + \frac{1}{2}\lambda^2\frac{\mathbf{g}^{\mathrm{T}}\mathbf{Hg}}{|\mathbf{g}|^2}$$

This is the quadratic analytical approximation and the term $\mathbf{g}^{\mathrm{T}}\mathbf{Hg}/|\mathbf{g}|^2$ measures the curvature along the search direction $\mathbf{u}$. The value of λ which produces minimum E is

$$\lambda_{\min} = \frac{|\mathbf{g}|^3}{\mathbf{g}^{\mathrm{T}}\mathbf{Hg}}$$

so no search or additional function evaluations are needed to determine $\lambda_{\min}$. The next approximation to the minimum is $\hat{\mathbf{D}} = \mathbf{D} + \boldsymbol{\delta}$. Substituting for $\boldsymbol{\delta}$ yields

$$\hat{\mathbf{D}} = \mathbf{D} - \frac{|\mathbf{g}|^2\mathbf{g}}{\mathbf{g}^{\mathrm{T}}\mathbf{Hg}}$$

This formula appears very familiar in comparison to the single-variable formula,

$$\hat{x} = x - \frac{E'(x)}{E''(x)}$$

Example 6.4: Continuing with the function in Example 6.2, at point A:

$$\mathbf{D}_A = \begin{Bmatrix} 1 \\ 1 \end{Bmatrix} \qquad \mathbf{H}_A = \begin{bmatrix} 38 & 12 \\ 12 & 8 \end{bmatrix}, \qquad (\mathbf{g}^T\mathbf{Hg})_A = 23128.0$$

and $\lambda_{min} = 0.5547$, thus giving an estimate of the minimum $\mathbf{D}_C = \begin{Bmatrix} 0.4784 \\ 0.8104 \end{Bmatrix}$, which is shown as point C in Fig. 6.11.

If there is no information available about $\mathbf{H}$, then some approximation must be used. The next logical step is to determine the value of the objective function at an additional point, giving a third piece of information. This is equivalent to fitting a quadratic through a point, the slope at the point, and a second point. For example, use a guess, μ, for the value of λ and make a finite step for the second function evaluation:

$$\delta = -\mu \frac{\mathbf{g}}{|\mathbf{g}|}$$

The value of E at that point can be used to estimate $\mathbf{g}^T\mathbf{Hg}$. The quadratic approximation is written as

$$E\left(\mathbf{D} - \mu \frac{-\mathbf{g}}{|\mathbf{g}|}\right) = E(\mathbf{D}) - \frac{\mathbf{g}^T \mu \mathbf{g}}{|\mathbf{g}|} + \frac{\mu^2 \mathbf{g}^T \mathbf{Hg}}{2|\mathbf{g}|^2}$$

Solving for $\mathbf{g}^T\mathbf{Hg}$ and substituting into the equation for λ_{min} yields

$$\lambda_{min} = \frac{\mu^2|\mathbf{g}|}{2}\left(E\left(\mathbf{D} - \frac{\mu\mathbf{g}}{|\mathbf{g}|}\right) - E(\mathbf{D}) + \mu|\mathbf{g}|\right)^{-1}$$

This avoids the necessity of completely evaluating $\mathbf{H}$. The obvious initial guess for μ_k is λ_{k-1}, the value calculated at the last step. A typical convergence test is based on λ, which is a measure of the step size.

Example 6.5: Continue with the function from Example 6.2, starting from point A, where $\mathbf{D}_A = \begin{Bmatrix} 1 \\ 1 \end{Bmatrix}$. Using a value of $\mu = 2$ leads to $E(\mathbf{D} + \delta) = 8.6245$, which leads to an approximate value of

$$\mathbf{g}^T\mathbf{Hg} \approx 11355.0$$

and

$$\lambda_{min} \approx 1.1297$$

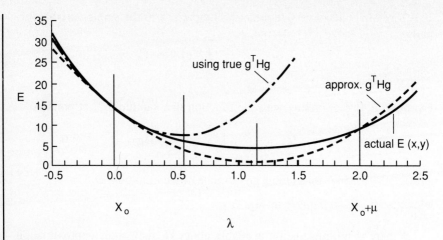

Figure 6.12 Line-search approximations.

and an estimate of the minimum at point D,

$$\mathbf{D}_D = \left\{ \begin{array}{c} -0.0620 \\ 0.61390 \end{array} \right\}$$

Note that smaller values of μ cause the approximate of be more accurate. But in this case, the estimate of the minimum is better with a less accurate value of $\mathbf{g}^T\mathbf{Hg}$, because the higher-order terms are strong and the trial points "span" the minimum. Contours for the objective function, the search direction $\mathbf{u}$, and predictions of the minimum are shown in Fig. 6.11. Fig. 6.12 illustrates the variation of the objective function and the analytical approximations along the search direction from the previous examples.

Quasi-Newton (Variable Metric) Second-Order Methods

Convergence is greatly improved by using all of the information contained in the Hessian (instead of only the curvature along $\mathbf{u}$) and the direction of steepest descent. Returning to the Taylor series expansion of the objective function,

$$E(\mathbf{D} + \boldsymbol{\delta}) = E(\mathbf{D}) + \mathbf{g}^T\boldsymbol{\delta} + \frac{1}{2}\boldsymbol{\delta}^T\mathbf{H}\boldsymbol{\delta} + \cdots$$

Truncating the Taylor series is equivalent to approximating the true objective function by a quadratic bowl that is tangent and has matching curvature. In other words, the level curve through the second order is an ellipse. The center of that ellipse is the minimum of the quadratic bowl. The step $\boldsymbol{\delta}$ directly to the minimum is

$$\boldsymbol{\delta} = -\mathbf{H}^{-1}\mathbf{g}$$

This is effectively a multidimensional Newton's method. The approximation comes about because the Hessian at the point $\mathbf{D}$ is not exactly the Hessian at the minimum. A variation on the technique is to use $\boldsymbol{\delta}$ not for a step but simply to produce a direction and go ahead and perform a line search in direction $\boldsymbol{\delta}$.

Example 6.6: Continuing with the function in Example 6.2, at $\mathbf{D}_A = \left\{ \begin{matrix} 0 \\ 0 \end{matrix} \right\}$, the inverse of the Hessian is

$$\mathbf{H}_A^{-1} = \begin{bmatrix} 0.04396 & -0.06593 \\ -0.06593 & 0.20879 \end{bmatrix}$$

which gives

$$\boldsymbol{\delta}_E = \left\{ \begin{matrix} -0.43956 \\ -0.21978 \end{matrix} \right\} \quad \text{and} \quad \mathbf{D}_E = \left\{ \begin{matrix} 0.56044 \\ 0.78022 \end{matrix} \right\}$$

The point $\mathbf{D}_E$ is plotted in Fig. 6.11. Note that the resulting step is better than one based on $\mathbf{u}$; however, because the Hessian is so different from $\mathbf{H}_0$, the actual step is not as good as those resulting from the other methods discussed.

Quasi-Newton, or variable-metric, methods determine the search direction $\mathbf{u}_k$ by multiplying the gradient of the function E by the inverse of a matrix $\mathbf{B}_k$ that approximates the Hessian matrix of E at $\mathbf{D}_k$:

$$\mathbf{u}_k = -\mathbf{B}_k^{-1} \cdot \mathbf{g}_k$$

If the second partial derivatives are not available, then a suitable approximation is made and $\mathbf{B}_k$ is updated (the *Hessian update*) during every iteration step by a correction of the form

$$\mathbf{B}_{k+1} = \mathbf{B}_k + \Delta\mathbf{B}_k$$

Also, $\mathbf{B}_k$ must remain symmetric and positive definite, and the *quasi-Newton condition* must be satisfied:

$$\mathbf{B}_{k+1}\boldsymbol{\delta}_k = \mathbf{q}_k$$

where

$$\boldsymbol{\delta}_k = \mathbf{D}_{k+1} - \mathbf{D}_k$$
$$\mathbf{q}_k = \mathbf{g}_{k+1} - \mathbf{g}_k$$

The most common method of satisfying these requirements employs the *BFGS-update*:

$$\mathbf{B}_{k+1} = \mathbf{B}_k + \frac{\mathbf{q}_k \mathbf{q}_k^{\mathsf{T}}}{\mathbf{q}_k^{\mathsf{T}} \boldsymbol{\delta}_k} - \frac{\mathbf{B}_k \boldsymbol{\delta}_k \boldsymbol{\delta}_k^{\mathsf{T}} \mathbf{B}_k}{\boldsymbol{\delta}_k^{\mathsf{T}} \mathbf{B}_k \boldsymbol{\delta}_k}$$

One could define any symmetric, positive-definite matrix as the starting matrix $\mathbf{B}_0$, for example, the identity matrix.

For certain problems, the number of iterations to the minimum are very limited. Specifically, if E is a strictly convex quadratic function and if the exact line search for determining λ^k is used, then the search directions u_k are conjugate with respect to $\mathbf{B}$, and the algorithm terminates in at most n iterations. This guarantee of convergence in n iterations makes this a highly recommended algorithm.

Example 6.7: Rosenbrock's Function. A classical test function is

$$E(\mathbf{D}) = 100(y - x^2)^2 + (1 - x)^2$$

The minimum of the function is $E_{\min} = 0$, which occurs at $(1, 1)$. Rosenbrock's function is a poorly scaled objective function that can be geometrically interpreted as a slowly falling curved valley with very steep sides.

The motivations behind choosing this function include the following:

- A major requirement of an optimization algorithm is the ability to move along "a narrow valley." A narrow valley is the topological interpretation of the situation that occurs when the spectral radius of the Hessian (the ratio of the Hessian's maximum and minimum eigenvalues) is large. An efficient algorithm will produce a large component of the search direction down the length of the valley rather than across the valley.

- Methods that neither use nor approximate second-order information to determine the search direction are dependent on the relative scaling of the design variables. For long steep valleys, first-order methods converge too slowly to be effective. Observing the iterative process can show whether an algorithm is linear, quasi-Newton, or Newton.

The gradient of Rosenbrock's function is

$$\mathbf{g} = \left\{ \begin{array}{c} 400x^3 - 400xy + 2x - 2 \\ -200x^2 + 200y \end{array} \right\}$$

and the exact Hessian is

$$\mathbf{H} = \left[\begin{array}{cc} 1200x^2 - 400y + 2 & -400x \\ -400x & 200 \end{array} \right]$$

For future reference, at the minimum the gradient is

$$\mathbf{g}|_{\min} = \left\{ \begin{array}{c} 0 \\ 0 \end{array} \right\}$$

and the Hessian is

$$\mathbf{H}|_{\min} = \left[\begin{array}{cc} 802 & -400 \\ -400 & 200 \end{array} \right]$$

Consider a starting point on the steep side of the valley, such as point $P_{A0} = \{0.5, 0.5\}$ in Fig. 6.13. At this point the direction of steepest

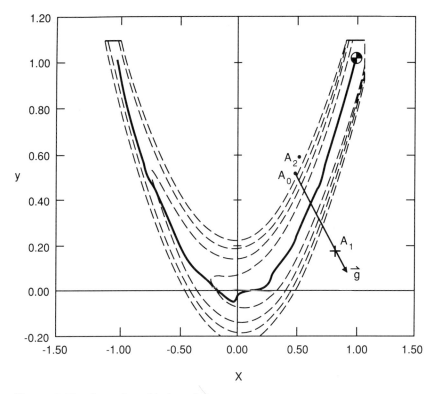

Figure 6.13 Rosenbrock's function.

descent is

$$-\mathbf{g}_{P_A} = \left\{ \begin{array}{c} 51 \\ -50 \end{array} \right\}$$

and the Hessian is

$$\mathbf{H}_{P_A} = \left[\begin{array}{cc} 102 & -200 \\ -200 & 200 \end{array} \right]$$

The next approximation, using a step based on first-order steepest descent, is

$$\mathbf{P}_{A_1} = \left\{ \begin{array}{c} 0.84 \\ 0.17 \end{array} \right\}$$

which shows that the direction of steepest descent is toward the valley floor, not toward the minimum. The approximation using a step based on second-order information is

$$\mathbf{P}_{A_2} = \left\{ \begin{array}{c} 0.503 \\ 0.58 \end{array} \right\}$$

6.5   CONSTRAINED OPTIMIZATION

Although unconstrained optimization is easier to present, problems with constraints are much more typical of engineering design. As discussed in Section
6.1, constraints fall into threee categories. The first is bounds on the design
variables. The second is equality constraints, each of which effectively reduces the dimension of the design space by one. Of course, eliminating one
design variable algebraically, if possible, is the best way to handle equality
constraints. Inequality constraints are the third category. If each variable is
assumed to have upper and lower limits, then a feasible region is defined.
Such bounding limits are usually treated separately. As shown in Fig. 6.14,
using inequality constraints may then reduce the feasible region:

$$\text{minimize } E = f(\mathbf{D})$$

subject to

$$g_i(\mathbf{D}) = 0, \qquad\qquad i = 1, \ldots, N_e$$
$$g_i(\mathbf{D}) \leq 0, \qquad\qquad i = N_e + 1, \ldots, N$$
$$\mathbf{L} \leq \mathbf{D} \leq \mathbf{U},$$
$$\mathbf{D} \in R^n,$$

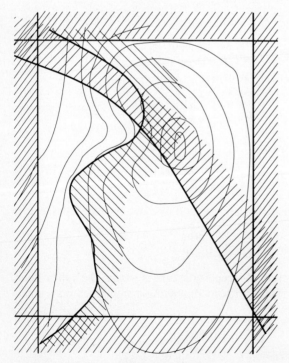

Figure 6.14   A constrained region.

Relative minima are more common in constrained problems. The minimum could be at $\nabla E = 0$ or along a boundary. If located on a boundary, then the minimum must occur either at a point where the contour lines of the objective function and constraint line are tangent, or at the intersection of two constraints.

For one active constraint, there will be a value for λ such that

$$\nabla E = \lambda \nabla g$$

that is, the contours are tangent to the constraint, and E and g increase in opposite directions, as shown in Fig. 6.15. In this figure, the objective function consists of an elliptical bowl. The curves for the constraints $g_1 = 0$ and $g_2 = 0$ are drawn and the nonfeasible sides $g_1 > 0$ and $g_2 > 0$ are shaded grey. Note that the gradient ∇E is perpendicular to the constraint.

For two active constraints, there will be values λ_1, λ_2 such that

$$\nabla E = \lambda_1 \nabla g_1 + \lambda_2 \nabla g_2$$

The three vectors at the constraint junction solve a vector sum of zero.

The standard approach to constrained problems is to modify the objective function to include the effect of the constraints. As described previously, this new function is a descent function. A constraint's contribution to a descent function can be interpreted by visualizing the constraint as a surface in its own right (Fig. 6.16), where the part of the surface below zero has been drawn dashed for clarity.

The constraint can therefore be evaluated at any location in design space, **D**, and the value of the constraint function at that point is in some sense a measure of how much the constraint has been violated. Like the gradient of the objective function, the gradient of each constraint is of interest also.

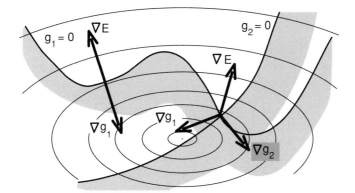

Figure 6.15   Gradients of the objective function and constraints are related when the minimum occurs along a constraint.

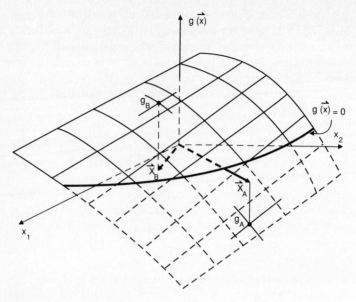

Figure 6.16 Visualizing a constraint as a surface.

Exterior Penalty Functions

The objective function can be penalized, or made larger, if a constraint is violated. The value of the constraint function measures how much the constraint has been violated. The descent function is formed by adding a penalty. Instead of minimizing $E(\mathbf{D})$, minimize

$$E(\mathbf{D}) + r \sum_j \delta_j g_j(\mathbf{D})^z$$

where

$$\delta_j = \begin{cases} 0, & \text{if } g_j(\mathbf{D}) \le 0 \\ 1, & \text{if } g_j(\mathbf{D}) \ge 0 \end{cases}$$

The constant r serves to weight the penalty. Of course, one could use $\sum_j r_j \delta_j g_j^z$, but choosing the individual r_j would be more difficult. Any implementation must also choose a value for z. Figure 6.17 illustrates the results for various values of z. The usual approach uses $z = 2$.

- Using $z = 0$ simply adds r if the constraint is violated.
- Using $0 \le z \le 1$ may fail to penalize sufficiently.
- Using $z = 1$ yields discontinuous first derivatives along the boundary.
- Using $z \ge 1$ gives continuous derivatives if E and g are differentiable.

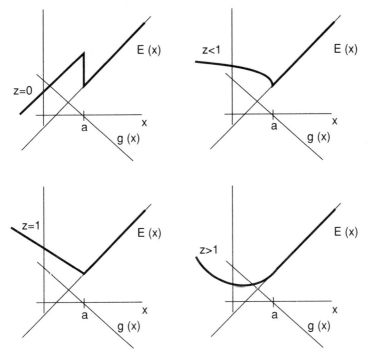

Figure 6.17 Exterior penalty functions for $g(x) = a - x$.

An algorithm would proceed as follows:

- Assign an initial (small) value for r, $r \leftarrow r_0$.
- Take an initial feasible guess $\mathbf{D} \leftarrow \mathbf{D}_0$.
- Minimize $E + r \sum_{j=1}^{m} \delta_i g_j^2$.
- if $\mathbf{D}_{\min}$ is not acceptable:
  - $r \leftarrow cr$
  - $\mathbf{D}_0 \leftarrow \mathbf{D}$
- Loop to minimize the preceding step above.

Observe that although larger values for r produce a minimum closer to the true constrained minimum, the descent function is harder to minimize because it is steeper. Smaller values for r give a poor approximation that minimizes more easily.

The implementation is such that exterior penalty functions are activated only when the constraint is violated. Thus the solution will always violate the constraints (although only slightly).

Interior Penalty Functions

The purpose of the interior penalty function method is to penalize the objective function whenever the **D** approaches the constraint. The penalty function should be very large at the constraint and reduce quickly as **D** moves away from the constraint into the feasible region:

$$\text{minimize } E(\mathbf{D}) + r \sum_{j=1}^{m} \frac{1}{-g_j(\mathbf{D})}$$

As the constraint boundary is approached, the term $1/-g_j(x)$ approaches infinity. Remember that the feasible region is such that $g_j(x) < 0$, which is the reason for the sign change in the equation above. Figure 6.18 illustrates an interior penalty function for a one-dimensional problem.

The usual approach with interior penalty functions is to choose a large value for r and minimize. Once convergence is achieved, reduce r and minimize again. This process is repeated until r is sufficiently small.

All constraints are always active and therefore must be evaluated. The resulting minimum will lie within the allowable region of feasible designs that satisfy all constraints.

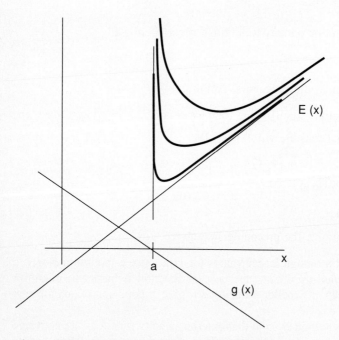

Figure 6.18 Interior penalty functions for various
values of r and $g(x) = a - x$.

Example 6.8: A Two-Bar Truss. Consider the two-bar truss shown in Fig. 6.19. The objective is to determine the height and diameter of the circular members that give a minimum weight truss that can carry the specified load without either plastic yielding or Euler column buckling.

The parameters are

$$P = 33 \text{ kips}$$
$$B = 30 \text{ in}$$
$$t = 0.1 \text{ in}$$
$$Y = 100 \text{ ksi}$$
$$E = 30 \times 10^3 \text{ ksi}$$
$$\rho = 0.3 \text{ lb/in}^3$$
$$1.0 \leq d \leq 3.0$$
$$10.0 \leq H \leq 35.0$$

The design vector is

$$\mathbf{D} = \left\{ \begin{array}{c} d \\ H \end{array} \right\}$$

The objective function, the total weight of the truss, is

$$\text{weight} = \rho 2\pi \, dt (B^2 + H^2)^{1/2}$$

The stress in each member is obtained with

$$\sigma = \frac{P(B^2 + H^2)^{1/2}}{\pi t H d}$$

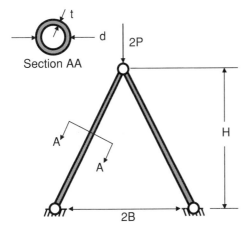

Section AA

A

A

2P

H

2B

Figure 6.19 A truss.

and the Euler column buckling load translates into a buckling stress of

$$\sigma_b = \frac{\pi^2 E(d^2 + t^2)}{8(B^2 + H^2)}$$

In this problem, the stress σ is a performance variable, introduced only to make the constraints more easily written as

$$\sigma \leq Y$$
$$\sigma \leq \sigma_b$$

The total constraint set is

$$H - 35 \leq 0 \qquad g_1(\mathbf{D}) \leq 0$$
$$-H + 10 \leq 0 \qquad g_2(\mathbf{D}) \leq 0$$
$$d - 3.0 \leq 0 \qquad g_3(\mathbf{D}) \leq 0$$
$$-d + 1.0 \leq 0 \qquad g_4(\mathbf{D}) \leq 0$$
$$\frac{P(B^2 + H^2)^{1/2}}{\pi t H d} - Y \leq 0 \qquad g_5(\mathbf{D}) \leq 0$$
$$\frac{P(B^2 + H^2)^{1/2}}{\pi t H d} - \frac{\pi^2 E(d^2 + t^2)}{8(B^2 + H^2)} \leq 0 \qquad g_6(\mathbf{D}) \leq 0$$

Figure 6.20 illustrates the objective function and the two constraints g_5, and g_6. Figure 6.21 shows a series of four minimization problems using exterior penalty functions where $z = 2$, and $r = 10^{-10}, 10^{-9}, 10^{-8}$, and 10^{-7}, respectively. The three minimization problems shown in Fig. 6.22 are based on interior penalty functions having values $r = 10^7, 10^6, 10^5$, respectively.

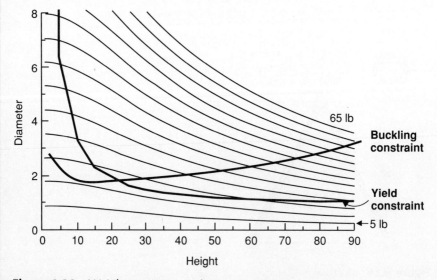

Figure 6.20 Weight contours and two constraints for a truss.

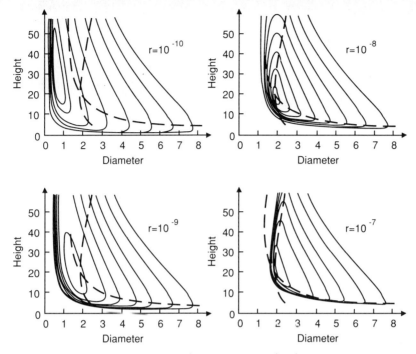

Figure 6.21   Truss contours with exterior penalty functions.

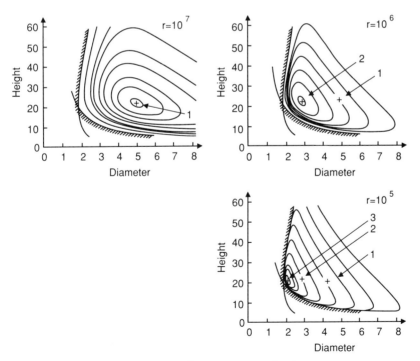

Figure 6.22   Truss contours with interior penalty functions.

219

Linear/Quadratic Approximation Methods

At each iteration step, a linear/quadratic approximation method requires the solution of a linear/quadratic subproblem to determine the search direction. Subsequently, a descent function is minimized along this search direction, thereby leading to a new iteration.

The *linear programming (LP) subproblem* at the kth iteration is defined as

$$\text{minimize } \mathbf{l}_0^{\mathrm{T}} \mathbf{u}^k$$

$$\text{subject to} \quad g_i(\mathbf{D}^k) + \mathbf{l}_i^{\mathrm{T}} \mathbf{u}^k = 0, \qquad i \in I_1$$

$$g_i(\mathbf{D}^k) + \mathbf{l}_i^{\mathrm{T}} \mathbf{u}^k \leq 0, \qquad i \in I_2$$

$$\left\| \mathbf{u}^k \right\|_2 \leq \epsilon$$

where $\mathbf{u}^k$ is the search direction, $\mathbf{g}_0$ is the gradient of the cost function, $\mathbf{l}_i$ is the gradient of the ith constraint, ϵ is the limit on change in design, and I_1 and I_2 are the active constraint *index sets* for the equality and inequality constraints, respectively.

The *quadratic programming (QP) subproblem* is similarly defined as

$$\text{minimize } \mathbf{l}_0^{\mathrm{T}} \mathbf{u}^k + \frac{1}{2} \mathbf{u}^{k\mathrm{T}} \mathbf{B} \mathbf{u}^k$$

$$\text{subject to} \quad g_i(\mathbf{D}^k) + \mathbf{l}_i^{\mathrm{T}} \mathbf{u}^k = 0, \qquad i \in I_1$$

$$g_i(\mathbf{D}^k) + \mathbf{l}_i^{\mathrm{T}} \mathbf{u}^k \leq 0, \qquad i \in I_2$$

The different linear/quadratic approximation methods differ in their definition and solution of LP or QP subproblems. For example, the definitions of the index sets I_1 and I_2, matrix $\mathbf{B}$, and ϵ can be different in the different algorithms. These definitions affect the search direction and the convergence rate of an algorithm.

The *Gradient Projection method*, by its simple definition of the active set (index sets I_1 and I_2), determines an approximate search direction in closed form. The linearized inequality constraints are treated as equalities at any iteration, and the search direction is obtained by projecting the minimum of the quadratic objective function of QP on the linear manifold of the active constraints. If the new iterate is feasible but violates the optimality conditions, a constraint is dropped from the active constraint and the whole procedure repeated. The reader is referred to Luenberger or Haug and Arora for a detailed description of this method.

The method of *Wilson, Han, and Powell* defines and solves the QP problem at each iteration step. All the equality and inequality constraints are included in the index sets I_1 and I_2, and the matrix $\mathbf{B}$ is taken as the Hessian of the Lagrangian or its approximation. In the latter case, the $\mathbf{B}$ matrix is updated using the BFGS formula (the quasi-Newton update procedure mentioned earlier). The step length λ is obtained by a quadratic interpolation of a nondifferentiable penalty function.

The *Pshenichny Linearization method* also solves a QP subproblem at each iteration step. The **B** matrix is defined as the identity matrix. However, by choosing an approximation to the Hessian of the Lagrangian from **B**, a variable metric algorithm for constrained optimization can be obtained. In this event, the Hessian approximation is updated using the BFGS formula.

The index sets I_1 and I_2 are defined as follows:

$$I_1 = \left\{ i : |g_i(\mathbf{D}^k)| + \epsilon(\mathbf{D}^k) \geq 0, \quad i = 1, \ldots, m_e \right\}$$
$$I_2 = \left\{ i : g_i(\mathbf{D}^k) + \epsilon(\mathbf{D}^k) \geq 0, \quad i = m_e + 1, \ldots, m \right\}$$

The value of ϵ used in *epsilon active constraints* comes from the *maximum constraint violation*. Specifically, the constraint-checking parameter, $\epsilon(\mathbf{D}^k)$, is defined using any specified positive constant δ as

$$\epsilon(\mathbf{D}^k) = \delta - F(\mathbf{D}^k)$$

where $F(\mathbf{D}^k)$ is the maximum constraint violation,

$$F(\mathbf{D}^k) = \max \left\{ 0, |g_1(\mathbf{D}^k)|, \ldots, |g_{m_e}(\mathbf{D}^k)|, g_{m_e+1}(\mathbf{D}^k), \ldots, g_m(\mathbf{D}^k) \right\}$$

The step length λ_*^k is determined by minimizing the *Pshenichny descent function*, $\phi(\mathbf{D})$, defined as

$$\phi(\mathbf{D}) = E(\mathbf{D}) + R \cdot F(\mathbf{D})$$

where R is selected to satisfy the condition

$$R \geq r, \qquad r = \sum_{i \in I_\epsilon} |\mu_i|, \qquad I_\epsilon = I_1 \cup I_2$$

where μ_i are the Lagrange multipliers of the linearized constraints of the QP subproblem. The step length is chosen as $\frac{1}{2^i}$ where i is the smallest integer such that the *stopping criteria*,

$$\phi\left(\mathbf{D}^k + \frac{1}{2^i}\mathbf{d}^k\right) \leq \phi(\mathbf{x}^k) - \frac{1}{2^i}\lambda\|\mathbf{d}^k\|^2$$

is satisfied. The reader is referred to Pshenichny for a detailed description of this method.

The Reduced-Gradient Methods

By introducing nonnegative slack variables to convert inequality constraints to equalities, the original design optimization problem is equivalent to an optimization problem having only nonlinear equality constraints and

the bounds on the variables, the *Generalized Reduced Gradient (GRG)
formulation:*

$$\text{minimize } E(\mathbf{D})$$
$$\text{subject to } \quad g_j(\mathbf{D}) = 0, \qquad j = 1, \ldots, m$$
$$\mathbf{D} \in R^n$$
$$\mathbf{l} \leq \mathbf{D} \leq \mathbf{u}$$

Let $\mathbf{D}$ be any feasible design in the GRG formulation. This design variable
vector can be partitioned into the so-called basis variable $\mathbf{D}_b \in R^m$ and
a nonbasis variable $\mathbf{D}_{nb} \in R^{n-m}$. The upper and lower bounds on design
variable vector $\mathbf{D}$ are analogously partitioned. The Jacobian matrix $\mathbf{J}$ of
constraints is also partitioned as follows:

$$\mathbf{J_D D}^k = \left[\mathbf{J_{D_b}}(\mathbf{D}^k) \quad \vdots \quad \mathbf{J_{D_{nb}}}(\mathbf{D}^k) \right]$$

If the basis variables are chosen so that the square matrix $\mathbf{J_{D_b}}(\mathbf{D}^k)$ is non-
singular, then the equation

$$g_j(\mathbf{D}_b, \mathbf{D}_{nb}) = 0, \qquad j = 1, \ldots, m$$

can be solved, at least conceptually, to obtain $\mathbf{D}_b$ for any given nonbasis
variables $\mathbf{D}_{nb}$. Thus the GRG formulation is transformed into a simpler
reduced problem:

$$\text{minimize } E_*(\mathbf{D}_{nb}^k)$$

subject to

$$\mathbf{D}_{nb}^k \in R^{n-m}$$
$$\mathbf{l}_{nb} \leq \mathbf{D}_{nb} \leq \mathbf{u}_{nb}$$

and $\mathbf{D}_b^k(\mathbf{D}_{nb}^k)$ is a solution of simplified GRG equations for a given independent variable $\mathbf{D}_{nb}^k$. The gradient of E_* is also known as the reduced gradient
of E.

The generalized reduced-gradient method aims to solve the GRG re-
duced function, at a feasible iterate, $\mathbf{D}^k$, partitioned into $\mathbf{D} = [\mathbf{D}_b^k, \mathbf{D}_{nb}^k]$.
Then either the steepest-descent, or the conjugate gradient, or the quasi-
Newton method is employed to compute a direction vector $\mathbf{d}^k \in R^{n-m}$.
This direction, when projected on the subspace defined by the bounds in the
GRG reduced problem, is the search direction $\mathbf{d}^k$.

A one-dimensional line search procedure is then applied to get the approximate solution of

$$\text{minimize } f_*(\mathbf{D}_{nb}^k + \lambda \mathbf{u}^k), \qquad \lambda > 0$$

During this minimization process, the system

$$\mathbf{D}_b^k : g_j(\mathbf{D}_b, \mathbf{D}_{nb} + \lambda \mathbf{d}) = 0, \qquad j = 1, \ldots, m$$

has to be solved for some values of λ. Some of the basis variables might violate their bounds during the solution process. The reader should refer to Luenberger or Ragsdell for a detailed description of this method.

Summary of Methods

Four general nonlinear constrained-optimization algorithms are available: the Cost Bounding Algorithm (CBA), the Recursive Quadratic Programming Algorithm (RQP), the Generalized Reduced Gradient (GRG) Algorithm, and the Sequential Quadratic Programming (SQP) Algorithm. To solve mildly nonlinear problems, the Method of Centers (CEN), and a Sequential Linear Programming (SLP) Algorithm can be used. Finally, linear programming algorithms are available to solve linear optimization problems. Several versions of the gradient and variable metric algorithms can then be implemented for unconstrained optimization.

The CBA, RQP, and SQP algorithms are classified as quadratic approximation methods; the CEN and SLP, as linear approximation methods. The GRG algorithm, however, belongs in the category of reduced-gradient methods.

Usually the functions that appear in a design optimization problem are very nonlinear in nature. For such problems, any algorithm that assumes near linearity of the design functions will perform poorly. Hence, the GRG and SQP algorithms are generally preferred over the SLP and CEN algorithms in a real-life design optimization situation.

Example 6.9: Optimization of a Heat Sink. A small heat sink for cooling electronic equipment is shown in Fig. 6.23. The heat sink has 20 fins, all 1 mm thick with 3 mm spacing between the fins, and outside dimensions as shown. The heat sink can be parameterized by the thickness of the base plate B. The boundary conditions are insulated on all surfaces, except for the applied heat flow at the center and the surfaces of the fins. The fins provide convective cooling to fan-driven air with flow rate V. In this problem, the quantity to minimize is the temperature at the center of the applied heat flow T_P. An optimization problem is expected because a very thin base ($B < 1$) will provide low conductivity (high resistance) to the fins, and hence, large T_P. On the other hand, a very thick base ($B > 1$) will provide very little surface for convective heat transfer, again resulting in large T_P. There will be an optimum value for B that produces minimum T_P. The fan is assumed to be predetermined with known pressure and flow-rate characteristics. The pressure and flow-rate characteristics for the heat sink are assumed to have been measured experimentally and are as given. Therefore, equating the pressure drops produces an equality constraint between the thickness B and the flow rate V, reducing the problem effectively to a single-degree-of-freedom problem. However, the following explanation treats the problem as a two-degree-of-freedom problem with an equality constraint.

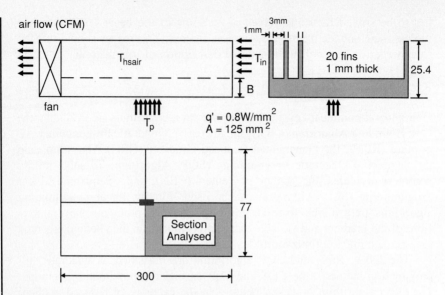

Figure 6.23 A heat sink's geometry and boundary conditions. All dimensions are in millimeters.

The optimization problem is formulated as

$$\text{minimize } T_P$$

subject to

$$\Delta P_{hs} - \Delta P_{fan} = 0$$
$$0 \leq B \leq 25.4$$
$$0 \leq V \leq 10$$

where

$$
\begin{aligned}
B &= \text{base thickness} \\
T_{in} &= 0° \text{ inlet temperature} \\
T_{hs,air} &= \text{average temperature across heat sink} \\
T_P &= \text{temperature of heat sink at point P} \\
K_{hs} &= 0.25 \text{ thermal conductivity} \\
q' &= 0.8 \text{ W/mm}^2 \text{ (heat flux through base)} \\
A &= 125 \text{ mm}^2 \text{ (Area through which } q' \text{ acts)} \\
V &= \text{volumetric air flow rate (ft}^3\text{/min)} \\
H &= \text{heat transfer coefficient [W/(°C mm}^2\text{)]} \\
\Delta P_{hs} &= \text{air pressure drop across heat sink} \\
\Delta P_{fan} &= \text{pressure difference across the fan}
\end{aligned}
$$

and,

$$T_P = T_{in} + \frac{q'A}{V} + \Delta T_{hs,air-P}$$

$$\Delta P_{hs} = 2.04(25.4 - B)^{-2.28}(V^{1.78})$$

$$\Delta P_{fan} = 0.2 - 0.009V - 0.001V^2$$

$$H = (4.84 \times 10^{-5})(2.54 - B)^{-0.53}(V^{0.42})$$

The temperature T_P was determined by a finite-element analysis of one quarter of the heat sink.

This is a very realistic optimization problem in that a contour plot of the objective function is not available. Each function evaluation required a finite-element run (approximately 10 minutes). Figure 6.24 shows the design space (V versus B), the locus of the equality constraint, and the trial points used by a Successive Quadratic Programming Algorithm. In this example, derivatives were not available in closed form, so they all had to be determined by finite-difference techniques, with the resulting extra function

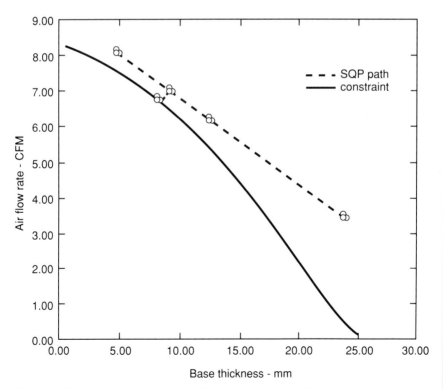

Figure 6.24   Convergence for SQP algorithm using 24 function evaluations and eight-gradient evaluations.

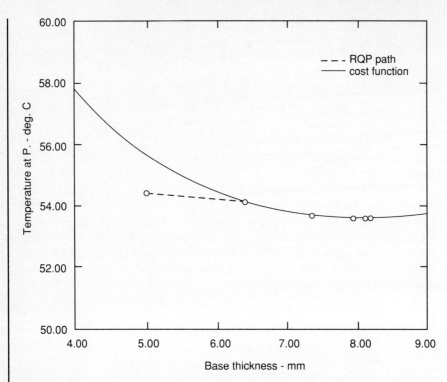

Figure 6.25   Convergence for RQP algorithm using 18 function
                    evaluations and six gradient evaluations.

evaluations. Figure 6.24 also shows the location of these evaluations. Figure
6.25 illustrates the relationship between the cost function and the base thickness, assuming that the equality constraint always satisfied. The search path
for a Recursive Quadratic Programming algorithm (RQP) is also plotted.

The analysis dominated the solution time required by this problem. Each
evaluation of the objective function (a finite-element problem) required approximately 10 minutes on an IBM 4341-12 processor. The efficiency of an
optimization algorithm's implementation can be viewed simply as the total
number of function evaluations.

6.6   PROGRAM ORGANIZATION

Regardless of the manner of implementation, the basic elements of an optimization procedure are the initialization, the optimizer, the analyzer, and the
terminator. These are organized in an iterative loop as shown in Fig. 6.26.

Three ways to organize these elements are as a "black box," with the
subroutine approach, or with a programming system.

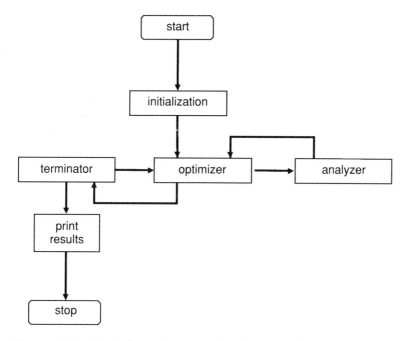

Figure 6.26 Basic flow of an optimization procedure.

Black Box

It is possible to obtain optimization programs that are almost completely self-contained. In such cases, the program is providing the interface that allows the designer to specify initial guess values, step sizes, tolerance, and so on; the user usually controls the package by keyboard commands. The objective function and constraint functions are almost always provided through a user-written subroutine with a specified name and argument list, as shown

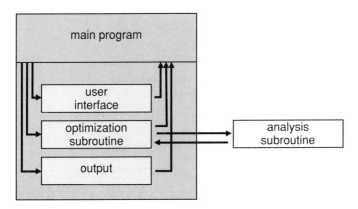

Figure 6.27 A main program with user-supplied subroutines.

in Fig. 6.27. This requires the use of a compilation and linking step whenever the problem is changed; and in this case, a change can be something as simple as adding a constraint or changing the value of a parameter. Examples of "black box" packages are IDESIGN and OPTDES.BYU.

Subroutine Approach

In this case, the optimization subroutine implements a search algorithm that seeks a constrained minimum in n-dimensional design space. The user must furnish an analysis subroutine suitable for the problem at hand and a main program that can accept input, call the search subroutine, and generate output. The search subroutine will execute the analysis subroutine, passing to it the values of the design variables and receiving the values of the objective functions and constraints, as shown in Fig. 6.28.

In an alternate version, the search subroutine does not actually call the analysis subroutine. Instead, it returns control to the main program after the new set of design variables is computed. The analysis information is expected to come from the main program, and is usually provided by a procedural call from that point, (see Fig. 6.29). However, in this version, the user must build into the main program the entire logic of the iteration and the terminator.

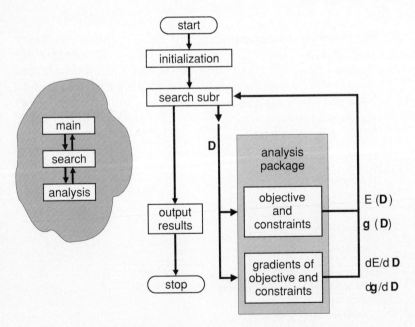

Figure 6.28   A procedure with an analysis subroutine called by a search subroutine.

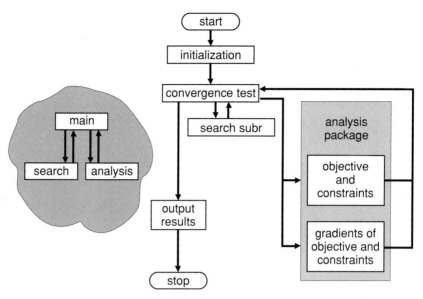

Figure 6.29   A procedure with an analysis subroutine
called by the main module.

The subroutine approach gives the user the freedom to craft a complete program pertinent to the problem at hand. The variation of parameters is easily handled, but a change in the objective function requires compilation and linking.

This is the approach that would be used either with procedures taken from popular numerical methods libraries such as Linpack or IMSL, or with specific library routines such as NPSOL. Many textbooks on optimization now provide such subroutines in an appendix or separately.

This implementation has the advantage of modularity. The optimization search procedures are implemented in a very portable language (usually FORTRAN), and all system-dependent features such as file I/O or user interaction are left to the programmer. This means that the user can customize to the particular installation. Also, the user can focus on the software that models the physics for the analysis part of the problem.

However, in some cases the analysis procedure cannot be invoked through a subroutine call. An extensive analysis program may be necessary; and if this program is not developed by the user, it probably has to be executed as an independent program. The best example of this would be a commercial finite-element program that cannot be installed as a callable subroutine. Although finite-element programs are the most common examples, many others can be cited, such as a dynamic system simulation package (as discussed in Chapter 4) or a kinematic analysis program. Some programs in this category

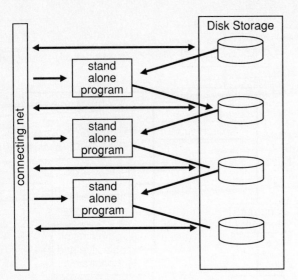

Figure 6.30   Programming system.

now provide optimization by including a subroutine that implements a specific algorithm. However, there is a different approach that should be taken to provide the best environment to the design engineer.

Programming System

In comparison with the main program and subroutine arrangement, the programming system provides greater application flexibility. The analyzer is no longer required to be a subroutine, which allows the use of large stand-alone commercial programs or even collections of large programs. This approach isolates the definitions of the analysis variables, analysis functions, design variables, and design functions (objective and constraints) in separate problem-dependent, user-supplied programs (see Fig. 6.30).

Unfortunately, the programming system has some major difficulties, which include the following: (1) the disk storage database system containing the data that must be communicated between the various entities, and (2) the flow control provided by the connecting network. These aspects are highly system-dependent and are virtually impossible to implement independent of the operating system of the target machine.

6.7   COMPONENTS OF THE PROGRAMMING SYSTEM

Current trends in CAD systems relate to the programming system architecture. As discussed elsewhere in the book, this trend can be seen in almost all analysis areas (not just optimization). Therefore, this implementation will be discussed in more detail. The components of the programming system are the analyzer, optimizer, pre- and postprocessors, terminator, and connecting network. The optimizer and terminator function as previously discussed. However, the other components have much more elaborate functions.

Analyzer

The function of the analyzer is the same as that of the analysis subroutine discussed earlier. This function can be addressed in more detail by choosing a particular domain, such as structural applications, to discuss. In this case, the analyzer would be a finite-element program.

The input to a structural application consists of structural cross-section dimensions, material properties, element connectivity data, nodal point coordinates, and loads. The analysis function consists of determining quantities such as displacements, internal forces, stresses, eigenvalues, and eigenmodes for vibration and buckling, and so forth.

Since the analyzer is to be executed many times in the loop, it is obviously advantageous if the code is divided into nonrepeatable and repeatable parts. The nonrepeatable part is executed outside of the optimization loop once, and the repeatable part is included within the loop. The analyzer should be able to calculate the gradients of the objective function and the constraints. Efficiency is improved if the analyzer has the ability to perform rapid reanalysis and design modification. In the structural example, such ability would include partial remeshing, stiffness matrix modification, and approximate reanalysis.

Interface Processors

These processors can be viewed as filters between the optimizer and the analyzer. The capabilities resulting from adding these two processors provides the basis for the system's adaptability. The preprocessor converts the variables of the optimization process (the current vector in design space) to a set of input parameters written in a format appropriate to the analyzer. The postprocessor computes the objective function from the detailed results produced by the analyzer. Furthermore, gradients and constraints and their gradients are computed and provided in a format required by the optimizer.

Connecting Network

The connecting network must execute the programs in a computational sequence and perform the logical functions required by the sequence, such as branching on an if-test, looping, or skipping to a labeled section, and storing (permanently or temporarily) and retrieving data input (both external or generated by the programs).

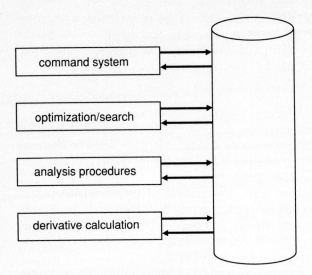

Figure 6.31   A disk-based programming system.

Three possible command language options are

- Operating system at the macro level (e.g., UNIX shell, VMS DCL, or CMS Rexx)
- Computed special-purpose language
- Menu-driven interactive

Figure 6.31 illustrates a disk-based programming system.

6.8   ARTIFICIAL INTELLIGENCE IN DESIGN OPTIMIZATION

The preceding material has discussed how the analyses and optimization techniques can be coupled to form a process. Of course, the direction in which the design develops is then influenced by the results of the data processed. However, at the metaprocess level discussed in the beginning of the book, it is also desirable to have the form of the process itself affected by the data. The design process would then adapt ("learn") as it proceeds. The field of artificial intelligence has been developing techniques for incorporating knowledge and reasoning into programs. Many of them are applicable to the optimization process.

Because optimization is an iterative process, two types of historical information can be collected. The first is the history of the investigation of the specific problem at hand: the design variables chosen, the resulting objective function value, and the constraints violated. The second is the metahistory, the history of the previous histories of problems addressed. This information can be used to adjust tuning parameters for specific algorithms, or even to choose between competing algorithms and switch strategies in midstream.

The most typical need for "outside" interference would stem from convergence problems within a specific algorithm. Many parameters influence the numerical behavior of an algorithm, so the actual performance of an implementation can be quite different from the theoretically expected behavior. Truncation error, round-off error, and division by zero are difficulties that may arise from numerical implementation.

6.9   PERFORMANCE EVALUATION

Some of the key issues in the evaluation of the performance of design optimization procedures include

- *Objectives of testing:* What should be tested? User-oriented features and safety provisions to serve the general user, or the underlying algorithmic ideas?

- *Computational environment:* The test results may depend on the computers and compilers used. Interactive optimization software will be required so that the course of computations and the degree of improvement can be followed.

- *Selection of test problems:* The question of whether to select problems of known mathematical structure or real-life problems is a point of concern.

- *Analysis of test results:* The test results need to be formally analyzed, and the codes need to be ranked and rated under the various performance criteria.

- *Performance criteria:* An accepted set of performance criteria may include efficiency, robustness, ease of use, and program organization. The quantification of these criteria, when making comparisons between codes, is difficult. Efficiency can be expressed in execution times (highly machine-dependent) or in equivalent function evaluations. Ease of use (documentation, input/output facilities, numerical differentiation, graceful termination) and program organization (modularity and protability) are not easy to assess.

The performance criteria used to make a comparative study of codes can be divided into two categories:

- Those criteria that are used to compare the underlying algorithmic details in a code.

- Those criteria that are used to compare features of the code such as "ease of use" and "program organization." This includes the number of input parameters to be set, the length of the data preparation phase, the facilities for numerical differentiation, output facilities, the programming language, and the modularity and portability of the code.

The computational expense of a design optimization problem depends only on the efficiency of the algorithm employed to solve the problem. The code-related features are desirable, but do not influence the efficiency of the optimization problem solution process. Hence, greater importance should be given to the evaluation of criteria used to compare the algorithmic performance than to the code-related features.

6.10   A SET OF PERFORMANCE CRITERIA

In this section a set of four performance criteria are developed that are deemed relevant to the evaluation of algorithmic performance alone.

Domain of Applications

The domain of applications refers to the class of problems for which the method is designed. The methods considered for evaluation here require the problems to have functions that are twice-continuously differentiable. The gradients of the active constraints should be linearly independent at the optimum, in other words, the constraints should satisfy the Kuhn-Tucker first-order constraint qualification.

It is important to note that the methods considered for evaluation converge to a local optimum point only. In order to prove that the optimum point obtained is a global minimum, either one must show that the problem is convex, or one must search the design space completely, starting from different points in the hope of finding a more optimal point.

Robustness

Robustness is the power to solve problems in the domain of applications with the required accuracy. This power is usually measured in terms of the percentage of problems that have "reasonably" been solved, even if the required accuracy is not fully obtained.

Accuracy

Numerical accuracy is a measurement of the algorithm's ability to compute a known optimum solution. Usually the optimum solution for real-life problems is not known. Thus, it may not be possible to evaluate the accuracy of an algorithm with the solution obtained for a real-life problem.

Efficiency

Efficiency is the effort necessary to solve problems in the domain of applications with the required accuracy. It is usually measured in terms of the time required for execution and the number of function and gradient evaluations.

Frequently, design optimization problems involve implicit functions that are evaluated as results of an analysis. This would occur, for example, when optimizing stresses that were calculated using some numerical method. Also, the derivative of these functions may need to be determined numerically through finite differences. This would result in additional function evaluations (as many as the number of design variables) through calls to the analysis routine. In complex engineering systems, it is reasonable to assume that the analysis time overwhelmingly dominates the optimization time. Hence, the number of function and gradient evaluations provide a measure of the efficiency of design optimization algorithms. To evaluate this efficiency, one could compute an equivalent number of function evaluations, obtained as a weighted sum of the number of function and gradient evaluations. Then this equivalent number of function evaluations could be used to compare the efficiency of algorithms. Alternatively, the gradients could be computed by finite differences, and the number of function evaluations could then be taken as the measure of overall efficiency.

In a similar manner, where gradients are evaluated by finite differences, the number of function evaluations per iteration is a measure of the efficiency of the line-search algorithm.

6.11 GEOMETRIC INTERPRETATION OF THE BEHAVIOR OF ALGORITHMS

Many optimization algorithms possess characteristic features that make it possible for an evaluator of algorithms to classify the algorithms on the basis of such characteristics. An example of a characteristic feature might be the observed peculiarity in the geometric trajectory that the algorithm exhibits while solving a test problem. A study of the geometric trajectory may also provide an understanding of the reasons for the efficient or inefficient performance of an algorithm. This section will study the geometric trajectories exhibited by a few of the optimization methods.

The basis for classifying the algorithms, through a study of the geometric trajectory, follows.

Line-Search Algorithms

The way a line-search algorithm works can be understood by studying the points at which the function evaluations were made by the code, while solving the optimization problem. This approach works because most line-search algorithms choose a step length based on the minimization of a descent function along the search direction. And, this minimization is usually performed using a method that needs function value evaluations only. Even a gradient-based descent-function minimization algorithm would usually need to evaluate the function values, at points where the gradients are evaluated.

Unconstrained Optimization Algorithms

- For reasons mentioned earlier, only a method that generates or uses second-order information can calculate a search direction down a narrow valley. A steepest descent direction will be orthogonal to the most efficient direction down the valley.

- The conjugate gradient method is an example of the conjugate direction methods. The nature of the trajectory of a traditional conjugate gradient method is cyclic (see section 4.8.3.3 of Gill, Murray, and Wright). The conjugate gradient method terminates in finite number of iterations for quadratic functions. However, the finite termination property of the method is not valid for nonquadratic functions. For these nonquadratic functions, the search direction is set to the steepest descent direction after n line searches, where n stands for the number of design variables. This strategy is known as restarting; the conjugate gradient method that restarts with the steepest descent direction every n iterations is known as the traditional conjugate gradient method. The cyclic nature of the conjugate gradient method is due to its restarts. When the conjugate gradient method is used to solve Rosenbrock's function, one would expect the algorithm to restart every two iterations. In other words, the algorithm would take steepest descent steps every two iterations.

- The quasi-Newton condition mentioned earlier determines the updated Hessian, based on the curvature information from the previous iterations. This curvature information is in turn based on a quadratic approximation to the function. The Newton algorithm determines the curvature information at every iteration, through the analytically determined Hessian of the function. If the analytically determined Hessian at a point is nearly equal to the updated Hessian obtained through the quasi-Newton condition, then the quasi-Newton search direction will be similar to the Newton search direction. However, the quasi-Newton algorithm will exhibit poor behavior at regions where curvature is changing rapidly, because in these regions, the updated Hessian, which was obtained on the basis of the curvature information from the previous iterations, would not accurately represent the actual curvature. Hence, for the Rosenbrock's function, one would expect any quasi-Newton algorithm to exhibit slow convergence in the neighborhood of the origin, where the curvature changes most rapidly.

Constrained Optimization Algorithms

In general, it is difficult to classify the constrained algorithms on the basis of the trajectory that was generated for the solution of a constrained problem. Some constrained algorithms, however, do possess characteristic trajectories:

- The reduced gradient method requires strict feasibility at every iteration. To satisfy this feasibility requirement, the iterates of this method tend to follow a path tangential to the constraints.

- From an infeasible design the gradient projection method will take a step tangential to the constraint. The method then performs a series of orthogonal iterations to return to the feasible region. From a feasible design, the step taken by the method is essentially unconstrained.

In both the reduced gradient method and the gradient projection method, the active constraints are treated as equalities for the purpose of computing the search direction and correcting back to feasibility. This is why the methods tend to follow a tangential path to the solution.

6.12   TEST PROBLEMS: REAL LIFE VERSUS HAND SELECTED

Any development or comparison of design optimization software must be based on extensive numerical tests. These numerical tests depend on test problems (in the form of the NLP Model) implemented in an appropriate way, about whose mathematical structure as much as possible is known. Many test problems used to test and compare optimization programs are so-called "real life" problems, which are believed to reflect the typical structures of practical design optimization problems. But this class of test problems has some disadvantages, since their precise solution is not known a priori; so the performance of the code cannot be related to the achieved accuracy. Thus the comparative performance evaluation of the optimization codes should be based on both hand-constructed test problems with known mathematical structure and real-life problems. Schittkowski's book (see Annotated References) is an excellent source on hand-constructed test problems for optimization codes.

The definitions of active sets are usually not identical in the constrained optimization algorithms. Most direct and constrained minimization algorithms intended to solve the nonlinear programming problem (NLP Model), formulate a simpler subproblem at each iteration step. This subproblem is then solved to obtain the search direction. The subproblems formed in the different constrained algorithms, upon reduction of the original nonlinear programming problem, are usually not the same. Moreover, an algorithm may choose to formulate different subproblems at different iterations, based on conditions at that iteration, such as the amount of constraint violation.

Hence, it would be difficult to make any conclusion about an algorithm's potential by studying its performance in a constrained test problem. Comparisons between the algorithms would be difficult, because no two algorithms are likely to generate similar search directions. Furthermore for a constrained test problem, it would be very difficult to deduce the inner workings of a constrained algorithm from its observed trajectory in the design space. If it were possible to reduce the performance of the constrained algorithms to a common denominator, then the comparisons could be made on their relative merits. An unconstrained test problem essentially provides the means for this reduction of constrained algorithms to a common basis. It may be possible to understand the working of the constrained algorithm with a simple study of the trajectory of the algorithm for an unconstrained test problem.

Most design optimization methods, when used to solve an unconstrained problem (using a dummy constraint), behave identically to one of the unconstrained optimization methods. For example:

- The gradient projection algorithm will exhibit similar behavior to the steepest-descent method for unconstrained optimization, if the approximate Hessian matrix of the Lagrangian is not supplied to the QP subproblem. Otherwise, it will behave as a variable metric algorithm for unconstrained optimization. This QP subproblem is solved at every iteration of the gradient projection algorithm.
- The PLBA algorithm (a second-order implementation of the Pshenichny's Linearization method) and the method of Wilson, Han, and Powell exhibit similar behavior to the variable metric method for unconstrained optimization.
- The GRG algorithm exhibits similar behavior to the underlying unconstrained optimization method used to minimize the reduced function f_*.

Any conclusion drawn from the efficiency of the line search algorithm, when based on the results of an unconstrained problem, is valid for a constrained optimization problem, also. Therefore, testing the constrained optimization code on an unconstrained optimization problem provides an understanding of the method used by the code to determine the search direction. This insight yields a basis for comparing the various codes, because the relative performances of the various unconstrained optimization methods is well documented.

6.13   SYSTEM GOALS

The goals of an optimal design system include the following:

- The system should identify discrepancies in the gradient calculation of cost and constraint functions.
- The system should illustrate flaws in the problem formulation (for example, a lack of a feasible region in design space) by identifying the constraints that cannot be satisfied.

- The system should classify the problems as linear, mildly nonlinear, highly nonlinear, unconstrained, or constrained, and select the appropriate algorithms to solve the problem.
- The system should identify design variables that have the most or least influence on the design process.
- The system should provide consultive support to improve the starting design without doing any optimization, by observing the variation (sensitivities) of all constraints with respect to each design variable. For example, if the sensitivities of all the inequality constraints with respect to a particular design variable are negative at a given starting point, the design can be moved into the feasible region by increasing that design variable alone. Thus the system can also help change the starting point, if a particular algorithm performs better from a feasible or infeasible starting point.
- The system should use the information from previous iterations to adjust parameters and improve the efficiency of the iterative process.

Example 6.10: Database for FEM-Optimization Processes. A central database that allows interaction between a finite-element analysis program and an optimization program so as to improve design iteratively is essential for an optimal design system. The central database is also essential to facilitate the flow of data between the various modules that make up the finite element analysis program or the optimization program. For example, the database is needed to transfer the current values of the objective function, constraints, and design variables between the optimizer and the terminator modules.

The database essentially consists of direct-access files that store

1. Nodal information for ease of reanalysis
2. Elemental information
3. Material properties
4. Loading information
5. Local/global stiffness matrices
6. Decomposed stiffness matrix
7. Deflections for all active loading cases
8. Stresses for all active loading cases
9. Objective function, constraint functions, and optimization parameters
10. Gradients of the objective function and constraint functions
11. History files containing histories of the design variables, the objective function and its gradient, the constraints and their gradients, the convergence parameter, the maximum constraint violation, and the Lagrange multipliers

6.14   REQUIREMENTS OF THE OPTIMAL DESIGN SYSTEM

The following are some of the user-oriented features that are required in optimization software intended for general use.

Input Features

Input features include the following:

- Able to assign a description to the names of the variables and constraints. For example, given that design variable 1 corresponds to a geometrical parameter such as the diameter of a column, the program should be able to associate the description "diameter" with design variable 1.

- Able to specify the type for each problem function and variable, independent of the order in which they appear in the list of functions and variables. Function types include objective, equality, lower bounded, upper bounded, both upper and lower bounded, and function to be ignored. Variable types are free, fixed, lower bounded, upper bounded, and both upper and lower bounded.

- Requires only one user-provided routine to compute the values of the problem functions. If the derivatives are needed, then the system should provide an option to compute them automatically.

- Capable of run time revision which allows modification of some problem data after the given problem has been solved, but leaving all the rest unchanged. Such a facility permits a sequence of different problems to be solved in one run.

- Error checking and direct echoing of all input data.

- Has default values for all system-dependent parameters like the largest allowable integer, unit round off, and so on. Default values for all the algorithm-dependent parameters, such as the value of step size, convergence parameter value, delta for finite differences, and so forth. Defaults for some of the other inputs required by the program, such as the amount of algorithmic data that the program should output during one iteration of optimization. These default values minimize the amount of input required from the occasional user, and yet retain for the sophisticated user, a high degree of control enabling the user to "tune" the algorithm for specific application.

- Capable of symbolic differentiation as performed by programs such as Macsyma, Mathematica, or REDUCE.

- Has program file operation for each module of the system; in other words, the system should be capable of executing a given task by reading the input commands from a file instead of the keyboard. This characteristic enables automated playback and automated task execution (for those tasks that allow easy program file generation).

Output Features

Output features include

- Tabular formats for the output of initial data and final solution information, which allows easy inspection of output for large problems
- Multiple print levels, to facilitate both production and debugging runs
- Dump and restart capabilities, to facilitate long runs and recover from error conditions
- Availability of a periodic detailed printout for every kth iteration
- Ability to change print levels after a specified number of iterations
- Graphical representations of the design space when design space has three or fewer dimensions
- Plots of the "history" of the design evolution, in other words, graphically examines the change in constraints or objective as optimization proceeds
- Availability of a record of all design decisions made at the terminal
- Ability to save or recall promising designs for further reference or optimization

Problem-Solving Capability

The problem-solving capabilities in an optimal design system are based on

- Ability to solve unconstrained problems efficiently
- Capability for handling nonlinear equality constraints efficiently
- Ability to start from feasible or infeasible points
- Ability to deal with bounds on the variables with implicit program logic, in other words, without counting them as g_i constraints
- Ability of an option to check any user-provided analytic derivation computations
- Capability to handle large sparse (Hessian) problems efficiently by exploiting sparsity
- Speed and robustness
- Capability to find an initial feasible design for algorithms requiring it
- Ability to redefine the design problem by
  - Changing the design variables
  - Changing which functions will form the objective and constraints
  - Changing the allowable values on constraints or upper and lower bounds on design variables
- Ability to examine a particular optimal solution's sensitivity to changes in design variables, by observing the derivatives of the objective function with respect to the design variables at the optimum
- Ability to examine the sensitivity of a particular optimal solution to changes in constraint value, by observing the values of the Lagrange multipliers at the optimum

6.15 ANNOTATED REFERENCES

Arora, Jasbir. *Introduction to Optimum Design*. New York: McGraw-Hill, 1989.

Excellent book with many examples and problems. Extensive bibliography.

Choi, K. K., Haug, E. J., Hou, J. W., and Sohoni, V. N. "Pshenichny's Linearization Method for Mechanical System Optimization," *Journal of Mechanisms, Transmissions and Automation in Design*, Vol. 105 (March 1983).

Flouda, C. A., and Pardalos, D. M. "A Collection of Test Problems for Constrained Global Optimization Algorithms," *Lecture Notes in Computer Science*, Vol. 455. New York: Springer-Verlag, 1990.

Forsythe, G. E., Malcom, M. A., and Moler, C. B. *Computer Methods for Mathematical Computing*. Englewood Cliffs, N. J.: Prentice-Hall, 1977.

This is a classic book for numerical methods algorithms, including least square, splines, integration, and matrix decomposition. Contains FORTRAN listings of very good subroutines in each area.

Gabriele, G. A., and Ragsdell, K. M. "The Generalized Reduced Gradient Method: A reliable tool for optimal design," *Journal of Engineering for Industry*. ASME, series B, Vol. 99, No. 2 (May 1977), pp. 394–400.

Gill, P. E., Murray, W., and Wright, M. H. *Practical Optimization*. New York: Academic Press, 1981.

Haug, Edward J., and Arora, Jasbir S. *Applied Optimal Design: Mechanical and structural systems*. New York: Wiley Interscience, 1979.

Haug, Edward J., Choi, Kyung K., and Komkov, Vadim. *Design Sensitivity Analysis of Structural Systems*. New York: Academic Press, 1986.

Himmelblau, D. M. *Applied Nonlinear Programming*. New York: McGraw-Hill, 1972.

Hock, W., and Schittkowski, K. "Test examples for nonlinear programming codes," *Lecture notes in Economics and Mathematical Systems*, No. 187. New York: Springer-Verlag, 1981.

Lootsma, F. A. "Comparative performance evaluation, experimental design, and generation of test problems in nonlinear optimization," *Computational Math Programming*. K. Schittkowski (Ed.). New York: Springer-Verlag, 1985.

Luenberger, D. G. *Introduction to linear and nonlinear programming*. Reading, Mass.: Addison-Wesley, 1973.

Papalambros, Panos Y., and Wilde, Douglass J. *Principles of Optimal Design: Modeling and computation*. New York: Cambridge University Press, 1988.

Press, W. H., Flannery, B. P., Teukolsky, S. A., Vetterling, W. T. *Numerical Recipes in C: The Art of Scientific Computing*. New York: Cambridge University Press, 1988.

Rosenbrock, H. H. *Computer Journal*, Vol. 3 (3) (October 1960), pp. 175–184.

Schittkowski, K. "Nonlinear programming codes—Information, tests, performance," *Lecture notes in Economics and Mathematical Systems*, No. 183. New York: Springer-Verlag, 1980.

Wilde, D. J. *Optimum Seeking Methods*, Engelwood Cliffs, N. J.: Prentice-Hall, 1964.

Wilde, Douglass J. *Globally Optimal Design*. New York: Wiley, 1978.

6.16   PROJECTS

Project 6.1   Optimum Sailing

Problem Statement   Determine the heading angle and sail angle needed to produce the maximum velocity into the upwind direction (velocity made good is V_{mg}).

The most critical measure of a sail boat is its performance into the wind. The helmsman must decide how close to hold the boat's heading into the wind and the angle of attack for the sail. Sailing too far off the wind means that velocity can be high; however, most of it is not contributing to productive motion. Holding too close into the wind means that the actual velocity can drop considerably. Note that the following analysis neglects the very important effects of boat heel angle and hull sideslip.

Analysis   Several vector diagrams are useful in understanding this problem (Figures 6.32 and 6.33). The apparent wind is a function of true wind, heading, and ship speed.

$$\vec{V}_A = -(V_T \cos \gamma + V_S)\vec{n}_2 + V_T \sin \gamma \vec{n}_1$$

The magnitude of $\vec{V}_A$ and the angle of β can be found from the preceding equation. The angle of attack of the sail is given by

$$\alpha = \beta - \delta$$

The aerodynamic forces (F_L and F_D) are parallel and perpendicular to the

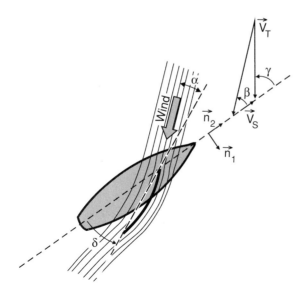

Figure 6.32   Kinematics for apparent wind.

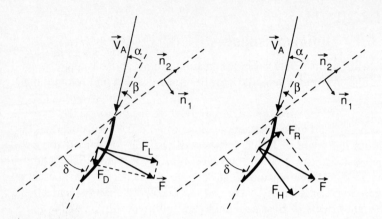

Figure 6.33 Sail force components relative to apparent wind and relative to hull.

apparent wind and are given in terms of lift and drag coefficients:

$$F_L = 0.0019V_A^2 S_A C_L$$

$$F_D = 0.0019V_A^2 S_A C_D$$

with F measured in pounds, V_A in ft/s, and S_A in ft^2. A typical sail area for a 5.5-meter yacht would be 300 ft^2. Figure 6.34 shows C_L and C_D for various values of α.

To determine the effect on performance, these forces must be resolved into components that are parallel and perpendicular to the hull (F_R and F_H):

$$F_R = F_L \sin\beta - F_D \cos\beta$$

$$F_H = F_L \cos\beta + F_D \sin\beta$$

The boat speed is limited by the hull drag:

$$F_{HD} = AV + BV^2 + CV^3 + DV^4 + EV^5 + FV^6$$

Typical coefficient values for a 5.5-meter yacht are

$$(13.47, -11.50, 3.926, -0.5703, 3.718 \times 10^{-2}, -8.6 \times 10^{-4})$$

Boat speed can be determined by a force balance, $F_R = F_{HD}$.

Several graphs can be used to help understand this performance problem:

1. Polar performance plot of V_S (assuming that optimum δ is used for each value of γ). See Fig. 6.35.

2. F_R versus F_H for constant β as α varies. See Fig. 6.36.

3. Lines of constant V_{mg} in an α versus γ plot.

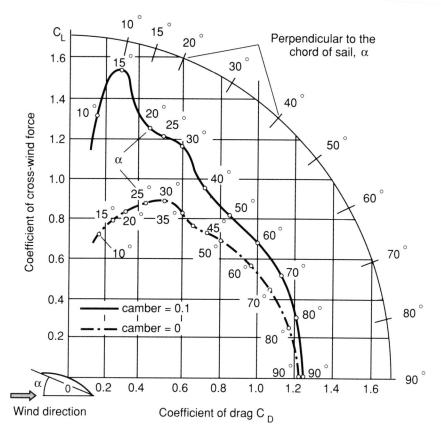

Figure 6.34 Measured sail performance with components relative
to wind. Note that sail aspect ratio = 5.

Suggested Procedure

1. Determine an analytical relationship for $C_L = f(\alpha)$ and $C_D = F(\alpha)$.
2. Given values for γ, and δ, determine $\vec{V}_s$ and V_{mg}. ($V_{mg} = V_S \cos \gamma$.)
3. Use an optimization procedure to maximize $V_{mg} = f(\gamma, \delta)$.
4. Produce any useful auxiliary plots needed to interpret the result (see
    Figures 6.34–6.36).
5. You may wish to make an interactive program that determines boat
    performance given user inputs for γ and δ.

Notation

V_T True wind velocity

V_{mg} Velocity made good

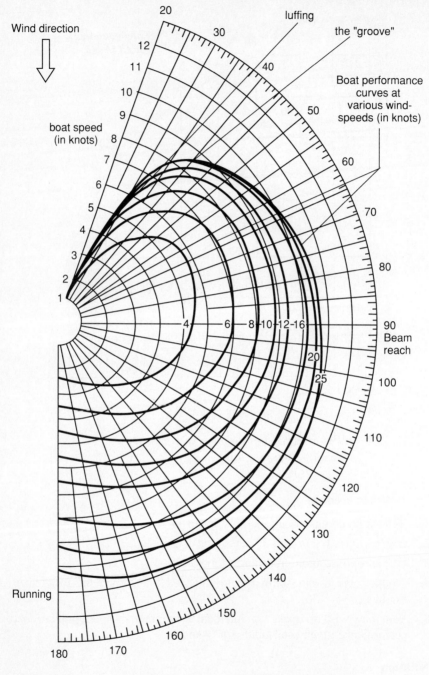

Figure 6.35 Maximum velocity as a function of the course
relative to wind and wind velocity.

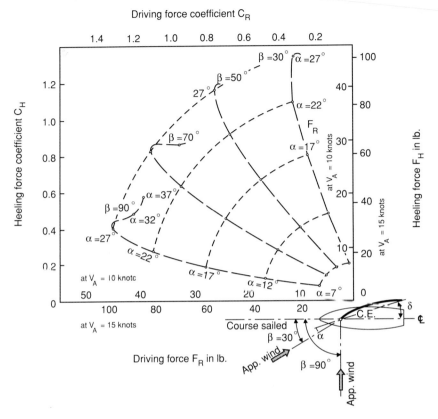

Figure 6.36   Force components relative to hull for different angles of apparent wind and for different sheeting angles.

V_S	Ship velocity through water
V_A	Apparent wind velocity
F_L	Lift force (direction of V_A)
F_D	Drag force (perpendicular to V_A)
F_R	Driving force (direction of V_S)
F_H	Heeling force (perpendicular to V_S)
F_{HD}	Hull drag force (direction of V_S)
α	Angle of attack of sail
β	Angle of the course relative to apparent wind
γ	True course relative to true wind
δ	Sheeting angle (sail relative to hull)
C_L	Lift coefficient
C_D	Drag coefficient
S_A	Sail area

Additional Reading

Chapelle, Howard I. *The Search for Speed Under Sail, 1700-1855*. New York:
W. W. Norton, 1984.

Good source of figures for ship hulls and rigging diagrams.

Curtiss, H. C., Jr. "Upright Sailing Craft Performance and Optimum Speed to Wind-
ward," *Journal of Hydronautics*. Vol. 11, No. 2 (April 1977), pp. 42–48.

Analytical treatment of sailing.

Davis, Charles G. *American Sailing Ships*. New York: Dover, 1984.

Good source of figures for ship hulls and rigging diagrams.

Kay, H. F. *The Science of Yachts, Wind, and Water*. Tuckahoe, N. Y.: John de Graff,
1971.

Kinney, F. S. *Skene's Elements of Yacht Design*. New York: G. P. Putnam, 1973.

Marchaj, C. A. *Sailing Theory and Practice*. New York: Dodd Mead, 1964.

Marchaj, C. A. *Aero-Hydrodynamics of Sailing*. New York: Dodd Mead, 1979.

Marchaj, C. A. *Seaworthiness: The Forgotten Factor*. Camden, Maine: International
Marine Publishing Co., 1986.

Project 6.2   Extreme Range and Endurance Aircraft

Problem Statement   An international prize was offered for the first non-
stop and nonrefuelled circumnavigation of the globe. The ground rules were
that the vehicle must be classified as an airplane (no orbital spacecraft); the
vehicle must take off on its own power, and the vehicle cannot discard any
parts (fuel tanks, engines, landing gear, etc.). In the following version of the
problem, the designer must select a power plant and wing geometry (span
and chord). The design must minimize project cost and satisfy the constraint
criteria discussed below.

Note: The circumnavigation was accomplished by Burt Rutan's *Voyager*
in 12 days, flying 80-150 mph at 12,000 ft. As designed, *Voyager* had a crew
of two, twin engines in a pusher-puller configuration, a canard wingplan,
gross weight of 11,300 lb, fuel weight of 8400 lb, structural weight of 938
lb, wing span of 111 ft, and wing chord of 3 ft.

Problem Data

b		Wing span (m)
c		Wing chord (m)
$C_{d,par}$	0.009	Parasitic drag coefficient
C_d		Drag coefficient
C_L		Lift coefficient
$C_{L,max}$	1.20	Maximum lift coefficient before stall

E		Objective function
$K_{hp,to,W}$	745.7	Conversion constant horse-power to watts
K_{fab}	0.80	Fabrication cost weighting factor
P_{eng}		Engine power (hp)
$P_{min,cruise}$		Minimum cruise power
R	28,000 mi	Range (4.51×10^7 m)
R_e		Reynolds number
SFC	8.4×10^{-7} 1/m	Specific fuel consumption
t	0.12	Wing-mean-thickness-to-chord ratio
T		Flight time (s)
T_{max}	12 days	Maximum flight time
V_{climb}	2.8 m/s	Desired rate of climb
$V_{min,stall}$		Minimum stall velocity
$V_{min,cruise}$		Minimum cruise velocity
V_{ratio}		Ratio of volume of wing used by fuel
W_{crew}	1,500 N	Crew weight
$W_{fuselage}$	3,000 N	Fuselage weight
W_{struct}		Total structural weight
η_{prop}	0.90	Efficiency of propellor
η_{wing}	0.90	Efficiency of wing
μ	1.789×10^{-5} N s/m^2	Air viscosity at sea level
ρ_{wing}	0.06 N/m^4	Wing density factor
$\rho_{air,alt}$	0.819 kg/m^3	Density of air at altitude (4 km)
$\rho_{air,0}$	1.23 kg/m^3	Density of air at sea level

Analysis The fabrication cost is assumed to be a function of structural weight, while the operational cost is just the cost of fuel. The objective function is the weighted sum of the two partial costs:

$$E = f(b, c) = K_{fab}W_{struct} + (1 - K_{fab})W_{fuel} \quad \text{where} \quad 0 \le K_{fab} \le 1$$

Note that the design of a fuel efficient aircraft would bias the objective function towards the fuel cost ($K_{fab} = 0$). However, the aircraft is expected to fly only once after flight testing before ending up in the Smithsonian Air and Space Museum. Therefore, the objective function has been biased more towards fabrication costs.

The various weights relevant to the problem are given by

$$W_{struct} = W_{fuselage} + W_{engine} + W_{wing}$$
$$W_{landing} = W_{struct} + W_{crew}$$
$$W_{takeoff} = W_{landing} + W_{fuel}$$

The weight of the engine is determined by the horsepower requirements

$$W_{engine} = f(P_{engine})$$

Table 6.2 gives three possible engine choices. Budgetary restrictions do not allow for new engine development. Data for jet engines are not given due to poor takeoff performance and the jet's requirements for high speed and high altitude for efficiency. The internal combustion engines are assumed to operate at a constant specific fuel consumption because the engine always can be leaned for maximum efficiency. The wing weight is given by wing dimensions and the wing density factor:

$$W_{wing} = \rho_{wing} c b^3$$

The fuel weight is found from the Breguet range equation:

$$R = \frac{\eta_{prop}}{SFC} \frac{C_L}{C_d} \ln \frac{W_{struct} + W_{fuel}}{W_{struct}}$$

where

$$\frac{C_d}{C_L} = 2 \sqrt{\frac{C_{d,par}}{\pi \eta_{wing} b/c}}$$

The design must satisfy the several constraints. First, the dimensions must be realistic: $c > 0.0$; $b > 0.0$. There must be sufficient room in the wing to store fuel:

$$V_{wing} \geq V_{fuel} \quad \text{where } V_{fuel} = \frac{W_{fuel}}{g \rho_{fuel}}, \quad V_{wing} = bc^2 t_{wing}$$

The thickness of the wing is given as a fraction of the chord.

The optimal lift coefficient must be well below the maximum (stall) lift coefficient, $C_{L,opt} \leq 0.5 C_{L,max}$:

$$C_{L,opt} = \sqrt{\pi \eta_{wing} \frac{b}{c} C_{d,par}}$$

$$C_{d,max} = C_{d,par} + \frac{C_{L_{max}}^2}{\pi \eta_{wing} b/c}$$

Engine	hp	Weight (lb)
C0235	110	320
I0360	200	380
I0540	300	440

Table 6.2   Engine power and weight.

Power requirements can be determined from

$$P = \rho_{\text{air}} V^3 bc C_d$$

There must be sufficient power at takeoff: $\eta_{\text{prop}} P_{\text{eng}} \geq P_{\text{takeoff}}$. Note that takeoff occurs at sea-level, $V = V_{\text{max,stall}}$, and maximum drag $C_{d,\text{max}}$. In addition to simply maintaining flight in this situation, the value of P_{takeoff} must include the climb power ($W_{\text{takeoff}} V_{\text{climb}}$).

There must be sufficient power at maximum optimal cruise velocity: $\eta_{\text{prop}} P_{\text{eng}} \geq P_{\text{max,cruise}}$, which occurs at altitude and uses $C_{d,\text{par}}$.

The relationship between weight, velocity, and lift coefficient is

$$C_L = \frac{2W}{\rho b c V^2}$$

which can be rearranged to yield

$$V = \sqrt{\frac{2W}{\rho b c C_L}}$$

Working from this equation,

$$V_{\text{max,stall}} = f(W_{\text{takeoff}}, \rho_{\text{air},0}, C_{\text{L,max}})$$
$$V_{\text{max,cruise}} = f(W_{\text{takeoff}}, \rho_{\text{air,alt}}, C_{\text{L,opt}})$$
$$V_{\text{min,stall}} = f(W_{\text{landing}}, \rho_{\text{air},0}, C_{\text{L,max}})$$

The flight time must be within the window $T < 12$ days. Flight time can be estimated using the Breguet endurance formula:

$$T = \frac{\eta_{\text{prop}}}{SFC} \frac{C_L}{C_d} \sqrt{2\rho_{\text{air}} bc C_L} \left(\frac{1}{\sqrt{W}_{\text{landing}}} - \frac{1}{\sqrt{W}_{\text{takeoff}}} \right)$$

The airfoil should operate above turbulent Reynolds number to prevent boundary layer seperation: $R_e > 1.0 \times 10^6$. Minimum Reynolds number occurs at landing, sea level, and $V_{\text{min,stall}}$.

Optional Considerations   Consider the effects of changing the parameters given. For instance, a flight time of 12 days may be too long. The parameters assumed one crew member at 100 kg using 5 kg of consumables per day.

Explore the design space by making different initial guesses. Graph the search procedure of the optimization procedure. Can you say with confidence that a global minimum has been achieved?

Consider the scenario where the fuel is donated by a major oil company as part of a public relations and sales campaign. How are the optimum power plant size and wing dimensions changed?

An entrepeneur speculates that a lucrative venture would be leasing this aircraft to eccentric pilots who want to fly around the world. Which design do you recommend to make his business most profitable?

Project 6.3 Fully Stressed Grillage

Problem Statement Determine the cross-sectional properties for a minimum weight, simple elastic grillage that carries a uniformly distributed load.

Problem Data The grillage configuration is shown in Fig. 6.37.

Analysis Grillages can be found in factories, process plants, ships, and bridges. The grillage discussed here consists of two beams of different length that are orthogonally oriented, rigidly attached at midspan, and simply supported at the ends. The beams carry a uniformly distributed load as shown. Each beam belongs to a family of standard cross-sectional shapes. Empirical relationships in the literature give moment of inertia and section modulus as functions of cross-sectional area. Alternatively, cross-sectional shapes can be assumed and the sectional properties calculated. The stress is of concern at the point of intersection and at an interior point along each beam where bending stress is maximum. Minimize the volume, subject to stress constraints.

Optional Exercises Does the problem have several minima? How does the solution depend upon the aspect ratio of the grillage?

Additional Information

Moses, F., and Onoda, S. "Minimum Weight Design of Structures with Application to Elastic Grillages," *International Journal of Numerical Methods in Engineering*, Vol. 1 (1969), pp. 311–331.

Clarkson, J. *The Elastic Analysis of Flat Grillages*. New York: Cambridge University Press, 1965.

Burns, S. A., and Locascio, A. "A Monomial-Based Method for Solving systems of Nonlinear Algebraic Equations," *International Journal for Numerical Methods in Engineering*, Vol. 31 (7) (1991), pp. 1295–1318.

Burns, S. A. "Visualizing Iterative Behavior in Engineering Design Optimization Processes," (January 1991),

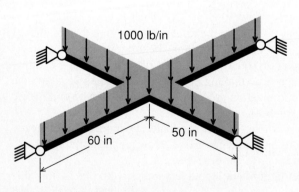

Figure 6.37 An elastic grillage structure.

Project 6.4   Column Design

Problem Statement   Determine the dimensions for a minimum weight, hollow cylindrical column. Determine R and t, subject to stress constraints and Euler and local buckling constraints.

Problem Data

σ_y	36×10^3 psi	Yield stress
E	3×10^7 psi	Young's modulus
ρg	0.283 lb/in^3	Density
k	0.6	Buckling coefficient
L	144 in	Column height
P	25×10^3 psi	Load
R		Column radius
t		Column thickness

Analysis   The local stress in the column can be expressed as

$$\sigma = \frac{P}{A}$$

Assuming that $t \ll R$, cross-sectional properties are

$$A = 2\pi R t \qquad I = \pi R^3 t$$

Local yielding will occur if the stress exceeds the yield stress. The Euler column buckling load is

$$P_{cr} = \frac{\pi^2 E I}{4L^2}$$

The critical buckling stress for local buckling in a tubular shell is

$$\sigma_{cr} = \frac{k E t}{R}$$

where k is a coefficient, approximately equal to 0.6 for steel.

   The optimal design problem is to select the design variables R and t to minimize the total weight of material in the column, subject to the above constraints.

Comments   This problem is only two dimensional and the computational requirements are trivial. If a contour plotting program is available, plot the objective function, constraints, and trajectory of the optimization algorithm.

Project 6.5   Optimum Selection of Gas Compressors

Problem Statement   A combination of centrifugal and reciprocating compressors are to be used to compress gas. Select the pressure ratios for each compressor to minimize the total initial cost.

Problem Data

p_0	25	psia	Intake pressure for centrifugal compressor
p_1			Intake pressure for reciprocating compressor (psia)
p_2	2,500	psia	Outlet pressure for reciprocating compressor
t_0	120	°F	Intake temperature for centrifugal compressor
t_1	120	°F	Intake temperature for reciprocating compressor
t_2	2,500	°F	Outlet temperature for reciprocating compressor
Q_0	500	ft³/s	Volumetric flow rate, centrifugal compressor inlet
Q_1			Volumetric flow rate, reciprocating compressor inlet (ft³/sec)
C_c			Centrifugal compressor cost ($)
C_r			Reciprocating compressor cost ($)

Analysis   A flow rate of 500 ft³/s of natural gas at 120°F and 25 psia is to be compressed to a final pressure of 2,500 psia. The available commercial compressors are either centrifugal or reciprocating. The centrifugal compressor can handle a large volume flow rate but can develop only a low pressure ratio per stage. The reciprocating compressor can develop high pressure ratios but is suited to low volume flow rates. The best attributes of each can be exploited by combining both types of compressor. First, a centrifugal compressor is used to handle the initial volume. Second, an intercooler cools the gas back to 120°F. Finally, a reciprocating compressor provides the remainder of the pressure increase.

The initial cost of each compressor is a function of the pressure ratio and flow rate:

$$C_c = 2Q_0 + 1,600\left(\frac{p_1}{p_0}\right)$$

$$C_r = 6Q_1 + 800\left(\frac{p_2}{p_1}\right)$$

where C, Q, and p have units as given above.

Assume that the gas behaves as a perfect gas. Assume a zero pressure drop across the intercooler.

Comments   The resulting cost equation is relatively simple, and calculus can determine the optimum. However, this is a good simple problem for a one-dimensional search program. A more detailed equation of state for natural gas or a more detailed cost equation can be determined (possibly using the curve fit techniques from Chapter 2).

C H A P T E R

7
Graphics

7.1 INTRODUCTION

Understanding physical systems requires more information than is contained in the symbolic language of mathematics and physics. Although mechanical engineering problems involve geometry, engineering problems also contain information that would be communicated more efficiently graphically than symbolically in words or equations. This chapter will deal with the use of graphics as an output channel for the computer system. In addition, it will discuss the methods and techniques used to produce images on a screen (the primary but not the only output device).

Of course, it is very difficult to separate the elements of the picture from their content. However, as much as possible of the content will be considered later. For instance, Chapter 8, Visualization, will address the methods for describing data and the display of numerical information, including plotting, graphing, surface plots, and contour plots. And Chapter 9, Geometry, will discuss the methods for describing geometry and the display of physical objects, which includes the topics of splines, surfaces, patches, solids, and so on, as well as data structures for storing and manipulating geometry. Implementation of data structures is discussed in Chapter 10. The optimum use of graphics requires an interactive application; however, in keeping with the trends in the field, the interactive nature will be kept separate, and its discussion deferred until Chapter 11.

On the other hand, this chapter's primary focus is the display of graphical entities on the screen. Types of entities include points, lines, areas, and text. Generally, surfaces and volumes are displayed by either lines or filled areas. Some systems do not treat text as a distinct type but instead consider text as points or lines. This chapter, however, will distinguish between text and the other entities because most graphics packages make such a distinction. We will not concern ourselves with details about the hardware that produces the image other than to point out aspects that limit how the hardware can be used.

To the developer, graphics has the characteristics of both program and data more so than in other areas of CAD. In one sense, creating an effective computer graphics image can be viewed as generating data to be processed by the graphics package. This approach focuses on the information content in a specific image. However, the "data" is more than point/line coordinates, and in most cases, it contains instructions to the display programs regarding style and other nongeometric information. Furthermore, effective mechanical CAD is not a single image in isolation. Designing with CAD creates a sequence of images and the associated user interaction with those images. Thus the focus shifts to the programming aspects, and graphics becomes more than just the image. The key to grasping both the programming and the visual aspects of computer graphics is to develop a mental construct. This chapter will accomplish that by tracing the evolutionary process by which modern computer graphics was developed.

Classifications of Graphics Software

Graphics software can be divided into three categories. At the most fundamental level is the device-dependent software that generates the machine code commands (often called escape codes) to activate the peripheral graphic device such as the CRT or plotter. This level of software is often commonly referred to as "device drivers," reflecting that such software is very hardware specific. Section 7.5 contains an example.

At the intermediate level is development software, which provides windowing, viewporting, transformations, display structures, and menu management. These are the so-called device-independent graphics packages that are intended to ease the application programmer's task. Typically, such packages are available on a wide range of hardware. Examples would include GKS, PHIGS, HOOPS, PLOT-10, NCAR plotting package, GL 2, Renderman, and so forth. These packages are all libraries of subroutines, and the user must write a program in a classical programming language. Typically, bindings (procedure names and argument definitions) are provided for FORTRAN, PASCAL, and C.

Frequently such a package will generate a data set that represents the final image. This data set (sometimes a data file) will use a very fundamental language (usually proprietary) that is generally referred to as metacode. The metacode file can be stored, transmitted over a network, or drawn on a peripheral device. The metacode definition is usually very primitive (draw line, draw pixel, write text), which makes the metacode translator (device driver) easier to write. An example of a sophisticated metacode definition is the PostScript language.

At the highest level are completely packaged application programs, which (among other things) produce graphical images for specific problems such as data plotting, finite-element modeling, solid modeling, and simulation. Examples include Cricket-Graph, AutoCAD, CATIA, CADAM, PATRAN, and Mathematica. These are the independent, stand-alone programs that are very general purpose, and have a wide range of functionality, but are not easily adapted. Also, at this level hardware portability typically decreases.

The focus of this chapter is what happens inside packages at the device-independent level. Although likely never to write such a subroutine library, a good CAD engineer will use such libraries frequently, and therefore needs to understand their internal workings and limitations. Furthermore, since application programs are built upon graphics libraries, understanding the fundamentals can be useful to the user of application programs.

7.2 HISTORICAL DEVELOPMENT

The characteristics of graphics packages can be best understood by tracing the evolution of these programs. The beginnings of computer graphics can be traced to two seminal projects.

The first was a research project in artificial intelligence conducted by the Rand Corporation in the 1950s for the Department of Defense (McCorduck, 1979). During World War II, and especially during the Battle of Britain, air defense had hinged on ground-based radar and ground-guided intercept. After the end of World War II, the discipline of operations research began to receive increased attention. Of particular interest was the organization and management of the ground-control center for local air-defense missions.

The Rand Corporation investigated different operational strategies for such ground-control centers. Obviously, it was impractical to have many aircraft flying around just to generate the information flow to exercise the ground-control center. At the time, the concept of simulation was just being developed; therefore, the primitive computers of the day were used to simulate the air traffic environment. It is interesting to note that the researchers did not attempt to simulate the interactions within the control center but chose instead to have human participants. This probably indicates the low level of experience with simulation.

One approach was to have the computer print out the aircraft locations and use traditional plotting-board activities to communicate with the control center. However, at that point radar was beginning to be the principal source of information. Radar displays were still very primitive, and aircraft were simply blips on a CRT. The key concept was to have a computer simulate the radar screens, using digital-to-analog conversion to drive the CRT display. This was not planned as part of the research project but came about by serendipity. At this point, the output was truly analogous to a primitive radar display. In a similar fashion, a stock market simulation could produce results on an actual "ticker tape" display; or an aircraft simulation could drive the dials on an actual aircraft instrument panel.

Eventually the graphics system was implemented as Project SAGE (for Semi-Automated Ground Environment), which linked all North American radar sites. Aircraft targets were represented symbolically on the graphics screen, and the operator assigned the intercept using a "light gun," a hand-held precursor to the light pen.

The second project was the Sketchpad Program developed by Ivan Sutherland at MIT in 1965. MIT Lincoln Labs designed and developed a computer to investigate human-machine interaction through a wide selection of switches, knobs, a point-plotting display, and a light pen. Sutherland, as a graduate student, produced the first complete working CAD software package, Sketchpad. Commands were entered via keyboard and coordinate values were indicated by the light pen. Objects could be drawn, stored as primitives, and then scaled, rotated, and duplicated. It is important to note that the graphics were produced interactively and in real time. For the next few years, CAD application development focused on pen-plotter graphics for drafting. However, Sutherland's dissertation, "Sketchpad: A Man-Machine Graphical Communication System," launched the field of interactive computer graphics.

7.3   HARDWARE

Graphics hardware can be classified by two characteristics: the permanence of the display (static or dynamic) and whether the device is inherently analog or digital (vector or raster).

Graphics displays may be either static or dynamic. Graphics on a static display are cumulative over time until something akin to a reset occurs specifically. For example, the lines on a pen plotter are permanent until the paper is changed, and the lines on the screen of a storage oscilloscope (or direct view storage tube) are permanent until the screen is discharged. Pixels set on a raster display will remain set until the screen is reset. (At the lowest level of hardware, a raster pixel is transient in that a continuous sweep of the screen is necessary, as in a TV. However, the raster display is not a television screen but a combination of the screen and "screen memory." The bits in screen memory retain their value until changed, so the raster display can be treated as a permanent display.)

Conversely, the lines on an ordinary oscilloscope fade out depending upon the persistence of the phosphor. Historically, graphics began with cumulative displays, because among other reasons, the computer speed was too slow to regenerate complete pictures fast enough to sustain a continuous image. With increasing computer speed, the vector refresh calligraphic displays began to see more use in the late 1970s. At the crudest level, a vector refresh calligraphic display is analogous to forming a line by moving a flashlight rapidly from side to side. More complex images only require firm control and higher speed. Given the continuous process of "redrawing," it was extremely easy to change the image rapidly. Although vector refresh displays were very fast, they did not provide sufficient color range. Most were only white lines on a black background. The fundamental characteristics were images made up to straight line (vector) strokes (calligraphic). Further increases in computer speed have allowed color raster displays to emulate the transience of the vector refresh displays.

Analog devices operate in floating point and appear to be infinitely addressable (or at least almost so). For the mechanical engineer, an analog device is attractive because the information dealt with is floating point values. Typical engineering geometry occurs in a continuous spatial domain, so integer spatial coordinates are not attractive. Examples of analog devices are standard oscilloscopes, x-y pen plotters, and vector refresh displays (also called calligraphic or stroke displays). With continual advancement in VLSI design, digital displays have passed the capabilities of analog displays. Calligraphic screens have been developed that use digital screen addresses, usually 0-4095. Digital displays are addressable with a finite resolution that is sufficiently fine as to appear to have infinite resolution. For example, a color raster screen easily provides $1,024 \times 1,024$ resolution. Laser printers provide 300 dpi resolution over $8\frac{1}{2}$ by 11 inches or $2,550 \times 3,300$ resolution. It is important to note that the characteristics of a device might not be readily apparent to a casual observer. An x-y plotter driven by a stepping motor would be a digital device.

The common graphic devices used now can be described as digital and transient. The graphics screen consists of finite pixels and is repetitively scanned from the screen memory. However, to the CAD designer/user, the device is made to appear to be analog and permanent. The display is cumulative: A line remains until removed. The graphics library will achieve this fundamental change. Henceforth in this chapter, the graphic screen will be treated as a permanent media able to display lines defined with floating-point numbers.

7.4 GEOMETRIC TRANSFORMATIONS

Graphical information is seldom rendered onto the display in raw form. Engineers deal with measurements ranging from angstroms (atomic) up through light-years. Displays are two dimensional, while the physical world of engineers is three dimensional. This section will present the mathematics used to transform graphical information. Interactive computer-aided design depends on the ability to modify portions of the display or the total image. Section 7.5 will discuss the organization of the images and how transformation can be applied to portions of a display.

The variety of transformations imaginable is infinite. This characteristic is easily seen after a few minutes spent with a deformable object such as a rubber eraser. A basic set can be defined from the fundamental rigid body motions (translation and rotation) and the fundamental elastic deformations (normal strain and shear strain). Note that a normal strain is equivalent to a scale change. Each of these is a mapping operation, transforming all points

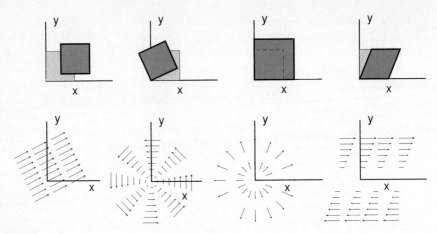

Figure 7.1   Fundamental transformations: translation,
rotation, scale, and shear.

in the x-y plane as shown in Fig. 7.1. For each transformation, a square
has been drawn in the initial position with a light gray fill and in the final
position with a dark gray fill. The transformation is represented as a field of
vectors. Note how each transformation is relative to the origin.

Vector Formulation

As will be discussed in Chapter 9, Geometry, all geometric forms build upon
point data. A point in three space is representable as a 3-tuple of numbers
that also represents the "position" vector from the origin to that point. A
typical engineering analytical approach would represent the transformation
of interest using traditional vector algebra.

Translation is simply a vector addition operation and uniform scale is a
scalar multiplication (using a positive scalar). Unfortunately, rotation is not
easily handled. A rotation θ about an axis $\vec{n}_r$ applied to the target $\vec{V}$ can be
defined as an operator ($\hookrightarrow$) as

$$(\theta \vec{n}_r) \hookrightarrow \vec{V} = \cos(\theta)\vec{V} + \sin(\theta)\vec{n}_\kappa \times \vec{V}$$

For example, a translation in x and y, scale by a factor of 0.5, and a
$90°$ rotation about the z axis (in that order) would be

$$\vec{V}^* = \left\{ \begin{array}{c} 0.0 \\ 0.0 \\ \pi/2 \end{array} \right\} \hookrightarrow 0.5 \left(\vec{V} + \left\{ \begin{array}{c} 0.6 \\ 0.75 \\ 0.0 \end{array} \right\} \right)$$

Note that this book will treat vectors as vertical columns. The alternative of
using row notation is discussed at the end of this section, in the subsection
on coordinate systems.

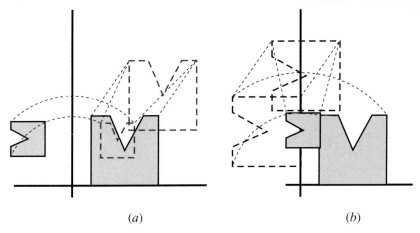

(a)   (b)

Figure 7.2 Transformations are not cummutative. (a) shows a translation,
scale, and rotation. (b) shows the same transformations
applied in order of rotation, translation, and scale.

Figure 7.2(a) shows the preceding transformation applied to a shape;
Fig. 7.2(b) shows the same transformations used in a different order. The
initial and final objects are filled in Fig. 7.2 while the intermediate shapes
are dashed.

Because the vector cross-product is not commutative, it should be clear
that transformations are generally not commutative. This approach, while
natural to mechanical engineers raised on a diet of vector calculus from fundamental mechanics, is not typically used by graphics programmers. The
rotation operator is clumsy, and nonuniform scale and shear transformations
will be also. A scale of 0.5 in the x direction but 0.8 in the y direction is
a vector requiring a vector operation rather than scalar multiplication. Just
as importantly, the perspective projection, used to add a three-dimensional
feel to two-dimensional images, is not easily handled in this format. For
efficiency in computer graphics applications, it is more desirable to compose
a single operation than to use the set of vector addition, scalar multiplication,
vector cross-product, and the rotation operation. The solution is to use 4×4
transformations based only on matrix multiplication and homogeneous coordinates. These concepts will be defined by example in the following subsections.

Two-Dimensional Transformations

A vector $\vec{V}$ with coordinates (a, b), rotated by an angle θ about a line passing
through the z-axis will have coordinates $(a \cos \theta - b \sin \theta, a \sin \theta + b \cos \theta)$,
as shown in Fig. 7.3. This can be written simply using matrix notation as

$$\vec{V}^* = \begin{bmatrix} \cos \theta & -\sin \theta \\ \sin \theta & \cos \theta \end{bmatrix} \begin{Bmatrix} a \\ b \end{Bmatrix}$$

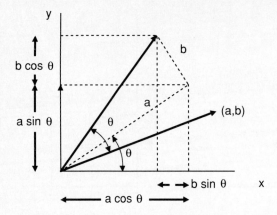

Figure 7.3 Rotation about the *z*-axis.

Now the complex vector notation for a rotation simply becomes a matrix multiplication. Note that the angle θ appears in more than one location and the vector for the rotation axis does not appear explicitly. Consistent with this approach, scale transformations are multiplication by a diagonal matrix, although translations still are vector addition. Translation operations can be unified by including an extra coordinate that is usually unity (homogeneous coordinates). The rotation transformation becomes

$$\vec{V}^* = \begin{bmatrix} \cos\theta & -\sin\theta & 0 \\ \sin\theta & \cos\theta & 0 \\ 0 & 0 & 1 \end{bmatrix} \begin{Bmatrix} a \\ b \\ 1 \end{Bmatrix}$$

The matrix form of the scale transformation becomes

$$\vec{V}^* = \begin{bmatrix} s_x & 0 & 0 \\ 0 & s_y & 0 \\ 0 & 0 & 1 \end{bmatrix} \begin{Bmatrix} a \\ b \\ 1 \end{Bmatrix}$$

and the translation transformation becomes

$$\vec{V}^* = \begin{bmatrix} 1 & 0 & r_x \\ 0 & 1 & r_y \\ 0 & 0 & 1 \end{bmatrix} \begin{Bmatrix} a \\ b \\ 1 \end{Bmatrix}$$

Interestingly, any arbitrary matrix of the form

$$\begin{bmatrix} a & b & c \\ d & e & f \\ 0 & 0 & 1 \end{bmatrix}$$

represents a valid transformation matrix that can be viewed as the product of the defined fundamental transformations: translation, scale, rotation, and shear. An arbitrary 2×2 matrix can be considered as a combination of diagonal, symmetric, and skew symmetric terms. The diagonal terms are seen to result from scale; the off-diagonal skew symmetric terms, from rotation, and the off-diagonal symmetric terms, from shear. One form of the shear transformation matrix is

$$\begin{bmatrix} \cos a & \sin a & 0 \\ \sin a & \cos a & 0 \\ 0 & 0 & 1 \end{bmatrix}$$

The standard forms of the shear matrix are as follows. Shearing along the x axis is obtained using the matrix

$$\begin{bmatrix} 1 & \tan \gamma & 0 \\ 0 & 1 & 0 \\ 0 & 0 & 1 \end{bmatrix}$$

while shearing along the y axis is obtained using

$$\begin{bmatrix} 1 & 0 & 0 \\ \tan \gamma & 1 & 0 \\ 0 & 0 & 1 \end{bmatrix}$$

In the preceding, γ represents the amount of rotation of a line perpendicular to the shear axis.

Note that each transformation leaves the third coordinate at a value of 1. A series of transformations is then simply a sequence of matrix multiplications, (remember that matrix multiplication is *not* commutative). Multiple transformations are discussed later in this section.

Three-Dimensional Transformations

The generalization to three dimensions is straightforward (as long as the rotation is about one of the fundamental basis axes). Note that although the rotation about an arbitrary axis is a matrix multiplication, the matrix is not obvious. For example, the rotation matrices for a rotation about the x axis, y axis, or z axis, respectively, are

$$\begin{bmatrix} 1 & 0 & 0 & 0 \\ 0 & \cos \theta_x & -\sin \theta_x & 0 \\ 0 & \sin \theta_x & \cos \theta_x & 0 \\ 0 & 0 & 0 & 1 \end{bmatrix}, \quad \begin{bmatrix} \cos \theta_y & 0 & -\sin \theta_y & 0 \\ 0 & 1 & 0 & 0 \\ \sin \theta_y & 0 & \cos \theta_y & 0 \\ 0 & 0 & 0 & 1 \end{bmatrix},$$

$$\begin{bmatrix} \cos \theta_z & -\sin \theta_z & 0 & 0 \\ \sin \theta_z & \cos \theta_z & 0 & 0 \\ 0 & 0 & 1 & 0 \\ 0 & 0 & 0 & 1 \end{bmatrix}$$

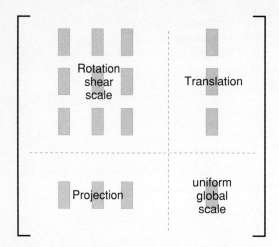

Figure 7.4   General form for a transformation matrix.

The translation matrix is

$$\begin{bmatrix} 1 & 0 & 0 & r_x \\ 0 & 1 & 0 & r_y \\ 0 & 0 & 1 & r_z \\ 0 & 0 & 0 & 1 \end{bmatrix}$$

and scaling of s_x, s_y, and s_z can be produced by

$$\begin{bmatrix} s_x & 0 & 0 & 0 \\ 0 & s_y & 0 & 0 \\ 0 & 0 & s_z & 0 \\ 0 & 0 & 0 & 1 \end{bmatrix}$$

Three-dimensional manipulations can therefore be unified into a matrix transformation that is applied by matrix multiplication. The general form for a transformation matrix is shown in Fig. 7.4. The use of the fourth row for projection transformation is discussed later.

The transformation matrices which have been developed are "affine transformations." They are constant in that the entries are not functions of any spatial coordinates: Straight lines will remain straight; parallel lines will remain parallel, and all intersection points will be preserved.

Of course, an infinite number of transformations are possible, particularly if the transformation field is nonuniform. For example, a rotation about the z axis, in which $\theta = 4z$, will produce a uniform twist. Graphics packages usually support only translation, rotation, scale, and perspective.

Multiple Transformations

Except for translation, all transformations presented in this chapter are applied relative to the origin because the origin $\{0 \quad 0 \quad 0\}^{\mathrm{T}}$ remains unchanged. However, most applications require a richer set of transformations. These are more difficult to develop as single transformations but can be effectively achieved through concatenation of simple transformations. Again for simplicity, we will work out an example in two-dimensions. A unit square, centered on $\{1 \quad 1\}^T$, and scaled using the transformation

$$\begin{bmatrix} 2 & 0 & 0 \\ 0 & 2 & 0 \\ 0 & 0 & 1 \end{bmatrix}$$

will have its center moved to $\{2 \quad 2\}^T$. A body-centered scaling is achieved by translating the center to the origin, scaling, and translating back:

$$\begin{bmatrix} 2 & 0 & -1 \\ 0 & 2 & -1 \\ 0 & 0 & 1 \end{bmatrix} = \begin{bmatrix} 1 & 0 & 1 \\ 0 & 1 & 1 \\ 0 & 0 & 1 \end{bmatrix} \begin{bmatrix} 2 & 0 & 0 \\ 0 & 2 & 0 \\ 0 & 0 & 1 \end{bmatrix} \begin{bmatrix} 1 & 0 & -1 \\ 0 & 1 & -1 \\ 0 & 0 & 1 \end{bmatrix}$$

Various notations can be developed to denote operation, axis, and amount. None has found universal use because each one is used only for conceptual discussion. In reality these are software operations. However, if $T(r_x, r_y)$ denotes a translation and $S(s_x, s_y)$ denotes a scale, then the net transformation can be written as

$$T_{net} = T(1, 1) \cdot S(2, 2) \cdot T(-1, -1)$$

In the preceding, translations have two components and hence, two parameters. An alternative form uses a subscript to denote the axis and a single parameter for the amount

$$T_{net} = T_y(1) \cdot T_x(1) \cdot S_x(2) \cdot S_y(2) \cdot T_y(-1) \cdot T_x(-1)$$

The sequence of primitive transformations is not unique. For example,

$$T_{net} = T(-1, -1) \cdot S(2, 2) \quad \text{or} \quad T_{net} = S(2, 2) \cdot T(-0.5, -0.5)$$

will achieve the same result. The reader should verify that the final matrix product is the same for either case.

Inverse transformations can be determined in two different ways. A sequence of individual "inverse" transformations can be constructed, carefully maintaining reverse order:

$$T(a, b)^{-1} = T(-a, -b) \quad \text{and} \quad S(a, b)^{-1} = S(1/a, 1/b)$$

To invert T_{net}, as given previously, use

$$T_{net}^{-1} = T(1, 1) \cdot S(0.5, 0.5) \cdot T(-1, -1)$$

Alternatively, the net matrix can be determined by matrix multiplication and then inverted:

$$\begin{bmatrix} 2 & 0 & -1 \\ 0 & 2 & -1 \\ 0 & 0 & 1 \end{bmatrix}^{-1} = \begin{bmatrix} 0.5 & 0 & 0.5 \\ 0 & 0.5 & 0.5 \\ 0 & 0 & 1 \end{bmatrix}$$

A similar strategy of concatenated transformations can be adopted to rotate an object about object-fixed reference frames; in other words, translate object reference frame to origin; rotate to align axis in question with one of basis axes in design space; rotate; undo axis rotation, and undo translation.

One of the important issues in computer graphics programming is how to combine the fundamental operations to achieve typical engineering operations. Graphics packages do not usually provide this variety of useful transformations. The following exercises are academically useful in two dimensions, but if solved in three dimensions, can lead to a useful set of procedures (toolsmithing).

■ **EXERCISE 7.1:** Develop a transformation matrix for rotation θ about an arbitrary axis, through the origin, denoted by a unit vector $\vec{n}$.

$$\vec{n} = \left\{ \begin{array}{c} n_1 \\ n_2 \\ n_3 \end{array} \right\}$$

Note that a vector $\vec{P}$ rotated to $\vec{P}^*$ is given by $\vec{P}^* = \vec{P} \cdot \vec{n}\vec{n} + (\vec{P} - \vec{P} \cdot \vec{n}\vec{n})\cos\theta + (\vec{n} \times \vec{P})\sin\theta$.

■ **EXERCISE 7.2:** Develop a transformation matrix for rotation about a basis axis ($\vec{n}_x$, $\vec{n}_y$, or $\vec{n}_z$) through an arbitrary point $\vec{r}$.

■ **EXERCISE 7.3:** Develop a transformation matrix for rotation about an arbitrary axis $\vec{n}$ through an arbitrary point $\vec{r}$.

■ **EXERCISE 7.4:** Develop a 2-D transformation matrix for a reflection through the y-axis (or in 3-D through the y-z plane).

■ **EXERCISE 7.5:** Develop a transformation matrix for reflection through an arbitrary plane in three-dimensional space. A plane can be specified in plane normal form as $ax + by + cz + d = 0$ where $\{a \quad b \quad c\}^T$ is a unit vector normal to the plane.

■ **EXERCISE 7.6:** Develop a transformation matrix for shear along an arbitrary plane in 3-D space.

■ **EXERCISE 7.7:** For which transformations are the angles preserved? For which transformations are the areas preserved? Which transformations are commutative?

■ **EXERCISE 7.8:** Show that a rotation is equivalent to a combination of scaling and shearing transformations.

■ **EXERCISE 7.9:** Develop the transformation matrix for a sequential series of three rotations Θ_X, Θ_Y, and Θ_Z about axes X, Y, and Z fixed in space.

■ **EXERCISE 7.10:** Develop transformations matrices for a sequential series of three rotations θ_x, θ_y, and θ_z about axes x, y, and z fixed in a body.

■ **EXERCISE 7.11:** Consider a body (possibly a cube) that has been rotated through angles θ_x, θ_y, and θ_z about axes x, y, and z fixed in the body. Now rotate the body an additional $\delta\theta_y$.

Perspective Transformations

Trying to achieve three-dimensional perception in two dimensions is not easy. The transformations that have been presented are not sufficient for projection because three-dimensional data remains three dimensional. Ultimately, a two-dimensional set of coordinates is required.

Traditional drafting has produced several standardized two-dimensional projections from three dimensions. The most simple is an *orthographic projection*. This is equivalent to ignoring the z coordinate. In orthographic projection, all points project along parallel lines onto the x, y projection plane (the screen). The standard top, front, and side views in drafting are orthographic projections. The common isometric view is also an orthographic projection looking down the line through the points $\{0 \quad 0 \quad 0\}^T$ and $\{1 \quad 1 \quad 1\}^T$. In passing, it is interesting to note that another family of projections ("oblique" projections) are generated when all points project along parallel lines that are not perpendicular to the projection plane. The cavalier and cabinet projections are members of this family. These projections were developed not only to provide a sense of depth, but also to use parallel lines, and thus, to be relatively easy to construct on a drawing board.

A more important projection is based on the perspective transformation. In a perspective projection, all projection lines converge on a single point. In computer graphics, the projection point is usually referred to as the eye location or camera location. If perspective projection is to be used efficiently, it must be implemented as a transformation based on a matrix multiplication. This requirement is the second reason for the use of the homogeneous coordinate. In all previous transformations, the final coordinate retained a value of 1.0. In perspective, it generally does not. Before display, the value of the final coordinate can be used to scale the homogeneous coordinates to produce the displayed coordinates:

$$\text{Given} \begin{Bmatrix} x \\ y \\ z \\ w \end{Bmatrix}, \qquad \begin{Bmatrix} x^* \\ y^* \\ z^* \end{Bmatrix} = \begin{Bmatrix} x/w \\ y/w \\ z/w \end{Bmatrix}$$

For clarity, we will begin by considering projection in two dimensions (x and z), as shown in Fig. 7.5, looking at the x axis from along the z axis. In this simple case the projection plane becomes a line. The orthographic and perspective projections are drawn. The eye location has been placed on the z axis at a distance d, and the projection plane is chosen as the line $x = 0$. Note that an orthographic projection just ignores the z value and

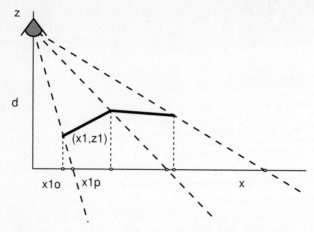

Figure 7.5 Orthographic and perspective projection in two dimensions.

that the projection lines are parallel. In the perspective projection, all lines pass through the eye (or camera). The projection line through a point x_1, z_1 can be parameterized as

$$z = (1 - t)d + tz_1$$
$$x = tx_1$$

The eye is at $t = 0$ and the point to be projected is at $t = 1$. The projected value will be $x(t_p)$, where $t_p = d/(d - z_1)$ is the value of t that is in the projection plane $y = 0$. Therefore $z_p = 0$ and

$$x_p = \frac{1}{1 - z_1/d} x_1$$

A transformation matrix that produced a homogeneous coordinate of $1 - z_1/d$ would then give the correct value after the final division described above. The transformation matrix in this case would be

$$\left\{ \begin{matrix} x \\ z \\ w \end{matrix} \right\} = \left\{ \begin{matrix} x_1 \\ 0 \\ 1 - z_1/d \end{matrix} \right\} = \begin{bmatrix} 1 & 0 & 0 \\ 0 & 0 & 0 \\ 0 & -1/d & 1 \end{bmatrix} \left\{ \begin{matrix} x_1 \\ z_1 \\ 1 \end{matrix} \right\}$$

The generalization to three dimensions is straightforward. The y component is projected using the same homogeneous coordinate:

$$\left\{ \begin{matrix} x \\ y \\ z \\ w \end{matrix} \right\} = \begin{bmatrix} 1 & 0 & 0 & 0 \\ 0 & 1 & 0 & 0 \\ 0 & 0 & 0 & 0 \\ 0 & 0 & -1/d & 1 \end{bmatrix} \left\{ \begin{matrix} x_1 \\ y_1 \\ z_1 \\ 1 \end{matrix} \right\}$$

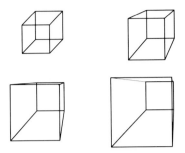

Figure 7.6   Varying perspectives.

The foreshortening perspective is controlled by relative distances between the eye, the data points, and the projection plane. Figure 7.6 shows a cube with unit length sides with various amounts of perspective.

Theoretically, the projection plane is unbounded. Because the screen is limited, projections are usually clipped to a rectangular window in the projection plane. The window can be specified in several ways. A common way is (x_{left}, y_{bottom}) and (x_{right}, y_{top}). In actuality, this is a six-sided volume as shown in Fig. 7.7, the faces of which are usually referred to as the left, right, top, bottom, hither, and yon planes. These form the *frustrum of vision*. The topic of clipping is a specialty topic for computer graphics implementations. It is sufficient now to assume that objects can be clipped to the boundaries of the frustrum of vision.

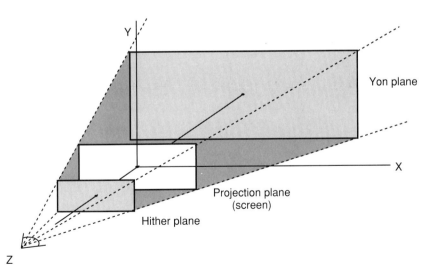

Figure 7.7   Frustrum of vision.

Finally, the rectangular window into design space must be mapped onto a region of the screen that is usually referred to as the viewport. Viewports are usually specified by corner locations or by one corner and length/width. Viewport corners are usually specified in screen coordinates, either [0,1] floating-point normalized device coordinates (NDC) or integer pixel numbers. The reader should note that a window can be distorted by mapping to a viewport with a different aspect ratio. As a result, a circle in design space may not appear as a circle. Also, left-to-right and top-to-bottom reflections are possible, given poorly specified viewports. Consider the following window and viewport combinations:

Window		Viewport	
(−30.0, −30.0)	(50.0, 50.0)	(0.2, 0.2)	(0.5, 0.5)
(−30.0, −30.0)	(50.0, 50.0)	(0.2, 0.2)	(0.5, 1.0)
(−30.0, −30.0)	(50.0, 50.0)	(0.5, 0.5)	(0.2, 0.2)
(50.0, 50.0)	(−30.0, −30.0)	(0.2, 0.2)	(0.5, 0.5)

The process of going from design space coordinates to screen coordinates is a series of transformations and operations. The total flow of data manipulation is shown in Table 7.1. The overall sequence is as follows:

1. The object's geometry is defined in convenient 3-D local coordinates. Although it is usually thought of as cartesian, this local reference frame geometry could be cylindrical or spherical. Within a work cell simulation

Transformation	Coordinates	Reference Frame
	x_i, y_i, z_i	Object
Modeling	↓	
	x, y, z	Design Space
Viewing	↓	
	x_c, y_c, z_c	Camera
Window	↓	
Clip	↓	
Perspective	↓	
	ξ, η	View Plane
Viewport	↓	
		Image Space
	ξ, η	Normalized Device Coordinates
		Screen Space
	↓	
	ξ, η	Device Coordinates

Table 7.1 Graphic display pipeline.

this object could be an individual segment of a robot arm or the work piece or the workbench.

2. Transformations such as scale, translate, and rotate are used to assemble in 3-D design space. This is the collection of the individual parts into a global reference frame. For the work cell example, this is fixed in the room.

3. The viewing transformation maps to the camera reference frame, which determines the point from where design space is viewed. This camera location may need to change if the user wants to see the scene from another side. Alternatively, the camera could be fixed to the gripper or paint sprayer on a robot arm.

4. Clipping to the frustrum of vision limits the display to a window in camera space. This transformation contains the parameters of the lens or viewfinder of the camera.

5. Perspective transformation maps to the viewplane of camera (projection plane). This also represents the camera lens.

6. Viewport parameters lead to a mapping to the rectangular subsection of screen.

7. Coordinates are converted from float to integer.

8. Finally, the device driver produces the correct specific bit pattern.

Most graphics packages protect the user from details such as the location of the projection plane. In a typical situation the user can specify a camera location, a viewing direction, distances to the hither and yon planes along the viewing direction, and some measure of the angle of the frustrum of vision (usually corners of the window). The graphics package will then determine the appropriate collection of transformation matrices that concatenate to produce the final results.

Viewing (camera position and orientation) can be specified in several ways. The most comprehensive is based on location and direction as shown in Fig. 7.8. This method represents viewing as a bound vector requiring six numbers. Alternatively, the view can be assumed to be facing the origin and specified in spherical coordinates (two angles and a radius). This positioning specification is used by many visualization programs because the data can be placed at the origin. But spherical camera positioning is too limiting for CAD work. Note that the rotation angle about the view direction or eye vector $\vec{n}_{zc}$ can orient the "horizon" on the screen. In some viewing situations, a nonzero value may be useful.

Some graphics packages do not allow for a movable camera. Instead, the camera is fixed looking down the z axis in the negative direction. In such a system, movement of the camera is effectively achieved by transforming the entire "world." For example, a rotation of camera orientation of $10°\vec{n}_x$ is equivalent to a rotation of the world of $-10°\vec{n}_x$ passing through the camera

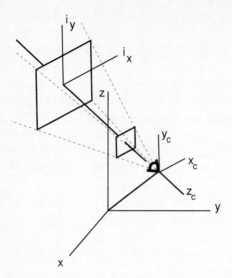

Figure 7.8 Camera positioning.

location. As discussed previously, this generally will require additional translations to implement. For example, if the camera is at $\{2 \quad 3 \quad 7\}^{\mathrm{T}}$, a "world" translation of $\{-2 \quad -3 \quad -7\}^{\mathrm{T}}$ causes later rotations to be relative to the camera position, not to the "world" origin.

Coordinate Systems

Engineers universally work in a right-handed coordinate system in which $\vec{n}_x \times \vec{n}_y = \vec{n}_z$. All of the material in this book is presented in a right-handed coordinate system; all commercial CAD/CAM systems use a right-handed coordinate system. However, computer graphics began by using a left-handed coordinate system, the x-axis being horizontal on the screen positive to the right, the y-axis being vertical on the screen positive up, and the z-axis being perpendicular to the screen and positive into the screen. The x, y definitions were natural. Positive z depth seemed to be naturally along the eye vector away from the eye, into the screen. Unfortunately, this led to a left-handed system. Most high-level graphics packages now use the standard right-handed reference system. However, the student is cautioned that lefthanded systems are still lurking about. Obviously, the transformation matrices for the preceding manipulations in a coordinate system of one sense are not necessarily valid for a coordinate system of the opposite sense. Scales and translations are correct, but rotations can differ in the sign of the sine terms, depending on the definition of positive rotation in a left-handed reference frame.

Also, conventions differ as to whether a point in homogeneous coordinates is written as

$$\begin{Bmatrix} x \\ y \\ z \\ w \end{Bmatrix} \quad \text{or} \quad \{ x \quad y \quad z \quad w \}$$

The only differences between row/column transformation formulations are transposition of the matrices and a reversal in the multiplication order from premultiplication to postmultiplication. Given the variety of conventions, students should avoid lifting a specific transformation matrix from a source and using it without further investigation.

7.5 STRUCTURE

A typical image may have literally thousands of points that must be transformed from several object spaces to screen space. Several matrices (from ten to one hundred) are ultimately involved in the transformation. It would not be efficient to repeat the separate matrix multiplications over and over. Most graphics packages will concatenate the transformation stream once, reducing the level of effort to a single 4×4 multiplication for each point. However, the original set of matrices must also be retained, because a modification of the scene (such as a rotation of an object about its local x-axis) will change a single transformation matrix within the overall collection of matrices. The transformations therefore have attributes of data (such as addressable, modifiable, and editable) and attributes of code (such as procedural interpretation, order dependence, etc.). We will study the structure that has developed for common use by discussing the evolutionary process by which it evolved.

At the most fundamental level of graphics processing is the "escape code." The first graphics devices worked through traditional digital/analog converters, as shown in Fig. 7.9; however, it quickly became common to use the standard ASCII terminal interface to communicate between the computer

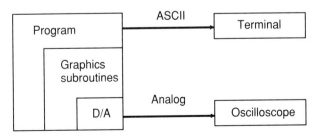

Figure 7.9 A primitive graphics configuration.

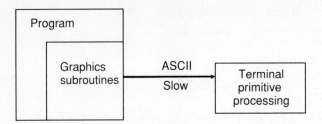

Figure 7.10   A common early graphics configuration.

and the graphics device, as shown in Fig. 7.10. The mainframe-terminal configuration was highly standardized at that time, and so it was important to avoid either a direct connection to the computer data bus or the requirement for a second terminal line for the graphics output. So-called intelligent terminals were developed that could divert the ASCII data stream from the terminal screen and use the alphanumeric information as graphics commands. In almost all cases, the command to divert began with the ASCII "escape" character.

For example, the data stream esc [H 10 , 20 ; would mean: Divert data stream, move cursor to screen coordinates ($x = 10$, $y = 20$), and end diversion. Alternatively, esc; might clear the graphics screen.

The function of the graphics device driver was to take floating-point screen locations; convert them to integer device locations; determine the correct "op code," assemble the escape sequence, and write it to the graphics device. Such a package could be written in a high-level language such as FORTRAN, given a knowledge of the ASCII character set and how to generate those characters in a FORTRAN WRITE operation. Because similar packages form the basis for all PLOT-10 compatible codes, it is worth considering how such a package might have been implemented.

A high-level graphics support package can be built upon subroutines designed to clear the screen, to set a matrix transform, to move to floating-point coordinates, and to draw to floating-point coordinates. Assume a device for which sequences begin with esc and terminate with ; and [H is the escape code for move and [J is the code for draw. This represents a pen plotter or storage tube display in which moves or draws are made from the current pen location. Furthermore, the following code assumes that graphics_unit is appropriately defined and assigned. Note that the transform is stored in a named common block and not passed through the argument list. A FORTRAN version of the move procedure is

```
subroutine move(x, y, z)

    real*4 x,y,z,a,b,c

    integer ix, iy

    common/transforms/tform
```

```
        call vector_matrix_multiply(x, y, z, tform, a, b, c)
        ix = fix(a)
        iy = fix(b)
        write (graphics_unit) esc,'[H', ix, iy,';'
    return
```

A simple draw procedure is

```
subroutine draw(x, y, z)
    real*4 x,y,a,b,c
    integer ix, iy
    common/transforms/tform
        call vector_matrix_multiply(x, y, z, tform, a, b, c)
        ix = fix(a)
        iy = fix(b)
        write (graphics_unit) esc,'[J', ix, iy,';'
    return
```

The process of generating a translation involves formation of the appropriate transformation matrix and then concatenation with the current transformation matrix:

```
subroutine set_translate (dx, dy, dz)
    real*4 dx, dy, dz
    real*4 tform(4, 4), temp(4, 4), product(4, 4)
    common/transforms/tform
        do i = 1, 4
            do j = 1, 4
                temp(i, j) = 0.0
            enddo
            temp(i, i) = 1.0
        enddo
        temp(1, 4) = dx; temp(2, 4) = dy; temp(3, 4)=dz
    call matrix_concat (temp, tform)
    return
```

The preceding subroutines assume the existence of useful matrix manipulation routines such as vector_matrix_multiply or matrix_concat. Note that these routines will not be general purpose but specifically designed for the 4 × 4 matrices.

```
subroutine matrix_concat (a, b)
    real*4 a(4, 4), b(4, 4), c(4, 4), sum
    integer i, j, k
        do i = 1, 4
            do j = 1, 4
                sum = 0.0
                do k = 1,4
                    sum = sum + a(i, k)*b(k, j)
                enddo
                c(i, j) = sum
            enddo
        enddo
        do i = 1, 4
            do j = 1, 4
                b(i, j) = c(i, j)
            enddo
        enddo
        return
```

Applying a rotation to the global transformation matrix could result in the following:

```
subroutine set_rotate (axis, theta)
    real*4 theta, temp(4, 4),tform(4, 4)
    character axis
    common/transforms/tform
        do i = 1, 4
            do j = 1, 4
                temp(i, j) = 0.0
```

```
        enddo
    enddo
    if (axis = 'x') then
        temp(2, 2) = cos(theta); temp(2, 3) = sin(theta)
        temp(3, 2) = -sin(theta); temp(3, 3) = cos(theta)
        temp(1, 1)= 1    ; temp(4, 4) = 1
    else if (axis = 'y') then
        temp(1, 1) = cos(theta); temp(1, 3) = sin(theta)
        temp(3, 1) = -sin(theta); temp(3, 3) = cos(theta)
        temp(2, 2) = 1   ; temp(4, 4) = 1
    else if (axis = 'z') then
        temp(1, 1) = cos(theta); temp(1, 2) = sin(theta)
        temp(2, 1) - -sin(theta); tcmp(2, 2) - cos(theta)
        temp(3, 3) = 1   ; temp(4, 4) = 1
    endif
    call matrix_concat (temp, tform)
    return
```

To draw a rectangle and then clear the screen and redraw it at a 45°
angle could be accomplished by

```
call screen_clear
call set_rotate('z', 0.0)
call move (0.0, 0.0, 0.0)
call draw (1.0, 0.0, 0.0)
call draw (1.0, 1.0, 0.0)
call draw (0.0, 1.0, 0.0)
call draw (0.0, 0.0, 0.0)

 .  .  .  .  .  .

call screen_clear
call set_rotate('z', pi/4.0)
call move (0.0, 0.0, 0.0)
```

```
call draw (1.0, 0.0, 0.0)

call draw (1.0, 1.0, 0.0)

call draw (0.0, 1.0, 0.0)

call draw (0.0, 0.0, 0.0)
```

Note that only one rectangle will appear on the screen at any given instant in time.

The reader should visualize the stream of ASCII character data that the preceding code generates. If we simplify the escape codes to clear C; move M, draw D, and drop the ; delimiters, then the data stream read from left to right is

C M 0 0 D 1 0 D 1 1 D 0 1 D 0 0 C M 0 0 D 0 1 D -1 1 D

-1 0 D 0 0

Note that for simplicity, actual integer screen coordinates (e.g., 0–1,024) have not been generated.

There is a definite structure to the data stream. Certain groups of characters are needed when drawing the box. Note that the specific character sequence for the box segments will be different because the box will have different screen coordinates in each case. This occurs because the matrix multiplications occur in the computer and not the terminal, as shown in Fig. 7.10. In a more complex picture, if only the square moved, then the bulk of the character stream representing the remainder of the image would not change.

The section of the data stream between screen clearings is referred to as the display list. Much of the research in computer graphics has been aimed at the structure of this display list and at transferring functions from the main computer processor to peripheral graphics processors. The programmer must view the display list simultaneously as both data and program: As data, the display list represents the information in the ultimate screen image and is generated by the user's program. As programming, it provides commands (escape sequences) for a programmable device, in this case, the dumb terminal. Intelligent terminals simply have a richer programming language (a wider set of escape sequences).

The next step in the evolutionary sequence was the development of the intelligent terminal, (see Fig. 7.11). The configuration of an intelligent terminal was generally characterized by a high-speed interface that allowed a rapid transfer of an entire display list, a transfer so rapid that it could be viewed as a parallel transfer. Then the intelligent terminal would traverse the display list and produce the image on the screen. This process might involve a rasterization of the point/line data. But the actual assembly of the display list was the function of the graphics package. Of course, always completely transferring the entire display list was too inefficient. Actual implementa-

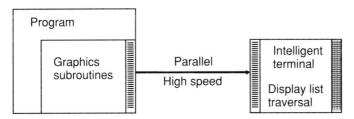

Figure 7.11   Intelligent terminal configuration.

tions transferred only data changes, in effect allowing the graphics package to "edit" the display list. This is yet another example of display list as a program.

Given this configuration, it was relatively easy to locate a general purpose CPU chip in the intelligent terminal and have the matrix multiplications for transformations, perspective, and clipping occur in the terminal, reducing the load on the main computer processor. Ways to structure the display list to represent this efficiently will be discussed later in this section. Conceptually, the escape codes are expanded to include functions such as

- Translate
- Rotate
- Scale
- Set color
- Set line type

Advances in VLSI design and fabrication have allowed for customized chips. A general-purpose CPU is not needed for the matrix multiplication, which can be done now with geometric processing chips. Other chips can be, and in some cases have been, developed for curved surface evaluation, color shading, and so forth. In all cases, this is simply a further enrichment of the command repertoire of the graphics device.

The advent of the workstation has removed the need for two copies of the display list. The special-purpose chips can now access the main memory of the workstation, and only a single copy of the display list is required, as shown in Fig. 7.12.

If the display list is viewed as a program, then the graphics support processing package can be viewed as a stand-alone process, the output of which is itself a program. This paradigm will be useful now in the following discussion of the display list and its structure.

Looking back at the sample program for generating the square, it is immediately obvious that the move/draw calls for the box should be localized to a procedure call and not repeated. This logical grouping of geometric

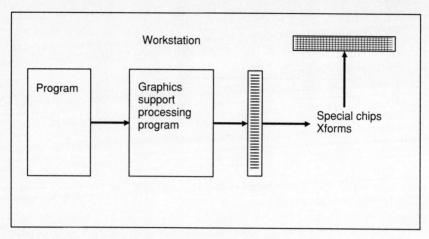

Figure 7.12 Workstation configuration.

entities is known as "segmentation." Various alternative data structures exist and will be discussed later; however, for now let us collect the move/draw calls into a subroutine called square:

```
subroutine square(a, b)
/* unit square with corner at a,b */
    real*4 a, b
    call move(a, b, 0.0)
    call draw(a + 1.0, b, 0.0)
    call draw(a + 1.0, b + 1.0, 0.0)
    call draw(a, b + 1.0, 0.0)
    call draw(a, b, 0.0)
    return
```

The main scrap of code now becomes

```
call screen_clear
call set_rotate('z', 0.0)
call square (1.0, 1.0)

. . . . . . .

call screen_clear
call set_rotate('z', pi/4.0)
call square(1.0, 1.0)
```

A rotating square is produced by

```
do while (true)
    call screen_clear
    call set_rotate('z', dtheta)
    call square(1.0, 1.0)
    enddo
```

Now consider the situation if several picture segments are involved. For simplicity, let us continue to limit ourselves to unit squares. The data stream between *screen clear* commands will have segments, each identifiable with an individual square. If a single square were to be transformed (translated, rotated, etc.), then the screen coordinates of all other squares would stay constant and not have to be transformed. However, in the example only a single transformation matrix has been maintained. Therefore, all move/draw coordinates downstream will be affected, which can be described as "stream of consciousness" display-list processing. A characteristic of this free-form display list is that transforms can be located arbitrarily. Similarly, the change of an attribute such as line color can be arbitrarily located, and that alteration is inherited throughout the rest of the display list until explicitly changed.

Structure is required for graphics data just as it is for programming languages. Program structures include procedures, loops, and branching. Currently, almost no graphics support packages implement loops or branching in the display list. However, these packages do include procedures that are useful for localizing variables such as the transformation or attributes such as color or line types.

Segmentation also allows for subroutine execution. A segment such as the square may be used (called) in other segments. In general, graphics packages have not implemented procedure calls with arguments. The segments have no variables that receive values at the time of calling. Attributes such as color, line style, and transformation matrix are inherited in the segments at calling and thus will change for different instantiations. This is analogous to a subroutine with no arguments but a set of common blocks to pass data. The scale of the square cannot be adjusted in the display list by a parameter as in the subroutine square; however, this can be achieved effectively by applying a transform to the segment.

The display list for a set of various scale squares is

```
set_scale(1.2)
square
set_scale(1.5)
square
```

```
set_scale(2.0)
```

```
square
```

This is similar to a program such as

```
call square(1.2, 1.2)
```

```
call square(1.8, 1.8)
```

```
call square(3.6, 3.6)
```

It is important to note a subtle difference. In the first case, the raw coordinates of the square remain at (0, 0), (1, 0), (1, 1), and (0, 1), and the square appears on the screen at different sizes because of matrix multiplications. In the second case, the arguments of the move and draw commands are different for each square.

Like general-purpose languages, display list languages do not require a GOTO statement. The concept of the label is useful in some cases, and some graphics packages will support the insertion of labels into the display list. These are almost always used for delete/replace operations, such as replacing a section of the display list between two labels with an alternative. However, if the graphics support package can efficiently handle many layers of segmentation, label capability is not necessary. Sections that might need to be replaced (and therefore need labels) can be localized to separate segments.

Viewing the display list as a program also highlights the command language aspects of attribute assignment. Line color is determined by a procedure such as set_line_color instead of requiring the programmer to refer to the actual data structure and memory location of the line color for the current segment. The programmer does not have to create many transformation matrices and remember what each one is storing. Most importantly, the programmer is relieved from the onerous task of memory management for a segmented display list with a constantly changing length.

If the display list is a program, then a good graphics support package must provide fundamental editing capability. At a minimum this will include the creation, deletion, and replacement of segments. If labels are not supported, then operations internal to a segment are not allowed and the preceding three functions are sufficient for all needs.

Before moving on to other topics, it is worth describing how the display list can be viewed as a data structure. Specifically, it is a tree or directed graph without loops. Each node of the tree represents a segment (a list of executable statements including subroutine calls). All attributes, including transformations, inherit downward from the root node. Attributes can be set on the edges of the graph and applied to all nodes below in the structure. However, attributes and transformations cannot be set within a node. Each segment is addressable by a name that traces its path from the root node, which is exactly analogous to the pathname for a file in a hierarchical file system. Implementation of data structures is discussed in Chapter 10.

Consider a primitive graphics terminal with the op codes given in Table 7.2. (Note that for simplicity, the escape signal and delimiter are not included.) The command sequence generated by the device driver for the example with the unit squares would be

```
C M 0 0 0 0 D 1 0 0 D 1 1 0 D 0 1 0 D 0 0 0 C Z 0.78589

M 0 0 0 D 1 0 0

D 1 1 0 D 0 1 0 D 0 0 0 E
```

Utilizing the subroutine concept, the display list for a rotating square in the previous example becomes a collection of programs. In the following example, the first word of each segment is the name of the segment used in procedural calls:

```
1 C S 2 C Z 0.78539 S 2 E

2 M 0 0 0 D 1 0 D 1 1 D 0 1 D 0 0 E

3 M 0 0 0 D 1 0 D 0 1 D 0 0 E
```

Note how easily the square (segment 2) can be replaced with the triangle (segment 3) by changing the target of the subroutine call in the main display list. The editing of these short programs is the editing capability provided by the graphics support package. It is important to note that the programmer is (unfortunately) never allowed to see the display list written as above. The programmer must infer the order and contents of the display list from the results seen on the graphics screen. Debugging of graphical programs would be much easier if the programmer had access to a "program listing."

The key to interactive dynamic graphics is the ability to make small changes in a complex display list or graphics structure that is then processed locally using customized hardware. The structuring of the display data is as vital to graphics as the structuring of procedures is to programming. Figure 7.13 outlines the hierarchical display structure for a multiengine transport; Fig. 7.14 shows each segment. Note that the most primitive segments (blade, nacelle, airfoil) have been drawn very simply because the level of detail does not affect the fundamental concept of hierarchical structure.

C	Clear Screen
D	Draw
M	Move
Z	Rotate about z Axis
S	Subroutine Call
E	End

Table 7.2 Simple graphics codes.

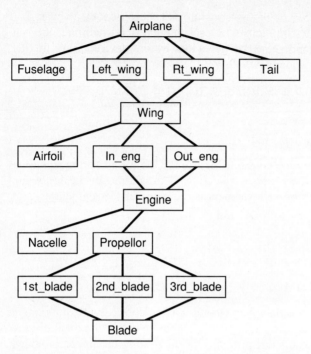

Figure 7.13 Hierarchial display list for an airplane.

7.6 THREE-DIMENSIONAL ENHANCEMENT

Several techniques can enhance the three-dimensionality of the display. The most effective technique, "kinetic depth," is the ability to dynamically rotate the image. If the user has control of the motion (direction and speed), then a three-dimensional effect will be clear, even with very sketchy graphics. A cloud of points that lie on the surface of a complex shape, such as a yacht hull or a human femur, can be confusing as a static image. But if the user is given interactive control of the real-time motion of the display, the three-dimensionality is striking.

Perspective is also more effective in a dynamic situation, when either translation or rotation of the data causes the perspective to change. The user obtains three-dimensional cues by comparing two images, just as a person would look at an object from two angles, even though the angles are almost the same. However, perspective must be used sparingly. Most engineers actually tend to prefer orthographic projections, and extreme amounts of perspective are confusing because of the distortion.

For line images, *intensity depth cueing* is a useful technique. The brightness of a line is adjusted by its z depth into the screen. Note that this introduces the z axis in screen coordinates. Lines of a constant z will have constant brightness. Those closer to the viewer (the hither plane) will be

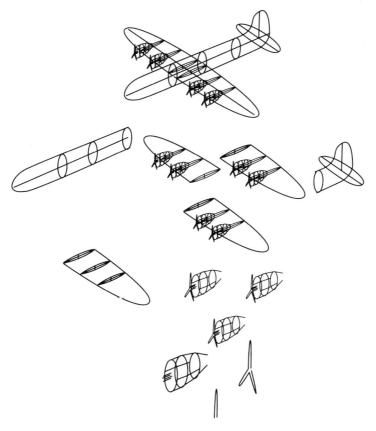

Figure 7.14 An airplane and its subsegments.

brighter, and this brightness will decrease for lines farther away. A line whose endpoints do not have the same z value will therefore have varying brightness along its length. In almost all cases, this variation is linear. Developers using depth cueing will need to consider how to specify the brightness variation with depth. Even if it is linear, at least two breakpoints could be specified, as in Fig. 7.15. It is unlikely that anything less than maximum brightness would be appropriate for the hither plane. However, minimum brightness at the yon plane is, in most cases, too low. This amount of dynamic range in brightness results in an image that appears to be murky or shrouded in dense fog. But the full range of brightness is useful for images in which the yon plane is realistically far away, as in civil engineering or architectural applications such as bridges and refineries. However, for most mechanical situations the objects are smaller, and depth cueing does not enhance the image.

It should be noted that the programmer is usually not given complete freedom of the functions shown in Fig. 7.15. In most cases, the user is

Brightness vs z depth

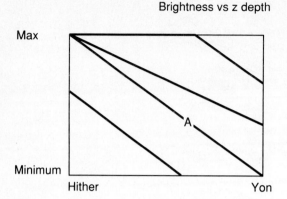

Figure 7.15 Alternative depth cueing functions.

limited to the fundamental depth cueing of curve A in Fig. 7.15. This makes the selection of the location of the hither and yon planes more critical. In addition to providing for clipping in the z direction, these planes also would control the depth cueing intensity. Most mechanical engineering applications can be handled satisfactorily by using the hither plane for clipping objects (clipping at the front of the screen) and using the yon plane location to control the dimness the back parts of the display. The yon plane should be so far away that it never clips objects. As far as the user is concerned, parts of the object that "protrude out of the screen" are not seen.

Under user control, hither and yon clipping can be extremely useful in producing an understandable image that is usable in an interactive environment. The ability to select lines or points with the cursor may require removing many other lines that seem to overlay the target (from a specific viewpoint). Hither and yon clipping is very effective for this. However, the engineer will not want intensity depth cueing as a yon plane is shifted to remove parts of the scene. This is one reason that intensity depth cueing is no longer extensively used; an additional reason is that color shading techniques have become more widespread. The topic of the "z-buffer," described in Section 7.9, is related to depth cueing.

7.7 COLOR TECHNIQUES

Ultimately, an image on the graphics screen is composed of either lines or filled regions of pixels. These entities can have various attributes, one of which (brightness) has already been discussed. In a graphics system with depth cueing, the z depth at which the entities are drawn is sometimes the only control over brightness. Other attributes of lines are line width and line type. Most graphics devices have hardware implementations for line width and type, and so these characteristics are easily handled by graphics packages. The final attribute for lines is color, and areas may have uniform or varying color that falls under the topics of shading and texturing. Flat shading uses a single color for the area; more advanced shading techniques produce smooth variations across the area. High-frequency (short period) variations can be used to produce textured effects.

Color can be specified in many ways, and each has been used by some graphics package. In discussing computer graphics color schemes, it is important to recognize that while the hardware implementations are fundamentally additive, the schemes used by artists, as well as those taught in grade school and high school, are subtractive. Display screen color (CRT) is fundamentally an additive process because direct light is used, whereas printing is a subtractive process based on dyes and reflected light. If the light sources of all colors are mixed together, the result will be white; as opposed to the situation with oil paints, where mixing all colors together results in "mud" (an approximation to black).

Physically, color monitors produce mixtures of red, green, and blue light on the screen. Sometimes there are three separate electron guns, but at other times sophisticated mask technology can be used. In any case, the hardware specification for any color is ultimately an RGB (red, green, blue) triplet. Conceivably, each component could be over the range [0.0, 1.0], but the digital nature of computing leads to an integer specification over the range [0, 256], or eight bits of color for each component and 24 bits of color overall. The range of eight is chosen because of the resolution of the human eye. If a series of filled rectangles are drawn with grey shading values of uniform increments, the stair-step nature of the brightness will not be noticeable if at least 256 levels are used. In fact, the range will look reasonably smooth at 128 levels, as shown by Fig. 7.16.[1]

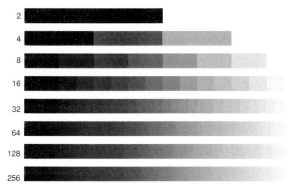

Figure 7.16   Grey shading at different resolutions.

---

[1]This figure was generated by Adobe Illustrator using programmed blends from black to white. However, the appearance is also affected by the rasterizing, typesetting, and printing steps.

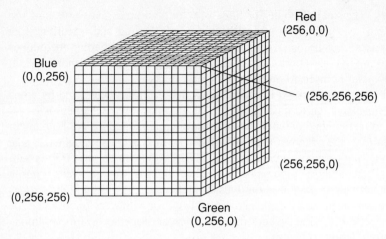

Figure 7.17   Color cube in red, blue, and green.

If color has three components, then all possible colors resolvable by the human eye can be displayed in a color cube, as shown in Fig. 7.17. A 24-bit color system provides 2^{24} or more than 16.7 million colors. A raster graphics display with a screen resolution of 1,280 by 1,024 has a total of about 1.3 million pixels. The palette has enough colors to assign a unique color to each pixel.

Effectively, a graphics display must provide a memory location for each pixel on the screen. If the screen is pure black and white, then only one bit is required, whereas for a 24-bit color display, 31.2 megabits or 3.9 megabytes will be required for screen memory. This voracious appetite for memory is why many graphics devices do not provide a full 24 bits for each pixel. Rather, a limited palette is used, and a color map (video lookup table) stores the correlation between integer pixel values and 24-bit RGB color.

For example, consider a system with four bits for each pixel. Although this system can display 16 different colors, each of the 16 can be a full RGB triplet. Sixteen colors can be useful for line drawings, but the dynamic range here is not sufficient for color shading.

On the other hand, a system with an eight-bit color display has enough range to provide an excellent monchrome image (remember Fig. 7.16). Since 128 shades appear to be fairly smooth, an eight-bit display can show two different colors with smooth variations. A common hardware implementation is a 10-bit palette (1,024 colors), which provides smooth shading for several colors simultaneously. Figure 7.18 shows how a color number in a location in screen memory becomes a colored pixel on the screen.

By now the reader should be aware that color control will probably be indirect. In many cases, the programmer must specify color attributes for objects by palette color number and separately specify how the palette is to be loaded. A common technique reserves one end of the palette for specific colors that are to be used (for example, on a menu, highlighting, etc.). Then,

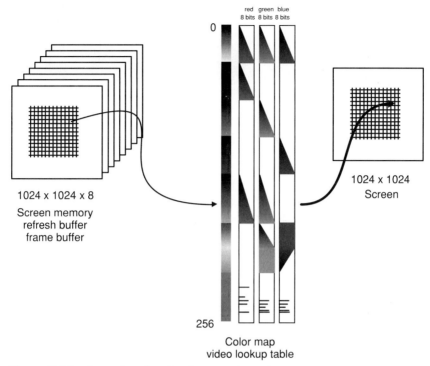

red green blue
8 bits 8 bits 8 bits

0

256

1024 x 1024 x 8

Screen memory
refresh buffer
frame buffer

1024 x 1024
Screen

Color map
video lookup table

Figure 7.18   A workstation implementation of
a 10-bit by 24-bit color map.

the programmer provides ranges of the palette that are loaded with uniformly
varying color, as shown in Fig. 7.19. This color map reserves some palette
slots for specific colors and then provides a grey scale, a monochrome red,
a monochrome green, a monochrome blue, a monochrome blue-green scale,
and a red-to-green spectrum.

Note that in the red-green spectrum, the red is held to full value for
half range, and the green is held to value for the other half range. The
alternative, a straightforward decrease in red and increase in green, leads to
reduced intensity in the midrange.

Color

Many different theories for color have been presented. Physicists and engineers usually trace color research back to Newton's experiments with prisms
and to work by British physicist David Brewster in 1831, who showed that
the three primary colors are red, yellow, and blue.

Color theories can be divided into additive and subtractive categories.
The former is applicable to direct light, such as that seen from a graphic
display. The latter is applicable to reflected light, such as sunlight from a

Figure 7.19   A 10-bit by 24-bit color map.

printed page, and pigment mixing. Both systems agree upon the fundamental three-dimensionality of color space; however, their differences center on the metric to be used to locate individual colors in that space. For example, the color cube in Fig. 7.17 is an imposition of a cartesian metric. In an additive system, mixing full red, green, and blue leads to white. In a subtractive system, a mixture of full red, green, and blue leads to black. The subtractive color cube was devised by Alfred Hickethier. Printers often use a subtractive color cube based on cyan, yellow, and magenta (CYM).

Artists and designers often prefer the hue-lightness-saturation (HLS) system credited to Wilhelm Ostwald. Hue is periodic around the color wheel $[0, 2\pi]$, and lightness and saturation span the range $[0, 1]$. Therefore an HLS triplet can be viewed as coordinates in a cylinder. The lightness varies along the vertical axis and the saturation changes from grey to pure color with radial distance from the axis. Because the ends of the cylinder are black or white, the HLS system is sometimes presented as a double cone, as shown in Fig. 7.20. An advantage of the HLS system is that the total luminence or lightness can be kept constant while varying the hue, which is not easily done in cartesian RGB space. This advantage is useful for pseudo-color shading of scalar distributions. The need for shading scalar distributions will be discussed in Chapter 8. Various 2-D representations are possible. One common approach includes the vertical axis and a diameter of the color wheel, which yields a rhombus shape with white at the top, black at the bottom, and complementary colors on each side. Alternatively, a plane

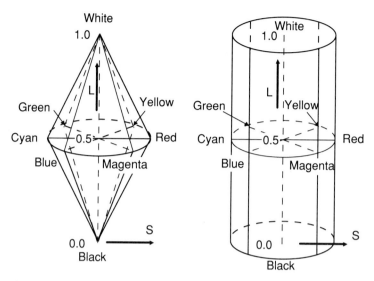

Figure 7.20   HLS double cone and cylinder.

perpendicular to the vertical axis will produce a circular cut of constant lightness and varying hue and saturation.

Munsell proposed a sphere (hue, value, chroma) similar to the double cone of Ostwald. In this scheme, the north pole is white, the south pole is black, and the equator is a color wheel with full saturation (or chroma). Munsell's scheme is seldom used.

A representation similar to HLS is the hue-saturation-value (HSV) system. This triplet has values $[0, 2\pi]$, $[0, 1]$, $[0, 1]$, as shown in Fig. 7.21. The

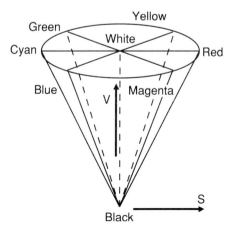

Figure 7.21   HSV color cone.

axis of either the HSV or HLS system corresponds to the gray diagonal of the RGB cube.

Different colors of equal luminosity will be indistinguishable in a black and white photo. The terms lightness and value are also used to describe this characteristic. However, luminosity as sensed to the human eye is color dependent: Yellow is most bright and violet is least bright. This can cause some distortion between pictures rendered in monochrome grey and the same images in the original color. These differences are important in generation of photo-realistic images but are of much less importance for CAD.

Saturation and intensity describe the absolute purity of a color. Although a pure color mixed with white or black will not change its hue, it will vary in saturation and lightness. A pure color mixed with a grey of the same lightness will only vary in saturation.

Consider the need to display a smooth spectrum of color between two values. This requirement occurs in shading of objects; but, as we will see in Chapter 8, Visualization, the extra dimensions provided by color are often used to represent quantitative conformations such as temperature, pressure, density, and so on.

The anchor points for the spectrum can be specified in any color notation. For example, consider interpolation from red to green. Table 7.3 lists the coordinates for both colors and their midpoints. Depending on the endpoints and reference frame, the interpolated spectrum will be different. Note that interpolation is not a straight line in HSV or HLS space because the fundamental basis is not cartesian. In most cases, this is only relevant to the generation of photo-realistic images, although it is one reason why data may appear different when displayed with different graphics packages.

No matter what color notation is used, a single color spectrum is analogous to the 3-D space curve discussed in Chapter 2 and Chapter 9. A two-dimensional spectrum is a surface, and surface representations will be discussed in Chapter 9. Color Plate 5 shows a spectrum between red, green, blue, and white generated as follows: A linear interpolation was made between red and blue and between green and white (16 steps). This step provides the horizontal top and bottom edges of the square in Color Plate 5. Linear "vertical" interpolation was used to fill in the interior of the square. This process a "bilinear" interpolation, which will be discussed in Chapter 9.

	Red	Median	Green
RGB	$\{1, 0, 0\}$	$\{0.5, 0.5, 0\}$	$\{0, 1, 0\}$
HLS	$\{0°, 1, 0.5\}$	$\{60°, 1, 0.5\}$	$\{120°, 1, 0.5\}$
HSV	$\{0°, 1, 1.0\}$	$\{60°, 1, 1.0\}$	$\{120°, 1, 1.0\}$

Table 7.3 Interpolated colors.

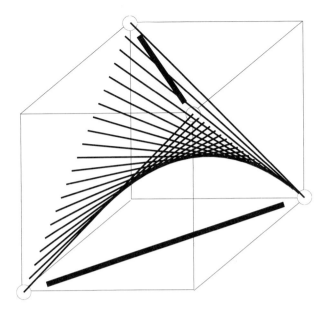

Figure 7.22   Bilinear interpolation in RGB associated with Color Plate 6.

It creates a "surface" in RGB space as shown in Fig. 7.22. The four corners of the "surface patch" are shown with the "vertical" interpolations.

Note that although the edges of the rectangle all lie on the faces of the RGB cube, the interior does not. This means that the diagonals will not lie on the faces of the RGB cube. The true linear interpolations between corners are also drawn in Fig. 7.22. Color Plate 5 shows the colors taken from the diagonals alongside a straightforward "linear" interpolation between the corner colors. The "sagging" toward grey can be seen.

Engineering CAD requires more colors than are available on many low-cost workstations. These extra colors can be effectively obtained by texture or bit mapping, also known as *color dithering*. Consider a display that can only show black or white (a binary display). If 8×8 "superpixels" are used, each superpixel has 64 possible levels of grey. More commonly, a display may be three bits deep, which allows for eight colors (the three primary, three secondary, white, and black). The RGB value of $\{0.5, 0.0, 0.0\}$ could be achieved by 32 pixels of pure red and 32 pixels of pure black. Of course the eye will be sensitive to the pattern in which these 32 pixels are chosen from the 8×8 super-pixel. Programming for color dithering is beyond the scope of mechanical CAD. However, the user should note that the technique may be used by a high-level graphics package to simulate full 24-bit color on a device with less capability. The use of super-pixels achieves the increased color range at the expense of spatial resolution.

We will conclude this by explicitly noting the connection between this section and the material in Chapters 8 and 9. A rapid review of the color plates discussed in Chapter 8 will show the need for multi-dimensional color interpolation. Any combinations of the patches discussed in Chapter 9 and the color spaces defined here can be used to generate a spectrum.

■ **EXERCISE 7.12:** Develop a conversion subroutine between RGB and HLS color systems.

Choice of Color

The CAD programmer will have to choose colors for objects and for menu items (text, lines, backgrounds). CAD users will usually want to adjust object colors, so the CAD programmer must also develop color editing tools. Once the fundamental object color is chosen, the graphics package will use a lighting model to determine the local color for individual parts of the images. The choice of color significantly affects the look and feel of a CAD program. Although this discussion could be reserved for Chapter 11, User Interfaces, it will be covered here. The following tips about color usage should be helpful to any CAD programmer or user:

- As a general rule of thumb, avoid the temptation to use a wide range of colors.
- Choose the background color first. This is analagous to selecting the colors for the wall and ceiling before picking trim colors. Background color is intended to fill the largest area. For background, light colors work better than dark colors, vivid colors are better than dull colors, and warm colors look better than cool colors.
- Choose the lightness (shade) before choosing hue. Think how the graphics would appear in monochrome grey. Varying the lightness will make the graphics seem to have more depth than simply varying the hue.
- However, if a variety of lightness is desirable, but the number of colors should be limited, then restrict either saturation or hue.
- Do not use the full range of hues; rather, pick one hue and then use the complementary hue.
- The human eye is least sensitive to blue, so do not depend on lightness to distinguish blue from black. Similarly, the pair formed by their complements, yellow on white, is a poor choice.
- Vivid colors must be used sparingly. A menu or image will appear less garish if pure colors are avoided.
- Make extensive use of achromatic color (a monochrome grey scale) instead of introducing many new hues.

The eleven colors in Table 7.4 provide good values for an initial palette. Note that they are not uniformly distributed around the color wheel and none is a pure primary color.

Cyan	Yellow	Magenta
0.0	1.0	1.0
0.0	0.9	0.7
0.0	0.9	0.45
0.0	1.0	0.1
0.45	1.0	0.0
0.8	1.0	0.0
1.0	0.7	0.0
1.0	0.0	0.5
0.8	0.0	0.75
0.7	0.0	1.0
0.2	0.0	1.0

Table 7.4 Recommended basic colors.

7.8 RENDERING

The techniques used to create images that are more realistic than straightforward line drawings can be grouped under the general heading of rendering.
At its simplest, this may require nothing more than removing hidden lines to
give the illusion of three dimensions (see Fig. 8.17). At the other extreme
is the goal of "photo-realism" or the production of a synthetic digital image
indistinguishable from a digital photograph. The latter is the subject of much
ongoing research in computer graphics, and besides being beyond the scope
of this book, will be beyond the scope of mechanical CAD for some time
to come. Photo-realism requires extensive computer resources, and its value
has not yet been demonstrated for mechanical design purposes. Of course,
design concerned with product appearance will use these techniques as they
become available. On the other hand, design concerned with function will
probably allocate the computing resources budget in areas other than enhanced
realism in display. However, a wide range of rendering techniques are available and are used frequently. These techniques can be broadly divided into the
categories of visibility, illumination, shading, and lighting, grouped as follows:

- Visibility
  - Hidden-line algorithms
  - Hidden-surface algorithms
        Backface cull
        Depth sort (painter's algorithm)
        z-buffer
- Illumination
  - Ambient
  - Lambertian
  - Phong

- Shading
  - Flat
  - Smooth, Gouraud
  - Phong
  - Ray cast
  - Radiosity
- Image characteristics
  - Shadow casting
  - Reflection
  - Transparency
  - Translucency
  - Refraction
- Lighting
  - Type
      Parallel
      Point
      Distributed
  - Location
  - Orientation
  - Intensity
  - Chromatic content

Visibility

Visibility algorithms generally seek to identify those aspects that would be visible from the particular camera location. A considerable body of literature exists in this area, much of it related to hidden line algorithms. The increased use of color raster displays has substantially reduced the amount of line drawing in design and so hidden line algorithms are of less importance. One way to achieve the appearance of a hidden line drawing for a surface model is to produce a shaded image using polygons with solid line edge attribute and white fill attribute.

If the image being created is based on polygons, then rendering is concerned with first, whether to draw the polygon, and second, what color it should be. The first concern is the hidden surface question. The hierarchical structure of the display often can solve many visibility questions. Even though the display list (see Fig. 7.13) has no particular order (left to right), the display process will traverse the tree and draw the polygons in a specific order. If done carefully, drawing polygons in the correct order can solve many visibility problems. However, this tactic is not always feasible, so it is important to know the alternatives.

The most easily implemented visibility algorithm is the *backface cull*. This method is based upon the simple fact that polygons have one outward-facing normal, and if this normal is facing away from the camera, the polygon is not visible. This is easily checked by a dot product between the polygon normal and the camera z-axis. If the camera faces in the negative z direction, then visibility requires $\vec{n}_{\text{poly}} \cdot \vec{n}_z > 0$. This check is easily implemented in hardware in the display pipeline and can be performed in "real time." This check requires the normal to the polygon, which for efficiency, should be precalculated and stored.

It is important to note that this method does not treat a polygon as a sheet of paper. The polygon is visible from only one side. The polygon is invisible (and hence transparent) from the other side, which can lead to some interesting effects. For example, consider a cube defined from six polygons. If depth clipping is used to remove the "front" of the cube, then the inside surfaces of the cube will not be seen.

If polygons are used to represent very thin objects and are intended to have both front and back visible (such as a sheet of paper, a thin shell, or a cube made from plates or shells), then two polygons must be defined at each location, one facing each way. Polygon direction is usually defined by the order in which the points or edges are entered, with the outward facing normal defined by the right-hand rule. For a convex polyhedral object, the backface cull is sufficient for visibility purposes. However, concave polyhedra or multiple objects will require more consideration.

As mentioned above, if the polygons are drawn in the "correct" order, then the visibility problem is solved. Working in camera space, one could sort the polygons in terms of increasing z value to obtain the correct order. This is referred to as a *depth sort* and is the core of the *painter's algorithm*. The computational effort is reduced if the algorithm is preceded by a backface cull. The painter's algorithm is sufficient if the polygons are convex and not interpenetrating.

For more complex visibility problems, the z-*buffer* method is preferable. For each screen pixel, a memory location is set aside in addition to the color value. This memory location stores the highest z value for the entity drawn at that pixel. The z-range from the frustrum of vision includes 0 through the maximum allowed by the depth of the z-buffer (usually 8 or 10 bits). The first step in generating a display is to set all z values to zero or maximum, depending upon the direction of positive z. If positive z is into the display, then the maximum value is used. If positive z is toward the camera, then 0 is used.

In the following discussion, let us assume that 0 is used. As each entity is drawn (point, line, or polygon), the x_c, y_c, and z_c value of each pixel is generated. Usually the z_c value is dropped, but now it is compared to the value in the z-buffer. If the z_c value is less than the z-buffer value, then that entity is considered obscured and is not drawn. If the z_c value is greater than the z-buffer value, then the entity is considered visible and drawn, and the z_c value is written into the z-buffer. This method can handle concave overlapping polygons and interpenetrating polygons. It is very fast and has been implemented in hardware to provide a "real-time" z-buffer. It should be noted that, in addition to any requirements for additional processing chips in the display pipeline, the typical z-buffer requires an additional eight bits per screen pixel. For a 24-bit color display, this requires an additional 1.3 megabytes of memory.

Before leaving visibility, it is worth mentioning methods for handling profile lines and facet lines. *Profile lines* are those lines that separate the object from the background or other objects. Another definition for profile lines are those lines for which the z value is discontinuous in a direction perpendicular across the line (in screen space). Obviously, profile lines depend on viewpoint; in addition, they are very easy to calculate for polyhedral objects. As we will see in Chapter 9, edges in polyhedral objects always connect two and only two faces. These faces each have polygon normals. For each edge in a polyhedral object, if the dot product between each normal and the camera z vector differs in sign, then the edge is a profile line. This is a quick way to detect profile lines.

Facet lines occur when a polyhedral object is used to represent an object that is intended to be smooth. The faceting of a circular cylinder is a prime example. Consider a circular cylindrical hole in a cube. A designer may wish to produce a line drawing of the hole with the circular edge drawn faceted (a sequence of straight lines), but not want to show the axial straight lines that separate facets. Note that the entire circular edge would not be a profile line and therefore cannot be drawn with that method. In a line drawing of a smooth, polyhedral object, some lines are actual edges and some are artifacts of the faceting process. The CAD user may wish to drop these lines in some automatic fashion because the degree of faceting may be user selectable. One method of removing these lines is to calculate the facet angle. The dot product of the normal for the polygon on each side of the edge will be a measure of the facet angle. Typically, a small angle indicates a facet that is part of a smooth surface, and a large angle indicates a true edge in the object. Some display algorithms may allow the user to set a facet angle that is used to drop facet lines.

Figure 7.23 shows a simple geometry with all lines drawn, hidden lines dashed, profile lines only, profile lines and lines that exceed a particular facet angle, and the "true" hidden line drawing. Additional line drawings can be found in Figures 8.2 and 8.9–8.17.

A quick-and-dirty hidden line algorithm can be implemented by combining a backface cull with a profile edge filter and a facet angle filter in parallel. That is, perform the backface cull, and then draw profile edges and edges that exceed the facet angle threshold.

Illumination

The objective of a shading algorithm is to determine what color to make each polygon (or possibly each individual pixel within the polygon). The following discussion will cover the shading algorithms for white light on

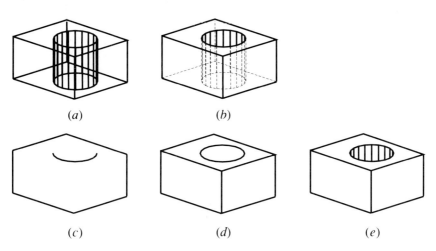

Figure 7.23 Line drawing for a simple part. (a) all lines (b) hidden lines
dashed (c) profile lines (d) profile lines and lines that exceed
a particular facet angle (e) the "true" hidden line drawing.

white objects. Only one intensity value will be developed for each polygon
and only one intensity value will be given for each source of light. For
chromatic light, three intensity equations will be needed for each component.
This will allow for effects such as those caused by blue light shining on red
surfaces.

The first shading to be considered is caused by ambient lighting. Each
polygon is considered to be illuminated with an intensity I_a that is independent of the polygon's orientation or location. However, the intensity of
the light reflected from the surface will depend upon the reflectivity of the
surface k_d. Ambient lighting is used to produce some light on back faces
of objects; otherwise, the back faces can become quite dark.

The diffuse reflection from a surface depends on the angle between
the surface normal and the direction to the light source. Lambert's cosine
law states that the intensity of reflected light is proportional to $\cos\theta$ where
θ is the angle of incidence. Note that this only applies for $-90° < \theta <
90°$. Otherwise, the polygon is not illuminated. The angle of incidence is
calculated from the polygon normal $\vec{n}_p$ and the vector to the light source $\vec{L}$.
The cosine of the angle is given by the dot product $k_d\vec{L} \cdot \vec{n}_p$. This term is
sometimes modified to include distance to the light source, $1/d^2$. However,
a distance dependence usually is not useful to design purposes. If the light is
far away, the effects from one side to the other of design space are negligible.
If the light source is close, the inverse square variation can be too large.
Including diffuse reflection, the polygon intensity is

$$I = I_a k_d + I k_d \vec{L} \cdot \vec{n}_p$$

Any object with a shiny surface will reflect some part of the incident light as well as the diffuse reflection just discussed. This *specular reflection* will have the color of the light source rather than the surface. The strength and dispersion of the specular reflection depends on the reflectivity of the surface; its intensity, on the angle between the camera axis and the axis for perfect reflection of the light $\vec{R}$. Phong developed a widely used illumination model that determines specular intensity as $k_s \cos^n \alpha$ where α is the angle mentioned above. The coefficient k_s is the material's specular-reflection coefficient, and the coefficient n determines how rapidly the highlight drops off. Figure 7.24 shows the geometry for illumination models. The Lambertian cosine dependence is drawn dashed. The Phong specular highlight function is shown as a function of α for values of $n = 1, 2, 5, 10$. Observe how the increase in the exponent n narrows the distribution of the specular reflection. For this model, it is important to emphasize that the surface color does not affect the color of the specular highlights; in other words, k_s is not dependent on the color of the surface. This is particularly true for shiny surfaces such as plastic.

After combining these phenomenon, the intensity can be calculated using

$$I = I_a k_d + I k_d \vec{L} \cdot \vec{n}_p + I k_s (\vec{R} \cdot \vec{n}_{zc})^n$$

where all vectors are normalized to unit vectors. For multiple lights, the effects are additive:

$$I = I_a k_d + \sum_{i=1}^{N_{lights}} \left(I_i k_d \vec{L}_i \cdot \vec{n}_p + I_i k_s (\vec{R}_i \cdot \vec{n}_{zc})^n \right)$$

The reader should remember that three separate instances of this equation are required for chromatic lighting.

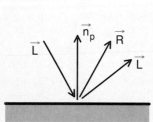 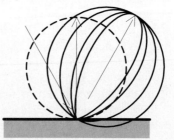

Figure 7.24   Illumination models are functions of the angle of incidence and the angle between the camera and the reflection vector. The Lambertian cosine function is drawn dashed. The Phong specular highlighting function $\cos^n \alpha$ is drawn for values of $n = 1, 2, 5, 10$.

In addition, other illumination equations have been developed. The most prominent are the Cook-Torrance-Sparrow model and the Hall model. The reader should refer to Foley, Van Dam, Feiner, and Hughes for further information.

Shading

A flat-shaded rendering is produced when each polygon has a single color determined by any of the previously discussed effects. For many cases this is sufficient, but for curved surfaces, the faceting is not acceptable. The number of facets could be greatly increased, but faster approximations are available.

A smooth-shaded image is obtained by interpolation of the shades set by a flat-shading algorithm. This requires interpolation within a polygon. If each node of a polygon were given a distinct intensity, then the internal pixel intensity could be interpolated from the nodal values. This is the *Gouraud shading* algorithm. Each node or polygon corner is given an intensity based on the shading algorithm described above. Because Gouraud shading has been implemented in hardware, it can be accomplished in "real time."

Gouraud shading is usually used for a polygon mesh (a collection of contiguous polygons). The intensity value must be set for each node in the mesh, usually by using a normal vector associated with each node. The nodal normal vector can be obtained by averaging the polygon normal for all polygons surrounding the node. However, Gouraud shading is not worthwhile for a single polygon unless the light source is close enough to allow each corner to have a different incident angle, and therefore, a different intensity.

Phong shading is an alternative to Gouraud shading. Rather than interpolating an intensity across a polygon, Phong shading interpolates the normal across the polygon. This "local" normal is used in the intensity equation given earlier. This approach will interpolate the effects of specular highlighting better than Gouraud shading.

The *ray cast algorithms* allow for individual treatment for each pixel rather than interpolation across a polygon and can provide significantly better images at substantial increased cost. Essentially, these algorithms trace a ray from the camera through each pixel in the view plane and into the object space. Eventually this ray will encounter a surface, at which point the process can spawn additional rays, both reflected and refracted. At each surface encounter, a local normal can be calculated and the intensity equation applied. This process continues for some predetermined number of encounters. The intensity for the pixel is determined as a function of the intensities contributed by each ray that has been spawned. It is important to note that more sophisticated rendering should be coupled with more sophisticated object models. For example, a ray cast image of a faceted curve surface is inferior to an interpolated image. The faceted model should be replaced with a curved patch model that provides accurate modeling of the local normal.

The most advanced rendering method is *radiosity* and has been described as almost diametrically opposite to ray tracing. Rather than being concerned with the light entering the camera, radiosity is first concerned with the distribution of light energy throughout the scene. Based on principles developed in the field of radient heat transfer, the energy is determined for every surface in the scene, which is modeled as a collection of ideal diffuse emitters and reflectors. The radiosity of a surface is a function of the radiosity of all other surfaces in the scene and depends on the emission of energy and reflection of incident energy. Each surface leads to a balance equation that includes all other surfaces. The radiosity values for all surfaces lead to a set of simultaneous equations that represents the total energy balance in the scene. This set of equations is linear and so matrix methods can be applied, resulting in the value for illumination intensity for each surface in the scene. Although substantial computation is required, the results are view-independent. Rendering the scene from different viewpoints can be done quickly; furthermore, radiosity provides the best means available to obtain photo-realism.

Various shaded images are discussed in Chapter 8 and can be found in Figures 8.2, 8.4, 8.13, 8.18, and Color Plates 1, 4, 5, 7, 8, 9, 10, 11, 12, and 16.

Image Characteristics

Several image characteristics are listed in the table at the beginning of this section. Of these, we will discuss shadow casting and transparency briefly. Shadows are extremely effective in producing the illusion of three dimensions and reality. However, shadow casting can be computationally expensive (particularly for multiple light sources). Many shadow casting methods produce shadows with sharp edges that are not realistic (except for harsh point lighting situations). The value of shadows can be seen by producing an image of an object floating above a plane, with and without the resulting shadow. The image with the shadow will be clearly superior.

It is worth mentioning a simple trick used for shadow creation. Determine the projection of the object as seen from the light source. Draw this projection (using a dark color) appropriately transformed onto the "floor." This is effectively a projection transformation onto a plane that is not normal to the camera z-axis. This is achieved by passing the same geometry through a second set of transformation matrices. After the shadow is drawn, the object can be drawn (see Fig. 7.25). This method can produce a shadow in "real time;" however; this method only works for situations in which an object would cast a shadow onto a flat plane. Although it can handle multiple objects, it cannot handle objects that shadow other objects.

Translucency and transparency are not used in a completely consistent fashion in rendering; rendering packages model both of these phenomena. Modeling translucency will include the optical effects of light transmission

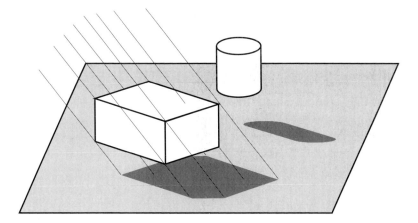

Figure 7.25 A simple shadow algorithm can be developed that uses transformations to "squash" an object onto the shadow plane and then draws each polygon filled and without a border.

through the intervening material, but this requires a solid model of the objects in question. The attenuation depends on the path length within the object and can be handled by ray cast techniques. In the case of transparency, the objective is to provide some ability to "see through" surfaces to what is behind them. This approach would treat objects as made of thin plastic shells, where the amount of transparency represents the transparency of the shell. There is no path length dependence. Although transparency can be handled by ray cast techniques, it is also handled easily by α-blending, an extension of the z-buffer. During a z-buffer check, the value of the existing intensity is averaged with the value of the new intensity. The weighting for this average provides a measure of the amount of transparency provided. Being a rather simple modification of the z-buffer, which has been implemented in hardware, the α-blend provides "real time" transparency.

Lighting

The illumination algorithms use lighting information that describes the light sources. Most rendering programs will provide a default set of lighting conditions, but the engineer may wish to change these to provide consistency between images generated by different programs or to highlight particular features of an image. The light source is specified by type, location, orientation, intensity, and chromatic content. Most rendering programs support a lighting scheme having multiple light sources.

The broadest classification of light sources is by type. The most commonly used is the parallel light source, which is equivalent to a point source at extremely large distance. All rays from a parallel light source enter the design space at the same angle. All rays from a point source emanate radially from that source, with equal intensity at all angles. The point source need not be within the volume of the space being rendered to produce effects different from those caused by a parallel source. A spotlight is represented if the intensity of light from a point source depends on the angle. The intensity is modeled as decreasing with the angle as measured from some orientation axis. The range of angle and rate of decrease must be specified. (For additional information, the reader should refer to Warn's work in this area.) The most difficult illumination to represent is a distributed light source. This could be distributed along a line (a neon tube) or over a surface (backlit frosted glass).

The location and orientation of a light source can be specified in much the same way as the camera location and orientation. Distributed sources will require further data specifying the shape of the source.

The light source can be specified by a single intensity if white light is assumed; however, remember that the chromatic content of colored light is specified by three intensity values. The basis for these three values depends on the color definition scheme being used.

The lighting model has a significant effect on the image. The importance of lighting is recognized by those agencies that produce product photos; these firms retain lighting specialists as well as photographers. Many programs use a default lighting scheme of ambient lighting and a single parallel white light along the camera axis. Substantial improvement is obtained by moving the light "off-axis," usually up and either to the left or right. Multiple sources can produce an esthetic image but for visualization purposes (refer to Chapter 8) may hinder viewer interpretation of the image. Some programs will use multiple lights with different colors as defaults. For example, Mathematica uses " . . . three point light sources, and no ambient component. The light sources are colored respectively red, green, and blue, and are placed at 45° angles on the right-hand side of the object."[2]

Exploitation of Structure

Rendering algorithms can become extremely computation-intensive. The trend in development is to move these algorithms into custom chips for increased speed. Hardware implementations have been developed for the most popular methods. Even so, any simplification of the problems will speed image generation. A substantial amount of the complexity arises because of the n^2 nature of rendering. Any entity may shadow, reflect, or light by reflection, any other entity. The imposition of structure can greatly reduce the number of interactions that must be considered. This is particularly important if images are to be produced at dynamic speeds; in which case, changes

---

[2]Steven Wolfram. Mathematica: A system for doing mathematics by computer 2d ed, New York: Addison-Wesley, 1991, p. 455.

from image to image may be small. As already discussed, a hierarchical structure is imposed on the graphic data. Another hierarchical structure can be imposed to represent the rendering interaction between objects. Such a structure could be based on location. For example, objects in the upper right quarter of the "screen" cannot obscure objects in the rest of the screen, and a visibility algorithm could substantially reduce the number of checks to be made. Similarly, a convex polyhedral object cannot obscure itself and so a backside cull would be sufficient for a hidden surface algorithm. In a scene consisting of convex polyhedra, individual polygons need only be checked against polygons that are part of other polyhedra.

In rendering, the imposition of structure can be described as partitioning. The problem is simplified substantially by partition into a set of subproblems. The real payoff occurs by hierarchically partitioning the problem. Successive levels of partition quickly reduce the amount of interaction in each partition. Of course, the overhead needed to achieve and manage partitioning is not negligible. As dynamic images change, the partitioning will change. This would imply the existence of some optimum level of partitioning; however, such discussions are beyond the level of this book.

One way to achieve partitioning is through the use of *extents*. These are entities that can be used as approximations for the object at each level of partition. To increase efficiency, the extents must be simpler than the objects themselves. Typical extents are bounding spheres and bounding boxes. To decide if one object obscures another, the extents can be tested against each other. If one of these extents does not obscure the other, then the corresponding object does not obscure the other. Simply checking against the six polygons of a bounding box can eliminate the need for checking against several hundred polygons.

The concept of extents can be usefully applied in other areas of computer-aided design. Consider collision detection in an NC machining simulation or a robotics simulation: The gripper, robot arm, workpiece, and environment descriptions can be quite complex. However, simple extents can be defined and checked for collision before more expensive computational algorithms are used. In finite-element mesh generation, given a complex part and an existing mesh, if a change is made to the part, extents could be used to determine which parts of the mesh must be changed. In a simulation with some moving and some stationary parts, extents can be used at each time step to determine the parts that need to be rendered again.

Summary

Rendering schemes are usually provided as part of the high-level graphics package. Often the CAD user will have two rendering environments available. One scheme will be based upon the high-level graphics package used to produce dynamic interactive images. This package will provide rendering based on the short cuts mentioned earlier (Gouraud shading, z-buffer, and α-blend). The second will use ray cast or radiosity methods to provide images after extensive computing. Frequently the former is used to determine view points and positioning before the expense of the latter. The reader will note that rendering cannot be completely decoupled from geometry because of the importance of surface normals for intensity calculations.

■ **EXERCISE 7.13:** Generate a polyhedral representation of a circular cylinder with *N* facets. Individually draw the wireframe image, the profile edges, and edges that exceed the facet threshold. Calculate each polygon color using flat shading or Phong shading. Calculate the point normal for use in a Gouraud shading algorithm.

■ **EXERCISE 7.14:** If a rendering package is available, generate a simple scene consisting of a cube and a right circular cylinder on a flat plane. Explore the effects of different surface properties, lighting parameters, and rendering methods. Prepare a brief report describing when each would be useful.

7.9 RASTER DISPLAY PECULIARITIES

Fundamentally, the CAD programmer works in a two- or three-dimensional floating-point universe. Among other things, this means that space is infinitely resolvable. In contrast, graphic displays have only finite resolution. For example, the universally used raster display has a finite resolution in each dimension. This means that eventually the floating-point representations must become integer screen coordinates. For computational efficiency, the float-to-fix conversion should happen early in the process so that as many operations as possible take place with integer numbers (e.g., matrix multiplications, etc.). However, analytical accuracy requires calculations in float representation until the very last minute. This can actually go so far as to describe screen coordinates as {[0.0, 1.0]; [0.0, 1.0]} rather than {[01023]; [01023]}.

CAD images are assembled from points, lines, and filled polygons. Point display is simply setting the color for a particular pixel. Ultimately, a line between two points is drawn as a series of pixels between two pixels. The integer address of each end is easily calculated. The Bresenham algorithm is usually used to set the intermediate pixels. Similarly, several algorithms have been developed to "draw" circles.

For raster screens with low resolution, a diagonal line will display a distinctive ragged appearance. Similarly, circles will not be smooth lines. Filled polygon edges will be similarly ragged. Smooth motion of a line or polygon will produce incremental changes as the pixel pattern along the edge changes. This forms part of the problem commonly referred to as "aliasing" or "the jaggies."

Antialiasing techniques can be used to remedy these problems. In effect, this technique sets adjacent pixels (but not on the line) to an intermediate color between line color and background color. This blurs the line and widens it, but also smooths it. Some graphics packages will provide antialiasing. If this feature is available, the CAD programmer must decide on a case-by-case basis whether the improved image quality is worth the increased computational effort and the increased time per image.

Graphics packages insulate programmers and users from these algorithms; however, these algorithms can be useful to CAD programmers. For example, remote sensing techniques such as computerized tomography, magnetic resonance imaging, and laser interferometry usually produce sampled data on a uniform cartesian grid. Such data is easily displayed as a digital image, simply by correlating each sample point with a pixel. However, for engineering design purposes, it can be useful to manipulate data along a line that is neither horizontal or vertical, as in a line integral or simply when plotting values. The fundamental graphics algorithms can be highly useful in these cases, and the CAD programmer should know of their existence.

7.10   SUMMARY

This chapter has briefly covered topics in computer graphics that are important to CAD programmers. As stated previously, a high-level graphics package can only be used effectively if the methods and concepts internal to that package are understood. The two most important concepts in such packages are transformation matrices and hierarchy.

All graphics packages will use homogeneous coordinates and sets of matrices to achieve affine transformations. Any of these transformations can be achieved rapidly, and the CAD programmer should look for ways to utilize these transforms and to understand how the particular graphics package concatenates these matrices.

Hierarchy and segmentation provide the only method of data structure control (Chapter 10 will discuss data structure further). However, because graphics packages cannot be developed or modified easily, the CAD programmer is restricted to the structural architecture used in the available graphics package. In the development of CAD applications, the choices about segmenting the graphics are some of the most significant decisions.

7.11   ANNOTATED REFERENCES

Ahuja, D. V., and Coons, S. A. "Geometry for Construction and Display," *IBM Systems Journal*, Vol. 7 (3/4)(1968), pp. 188–205.

Excellent development of homogeneous coordinate methods.

Badler, N. (ed). "Special Issue on Character Animation," *IEEE Computer Graphics and Applications*, Vol. 12(9) (November 1982), pp. 9–82.

Broad discussion of techniques for computer animation. A good introduction.

Biberman, L. M. *Perception of Displayed Information,* Plenum, NY, 1973.

Presents a discussion of human perception, crucial when designing graphic systems, but often overlooked.

Blinn, J. F., and Newell, M. E. "Clipping Using Homogeneous Coordinates," *Computer Graphics,* Vol. 12(3)(summer 1978), pp. 245–251.

The algorithm, and interesting pointers to the preceding literature.

Blinn, J. F. "Models of Light Reflection for Computer Synthesized Pictures," *Computer Graphics,* Vol. 11(12)(summer 1977), pp. 192–198.

Extensions to the Phong shading model.

Bresenham, J. E. "Algorithm for Computer Control of a Digital Plotter," *IBM Systems Journal,* Vol. 4(1)(1965), pp. 25–30.

Bresenham's raster line-drawing algorithm.

Bui-Tuong, P. "Illumination for Computer Generated Pictures," *Communications of the ACM,* Vol. 18(6)(June 1975), pp. 311–317.

Development of smooth "Phong shading" technique.

Chasen, S. H. *Geometric Principles and Procedures for Computer Applications.* Englewood Cliffs, N. J.: Prentice-Hall, 1978.

Discussion of the underlying mathematics, other than matrix transformations, necessary for graphics work.

Chasen, S. H. "Historical Highlights of Interactive Computer Graphics," *Mechanical Engineering,* Vol. 103 (1981), pp. 32–41.

Of historical interest.

Cook, R. L., and Torrance, K. E. "A Reflectance Model for Computer Graphics," *ACM Transactions on Graphics,* Vol. 1(1)(1982), pp. 7–24.

The basis for "Cook-Torrance" shading, the mainstay of many simple image generation and graphics systems.

Coons, S. A. "Computer Graphics and Innovative Engineering Design," *Datamation* (May 1966).

Historically interesting early overview of the field.

Crow, F. C. "A Comparison of Anti-aliasing Techniques," *IEEE Computer Graphics and Applications,* Vol. 1(1)(1981), pp. 40–48.

A survey article, useful for choosing appropriate antialiasing measures for given applications.

Encarnacao, J., and Schlechtendahl, E. G. *Computer Aided Design.* New York: Springer-Verlag, 1983.

Design-oriented graphics, including a discussion of device-independent graphics and the GKS system. Notable discussion of multivariate presentation graphics plotting.

Foley, J. D., Van Dam, A., Feiner, S., and Hughes, J. *Computer Graphics: Principles and Practice*. 2d ed. Reading, Mass.: Addison-Wesley, 1990.

One of the classic textbooks in the field, providing a solid grounding in just about everything needed to do graphics. New edition is greatly expanded.

Gayeski, D., and Williams, D. *Interactive Media*. Englewood Cliffs, N. J.: Prentice-Hall, 1985.

A discussion of modern and innovative forms of man-machine interaction.

Giloi, W. K. *Interactive Computer Graphics: Data Structures, Algorithms, Languages*. Englewood Cliffs, N. J.: Prentice-Hall, 1978.

A more traditional engineering perspective, that covers general data structures well. The graphics work is oriented towards vectors, rather than raster-scan techniques.

Gouraud, H. "Continuous Shading of Curved Surfaces," *IEEE Transactions on Computers*, (June 1971), pp. 623–629.

A fast, simple way of accurately shading simple curved surfaces with minimal calculation.

Greenberg, D. *The Computer Image*. Reading, Mass.: Addison-Wesley, 1982.

Excellent collection of graphic images, including a concise overview of the field and a good discussion of color.

Griffiths, J. G. "A Bibliography of Hidden-Line and Hidden-Surface Algorithms," *Computer Aided Design*, Vol. 10 (3) (May 1978), pp. 203–206.

Extensive pointers into the literature.

Guedj, R. A., et al (eds.). *Methodology of Interaction*. New York: North-Holland, 1979.

Proceedings of an IFIP workshop on user-machine interaction, which is often the weak link in graphics programs.

Hearn, D. D. and Baker M. P., *Computer Graphics*. Englewood Cliffs, N. J.: Prentice Hall, 1986.

Heckbert, P. "Color Image Quantization for Frame Buffer Display," *Computer Graphics*. Vol. 16(3) (summer 1982), pp. 297–307.

Discusses efficient and effective ways of displaying images with high-color resolution with a limited palette or color map. Both map color selection and dithering are discussed.

Jarvis, J. F., Jundice, C. N., and Ninke, W. H. "A Survey of Techniques for the Image Display of Continuous Tone Pictures on Bilevel Displays," *Computer Graphics and Image Processing*, Vol. 5(1)(March 1976), pp. 13–40.

Discussion of dithering and half-tone rendering of complex images.

Joblove, G. H., and Greenberg, D. "Color Spaces for Computer Graphics," *Computer Graphics* Vol. 12(3) (summer 1978), pp. 20–27.

Discussion of color spaces, solids, and conversions for color graphics processing.

Kerlow, I. V., and Rosebush, J. "Computer Graphics for Designers and Artists," New
   York: Van Nostrand Reinhold, 1986.

*A less mathematical discussion of graphics from a nonengineering background.
Discusses graphic design issues for several types of media. Beautifully illustrated.*

Lange, J. C., and Shanahan, D. P. *Interactive Computer Graphics Applied to Mechanical Drafting and Design.* New York: Wiley, 1984.

Contemporary look at the application of graphics to drafting.

McCorduck, P. *Machines Who Think.* New York: W. H. Freeman, San Francisco,
   1979.

*Interesting reading, notably in reference to early graphics work at the RAND Cor-
poration.*

Negroponte, N. "Raster-Scan Approaches to Computer Graphics," *Computers and
   Graphics*, Vol. 2(3) (1977).

Useful to offset the vector-oriented developments found in most graphics textbooks.

Newman, W. M., and Sproull, R. F. *Principles of Interactive Computer Graphics.*
   New York: McGraw-Hill, 1979.

*Besides Foley and Van Dam, the classic textbook in the field. Structured display
files are well covered. Unfortunately predates ray-tracing techniques. Has extensive
bibliography and references section.*

Rogers, D. F. *Procedural Elements for Computer Graphics.* New York: McGraw-Hill,
   1985.

*An excellent coverage of many of the most important algorithms and how-to ele-
ments of graphics, including a discussion of ray tracing/casting, and excellent references.*

Rogers, D. F., and Adams, J. A. *Mathematical Elements for Computer Graphics.* New
   York: McGraw-Hill, 1976.

*A more mathematical development of important concepts of geometry, including a
good development of 2-D and 3-D affine and perspective transformations.*

Rogers, D. F., and Earnshaw, R. A. *Techniques for Computer Graphics.* New York:
   Springer-Verlag, 1986.

*Proceedings of the International Summer Institute on the state of the art in Computer
Graphics. Contains several papers on recent hardware developments.*

Schachter, B. J. *Computer Image Generation.* New York: Wiley, 1983.

*An interesting and thorough discussion of flight simulation as an application of
sophisticated computer graphics.*

Sutherland, I. E. "Computer Displays," *Scientific American*, Vol. 222 (June 6, 1970),
   pp. 56–81.

The classic overview article in the field.

Sutherland, I. E. "SKETCHPAD: A Man-Machine Graphical Communication Sys-
    tem," *MIT Lincoln Labs Technical Report No. 296*, May 1965.

One of the earliest graphics systems demonstrated.

Sutherland, I. E., Sproull, R. F., and Schumacher, R. A. " A Characterization of Ten
    Hidden-Surface Algorithms," *ACM Computing Surveys*, Vol. 6(1)(March 1974),
    pp. 1–55.

Useful in tandem with Griffiths' bibliography above.

Torrance, K. E., and Sparrow, E. M. "Theory of Off-Specular Reflection From Rough-
    ened Surfaces," *Journal of the Optical Society of America*, Vol. 57(9) (1967),
    pp. 1105–1114.

A basis for shading of modeled solids.

Tufte, E. R. *The Visual Display of Quantitative Information*. Cheshire Conn.: Graphics
    Press, 1983.

A discussion of presentation graphics and design.

Watt, Alan. *Fundamentals of Three-Dimensional Computer Graphics*. Reading, Mass.:
    Addison-Wesley, 1989.

*Comprehensive introduction to color shading techniques, including reflection/shading
models, ray tracing, and radiosity.*

*The following publications should be read regularly by CAD developers for graphics
developments.*

ACM Transactions on Graphics. Association for Computing Machinery, monthly.

Computer Graphics. Special Interest Group on Computer Graphics, Association for
    Computing Machinery, monthly.

SIGGRAPH Proceedings. Association for Computing Machinery, annual.

7.12   PROJECTS

Project 7.1   Truss Display

Problem Statement   Develop a graphic display for the truss in Project 3.1.
Draw both undeformed and deformed shapes. This display program should
be data driven, using separate data files for truss shape and deflection.

Project 7.2   Sailboat Rigging Display

Problem Statement   Develop a graphic display of the rigging for a sailboat.

Project 7.3   Racetrack Display

Problem Statement   Develop a graphic display for the racetrack and vehicle from Project 5.2. Animate the display using a vehicle trajectory read
from a data file.

Project 7.4   Railroad Classification Yard Display

Problem Statement   Develop a graphic display for the railroad classification yard from Project 5.4. Animate the display directly from the simulation.
Expand the simulation to handle the input of a large group of cars, released
at a timing determined from Project 5.4. Each car should have a predetermined destination (holding track). You will have to develop software to
determine the switch settings as the cars pass through the switches.

Project 7.5   Frame Display

Problem Statement   Develop a graphic display for the frame in Project
6.4. "Animate" the display to show the trajectory through design space as
the optimization proceeds.

Project 7.6   Grillage Display

Problem Statement   Develop a graphic display for the grill from Project
6.5. "Animate" the display to show the trajectory through design space as
the optimization proceeds.

C H A P T E R

8
Visualization

"A mathematician, however great, without the help of a good drawing, is not only half a mathematician, but also a man without eyes."

Cigoli to Galileo, 1611

"No drawings are to be found in this book. The methods which I present require neither constructions nor geometrical or mechanical arguments, but only algebraic operations, subject to a regular and uniform process."

Lagrange, Mécanique Analytique 1788

8.1 INTRODUCTION

The preceding chapter dealt with the techniques for generating a graphic display of geometric data. This chapter will deal with the content of the display. A gallery of images will be provided in this chapter so that the reader can compare them and see examples of the different uses of color and style.

Each of these images is the result of a process of choosing among the many types of plots, colors, styles, rendering techniques, and viewing locations so as to best convey the underlying information to the viewer. This process includes all aspects of the design process. The "designer" must choose whether to use existing packages or write a custom program to display the data. The "product" (the image) will be assessed in terms of utility and appearance, which is similar to the architectural values of "commodity" and "delight." To a great extent, these two values are independent. That is, the images will display different degrees of functionality and of aesthetic appeal or elegance. However, this does not imply that the latter can be neglected in the pursuit of the former.

Major differences between computer graphics and visualization go far beyond the pure technical questions of producing lines and/or pixels of specific color so as to provide the illusion of three-dimensional shape and form. Unfortunately, addressing these issues is beyond the scope of this text. The CAD designer is strongly encouraged to spend time reading in this area, and Section 8.8 will provide an entry into the literature. Excellent sources include books by Tufte and by Kerlow and Rosebush.

8.2   CHARACTERISTICS OF VARIABLES

Before discussing the various types of graphs, plots, and displays, it is worthwhile to consider the characteristics of the data to be displayed. At the most fundamental level data can be either continuous or discrete. Discrete data may be taken from a set with limited membership (such as machining operations allowable on a specific NC mill) or have infinite range (as in the set of integers). Discrete variables with limited range are candidates for symbols. Some sets of discrete variables are orderable but others have no order other than based alphabetically on their names (the NC operations, for example). Small unorderable sets are usually displayed by symbols. Variables from larger orderable discrete sets are usually displayed by mapping onto a continuous variable and displayed as if continuous.

Characteristics of continuous variables include range, resolution, and distribution. These three characteristics interact to affect how the data can be displayed. Nonlinear distributions may call for nonlinear mappings (for example, the classical logarithmic scale). Other nonuniform distributions (e.g., bimodal) may require more imaginative mappings.

Data display is intended to highlight the relationships between the data, which in most cases implies a functional dependence. Therefore the variables that underlie the data can be characterized as independent or dependent variables. The types of displays that follow can be classified by the number of independent and dependent variables.

Independent Variables

Independent variables are almost always scalars. Occasionally, the independent variable is a vector (e.g., a position in a field, or velocity). Vectors, however, are rather easily treated as several scalars. It is extremely rare to encounter a tensor as the independent variable, but one such example would be the yield surface for some particular material. Consider the deformed shape of an object as a function of the yield surface for the object's material. Displaying the dependence would be an example of a tensor as independent variable.

The independent variable is most commonly mapped onto a spatial variable for display, using the graphics techniques discussed in Chapter 7. More precisely, the independent variables are embedded in 1-, 2-, or 3-space. (The graphics package performs an additional embedding into 2-D screen space.) The type of embedding is an important descriptor for the displays to be discussed.

If the independent variable is time, a transient animation may be used instead of a spatial embedding. However, given publishing limitations and most display limitations, time is usually also mapped onto a spatial variable.

If the independent variable is an orientation, it should be mapped as such. That is, the magnitude and direction of a velocity should be mapped in polar coordinates rather than cartesian. (Do not map direction to x and magnitude to y.) However, not all angles should be mapped in polar, cylindrical, or spherical coordinates. Nonrepeating angles (such as twist angles) must be mapped in some other fashion.

Dependent Variables

The dependent variables can also be scalar, vector, or tensor. The higher-order types are usually converted to several scalars. For tensors, this usually means the maximum and minimum principal values and the orientations of the principal directions. The latter is an example of an angle that should be mapped onto an angle in the display.

The dependent variable can be connected to any attribute of display. Most commonly this is a spatial location (the ordinate of a curve). Other alternatives are color, line type, line width, marker size, or marker orientation. Note that all of these attributes are continuously variable but one, line type. Line type and other style attributes can be used as symbols to display discrete variables from a limited set. It should also be noted that frequently color is treated as discrete rather than continuous. This usually is a reflection of the display capabilities (eight colors versus 256 colors).

8.3   TAXONOMY OF PLOTS

As previously mentioned, a plot can be characterized by the number of independent and dependent variables. The possible combinations are shown in Table 8.1. Sections 8.4–8.6 will discuss the appropriate plots for these combinations.

8.4   PLOTS WITH ONE INDEPENDENT VARIABLE

One Dependent Variable

In the case of one independent variable and one dependent variable, graphs or classical line plots are appropriate. These will not be discussed in detail here, but this does not imply that there is not much to discuss. The proliferation of

Number of independent variables	Number of dependent variables			
	1	2	3	4
1	Graphs	Multiple line graphs parametric lines	Multiple lines; parametric space curves	Parametric curves with attribute variation
2	Contour plots; surface plots; waterfall plots	Carpet plot; surface plot; with color variation	Parametric surface	Parametric surface with color variation
3	Isosurface plots; Volumetric rendering	Marker clouds	Marker clouds	?
4	?	?	?	?

Table 8.1   Taxonomy of plots.

current software in desktop publishing, spreadsheets, and graphing programs shows that there is much to be considered. Decisions must be made about axes, labeling, line types, symbols, type fonts, and so on. The dynamic range and resolution of the data affects the choice of scales, tick marks, and the values for tickmarks. All of these decisions will determine the aesthetics (delight) as well as the usability (commodity) of the plot.

Two Dependent Variables

If there are two dependent variables, multiple-line graphs can be employed. In addition, computer graphics has made possible an alternative, the classical line plot, $y = f(x)$, with an attribute varying to reflect the second dependent variable. This attribute could be color, line width, or dash length. A third possibility is a parametric line in a plane, $\{x, y\} = \mathbf{f}(s)$. The most obvious difficulty is indicating the value of s along the line, but this can be accomplished with annotated tick marks or simply equally spaced markers. Unfortunately, such a display may lead to inappropriate interpretations. For example, the viewer may interpret x as the independent variable.

Three or More Dependent Variables

If there are three dependent variables, again multiple-line graphs can be employed. Alternatively, a parametric space curve can be used, $\{x, y, z\} = \mathbf{f}(s)$.

If there are more than three dependent variables, an attribute can be attached to the space curve and allowed to vary along the curve, mapped from the fourth dependent variable. Markers with more than one degree of freedom can be attached to the curve.

8.5 PLOTS WITH TWO INDEPENDENT VARIABLES

One Dependent Variable

Scalar Function of Two Variables   Historically, a contour plot as in Fig. 8.1 has been used to display scalar distributions that vary over a twodimensional space. Uniformly spaced sample points in each dimension (a cartesian sampling array) are the easiest to handle. Nonuniform sample points are usually approached by interpolation onto a uniform grid (the difficult part) and then displayed using standard techniques. In many cases, the notation of $x = f(s, t)$ is preferable to $z = f(x, y)$ because it delays the embedding step. The distribution is usually visualized as a surface using the following techniques:

- Contour Plots
- Surface Plots
    - wire-frame
    - hidden-line
    - color-shaded
        - height-based
        - flat
        - smooth, Gouraud
        - Phong
- Marker Clouds
- Color Pixel Images

Figure 8.2 was generated using Mathematica and represents the function

$$\frac{1}{1 + 10(y - x^2)^2 + (1 - x)^2}$$

which is roughly the inverse of Rosenbrock's function (biased by 1 to avoid division by zero. The result is a narrow curving ridge with a relatively long flat top.

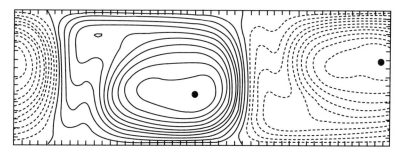

Figure 8.1   Contour plot.

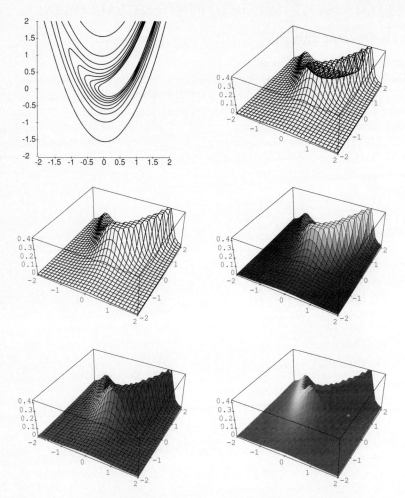

Figure 8.2   Scalar function of two variables. (a) Contour plot.
(b) Wire-frame surface plot. (c) Hidden-line image.
(d) Image with shading based on height. (e) Flat-shaded
image. (f) Image without mesh lines. These plots were
generated with Mathematica.

Figure 8.2a shows a contour plot of the function. This figure could be improved by labeling the contour lines. If a rectangular array of lines is used to connect the data points, and the dependent value of each (x, y) pair is mapped as $z = f(x, y)$, then the image in Figure 8.2b is obtained. Given a simple graphics support package, generation of images such as this is trivial, requiring only the sequential drawing of the lines. Note that the images can be simplified by drawing only lines of constant x or y. This is the waterfall plot to be shown later in this chapter.

Figure 8.2*c* shows the line drawing of the function with hidden lines removed. The front surface is more easily understood but at the price of reduced information about what is happening behind the ridge. Note how the grid lines provide pseudoshading for the front of the ridge (comparing right side to left side).

Figure 8.2*d* shows a shaded image of the distribution. Note that a shaded image will always have hidden lines removed because each polygon is filled with a color. In this case the color is based on height (z value). The more common alternative is to use a lighting model on the geometry of the surface that has been created and fill each polygon accordingly. Figure 8.2*e* shows the function with a single light source at location $(-10, 0, 1)^{\mathrm{T}}$. The light source has strength 0.8 on an range [0, 1], and ambient lighting of 0.2 is included. The right front of the ridge is dark because it faces away from the light. However, the ridge does not cast a shadow. The effect is more easily seen in Figure 8.2*f*, where the mesh lines have been removed. Unfortunately, the flat shading for each facet produces a very jagged effect. However, Gouraud shading for these polygons would smooth that. The next steps beyond that would be Phong shading, specular highlighting, surface texturing, and finally ray casting for true shadows.

The function value need not be mapped onto the z displacement of a surface. Mapping the function onto brightness produces a digital image similar to that obtained if Fig. 8.2*d* were viewed from directly overhead. In this case the function is evaluated in uniform steps, and "superpixels" are drawn. Obtaining the ultimate in resolution would require individual evaluation of each pixel of the screen. Removal of the mesh lines again has a significant effect on the image.

Figure 6.33 shows a variation of a scalar as a function of two independent variables. In this case, the wind velocity and the heading angle relative to the wind are the independent variables and the boat velocity is the dependent variable. Note that lines of constant wind velocity are drawn and the boat heading is plotted as an angle (polar coordinates). The dependent variable is then the radial coordinate in the polar coordinates. This kind of plot is more physically meaningful to a sailor. The alternative approach of plotting boat velocity as a function of wind velocity and heading angle, which would yield a contour plot of boat velocity, is not used.

The previous images all represented a rather simple function for comparison. Figure 8.3 shows a CT scan through the femurs of a human. The density is mapped to a 0–255 grey scale. The left half of Fig. 8.4 is a complete scan (512 × 512 pixels). The right half is a zoomed segment of the scan, displayed using squares ("superpixels") for each pixel from the scan. Bones show up with high density while air shows up at the low end of the scale. Different color maps can be used to create extremely different perceptions of the same set of data. A color map (Section 7.7) can be used to separate fat, muscle, and bone into different colors.

Figure 8.4 shows a set of data that represents the pressure within a fluid bearing on a connecting rod, as obtained by a finite-element

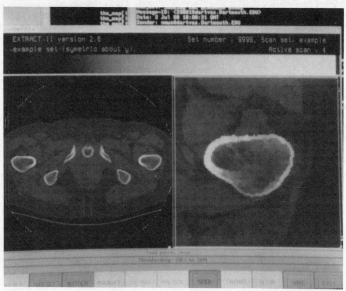

Figure 8.3   Computerized tomography, a display of radiographic density
using different color maps. Image courtesy of The Department
of Biomechanics, Hospital for Special Surgery.

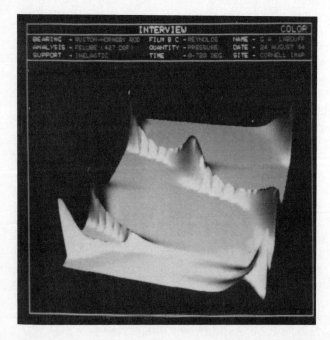

Figure 8.4   Surface plot for pressure distribution within fluid film of crank
end of a connecting rod. Image courtesy of Gary LaBouff.

analysis.[1] The fluid film is a cylindrical thin film and the circumferential centerline pressure is the quantity to be displayed in space and time. This line of pressure has been unwrapped for visualization purposes. In Fig. 8.4, left to right is 360° of bearing. The pressure varies transiently due to the engine cycle. In Fig. 8.4, front to back is one engine cycle. (On a four-cycle engine this represents 720° of crank angle motion.) This data also would have been appropriate for a "waterfall plot."

A surface was created by deforming a flat grid in θ, t space with the z coordinate mapping from the pressure. A light source was used for Gouraud shading of the four-sided polygons. The images were generated using the MOVIE-BYU package. Note that the ridges on the resulting surface don't cast shadows.

Prediction of cavitation is one aspect of the analysis of fluid film bearings. In this analysis, a pure zero pressure indicates cavitation. To highlight these regions, in Color Plate 1 the nodes with zero pressure have been colored red. Observe how well this emphasizes the size and location of the cavitation zone over time (front to back). Also, note that an artifact of the Gouraud shading is some "bleeding" of the red up onto the ridges. This is because nodes were set red and the polygons were interpolated, as opposed to polygon color being set and shaded based on the lighting model.

Figure 8.5 shows wing cross-sections, and Fig. 8.6 shows the pressure coefficient distribution over the top and bottom of a transonic wing. A continuous line is drawn through the values of the pressure coefficient at each of the 21 spanwise computational stations. The calculation was performed on a grid containing 147,456 mesh cells (2,560 of these abut the wing surface), using a cell-averaged finite-volume approximation to the Euler equations. A non-linear blend of second- and fourth- difference dissipation was added to stabilize the scheme. The solutions were converged using a diagonalized, alternating direction implicit, multigrid algorithm.[2,3]   This particular calculation required approximately 20 minutes of CPU time on a Cray Y-MP Supercomputer. However, adequate convergence could be achieved for most purposes in less than half the time.

Figure 8.6 is a version of the classical "waterfall plot." A more usual application of the waterfall plot would illustrate timewise variation, with a finite number of lines included. New lines are added to the front and old lines fall off the back as time progresses.

---

[1] G. A. LaBouff and J. F. Booker. "Dynamically Loaded Journal Bearings: A Finite Element Treatment for Rigid and Elastic Surfaces," *ASME Journal of Tribology*, Vol. 107 (October 1986), pp. 505–515.

[2] D. A. Caughey. "Diagonal Implicit Multigrid Algorithm for the Euler Equations," *AIAA Journal*, Vol. 26 (July 1988), pp. 841–851.

[3] Yoram Yadlin and D. A. Caughey. "Diagonal Implicit Multigrid Solution of the Three-dimensional Euler Equations," in *Proceedings 11th Conference on Numerical Methods in Fluid Dynamics, Lecture Notes in Physics*, D. L. Dwoyer, M. Y. Hussaini, and R. G. Voight, eds., Vol. 323 (1989), pp. 597–601.

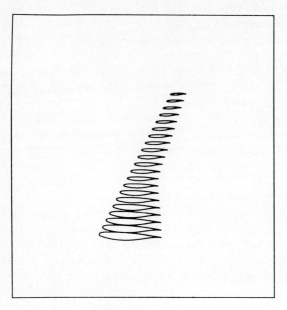

View of Wing

Lockheed Cranked Wing

Mach 0.805	Alpha 1.500	
Cl 0.5210	Cd 0.0259	Cm -0.7101
Grid 192x24x32	Work 199.95	Res 0.698E-05

Figure 8.5   Waterfall plot for cross-sections of transonic wing. Image
used by permission of Professor David Caughey.

Color Plate 2 shows an iteration map for the solution using Newton's
method of two coupled nonlinear equations[4] (from Project 3.1). Each pixel
represents a starting point for a Newton's method. The problem has five
possible solutions, each indicated by the hue of the pixel. The level or
value (the amount of black) is used to indicate how many iterations are
required for convergence from that pixel.

Two Dependent Variables

Figures 8.7 and 8.8 each show a "carpet plot" for two scalar variables as a
function of two independent variables. In this case, an optimum damped vibration absorber is specified for a damped single-degree-of-freedom system.[5] The

[4]S. A. Burns and A. Locascio. "A Monomial-Based Method for Solving Systems of Nonlinear Algebraic Equations," *International Journal for Numerical Methods in Engineering*,
Vol. 31(7) (May 1991), pp. 1295–1318.

[5]S. E. Randall, D. M. Halsted, D. L. Taylor. "Optimum Vibration Absorbers for Linear Damped Systems," *ASME Journal of Mechanical Design*, Vol. 103 (October 1981),
pp. 908–913.

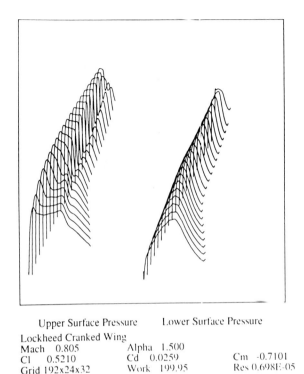

Upper Surface Pressure   Lower Surface Pressure
Lockheed Cranked Wing
Mach   0.805   Alpha   1.500
Cl   0.5210   Cd   0.0259   Cm   -0.7101
Grid 192x24x32   Work   199.95   Res 0.698E-05

Figure 8.6   Waterfall plot for pressure distribution at the top
                 and bottom of a transonic wing. Image used by
                 permission of Professor David Caughey.

independent variables are the primary damping ratio (ζ) and the mass ratio of the absorber relative to the primary system (μ). The independent variables are the optimum damping ratio for the absorber ($\zeta_{2\ opt}$), the optimum tuning frequency ratio ($\gamma = \omega_2/\omega_1$), the resulting amplitude ratio for the primary system, and the amplitude ratio for the absorber. The results are presented in the graphs in Figures 8.7 and 8.8. The mixture of independent and dependent variables in these graphs are unusual; typically, the independent variables are on the ordinate and abscissa and the dependent variables are on the carpet weave.

The data in Figures 6.31 and 6.32 are also candidates for a carpet plot display. Note that in Fig. 6.31, lines of constant camber are plotted with varying angles of attack α. The angle of attack is annotated, but the lines of constant α have not been drawn. In Fig. 6.32, lines of constant apparent wind β are drawn with values of α annotated. Note that the curves are such that mesh lines of constant α and β would fold over themselves and create a very confusing graph.

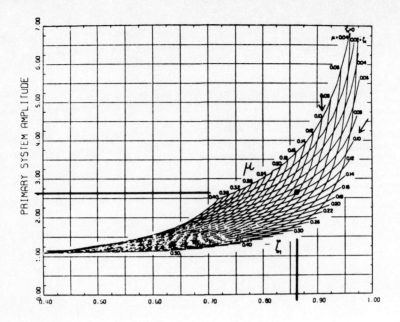

Figure 8.7   First carpet plot for an optimum vibration absorber.

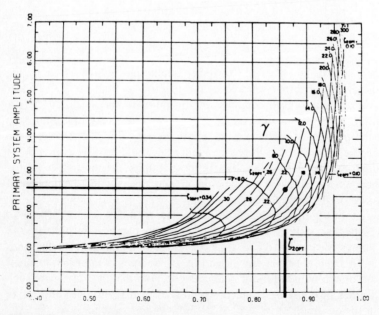

Figure 8.8   Second carpet plot for an optimum vibration absorber.

Three Dependent Variables

Two-Dimensional Geometry Embedded in Three Dimensions   The display of geometry is crucial to mechanical CAD/CAM systems. Chapter 9 will discuss the underlying methods for describing geometry in more detail. Typically, geometric parts classify into those consisting of smooth sculptured surfaces and those of a more regular, angular, and manufactured nature. In Figures 8.9-8.19, Figures 9.26-9.31, and Color Plates 3 and 4, watch for defining geometric entities such as splines, the amount of faceting in wire frame images, the use of hidden-line removal for image clarification, choice of wire-frame versus shaded image, and the use of color. Observe object color, line color, and background color, remembering that background colors that are aesthetically appealing on the screen differ from those that are aesthetically appealing on a printed image.

The use of patches to describe complex surface geometry is best understood by several examples. Figures 8.9 and 8.10 and Color Plates 3 and 4 represent a conceptual design for a joystick. Each patch is a Bezier patch (described further in Chapter 9), which can be shown by the defining points or in wire-frame mode by faceting the geometry. Figures 8.9 and 8.10 show wire-frame images with an increasing level of subdivision or faceting. Color

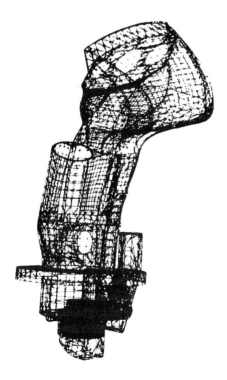

Figure 8.9   Coarse tesselation of a joystick handle.
Courtesy of Silicon Graphics, Inc.

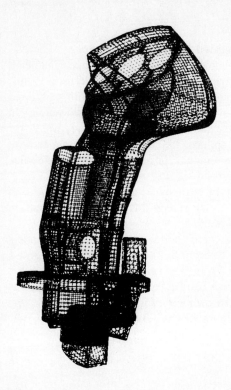

Figure 8.10   Fine tesselation of joystick handle.
                 Courtesy of Silicon Graphics Inc.

Plate 3 uses different colors to emphasize each patch's individuality. Note
that the patches are drawn not only with a filled border but also with a wire-
frame interior that provides some measure of transparency. Finally, Color
Plate 4 shows a shaded image with Gouraud shading for each facet.

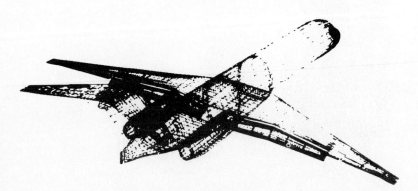

Figure 8.11   Wire-frame model of a transport aircraft. Courtesy of the
                 Douglas Aircraft Company, McDonnell Douglas Corporation.

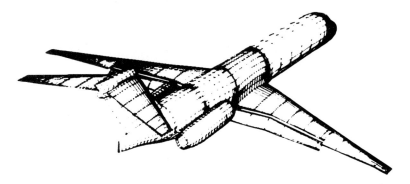

Figure 8.12   Hidden-line representation of a transport aircraft.
Courtesy of the Douglas Aircraft Company,
McDonnell Douglas Corporation.

Several images for a transport aircraft are shown in Figures 8.11–8.13. The patches in this case are bicubic parametric patches. An adaptive subdivision algorithm has been used to produce subdivision (faceting) only in areas of high curvature. The shaded model uses Gouraud shading for each facet. Finally, the pressure at each point of the surface is shown in Color Plate 6. This illustration uses a color spectrum to map the additional scalar variable onto the two-dimensional geometry embedded in three-dimensional space. This is discussed in a following section as two independent variables (u, v) and four dependent variables (x, y, z, p). The blending of color is provided by the Gouraud-shading capabilities of the graphics package. That is, the pressure is blended across the polygon rather than across the lighting intensity. The same function could have been used to produce a continuous color spectrum instead of the few bars shown. In images such as this, it is critical to include the color spectrum for the viewer's reference.

Figure 8.13   Shaded-surface representation of a transport
aircraft. Courtesy of the Douglas Aircraft
Company, McDonnell Douglas Corporation.

Figures 9.26–9.31 show the surface geometry for a fighter aircraft. (Note the vertical stabilizers have not been modeled.) The geometry was originally obtained as a set of x, y, z coordinates, conveniently grouped into cross-sectional planes. These points were joined to form splines, shown in Fig. 9.26. Since the aircraft is symmetric, only one half is modeled. A mirror function will be used to produce the complete model. On a color graphics display, different colors would have been used to help distinguish the individual patches. Figure 9.28 shows a zoom view of the area around the cockpit canopy; Fig. 9.29 shows a tesselated hidden-line image, and Fig. 9.30 shows a flat-shaded image. However, because of the restrictions on number of colors, each facet from Fig. 9.29 could not be rendered. A close look at the top of the wing reveals that it has been drawn with only two colors. This gives an apparent ridge line on the top of the wing that is purely a rendering artifact. Crucial to the creation of the geometry in this case is the tangency control between the individual patches.

Figure 9.31 shows a plastic model of the aircraft, which was made on an NC machine using the NC functions from within the CAD program. In order to save time, the distance between tool passes was set quite large, leaving very visible scallop height. (When using a ball mill, a slight ridge is always left between each tool path. The height of this ridge depends on the spacing between tool paths.)

Figures 8.14–8.17 show the surface geometry for a typical mechanical part. This part is to be manufactured by casting followed by machining of

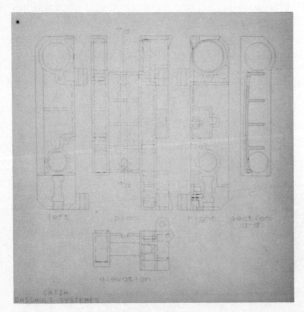

Figure 8.14   A Three-view drawing of a printer part.
Geometry courtesy of IBM. Image courtesy
of Integrated Mechanical Analysis Project.

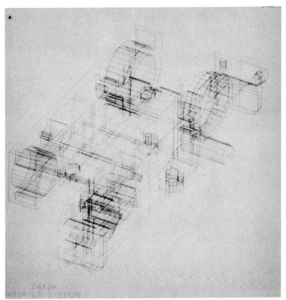

Figure 8.15 Wire-frame model of a printer part, with facet lines. Geometry courtesy of IBM. Image courtesy of Integrated Mechanical Analysis Project.

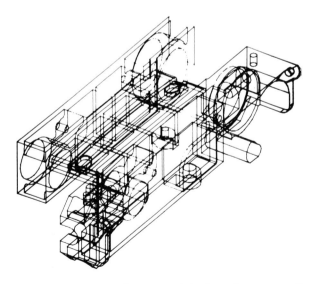

Figure 8.16 Wire-frame model of a printer part. Geometry courtesy of IBM. Image courtesy of Integrated Mechanical Analysis Project.

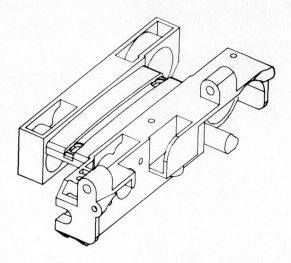

Figure 8.17   Hidden-line representation of a printer part.
Geometry courtesy of IBM. Image courtesy
of Integrated Mechanical Analysis Project.

certain key surfaces. The part model could be built with either a surface
representation or a solid representation using constructive solid geometry.
These alternatives are discussed in the next chapter. However, this particular
model was generated using a surface representation in CATIA. Figure 8.14
presents a classical set of multiple planar views. The wire-frame representation
is shown in Figures 8.15 and 8.16. The first shows facet lines for the
circular cylinderical surfaces. In many ways, these figure are more difficult
to interpret than multiple views. There are simply too many lines in Figure
8.16. The removal of hidden lines (Figure 8.17) simplifies the interpretation
of the geometry, but then, of course, nothing can be known about the
back side. Figure 8.18 shows a monochrome-shaded model. This image
provides the opportunity to comment on the value of color in essentially
monochromatic images. Figure 8.18 is much more attractive as a red object
on a white background with black facet lines. The graphic display used for
this image only permits 10 bits of color, and not all were assigned to a grey
scale, therefore, only a limited number of shades are available. Also, the
smooth continuous geometry is represented as faceted (note the cylindrical
surfaces) and displayed in a flat-shaded mode, which is emphasized by the
dark facet lines. The faceting would be less noticeable without these lines.
The amount of faceting is purely a function of the display and can be adjusted
without affecting the underlying geometric model; however, images with
fewer facets are displayed faster. Finally, Fig. 8.19 shows a plastic model of
the part that was machined on an NC mill using the data in the CATIA model.

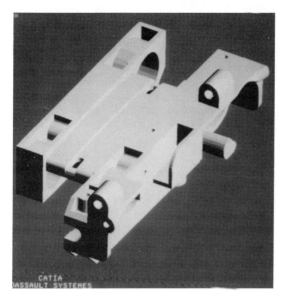

Figure 8.18 Shaded-surface representation of a printer part.
Geometry courtesy of IBM. Image courtesy of
Integrated Mechanical Analysis Project.

More Than Three Dependent Variables

Scalar Distributions over Two-Dimensional Geometry Embedded in Three-Dimensional Space   Color Plate 7 shows the stress distribution over the surface of the proximal portion of a human femur. In this case, three of the dependent variables are coordinates x, y, z of the surface u, v, and one of

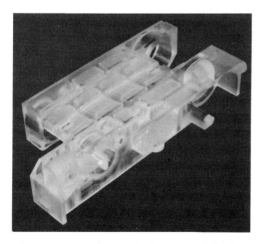

Figure 8.19 Photo of plastic model of a printer part. Photo courtesy
of Jon Reis. ©1990 all rights reserved.

Figure 8.20   Finite-element mesh for a plastic molded
part. Image courtesy of K. K. Wang.

the dependent variables is a tensor. The geometric surface is formed from the
mesh on the surface and then a scalar for one component of the stress tensor
(σ_{zz}) is used through a color map. The geometry consists of several bi-cubic
parametric patches. The image was generated using the PATRAN package.
Note that discrete values are used on the color map and smooth blending
of the color fringes is not employed. Also, observe the black background,
which is very effective on a display but less so on the printed page.

Color Plate 8 shows a surface-lighted model with contour lines for the
scalar variable. Color Plate 9 shows the distribution of von Mises stress using
a color spectrum. These images could have also shown the finite-element
mesh superimposed on the color shading.

Figure 8.20 shows a mesh for an injection-molded part. The pressure
distribution at the end of the injection cycle is shown in Color Plate 10. A
fourth independent variable for this problem is time. This can be shown by
either an animation loop or a series of frames at equally spaced time intervals.
The types of plots shown here work well for parts that are thin and thus approximately two-dimensional. Otherwise, only surface data can be displayed.

Color Plate 11 shows a scalar calculated from the stress tensor and shaded
over the surface of a mechanical part from a computer head drive assembly.

8.6   PLOTS WITH THREE INDEPENDENT VARIABLES

Any data set with three independent variables fills a volume, and therefore,
poses significant challenges for visualization. The data can be best thought

of as existing in a three-dimensional array. Two approaches exist: either create lower-order displays in some fashion (usually isosurfaces, or surfaces of constant value), or use volumetric rendering techniques.

One Dependent Variable

The case of one dependent variable is $x = f(r, s, t)$. Isosurfaces (surfaces with constant temperature, pressure, or density) are frequently used for such a case. Each surface is analogous to a contour line in a contour plot. Both multiple contours and multiple surfaces are required in those plots, which can be shown either on a single image using a transparency effect or in multiple images. However, the transparent images are probably more difficult to interpret.

The stress distribution shown in Color Plate 11 actually fills the interior of the part. If a scalar is extracted from the stress tensor and considered as volumetric data and used to adjust the color and transparency throughout the part, a representation such as in Color Plate 12 can be obtained.

Color Plate 13 uses isocontours for volume filling data. The scalar-dependent variable for fluid flow can be extracted from either pressure (a scalar), velocity (a vector), or vorticity (a vector).

Volumetric data can be acquired by remote sensing techniques such as computerized tomography. The density can be used to adjust the transparency and color each voxel (volume element) to simulate surfaces. Note that although there appear to be surfaces in these images, the underlying data is a full three-dimensional array of density, $d(i, j, k)$. The interpretation of such images is greatly enhanced by dynamic rotation during viewing.

Two, Three, or More Dependent Variables

The display of two dependent variables in a volume filling data set requires an innovative use of transparency. Obviously, two volumetric images could be created. However, this hampers comparison of the dependent variables. The alternative is to use marker symbols to indicate the two values. For example, a filled circle can be used, with the diameter linked to one dependent variable and the color linked to the second variable. Markers provide some measure of transparency because one can "see past them." Unfortunately, increased density of markers provides more spatial information to the user at the expense of less "transparency." Markers with several degrees of freedom can be designed quite easily; however, aesthetically pleasing, easily interpreted markers will require more thought. Most finite-element processing programs use markers to display stress tensors.

Figure 8.21 shows the distribution in the plane of the paper of the generalized inertia tensor for a robot arm.[6] The robot arm has been drawn for

---

[6]N. Kamikawa. *Dynamic Analysis and Design of Robotic Manipulators using Generalized Inertia Ellipsoids*, Master's thesis, Cornell University, Ithaca, N.Y., 1986.

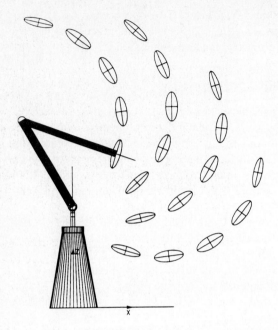

Figure 8.21   Two-dimensional distribution of a 2-D tensor
for generalized inertia of a robot arm.

clarity. The markers are drawn at equally spaced values of the joint coordinates for the robot arm, rather than at equally spaced x, y locations. At
each location, the generalized inertia tensor is shown by the ellipse marker.
The major and minor diameters of the ellipse are found from the principal
values and the major and minor axes are oriented to the principal directions.
By using joint coordinates to spot the markers, it becomes quite clear that
the principal directions are aligned with the natural directions of the robot
arm. This alignment would have been much harder to observe if the markers
had been drawn on a standard cartesian x, y spacing.

Figure 8.22 shows the distribution of the three-dimensional tensor. Only
one plane needed to be drawn because of radial symmetry (the third degree
of freedom being the cylindrical joint at the base of the arm). Note how
the marker was generalized for the higher dimension. In the absence of
radial symmetry, the display of several "layers" of markers would be much
more difficult to interpret. Several images would have been required and
the choice of orientation for the layers and viewpoints would have been
critical.

Figure 8.23 shows a representation of three dependent variables $\{x, y, z\}$
$= \mathbf{f}(r, s, t)$, in this case a volume filling finite element mesh to be used
for flow calculation around an aircraft wing fuselage combination. The rect-

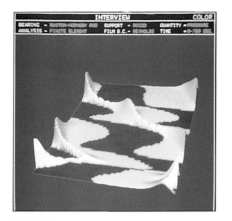

PLATE 1

PLATE 2

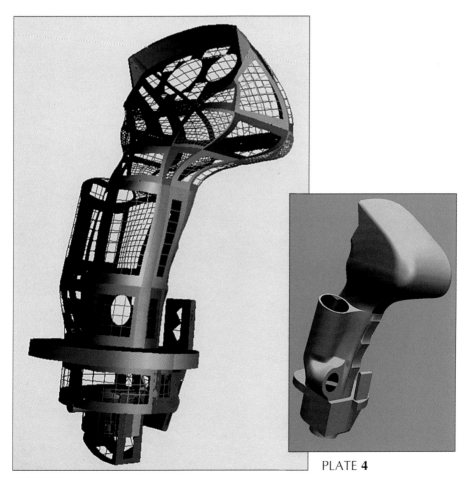

PLATE 3

PLATE 4

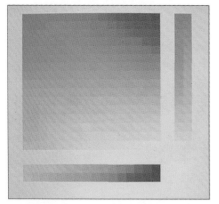

PLATE **5**

PLATE **6**

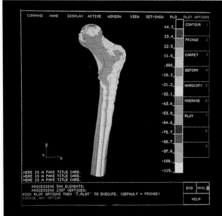

PLATE **7**

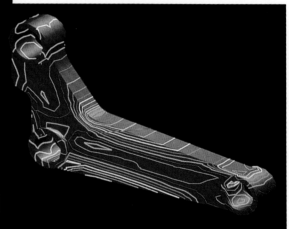

PLATE **8**

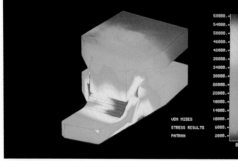

PLATE **9**

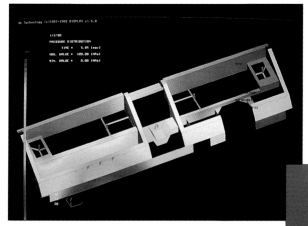

PLATE **10**

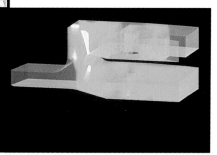

PLATE **11**

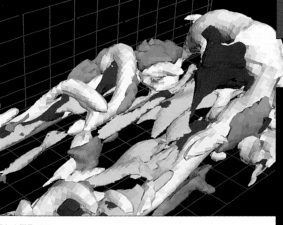

PLATE **13**

PLATE **12**

The images for plates 11 and 12 were created by Pixar. Data courtesy of Mr. Harris Hunt, PDA Engineering. © 1987 Pixar. All rights reserved.

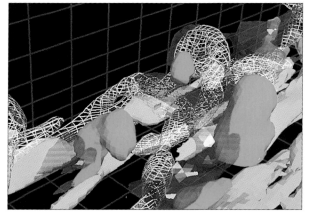

PLATE **14**

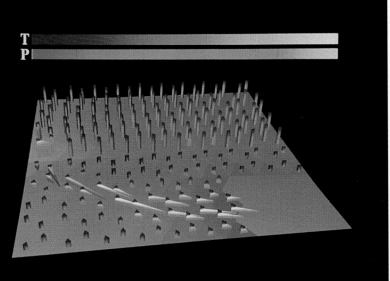

PLATE **15**

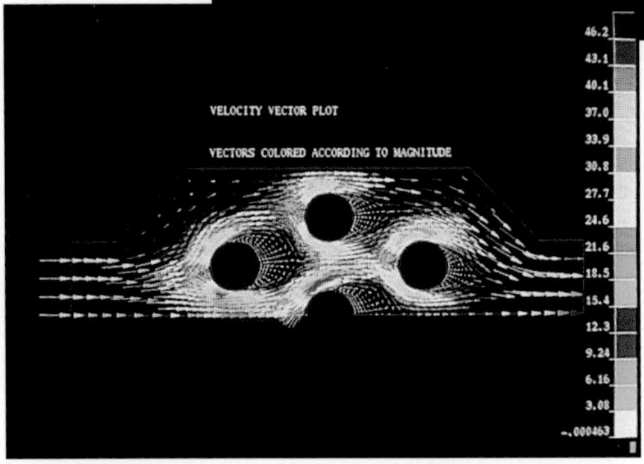

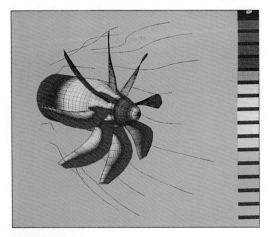

PLATE **16**

PLATE **17**

PLATE **18**

Figure 8.22 Three-dimensional distribution of a 3-D tensor for generalized inertia of a robot arm.

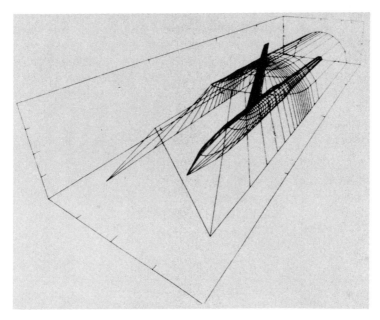

Figure 8.23 One plane of a volume-filling finite-element mesh. Image used by permission of Professor David Caughey.

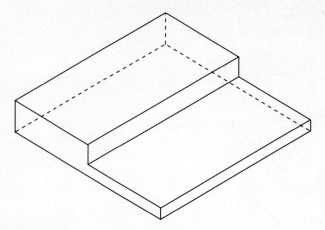

Figure 8.24 Geometry of a mold cavity.

angular box is shown for the x-, y-, and z-axes. A surface of a constant independent variable (possibly t) is shown and the grid lines for constant r, s are shown in that t-plane. The "fuselage" and wing have also been drawn. Because wire-frame display is used, there is no need for transparency on the constant t-plane.

Color Plate 16 shows a use of markers for two independent variables i, j and four dependent variables $x, y, \vec{V}$. Note how the location of the markers shows the grid used for the calculation. The direction and length of each arrow is tied to $\vec{V}$. The use of color in this case is redundant, but it does improve the drawing's aesthetic appearance. Color Plate 17 shows a similar situation for $x, y, z, \vec{V}$. The markers are only displayed along a cutting plane in full x, y, z space.

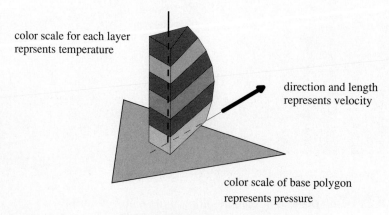

Figure 8.25 Definition of the injection molding glyph.

Color Plate 18 ribbons show the three-dimensional flow field; color is used to show pressure distribution. Color Plates 13 and 14 show representations of several scalar and vector fields that fill three-dimensional space. Note the use of multiple isosurfaces, color, markers (vector arrows), and cuts along values of a constant independent variable. Note that markers are frequently used along a plane of a constant independent variable.

Figures 8.24–8.29 provide one of the best illustrations of how to use markers to display several items of information. The objective is to display the temperature, pressure, and velocity of plastic filling a mold cavity shaped as shown in Figure 8.24. The values of the dependent variables are determined by a finite element solution. The independent variables are the three coordinates for spatial location in the finite element mesh (say i, j, k and time t). The dependent variables are x, y, z, T, P, and $\vec{V}$. At each i, j pair, the glyph in Figure 8.25 is drawn. The variable k is considered to run across the thickness of the cavity, and the seven layers in the glyph represent different values for k. The velocity vector $\vec{V}$ is mapped onto the direction and length of the glyph. Two color schemes are used to map the temperature and the pressure. The specific colors were selected to be mutually orthogonal. Figures 8.26–8.29 show four snapshots from an animation of the mold-filling sequence. Note how the thick part of the mold fills first, and then (see Fig. 8.29, Color Plate 15) the thin portion fills relatively quickly with a hot jet of flowing material.

Figure 8.26   Injection molding sequence, $T = T_1$. Image courtesy of Richard Ellson, Kodak Research Scientist; Donna Cox, Visualization Artist; Ray Idaszak, Visualization Research Programmer.

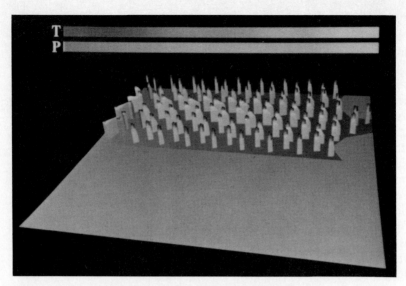

Figure 8.27 Injection molding sequence, $T = T_2$. Image courtesy of Richard Ellson, Kodak Research Scientist; Donna Cox, Visualization Artist; Ray Idaszak, Visualization Research Programmer.

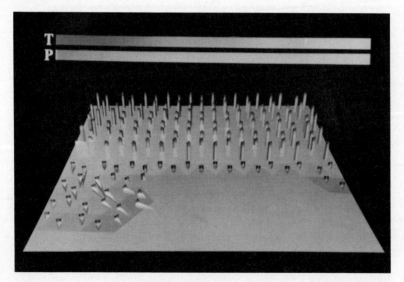

Figure 8.28 Injection molding sequence, $T = T_3$. Image courtesy of Richard Ellson, Kodak Research Scientist; Donna Cox, Visualization Artist; Ray Idaszak, Visualization Research Programmer.

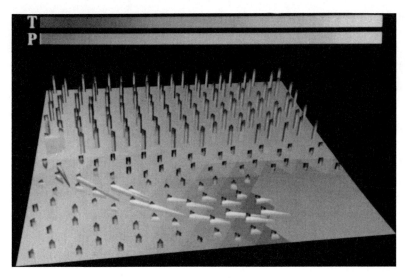

Figure 8.29   Injection molding sequence, $T = T_4$. Image courtesy of Richard Ellson, Kodak Research Scientist; Donna Cox, Visualization Artist; Ray Idaszak, Visualization Research Programmer.

8.7   SUMMARY

At this point a wealth of techniques exist to display data. However, how these techniques are used can either help or, in some cases, hinder the interpretation of the information content in the data.

Computer graphics has promoted many new techniques, including the following: color-shaded distributions of scalars over two-dimensional geometry that is embedded in three-dimensional space, volumetric visualization, and high-order glyphs. At the same time, other graphical techniques and plot styles (e.g., nomograms) are falling into disuse.

The most challenging visualization problems exist in two situations: first, when the same number of independent and dependent variables exist. Second, when more than three dependent variables occur.

Currently, software packages can be obtained that address plotting, contour and surface graphing; scalar distributions over two-dimensional surfaces embedded in three-dimensional space, and volumetric scalar distributions. Other display styles require user-created graphics programming.

8.8   ANNOTATED REFERENCES

Biberman, L. M. *Perception of Displayed Information*. New York: Plenum, 1973.

Presents a discussion of human perception, crucial when designing graphic systems, but often overlooked.

Friedhoff, R. and Benzon, W. *Visualization: The Second Computer Revolution*. Harry
    N. Abrams, Inc., 1989.

Kerlow, I. V., and Rosebush, J. *Computer Graphics for Designers and Artists*. New
    York: Van Nostrand Reinhold, 1986.

*A less mathematical discussion of graphics from a nonengineering background.
Discusses graphic design issues for several types of media. Beautifully illustrated.*

Krueger, M. W. *Virtual Reality II*. Reading, Mass.: Addison-Wesley, 1991.

Laurel, B. *The Art of Human-Computer Interface Design*. Reading, Mass.: Addison-
    Wesley, 1990.

Rheingold, H. *Virtual Reality*. New York: Simon & Schuster, 1991.

SIGGRAPH Video Review, Association for Computing Machinery, New York.

*Most of these tapes have material relevant to visualization. Specific tapes are #28
and #29 (1987), #30, #42, and #43 (1989), and #60 (1990).*

Tufte, Edward. *The Visual Display of Quantitative Information*. Cheshire, Conn.:
    Graphics Press, 1983.

*Excellent reference on theory and practice in design of data presentations. Examples
of both good and bad practice. Important discussion of design of graphs.*

Tufte, Edward. *Envisioning Information*. Cheshire, Conn.: Graphics Press, 1990.

*Excellent set of examples of visualization techniques. Not limited to computer-
generated images.*

*The following publications should be read regularly by CAD developers for devel-
opments in visualization.*

ACM Transactions on Graphics. Association for Computing Machinery, monthly.

Computer Graphics. Special Interest Group on Computer Graphics, Association for
    Computing Machinery, monthly.

SIGGRAPH Proceedings. Association for Computing Machinery, annual.

8.9   PROJECTS

Project 8.1   Interference Pattern

When experimenting with contour plotting programs, surface plotting programs, or digital image display programs, it is useful to have a reasonably
interesting but easily generated set of data. The most common set is probably the "sombrero," which has two parameters, λ, ω. In polar coordinates,
this can be written as follows.

$$z = e^{-\lambda r} \cos(\omega r)$$

A more interesting plot is obtained using the interference pattern between
two such shapes:

$$z = e^{-\lambda_1 r_1} \cos(\omega_1 r_1) + e^{-\lambda_2 r_2} \cos(\omega_2 r_2)$$

where r_1 and r_2 are measured from (x_1, y_1) and (x_2, y_2), respectively. Suggested values are

$$(x_1, y_1) = (1, 1)$$
$$(x_2, y_2) = (-1, -1)$$
$$\lambda_1 = \lambda_2 = 0$$
$$\omega_1 = \omega_2 = 1$$
$$-10 \le x \le 10$$
$$-10 \le y \le 10$$

Project 8.2   Pressure Distribution in a Fluid Film Bearing

Develop a display for the pressure distribution in a squeeze film damper, as discussed in Project 2.5.

Project 8.3   Performance Function Visualization

Develop a display for the performance or response variables as functions of either design variables or parameters from Projects 2.2, 2.4, 2.7, and 2.8.

Project 8.4   Performance Function Visualization

Develop a single display for the dependence between η, W, r, T_3 from Project 2.3.

Project 8.5   Objective Function Visualization

Develop a display for the objective function in Project 6.1, 6.2, 6.3, 6.4, or 6.5.

Project 8.6   Pressure Distribution on Sails

Problem Statement   Develop a visualization for pressure distribution on a mainsail and jib.

Analysis   This is an exercise in visualization of four dependent variables and two independent variables, specifically x, y, z, and $p = f(s, t)$. The pressure distribution can be determined in at least two different ways: First, contour plots have been published, see Marchaj (Project 6.1). Second, the pressure distribution at each cross-section of the sail (the z value) can be calculated independently of the fluid flow at other levels. The pressure distribution is determined for the flow around an infinitely long airfoil with the same cross-section as the sail shape at any particular level. This is essentially a two-dimensional problem. The entire sail pressure distribution is represented as a set of these 2-D approximations. The pressure distribution determined this way neglects any flow in the z direction due to taper of the sail. The 2-D problems can be solved by finite-difference techniques. Alternatively, if the sail is assumed to be a zero-thickness arc of a circle, solutions can be found in fluid dynamics or aerodynamics texts.

It is important to note that the techniques discussed above are applicable to individual airfoils (sails) and besides neglecting taper also, more importantly, neglect the interaction between the airfoils. A primary reason for the use of a foresail is to increase air velocity within the "slot" (the space between the foresail and mainsail) which substantially improves the performance of the mainsail.

Project 8.7   Patch Model Error Visualization

Problem Statement   Develop a visual representation of the errors in the geometric model for the sail developed in Project 9.2.

Comments   This project is essentially the same as Project 8.6, except for using geometric error instead of pressure. Visual representations such as this have been developed to display errors from ideal geometry caused by machining or tolerance variations.

C H A P T E R

9
Geometry

9.1 INTRODUCTION

Mechanical engineers are frequently concerned with questions pertaining to shape. This includes the shape of actual objects but also extends to the shape of conceptual entities. Many of the available analytical methods depend on conceptualizing a quantity as a shape that can help in interpretation. Examples include conceptualizing an optimization problem as locating the minimum of some surface, representing a scalar field as a set of equipotential lines or surfaces, or conceptualizing the frequency response of a system as a curve.

We will approach the geometry required for computer-aided design as a concept more general than modeling of physical objects. That is, all geometric entities, not just three-dimensional solids, will be dealt with in a consistent manner. As such, the 0-D point, the 1-D curve, the 2-D surface (patch), and the 3-D solid will be developed using a unified and extensible formulation.

In the field of computer-aided design, geometric models have usually been characterized in terms of wire frame, surface, or solid representations. The more general approach adopted in this chapter can be referred to as *nonmanifold modeling*, as opposed to manifold modeling, which is discussed in more detail in Section 9.8. The boundary of a manifold divides the space and unambiguously separates inside from outside. On the boundary of a manifold solid, the small area around any point is homeomorphic to a disk or "locally two-dimensional."

A geometric entity can be thought of as identifying a set of points from the set of all possible points. A manifold divides the space and thus can identify those points that are, and those that are not, in the set. A space of dimension n is divided or limited by an entity of dimension $n - 1$. For example, a 1-D space is divided by a 0-D point, a 2-D space is divided by a 1-D curve, and a 3-D space is divided by a 2-D surface. The most simple entity at each level is defined by the most simple entity at the next lowest dimension of space, starting from a point.

A curve can be limited (or bounded) by points. Two are required, and the result is a straight line. Two points can be said to define a bounded straight line. A surface can be limited (or bounded) by a closed curve. With straight lines three are required, yielding a triangle. A volume can be limited (or bounded) by a closed surface. Using triangles, four are required, yielding a tetrahedron.

Physical component models are usually developed as true solids. These might be machined objects with very regular surfaces, such as crankshafts and pistons. However, these "chunks" of material are defined more often than not by complicated sculptured surfaces (connecting rod, pump impellor, intake manifold within an engine head).

The aircraft industry relied extensively on surface modeling, primarily for its use in modeling aerodynamic surfaces such as wing sections, fuselages, rudders, and so forth. In addition, this approach was affected by the design of built-up structures fashioned from stringers and very thin skins.

The distinctions, however, are not cleanly defined. For instance, the automotive industry is very interested in the application of surface models for the aesthetic design and sheet metal forming of body panels. The aircraft industry is interested in solid models for landing gear components, engine components, and so forth.

Accurate shape representation is required for more than aesthetic visualization in design applications (conception, display, and modification of complex forms). A precise, unambiguous, and accurate model is required for both functional prediction (perhaps based on finite element analysis techniques) and for manufacturing purposes (such as numerically controlled machining).

Examples of objects include engine block castings, artificial hip and knee joints and models of the human skeletal system, automobile rearview mirrors, ship hulls, and aircraft wings.

9.2   REQUIRED FUNCTIONS

Using point, curve, surface, and solid entities, one may be required to perform the analytical operations of Table 9.1 and the manipulative operations of Table 9.2.

The analytic operations can be classified as unary (having only one operand) and binary (having two operands). Many of these functions are not well defined for all four types of entities. For example, the distance between two curves is not unique, although one may assume that the minimum distance is desired. Note that neither a point nor a solid has local tangent, normal, or curvature. Similarly the integral operations are not applicable to the point and the enclosed integral is not meaningful for a solid.

As shown in Table 9.2, manipulative operations are also unary and binary. The unary operations are straightforward, using techniques discussed in Chapter 7, although actual implementation will depend on the specific

	Unary
Local Tangent	Curve
	Surface
Local Normal	Curve
	Surface
Local Curvature	Curve
	Surface
Integral	Line Integral along Curve
	Surface Integral
	Volume Integral
Enclosed Integral	Integral over Area Enclosed by Curve
	Integral over Volume Enclosed by Surface
Centroids	
Weighted Integral	Moments of Inertia (line, area, volume)
	Binary
Distance	Point-to-Point
	Point-to-Curve
	Point-to-Surface
	Point-to-Solid
	Curve-to-Curve
	Curve-to-Surface
	Curve-to-Solid
	Surface-to-Surface
	Surface-to-Solid
	Solid-to-Solid

Table 9.1   Analytical operations.

Unary	Binary	Operands
Create	Intersection	Point-to-Point
Delete	Union	Point-to-Curve
Edit	Difference	Point-to-Surface
Move		Point-to-Solid
Rotate		Curve-to-Curve
Scale		Curve-to-Surface
Shear		Curve-to-Solid
		Surface-to-Surface
		Surface-to-Solid
		Solid-to-Solid

Table 9.2   Manipulative operations.

data structures used. The binary operations listed are based on the Boolean operations applicable in the mathematics of sets. For additional information, the reader should refer to the literature of the mathematical background in this area (Mortenson). Note that the list of operands is simply all possible combinations of entities.

Manipulative operations are useful not only for creation and modification of geometry, but also for design purposes. One may require the intersection of a line of sight with a true solid. Collision detection can be posed as an intersection problem, and generation of a cross-section is the intersection of a solid and a surface.

All of the analytical operations return information about the geometric entity, but the manipulative operations return another geometric entity. This is best seen by considering the intersection of two surfaces, which produces a curve (possibly a null curve).

However, the complication for CAD systems is that the operations may not produce a geometric entity of the same type. In mathematical terminology, the set of objects is not closed under the listed operations. Solid objects are closed under these three operations, as discussed in Section 9.8. However, neither the set of all surfaces, nor the set of all curves, nor the set of all points is closed under the listed operations. For example, consider two curves. The intersection of two curves is a point (possibly a null point). The union of two curves is a curve, but the difference between two curves is two curves (end-to-end) with an infinitesimal gap. The operations are not guaranteed to produce a well-formed curve. (Further study of all possible combinations of operations and entities in Table 9.2 will show that it is the difference operations that produce the most unusual and ill-defined geometry combinations.)

Although closure is desirable, it must be sacrificed to accommodate the mixture of geometric entities required. Even if each type of geometric entity were closed under the operations, we still would need to have operations that involve combinations of entities. The union of a curve and a surface produces a mixed entity, a curve, and a surface.

CAD systems cannot be limited to a set of one type of entity. Points are needed to specify locations; lines are needed to specify trajectories, directions, and intersections of surfaces; surfaces are needed to specify constraints and interfaces, cross-sections, and boundaries of solids, and solids are needed to specify physical objects.

9.3 NOTATION

Throughout this chapter, $\vec{Q}$ will represent the coordinates of geometry, and $\vec{P}$ will represent a finite set of data from which $\vec{Q}$ is developed.

$$\vec{Q}(s, t) = f(\vec{P}_{ij})$$

In the preceding equation, the subscripts of $\vec{P}$ identify the member of the finite set; $\vec{Q}$ is a function of one or two parametric variables, and both have three components:

$$\vec{P} = \left\{ \begin{array}{c} P_x \\ P_y \\ P_z \end{array} \right\} \qquad \vec{Q} = \left\{ \begin{array}{c} Q_x \\ Q_y \\ Q_z \end{array} \right\}$$

9.4 POINTS

Even though a point doesn't represent a physical object (having no mass or volume), it is invaluable to CAD modelers because it defines a location in space of N dimensions. As we will see, most higher-order entities are defined in terms of sets of points.

The most appropriate representation for a point in 3-D is as a triplet $\{x, y, z\}$ (assumed to be in a right-handed cartesian frame). A more general approach would define a point data structure that includes an identifier and the possibility of associating a scalar value with the point, so as to represent time, temperature, speed, and so forth. Data structures will be discussed in more detail in Chapter 10.

9.5 CURVES

The point is a zero-dimensional entity, and the number of its representations are relatively limited. A curve is a one-dimensional entity with many more types of representations. A curve is unbounded, but part of the definitions that follow involve bounding to a segment of the curve.

This section builds upon the material on parametric representation and various types of cubics and splines that was developed in Chapter 2. Before proceeding, it will prove invaluable to review the characteristics expected of curve generation procedures:

- Axis independence
- Multiple valued
- Global versus local behavior
- Variation diminishing

In design applications, a curve's geometry should be independent of the reference axes chosen to express it. This is best understood by a counterexample. A least-squares curve fit through a set of points is dependent on the choice of coordinate axes used, even for the same set of points. The ability to represent multiple-valued curves was cited in Chapter 2 as a prime reason for using parametric representation. Desired design modifications often are only local changes in the overall shape of the curve. For any representation scheme, it is important to know if a change in the parameters that specify a particular curve will produce a local modification or a global modification.

Variation diminishing refers to the capability to smooth out local irregularities in shape (or in geometry). As developed in Chapter 2, a high-order polynomial curve fit was shown to not be variation diminishing, but rather to be sensitive to the precise values of the control points.

The Straight Line

The most fundamental of all curves is the straight line. A common way to define a straight line is in terms of the endpoints $\{x_1, y_1, z_1\}, \{x_2, y_2, z_2\}$, or $\{\mathbf{Point_1}, \mathbf{Point_2}\}$. This highlights the fact that in almost all cases, we deal with curve segments, or finite portions of curves. The line itself is infinite in length and the endpoints are used to define the segment.

The following equations show two possible forms for a line. The first is based on two endpoints, and the second is based on endpoint, tangent direction, and length. It would appear that the latter is based on seven pieces of data and the former is based on only six; however, an implied constraint on the second equation is that the tangent vector is a unit vector. The latter form makes the bounding explicit.

$$\left\{\begin{matrix} x \\ y \\ z \end{matrix}\right\} = (1 - s)\left\{\begin{matrix} x_1 \\ y_1 \\ z_1 \end{matrix}\right\} + s\left\{\begin{matrix} x_2 \\ y_2 \\ z_2 \end{matrix}\right\}$$

$$\left\{\begin{matrix} x \\ y \\ z \end{matrix}\right\} = \left\{\begin{matrix} x_1 \\ y_1 \\ z_1 \end{matrix}\right\} + sL\left\{\begin{matrix} n_x \\ n_y \\ n_z \end{matrix}\right\}$$

General Space Curve

A general space curve can be described with the point, tangent, and length formulation by allowing the tangent to be a function of the arc length location. However, this is too general in most cases and so simplifications will be considered. The reader is referred to Mortenson for an excellent discussion of the general space curve.

Circular Arcs

A bounded portion of a circle forms a circular arc. Once again, the major issues are how such arcs are specified and limited. A circle in $\mathbf{R}^3$ can be specified by a center point, a radius, and a normal vector. Arcs (and more generally quadratics) are always planar. Section 9.6 provides definitions for a plane. Once limited to a plane, the circle can be defined by any of the methods listed in Table 9.3.

Table 9.3 illustrates the increasing complexity of definitions. A general-purpose CAD program would have to support almost all of these possibilities. Furthermore, the circle is just one of the family of quadratic curves (ellipse,

Radius, Tangent to Two Lines
Radius, Tangent to Two Arcs
Radius, Tangent to Two Curves
Radius, Tangent to a Line and Circle
Center, Tangent to a Circle
Center, Tangent to a Line
Passing through a Point, Tangent to Two Lines
Passing through a Point, Tangent to Two Arcs
Three Points
Tangent to Three Lines
Passing through Two Points, Tangent to a Line
Passing through a Point with a Specified Slope, Tangent to a Line
Passing through a Point, Radius, Tangent to a Line

Table 9.3 Methods of defining a circle.

parabola, and hyperbola), each of which has many alternative definitions. Instead of enumerating all possible definitions for entities, this chapter will discuss the underlying representation schemes.

Bézier Curve

The family of quadratic curves is not sufficiently general for curve definition. For example, quadratics are planar and do not exhibit inflection points. Bézier proposed to blend discrete point information into a curve. If the parametric dimension is denoted by s, the curve is defined from n control points $\vec{P_i}$ as

$$\vec{Q}(s) = \sum_{i=0}^{n} \Phi_i(s)\vec{P_i}$$

The blending functions $\Phi_i(s)$ are known as the Bernstein polynomials:

$$\Phi_i(s) = \frac{n!}{i!(n-i)!} s^i (1-s)^{n-i}$$

which are essentially binomial distribution functions. For example, if $n = 3$, then

$$\Phi_0(s) = 1(1-s)^3$$
$$\Phi_1(s) = 3(1-s)^2 s$$
$$\Phi_2(s) = 3(1-s)s^2$$
$$\Phi_3(s) = 1s^3$$

These basis functions are shown in Fig. 9.1.

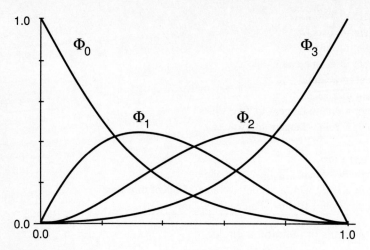

Figure 9.1   Degree three Bernstein basis functions.

Note that at $s = 0$ only Φ_0 is non-zero and in fact is precisely 1.0. This ensures that the curve will pass through P_0. Similarly at $s = 1$, $\Phi_3 = 1.0$ while the others are zero, and the curve interpolates $\vec{P}_3$. The other blending functions are maximum at the values of $s = \frac{1}{3}$ and $s = \frac{2}{3}$, respectively, causing the curve to approach $\vec{P}_1$ and $\vec{P}_2$. The curve generally will not pass through either point because the other blending functions are not zero.

A series of straight-line interpolations through the control points is the "control polygon." The Bézier curve is tangent to the first leg of the control polygon at $s = 0$ and tangent to the last leg at $s = 1$. Bézier curves require a minimum of four control points for independent control of slope at each end of the curve.

An example of a four-point Bézier curve is shown in Fig. 9.2, along with the control points and control polygon. A "fence" representation and the projection on the x, y plane is shown for clarity. Note that the curve passes through the endpoints, is "attracted to" the intermediate points, and is tangent to the directions defined by the line segments between points 0,1 and 2,3.

Multiple Bézier segments can be used to create composite curves. Continuity of tangency is preserved by controlling the tangent directions at the junctions, as shown in Fig. 9.3, where the open control polygon for each segment is shown. Specifically, the end segments of the control polygons must be collinear for tangent continuity.

Higher-degree Bézier curves are quickly developed by noting the pattern for the exponents of the terms s and $(1 - s)$ and using Pascal's triangle to find the binomial coefficients:

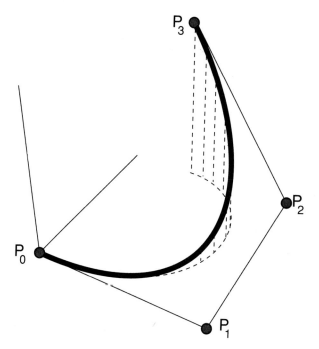

Figure 9.2   Sample 3-D Bézier curve.

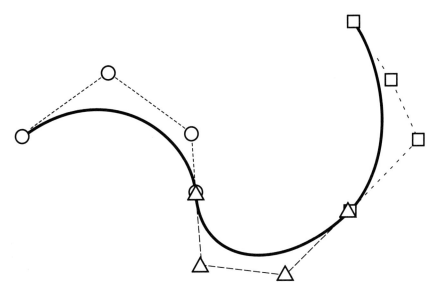

Figure 9.3   Composite Bézier curve.

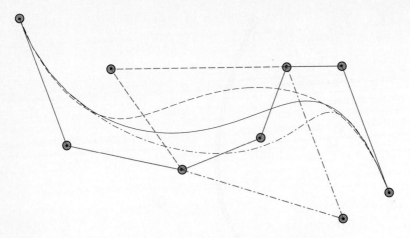

Figure 9.4   The global effect of change for the Bézier curve.

		1			order 0
	1		1		order 1
	1	2	1		order 2
1	3		3	1	order 3
1	4	6	4	1	order 4

Bézier curves have two distinct disadvantages: First, it is very difficult to make the curve interpolate (pass through) any specific points, other than the endpoints. A four-point interpolant can be reworked into Bézier form, but interactive control of the interpolant is more difficult. Second, the effect of moving a control point is global, as shown in Fig. 9.4, although the effect does decrease as one moves away from the control point. The solid line shows a Bézier curve through seven points. The control polygon is drawn in a light grey solid line. The dashed line (and control polygon) and the dash-dot line (and control polygon) show the effect of moving one control point. The Bézier curve is drawn with a very thin line to show that the changes extend along the entire length of the curve. This global effect occurs because the blending function for any particular control point is nonzero for the entire length of the curve [0, 1].

■ **EXERCISE 9.1:** Develop the algebraic form for the four-point Bézier curve. This form can be useful for reducing computation costs during curve evaluation, although the Bézier form is the most stable for evaluation purposes. Algebraic and geometric forms are discussed in Section 2.2.

■ **EXERCISE 9.2:** Plot the Bernstein polynomials for $n = 3$ and $n = 6$.

■ **EXERCISE 9.3:** Determine a "good" set of control points for a four-point Bézier representation for a 90° and a 180° circular arc. Using the known tangency at each end of the arcs, the problem can be reduced to determining a distance d along the tangent line at which to place the control points. The known symmetry about the normal through the middle of the arc will require symmetry in the control polygon. Therefore the problem has only one scalar value to be determined. An error ϵ can be determined, using the midpoint of the arc ($s = 0.5$), and the problem can be formulated as a root-finding problem ($\epsilon(d) = 0$). *Hint*: Locate the arc with the circular center at the origin.

■ **EXERCISE 9.4:** The Bézier curve will remain within the closed control polygon. Consider a Bézier curve with four control points arranged such that the control polygon forms a "figure 8." The curve will pass through the intersection of the 8. Determine the parametric coordinate s at that intersection.

■ **EXERCISE 9.5:** The Bézier curve can be developed with control points that are co-located. Plot the Bézier curve for three control points $\vec{P}_a, \vec{P}_b, \vec{P}_c$. Plot a four-point Bézier curve using the control points $\vec{P}_a, \vec{P}_b, \vec{P}_b, \vec{P}_c$; that is, the two interior control points are co-located. The "strength" of any control point can be increased by using this method.

B-Splines

A disadvantage of the Bézier curve is that any change in a control point will produce a global change over the entire curve, as was shown in Fig. 9.4. This discourages the use of very high-degree Bézier curves and encourages collections of low-degree curves. It is important to distinguish between a single Bézier curve of high order and an end-to-end collection of Bézier curves (as in Fig. 9.3). However, other basis functions can be used that will have a similar effect of blending a large number of control points but will limit the range of effect of any particular control point. The functions for the B-splines form a family of sets of functions, each set characterized by degree ($k - 1$) and producing a B-spline curve. Specifically, the degree $k - 1$ B-spline is based on blending functions $N_{i,k}(s)$:

$$\vec{Q}(s) = \sum_{i=0}^{n} N_{i,k}(s)\vec{P}_i$$

As in the Bézier curve, the B-spline is based on an open polygon with $n + 1$ points. However, the blending functions are nonzero over a range of k control points. For $k = n + 1$, the blending functions span the entire range, as in the Bézier curve. As the degree is decreased, the nonzero width of the basis functions narrows and the curve approaches each control point more closely. Ultimately, at degree 1 ($k = 2$), the spline degenerates into the open control polygon itself (linear interpolation between control points). The degree of the basis functions is $k - 1$.

A B-spline is developed as follows: The degree ($k - 1$) and number of vertices ($n + 1$) are chosen. (Note that the number of points will be $n + 1$

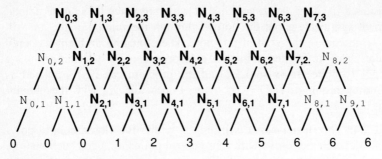

Figure 9.5   B-spline basis functions $N_{i,k}$.

because points are numbered from $\vec{P}_0$.) The parametric coordinate s will cover the range $0 < s < n + 1 - (k - 1)$. The *knot vector* $\{\alpha_0, \alpha_1, \ldots, \alpha_i, \ldots, \alpha_{n+k}\}$ is formed by the integers over the range of s, with an end multiplicity of k. For example, a degree 2 spline for five points would span $0 < s < 3$ and the associated knot vector would be

$$\{0 \quad 0 \quad 0 \quad 1 \quad 2 \quad 3 \quad 3 \quad 3\}$$

A degree 2 spline for four points would span $0 < s < 2$ and the associated knot vector would be

$$\{0 \quad 0 \quad 0 \quad 1 \quad 2 \quad 2 \quad 2\}$$

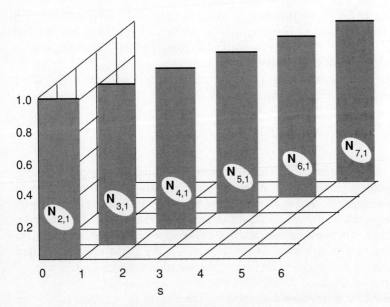

Figure 9.6   Degree 0 B-spline basis functions.

The B-spline is defined as

$$\vec{Q}(s) = \sum_{i=0}^{n} N_{i,k}(s)\vec{P}_i$$

and the weighting functions are defined in a recursive fashion:

$$N_{i,k}(s) = \frac{s - \alpha_i}{\alpha_{i+k-1} - \alpha_i} N_{i,k-1}(s) - \frac{s - \alpha_{i+k}}{\alpha_{i+k} - \alpha_{i+1}} N_{i+1,k-1}(s)$$

and

$$N_{i,1}(s) = \begin{cases} 1, & \text{if } \alpha_i < s < \alpha_{i+1} \\ 0, & \text{otherwise.} \end{cases}$$

This formulation uses the convention that $\frac{0}{0} = 0$.

The recursive nature of the definition is shown in Fig. 9.5, which represents the basis functions of a second-degree B-spline over eight points. The associated knot vector is $\{0, 0, 0, 1, 2, 3, 4, 5, 6, 6, 6\}$. The depth of the array of spline functions is determined by the degree of the spline, and the width is determined by the length of the knot vector. At the lowest level, the functions $N_{0,1}, N_{1,1}, N_{2,1}, \ldots$ are either 0 or 1 depending upon the value of the parametric variable s. Note that some of these may be zero always. The zero basis functions for the particular knot vector in Fig. 9.5 are shown in a lighter font.

Figures 9.6 and 9.7 show the zero- and first-degree basis functions that develop the second-degree B-spline basis functions over eight points, as shown in Fig. 9.8. For each increase in order, the nonzero width of the basis function increases, as shown in Figure 9.9. The basis functions do not always peak at a knot location. For example, if $k = 3$ and $n = 7$, then

$$N_{2,3} = \begin{cases} \frac{1}{2}s^2 & 0 < s < 1 \\ -s^2 + 3s - \frac{3}{2} & 1 < s < 2 \\ \frac{1}{2}(s - 3)^2 & 2 < s < 3 \end{cases}$$

which has a maximum value of 0.75 at $s = 1.5$.

As the degree of the B-spline is increased, the basis functions are nonzero over a larger parameter range, and therefore, the effects of changing a single point in the control polygon become less and less local. The central basis functions have the same shape, just shifted. However, the end conditions produce special basis functions, as shown in Fig. 9.8.

The B-spline will be contained within a polygon that can be generated from the control points. For a B-spline of degree $k - 1$, sequentially take k control points and form the convex hull. The B-spline will be contained within the superposition of these polygons. Figure 9.10 shows the superposition for six points and $k = 2, 3$, and 4. This figure illustrates how decreasing the degree of the B-spline requires the spline to pass more closely to the control points.

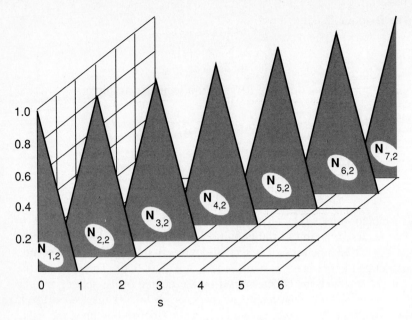

Figure 9.7   Degree 1 B-spline basis functions.

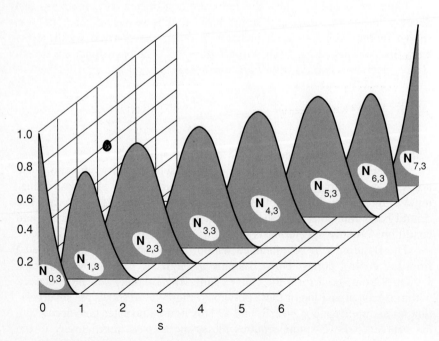

Figure 9.8   Degree 2 B-spline basis functions.

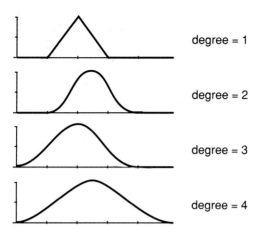

Figure 9.9 Higher-degree B-spline basis functions.

B-splines can be developed with multiple internal knots and for closed curves rather than the open curve segments presented in Fig. 9.10. These advanced topics will not be developed here, but for additional information, the interested reader should refer to Faux and Pratt, Farin, or Coons.

■ **EXERCISE 9.6:** Develop and plot the basis functions for a degree 2 B-spline through six points.

■ **EXERCISE 9.7:** Develop the basis functions for a B-spline curve of degree 3 through four points. Compare these to the degree 3 Bernstein polynomials.

■ **EXERCISE 9.8:** Develop the basis functions for a B-spline curve of degree 4 through five points. Compare these to the degree 5 Bernstein polynomials.

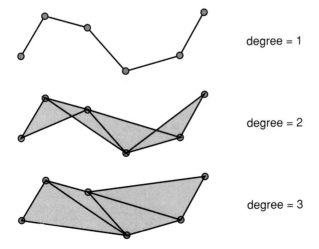

Figure 9.10 Convex hulls for increasing degree B-spline.

9.6 SURFACES

Plane

The simplest of all surfaces is the plane, which by definition is "flat." Even though this would appear to be rather limiting, reasonably complex and robust geometrical modeling programs can be built using flat planes. These polyhedral or faceted modelers use flat planes to represent even curved surfaces by discretizing to an appropriate level. Tesselation is discussed in Section 9.7.

An important issue to be addressed is how to define a plane. The CAD system designer must select one of these definitions for an internal representation, even if various definitions are supported for the user interface.

The most fundamental representation is the implicit plane normal form

$$ax + by + cz + d = 0$$

The coefficients have physical meaning in that $\{a, b, c\}^T$ is the unit vector which is normal to the plane, and d is the distance from the origin to the plane. Note that for the preceding interpretation of coefficients, the equation must be normalized so that $a^2 + b^2 + c^2 = 1$. Although this representation defines the orientation of the plane, it does not address the questions of limits.

As was the case with curves, only a finite portion of the infinite plane is of interest. As with the curve, a surface entity (2-D) will be limited by an entity of one less order (1-D), a curve. Any closed curve will suffice. Therefore the possibilities are limited only by the limitations of the previous section. However, if we intend to form surfaces from a collection of planar faces, we must require the limiting curves to be polygons, because only a straight line segment can be common to two planes.

Regardless of the number of edges and vertices in a nondegenerate closed planar polygon, only three noncollinear points are required to define the plane of the polygon. The direction cosines for the edges, the plane normal form, and other useful information can all be generated from the three-point definition. This concept is developed further in the case of a polyhedral data base in Example 10.2.

Patches

The term patch is usually reserved for the geometric description of nonplanar surfaces. Patches can be defined through *implicit representation* using any restricted set of functions $f(x, y, z) = 0$, which can include spheres, cylinders, tori, cones, and so forth. One analytic form is the general quadratic equation in x, y, z:

$$ax^2 + by^2 + cz^2 + 2fyz + 2gzx + 2hxy + 2px + 2qy + 2rz + d = 0$$

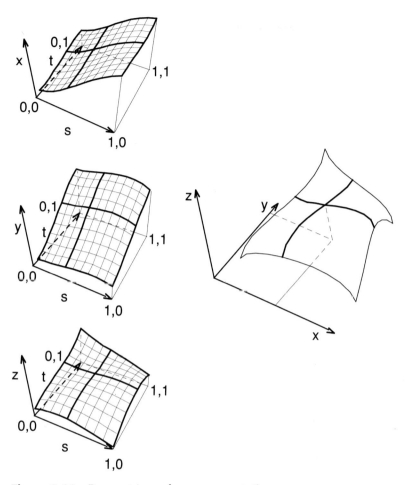

Figure 9.11 Parametric surface representation.

With appropriate coefficients this form can represent an ellipsoid, a hyperboloid of one or two sheets, a quadric cone, an elliptic paraboloid, a hyperbolic paraboloid, an elliptic cylinder, a hyperbolic cylinder, a parabolic cylinder, intersection planes, parallel planes, or coincident planes, as well as imaginary versions of many of these.

A *parametric representation* is more useful and is preferred for describing curves. It is multivalued and easily limited. In this case, each coordinate is treated as a function of two parameters (s, t), as shown in Fig. 9.11. The limits are generally normalized to $s, t \in [0, 1]$ or $s, t \in [-1, 1]$. Figure 9.12 shows the patch notation that will be used.

Parametric representations can be divided into three classes: cartesian product, lofting, and transfinite definition.

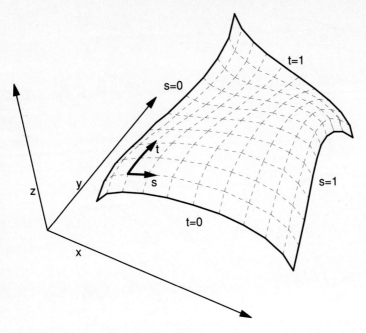

Figure 9.12   Surface patch notation.

The *cartesian product* (also known as tensor product) uses blending functions to define the patch in terms of point and tangent vector information. This has been called zero-variate information.

$$\vec{Q}(s, t) = \sum_i \sum_j \Phi_{ij}(s, t)\vec{P}_{ij}$$

Examples of this form include bilinear mapping, bicubic patches, Bézier patches, and B-spline patches.

The *lofting method* passes the surface through a family of curves:

$$\vec{Q}(s, t) = \sum_j \Phi_j(t)\vec{P}_j(s)$$

This has been called univariate information. This technique has found wide use in the aircraft and shipbuilding industries.

The *transfinite definition* is a blend of two families of curves:

$$\vec{Q}(s, t) = \sum_i \Phi_i(s)\vec{P}_i(t) + \sum_j \Phi_j(t)\vec{P}_j(s) - \sum_i \sum_j \Phi_{ij}(s, t)\vec{P}_{ij}$$

In the following subsections, we will develop a detailed example of each type of patch.

Example 9.1: Spherical Surface. As a running example throughout the chapter, we will consider a patch that represents a portion of a sphere. This is an appropriate example for several reasons, but the primary reason is that the

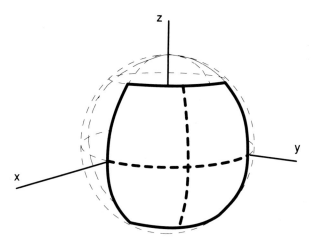

Figure 9.13 A segment of the surface of a sphere.

true shape of the desired surface is known both intuitively and analytically. The intuitive knowledge will help in visualizing the patches, and the analytical knowledge will help in developing the patch control data $\vec{P}$. The target surface is shown in Fig. 9.13, which represents the area from $0°$ to $+90°$ in longitude, as measured from the meridian in the x, z plane, and from $\pm 45°$ in latitude, as measured from the equator in the x, y plane.

Bilinear Mapping

Using the coordinates of the four corners, $\vec{P}_{00}, \vec{P}_{10}, \vec{P}_{01}, \vec{P}_{11}$, a cartesian product yields the bilinear patch. The bilinear patch is planar only if the four corner points lie within a plane. Otherwise, the patch generates a ruled surface, which means that the surface is composed of straight lines. Effectively, the patch uses straight-line interpolation to find the endpoints of a constant s line:

$$\vec{Q}(s, 0) = (1 - s)\vec{P}_{0,0} + s\vec{P}_{1,0}$$
$$\vec{Q}(s, 1) = (1 - s)\vec{P}_{0,1} + s\vec{P}_{1,1}$$

Then the patch uses straight-line interpolation between the endpoints:

$$\vec{Q}(s, t) = (1 - t)\vec{Q}(s, 0) + t\vec{Q}(s, 1)$$

Substitution leads to

$$\vec{Q}(s, t) = \vec{P}_{00}(1 - s)(1 - t) + \vec{P}_{01}(1 - s)t + \vec{P}_{10}s(1 - t) + \vec{P}_{11}st$$

which can be easily rewritten in matrix form as

$$\vec{Q}(s, t) = \{1 - s \quad s\} \begin{bmatrix} \vec{P}_{00} & \vec{P}_{01} \\ \vec{P}_{10} & \vec{P}_{11} \end{bmatrix} \begin{Bmatrix} 1 - t \\ t \end{Bmatrix}$$

Figure 9.14 shows a bilinear patch using four corners of a unit cube.

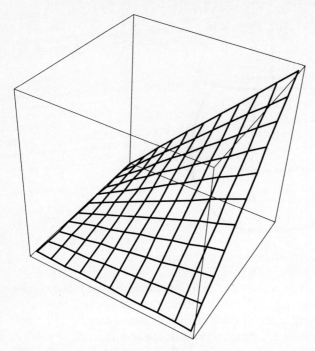

Figure 9.14 Sample bilinear patch.

Example 9.2: Bilinear Patch on a Sphere. For the spherical segment of Example 9.1, the bilinear mapping shown in Fig. 9.15 is based on the four corner points (which are coplanar).

$$\vec{P}_{00} = \left\{ \begin{array}{c} 0.707 \\ 0 \\ -0.707 \end{array} \right\} \qquad \vec{P}_{01} = \left\{ \begin{array}{c} 0.707 \\ 0 \\ 0.707 \end{array} \right\}$$

$$\vec{P}_{10} = \left\{ \begin{array}{c} 0 \\ 0.707 \\ -0.707 \end{array} \right\} \qquad \vec{P}_{11} = \left\{ \begin{array}{c} 0 \\ 0.707 \\ 0.707 \end{array} \right\}$$

Obviously, this planar surface patch is a rather poor approximation for a spherical surface over such a large angle.

Lofting in One Direction

In order to introduce additional curvature, the linear approximation along the edges can be generalized into four known functions, as shown in Fig. 9.16:

$$\vec{P}_1(s) = \vec{P}(s,0) \qquad \vec{P}_2(t) = \vec{P}(1,t)$$
$$\vec{P}_3(s) = \vec{P}(s,1) \qquad \vec{P}_4(t) = \vec{P}(0,t)$$

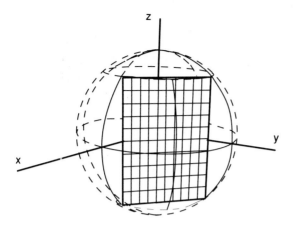

Figure 9.15 Sphere example: bilinear patch.

Using a linear loft in the t direction yields

$$\vec{Q}(s, t) = \vec{P}_1(s)(1 - t) + \vec{P}_3(s)t$$

Alternatively, a linear loft in the s direction yields

$$\vec{Q}(s, t) = \vec{P}_4(t)(1 - s) + \vec{P}_2(t)s$$

The bounding curves can be defined in any fashion and to any degree of complexity. However, the resulting patch is completely linear in the second direction unless a higher-order lofting function is used.

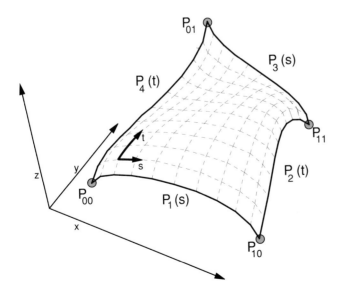

Figure 9.16 The Coons patch notation.

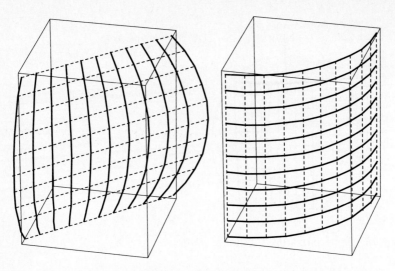

Figure 9.17 Sphere example: lofted patches.

Example 9.3: Linear Lofts on a Spherical Surface. Figure 9.17 shows
a linear loft in s and a linear loft in t for the spherical patch example. In
these cases the exact circular boundary is used, either

$$\vec{P}_1(s) = 0.707 \begin{Bmatrix} \cos(s\pi/2) \\ \sin(s\pi/2) \\ -1.0 \end{Bmatrix} \qquad \vec{P}_3(s) = 0.707 \begin{Bmatrix} \cos(s\pi/2) \\ \sin(s\pi/2) \\ 1.0 \end{Bmatrix}$$

or

$$\vec{P}_4(t) = \begin{Bmatrix} \cos((2t-1)\pi/4) \\ 0 \\ \sin((2t-1)\pi/4) \end{Bmatrix} \qquad \vec{P}_2(t) = \begin{Bmatrix} 0 \\ \cos((2t-1)\pi/4) \\ \sin((2t-1)\pi/4) \end{Bmatrix}$$

The four corners and the two edges are exact and the patch is not flat.
For this example, the error can be determined very easily at any parametric
location because the distance from the origin should be 1.0. For example,
at $(s, t) = (0.5, 0.5)$ the linear loft in s gives an error of

$$e = 0.293 = 1.0 - \left\| \begin{Bmatrix} 0.5 \\ 0.5 \\ 0.0 \end{Bmatrix} \right\|$$

and the linear loft in t gives an error of

$$e = 0.293 = 1.0 - \left\| \begin{Bmatrix} 0.5 \\ 0.5 \\ 0.0 \end{Bmatrix} \right\|$$

Bidirectional Lofting (Linear Coons Surface)

Additional interior curvature can be added by considering all four sides simultaneously: $\vec{P}(s, 0)$, $\vec{P}(s, 1)$, $\vec{P}(0, t)$, and $\vec{P}(1, t)$. This can be viewed as an average of the preceding linear lofts in s and t.

$$\vec{Q}(s, t) = \frac{\vec{P}_1(s)(1 - t) + \vec{P}_3(s)t + \vec{P}_4(t)(1 - s) + \vec{P}_2(t)s}{2}$$

However, even though the corners are correct, this straightforward average results in an edge that is the average of the correct edge and the linear loft between the two corners. The reader should superimpose the patches in Fig. 9.17 and visualize the process. For the general case, along the $s = 0$ edge,

$$\vec{Q}(0, t) = \frac{\left(\vec{P}_1(0)(1 - t) + \vec{P}_3(0)t\right) + \vec{P}_4(t)}{2}$$

which should be $\vec{Q}(0, t) = \vec{P}_4(t)$. The error for the fourth side is

$$e_4 = \frac{1}{2}\left(\vec{P}_1(0)(1 - t) + \vec{P}_3(0)t\right) - \vec{P}_4(t)$$

The errors for each side (1,2,3,4) are multiplied by $(1 - s)$, $(1 - t)$, s, and t, respectively, and subtracted from the average given above. After a bit of algebraic manipulation, and noting that

$$\vec{P}_{00} = \vec{P}_1(0) = \vec{P}_4(0)$$
$$\vec{P}_{10} = \vec{P}_1(1) = \vec{P}_2(0)$$
$$\vec{P}_{01} = \vec{P}_4(1) = \vec{P}_3(0)$$
$$\vec{P}_{11} = \vec{P}_3(1) = \vec{P}_2(1)$$

the resulting expression (the Coons patch) is

$$\vec{Q}(s, t) = \vec{P}(s, 0)(1 - t) + \vec{P}(s, 1)t + \vec{P}(0, t)(1 - s) + \vec{P}(1, t)s$$
$$- \vec{P}_{00}(1 - s)(1 - t) - \vec{P}_{01}(1 - s)t$$
$$- \vec{P}_{10}s(1 - t) - \vec{P}_{11}st$$

In compact notation this becomes

$$\vec{Q}(s, t) = \left\{ \begin{matrix} 1 - s & s & 1 \end{matrix} \right\} \begin{bmatrix} -\vec{P}_{00} & -\vec{P}_{01} & \vec{P}(0, t) \\ -\vec{P}_{10} & -\vec{P}_{11} & \vec{P}(1, t) \\ \vec{P}(s, 0) & \vec{P}(s, 1) & 0 \end{bmatrix} \left\{ \begin{matrix} 1 - t \\ t \\ 1 \end{matrix} \right\}$$

The Coons patch is an example of a transfinite representation in which each family consists of two curves ($i = 1, 2$; $j = 1, 2$).

Example 9.4: A Coons Patch for a Spherical Surface. The Coons patch for the spherical segment is shown in Fig. 9.18. The same edge functions

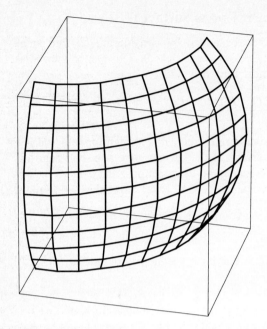

Figure 9.18 Sphere example: Coon's patch.

are used as in Example 9.3, namely the exact analytical edge equations. Visually the result is acceptable; however, most engineering analyses are not "visual."

■ **EXERCISE 9.9:** Determine the error for the approximate patch in Example 9.4. (Refer to Example 9.3 for a discussion of error determination.) This patch can be displayed as a contour plot in (s, t) space.

Bicubic Surface Patch

Analytical expressions for patch boundaries usually are not available. The reader should remember that frequently curves are generated by operations rather than by specification. If the general underlying representation for all curves is cubic, then one can build upon this and assume that the shape of the patch is of cubic order:

$$\vec{Q}(s, t) = \sum_{i=0}^{3} \sum_{j=0}^{3} \vec{a}_{ij} s^i t^j$$

Cubic space curves will form the boundaries of this representation. For example:

$$\vec{Q}(s, 0) = \vec{a}_{30} s^3 + \vec{a}_{20} s^2 + \vec{a}_{10} s + \vec{a}_{00}$$

Recalling the parametric cubic material in Section 2.2,

$$Q(s, 0) = a_0 + a_1 s + a_2 s^2 + a_3 s^3$$

and

$$\left\{ \begin{array}{c} Q(0) \\ Q(1) \\ dQ/ds\,(0) \\ dQ/ds\,(1) \end{array} \right\} = \begin{bmatrix} 0 & 0 & 0 & 1 \\ 1 & 1 & 1 & 1 \\ 0 & 0 & 1 & 0 \\ 3 & 2 & 1 & 0 \end{bmatrix} \left\{ \begin{array}{c} a_3 \\ a_2 \\ a_1 \\ a_0 \end{array} \right\}$$

Inverting the matrix gives

$$\left\{ \begin{array}{c} a_3 \\ a_2 \\ a_1 \\ a_0 \end{array} \right\} = \begin{bmatrix} 2 & -2 & 1 & 1 \\ -3 & 3 & -2 & -1 \\ 0 & 0 & 1 & 0 \\ 1 & 0 & 0 & 0 \end{bmatrix} \left\{ \begin{array}{c} Q(0) \\ Q(1) \\ dQ/ds\,(0) \\ dQ/ds\,(1) \end{array} \right\}$$

and

$$Q(s, 0) = \left\{ \begin{array}{cccc} s^3 & s^2 & s^1 & s^0 \end{array} \right\} \begin{bmatrix} 2 & -2 & 1 & 1 \\ -3 & 3 & -2 & -1 \\ 0 & 0 & 1 & 0 \\ 1 & 0 & 0 & 0 \end{bmatrix} \left\{ \begin{array}{c} Q(0) \\ Q(1) \\ dQ/ds\,(0) \\ dQ/ds\,(1) \end{array} \right\}$$

or

$$Q(s, 0) = \left\{ \begin{array}{cccc} s^3 & s^2 & s^1 & s^0 \end{array} \right\} \mathbf{M} \left\{ \begin{array}{c} Q(0) \\ Q(1) \\ dQ/ds\,(0) \\ dQ/ds\,(1) \end{array} \right\}$$

Continuing in this vein, the coefficients for $\vec{Q}(s, t)$ can be shown to be

$$\{\vec{a}_{ij}\} = \mathbf{M}\vec{\mathbf{B}}\mathbf{M}^{\mathrm{T}}$$

where the geometric coefficient matrix is

$$\vec{\mathbf{B}} = \begin{bmatrix} \vec{P}_{00} & \vec{P}_{01} & \left.\dfrac{\partial \vec{P}}{\partial t}\right|_{00} & \left.\dfrac{\partial \vec{P}}{\partial t}\right|_{01} \\[2ex] \vec{P}_{10} & \vec{P}_{11} & \left.\dfrac{\partial \vec{P}}{\partial t}\right|_{10} & \left.\dfrac{\partial \vec{P}}{\partial t}\right|_{11} \\[2ex] \left.\dfrac{\partial \vec{P}}{\partial s}\right|_{00} & \left.\dfrac{\partial \vec{P}}{\partial s}\right|_{01} & \left.\dfrac{\partial^2 \vec{P}}{\partial s\,\partial t}\right|_{00} & \left.\dfrac{\partial^2 \vec{P}}{\partial s\,\partial t}\right|_{01} \\[2ex] \left.\dfrac{\partial \vec{P}}{\partial s}\right|_{10} & \left.\dfrac{\partial \vec{P}}{\partial s}\right|_{11} & \left.\dfrac{\partial^2 \vec{P}}{\partial s\,\partial t}\right|_{10} & \left.\dfrac{\partial^2 \vec{P}}{\partial s\,\partial t}\right|_{11} \end{bmatrix}$$

Note the form of the geometric coefficient matrix. One partition contains corner information; two partitions (upper right and lower left) contain tangent information, and the fourth partition contains mixed partial second derivative vectors (called twist vectors). The vectors in the geometric coefficient matrix are shown in Fig 9.19.

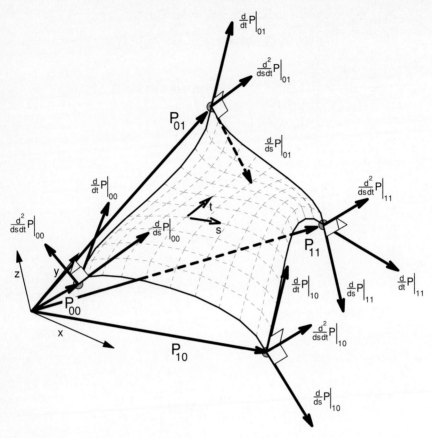

Figure 9.19 Cubic patch definitions.

Instead of following the derivation sketched above, one can consider that cubic expressions were used for the edges and a blend is obtained that satisfies the boundary conditions on all four edges. As in the Coons patch, this bicubic surface patch is achieved by considering extra contributions of the corners:

$$
\vec{Q}(s,t) = \begin{Bmatrix} s^3 \\ s^2 \\ s^1 \\ s^0 \end{Bmatrix}^{\mathrm{T}} \mathbf{M}
\begin{bmatrix}
\vec{P}_{00} & \vec{P}_{01} & \left.\frac{\partial \vec{P}}{\partial t}\right|_{00} & \left.\frac{\partial \vec{P}}{\partial t}\right|_{01} \\
\vec{P}_{10} & \vec{P}_{11} & \left.\frac{\partial \vec{P}}{\partial t}\right|_{10} & \left.\frac{\partial \vec{P}}{\partial t}\right|_{11} \\
\left.\frac{\partial \vec{P}}{\partial s}\right|_{00} & \left.\frac{\partial \vec{P}}{\partial s}\right|_{01} & \left.\frac{\partial^2 \vec{P}}{\partial s \partial t}\right|_{00} & \left.\frac{\partial^2 \vec{P}}{\partial s \partial t}\right|_{01} \\
\left.\frac{\partial \vec{P}}{\partial s}\right|_{10} & \left.\frac{\partial \vec{P}}{\partial s}\right|_{11} & \left.\frac{\partial^2 \vec{P}}{\partial s \partial t}\right|_{10} & \left.\frac{\partial^2 \vec{P}}{\partial s \partial t}\right|_{11}
\end{bmatrix}
\mathbf{M}^{\mathrm{T}} \begin{Bmatrix} t^3 \\ t^2 \\ t^1 \\ t^0 \end{Bmatrix}
$$

Note that each entry in the preceding equation is a vector. Alternatively, three versions can be written for the x, y, and z components.

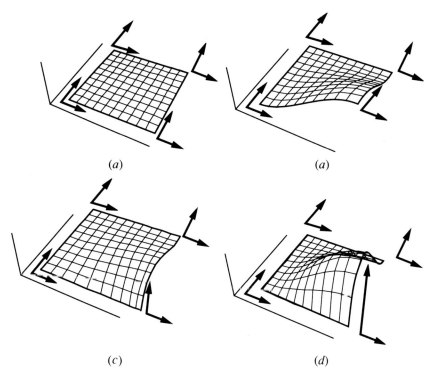

(a)   (a)

(c)   (d)

Figure 9.20 Cubic patch variations.

The individual effects of the corner, tangent, and twist vectors are shown in Figures 9.20 and 9.21. For clarity, a flat square patch (initially in the x, y plane) has been used as a reference. The tangent and twist vectors are

$$\frac{\partial \vec{P}}{\partial s}\bigg|_{00} = \frac{\partial \vec{P}}{\partial s}\bigg|_{10} = \frac{\partial \vec{P}}{\partial s}\bigg|_{01} = \frac{\partial \vec{P}}{\partial s}\bigg|_{11} = \begin{Bmatrix} 1 \\ 0 \\ 0 \end{Bmatrix}$$

$$\frac{\partial \vec{P}}{\partial t}\bigg|_{00} = \frac{\partial \vec{P}}{\partial t}\bigg|_{10} = \frac{\partial \vec{P}}{\partial t}\bigg|_{01} = \frac{\partial \vec{P}}{\partial t}\bigg|_{11} = \begin{Bmatrix} 0 \\ 1 \\ 0 \end{Bmatrix}$$

$$\frac{\partial \vec{P}}{\partial s}\bigg|_{00} = \frac{\partial \vec{P}}{\partial s}\bigg|_{10} = \frac{\partial^2 \vec{P}}{\partial s\,\partial t}\bigg|_{01} = \frac{\partial^2 \vec{P}}{\partial s\,\partial t}\bigg|_{11} = \begin{Bmatrix} 0 \\ 0 \\ 0 \end{Bmatrix}$$

In Fig. 9.20b the corner $\vec{P}_{10}$ has been changed in the z direction only. Note that the tangents remain constant. In Fig. 9.20c, the tangent vector $\partial \vec{P}/\partial t$ evaluated at 10 is changed to $\{0 \quad 1 \quad 1\}^T$ As with the cubic splines, the

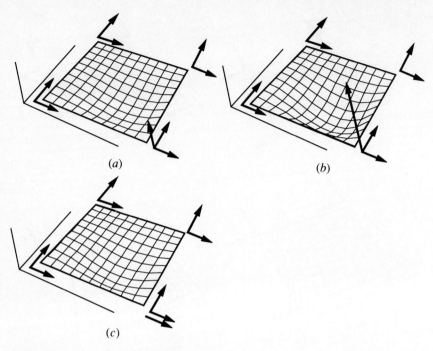

Figure 9.21 Cubic patch variations.

magnitude of this vector can be varied independent of the direction. In Fig. 9.20d, a value of $\{ 0 \quad 5 \quad 5 \}^{\mathrm{T}}$ is used. Note that all other tangent vectors are unchanged. The patch is still "square" if viewed from the z direction.

The effect of nonzero twist vectors is shown in Fig. 9.21. The original "flat" tangent vectors are used, and twist vectors $\partial^2 \vec{P} / \partial s\, \partial t$ evaluated at 10 of $\{ 0 \quad 0 \quad 1 \}^{\mathrm{T}}$ and $\{ 0 \quad 0 \quad 5 \}^{\mathrm{T}}$ are used in Fig. 9.21a and Fig. 9.21b, respectively. Note that in each case the twist vector is normal to the two tangent vectors, which deforms the interior of the patch in the $-z$ direction. Components of twist vectors that are not normal to the tangent vectors do not change the patch's shape, but they do warp the interior parameterization. Figure 9.20 shows that $\partial^2 P / \partial s\, \partial t$ evaluated at 10 = $\{0 \quad 1 \quad 0\}^{\mathrm{T}}$, and the patch is still flat. Usually, twist vectors are chosen perpendicular to the tangent vectors.

Example 9.5: Bicubic Patch. The purpose of this example is to show explicitly the data required to specify a bicubic patch (twelve vectors) and show that complex shapes can result. Figure 9.22 shows three views of the patch based on these control vectors.

$$\vec{P}_{00} = \left\{ \begin{array}{c} 0.1 \\ 0.1 \\ 0.1 \end{array} \right\} \quad \vec{P}_{10} = \left\{ \begin{array}{c} 0.3 \\ 0.8 \\ 0.5 \end{array} \right\} \quad \vec{P}_{01} = \left\{ \begin{array}{c} 0.8 \\ 0.2 \\ 0 \end{array} \right\} \quad \vec{P}_{11} = \left\{ \begin{array}{c} 0.8 \\ 0.8 \\ 0.1 \end{array} \right\}$$

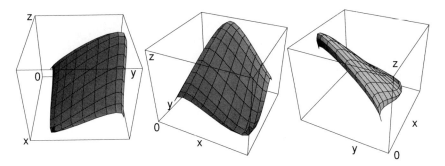

Figure 9.22 Three views of the bicubic patch from Example 9.5.

$$\left.\frac{\partial \vec{P}}{\partial s}\right|_{00} = \left\{\begin{matrix} 0.2 \\ 0.1 \\ 0.4 \end{matrix}\right\} \quad \left.\frac{\partial \vec{P}}{\partial s}\right|_{10} = \left\{\begin{matrix} 0.2 \\ 0 \\ -0.6 \end{matrix}\right\} \quad \left.\frac{\partial \vec{P}}{\partial s}\right|_{01} = \left\{\begin{matrix} 0.4 \\ -0.3 \\ -0.3 \end{matrix}\right\} \quad \left.\frac{\partial \vec{P}}{\partial s}\right|_{11} = \left\{\begin{matrix} 0.1 \\ 0 \\ -0.6 \end{matrix}\right\}$$

$$\left.\frac{\partial \vec{P}}{\partial t}\right|_{00} = \left\{\begin{matrix} 0 \\ 0.3 \\ 0.6 \end{matrix}\right\} \quad \left.\frac{\partial \vec{P}}{\partial t}\right|_{10} = \left\{\begin{matrix} 0 \\ 0.3 \\ 0.9 \end{matrix}\right\} \quad \left.\frac{\partial \vec{P}}{\partial t}\right|_{01} = \left\{\begin{matrix} 0 \\ 0.4 \\ 0.8 \end{matrix}\right\} \quad \left.\frac{\partial \vec{P}}{\partial t}\right|_{11} = \left\{\begin{matrix} 0.4 \\ 0.1 \\ -0.6 \end{matrix}\right\}$$

$$\left.\frac{\partial^2 \vec{P}}{\partial s \partial t}\right|_{00} = \left.\frac{\partial^2 \vec{P}}{\partial s \partial t}\right|_{10} = \left.\frac{\partial^2 \vec{P}}{\partial s \partial t}\right|_{01} = \left.\frac{\partial^2 \vec{P}}{\partial s \partial t}\right|_{11} = \left\{\begin{matrix} 0 \\ 0 \\ 0 \end{matrix}\right\}$$

■ **EXERCISE 9.10:** Using the known analytical representation for a sphere, determine the corner, tangent, and twist vectors for the spherical patch in Example 9.1. Determine the errors for the bicubic patch and compare them to those of Exercise 9.9.

■ **EXERCISE 9.11:** How can the values of the bicubic control matrix be selected to represent a triangular patch? For example, if $\vec{P}_{00}$ and $\vec{P}_{01}$ have the same coordinates, one has the beginnings of a triangular patch. How should tangent and twist vectors be assigned?

Bézier Patch

The Bézier patch is a cartesian product and a straightforward extension of the Bézier spline that uses two sets of Bernstein basis functions:

$$\vec{Q}(s,t) = \sum_{i=0}^{n}\sum_{j=0}^{m} \Phi_i(s)\Phi_j(t)\vec{P}_{ij}$$

For example, a quadratic basis leads to

$$\vec{Q}(s,t) = \left\{\begin{matrix} (1-s)^2 & 2s(1-s) & s^2 \end{matrix}\right\} \begin{bmatrix} \vec{P}_{00} & \vec{P}_{01} & \vec{P}_{02} \\ \vec{P}_{10} & \vec{P}_{11} & \vec{P}_{12} \\ \vec{P}_{20} & \vec{P}_{21} & \vec{P}_{22} \end{bmatrix} \left\{\begin{matrix} (1-t)^2 \\ 2t(1-t) \\ t^2 \end{matrix}\right\}$$

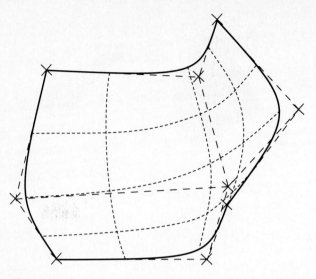

Figure 9.23   A 3 × 3 Bézier patch.

Note that the control matrix consists only of points. These points are often
presented as a "control net," as shown in Fig. 9.23. The control net is analogous to the control polygon for a Bézier curve. It should be noted that the
patch is tangent to the control net at the corners and that points internal to
the net help shape this patch. The Bézier patch can be of higher order. A
common form is the 4 × 4 net shown in Fig. 9.24, which allows independent
control of tangency at each corner. There is an obvious similarity between
these control points and the control values for the bicubic patch; for instance,
four points are available at each corner to determine position, tangent, and twist.

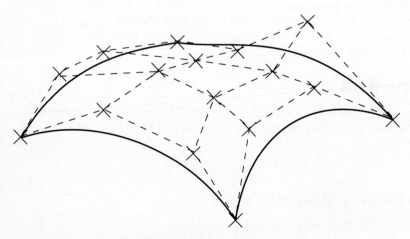

Figure 9.24   A 4 × 4 Bézier patch.

■ **EXERCISE 9.12:** The edges of the control net shape the edges of the patch. Determine the coordinates for a 3×3 Bézier patch for the spherical segment of Example 9.1. This problem is simplified substantially by its symmetry (only four points are "different"). Also, each edge lies in a plane and can be developed in two dimensions.

9.7 SURFACE MODELS

It is not possible to represent entities of interest in a mechanical design either with a single implicit representation or with a single patch. This means that an entity must be represented by a collection of patches. The representation of a physical object by its surface leads to a family of modelers, commonly referred to as *B-rep modelers* for "boundary representation modelers." Such representation is discussed in the next section. At this point, however, let us limit our focus to collections of surface, where our primary concerns are continuity and compatibility.

In most cases, the surface generated must be physically possible, in which case compatibility requires orientability and disallows self-intersection. Patches should be assembled such that common edges with other patches have compatible surface normals to either side of the edge.

Surface self-intersection problems are of two types: patch-to-patch intersection and patch self-intersection. The first subproblem is obvious. The second can occur with higher-order patches (e.g., Coons, bicubic, and Bézier). Self-intersecting edges will give rise to self-intersecting patches, as shown by Fig. 9.25. It is not sufficient to avoid self-intersecting edges, because in extreme cases, the control points can be defined so that the patch intersects itself internally (away from the edges).

Engineering usability requires further constraints on B-rep models. Functionality and aesthetics will often demand a higher level of continuity that the C^0 level described above. Proper selection of the control functions can provide C^1 or C^2 surfaces.

Multiple Patches

The procedure for generating a multiple-patch surface would proceed as follows:

1. Determine the points that form the surface in 3-D space.

2. Determine the boundaries of the proposed patches, and collect the points accordingly. Determine a curve fit of some kind through points that will form boundary of a patch. If necessary, reparameterize each "spline" into segments with parametric range [0, 1]. For example, a single spline may be fit for the whole length of the object to enforce the desired degree of continuity.

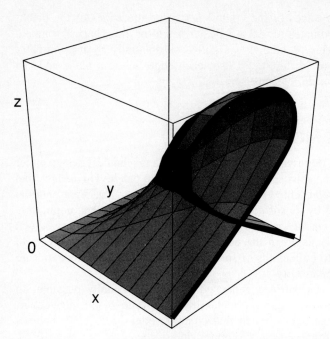

Figure 9.25 A self-intersecting bicubic patch with a self-intersecting edge along $s = 1$.

3. Form patches from the controlling points and the edge splines as appropriate. Note that the proper reuse of curves and slopes will provide the maximum continuity.

4. Tesselate each patch if necessary.

Figures 9.26 and 9.27 illustrate this process for an aircraft surface: Figure 9.26 shows the splines passed through the initial points in space, and Fig. 9.27 presents the boundaries of the patches. An enlarged view of the region around the cockpit is shown in Fig. 9.28. Due to symmetry, only half the surface is being modeled; reflection is used to produce the complete model. Figures 9.29 and 9.30 show tesselated representations with hidden-line removal and flat shading, respectively. The plastic model shown in Fig. 9.31 was machined using NC codes developed directly from the geometric model. In order to reduce machining time, the distance between tool passes was set quite large, leaving very visible scallop height.

Continuity

The degree of continuity achieved is an important consideration when connecting curves or patches. Continuity is characterized as C^0, C^1, ..., C^n where the nth derivative is continuous. However, different applications re-

Figure 9.26   Defining splines for fighter aircraft.
Image courtesy of Integrated
Mechanical Analysis Project.

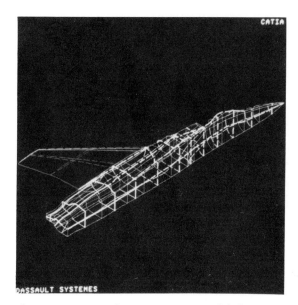

Figure 9.27   Patch representation of fighter aircraft.
Image courtesy of Integrated
Mechanical Analysis Project.

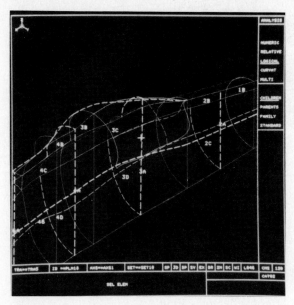

Figure 9.28 Patch representation around cockpit of
fighter aircraft. Image courtesy of
Integrated Mechanical Analysis Project.

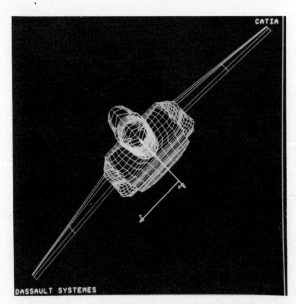

Figure 9.29 Tesselated model of fighter aircraft with hidden
lines removed. Image courtesy of Integrated
Mechanical Analysis Project.

Figure 9.30   Flat-shaded image of fighter aircraft. Image courtesy
of Integrated Mechanical Analysis Project.

quire different levels of continuity. For example, a surface model must be
at least C^0 for visual acceptability. Many shading algorithms, such as the
Gouraud or Phong methods, can smooth C^0 objects visually. However, if the
curve or surface is to be machined, at least C^1 continuity is desirable. Items
where visual aesthetics are important (automotive fenders and hoods) may
require up to C^3 continuity. Each of the models that has been discussed can
provide various levels of continuity. Each has a maximum level of continuity,
but without care, this can easily deteriorate until even C^0 is lost. Although
this is particularly true if types of curves or patches are mixed, it can happen
with use of a single type of entity.

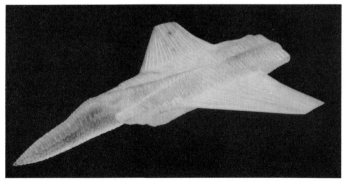

Figure 9.31   A plastic machined model of fighter aircraft. Image
courtesy of Jon Reis. ©1990 all rights reserved.

For example, consider two adjacent spherical patches (each similar to Fig. 9.13), one represented by a bicubic patch and the other, by a bilinear patch. The two corners will match, but the edges will not; therefore, the two patches are not C^0. A bicubic patch can be joined to a bilinear patch if the tangent vectors on the common edge are chosen so that the edge of the bicubic patch is linear.

Two patches that can be shown to share a common edge exactly will be C^0 (e.g., two Coons patches using the same edge expression). However, C^1 is more difficult to achieve. For example, a polyhedral surface is C^0 but not C^1. The requirements for patch-to-patch C^1 continuity can be developed by deriving expressions for the derivatives at arbitrary internal parametric locations, evaluating these at the edge, and requiring equality between these and expressions from the adjacent patch. This leads to constraint relationships on the defining quantities.

Figure 9.32 depicts a surface model of an automobile developed from a set of spatial coordinates. A high degree of continuity has been maintained.

Curve-to-curve continuity provides an easy example for a discussion of geometric (G) and parametric (C) continuity. Parametric continuity does not imply geometric continuity. Consider two curves, one in the x, y plane and one in the y, z plane as shown in Figure 9.33a. This curve has parametric continuity through the first derivative C^1: $\{ dx/ds \quad dy/ds \quad dz/ds \}_A^T \big|_{s=1}$ $= \{ dx/ds \quad dy/ds \quad dz/ds \}_B^T \big|_{s=0}$. However, viewed from along the y-axis, the curve does not have continuous slope; its slope is only G^0.

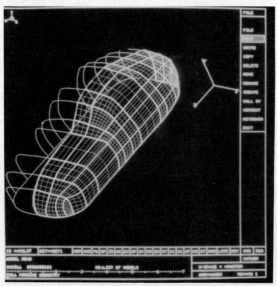

Figure 9.32 Automobile surface model. Image courtesy of Integrated Mechanical Analysis Project.

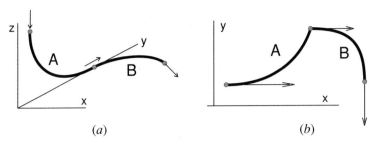

Figure 9.33 Examples of C^1 but not G^1 continuity.

If curve segments join, C^0 continuity is achieved. If directions of tangent vectors (but not necessarily magnitude) are identical then the curve has C^1 continuity. If the magnitude and direction of nth derivatives are equal, then the curve is called C^n continuous. However, C^1 does not imply G^1. If the magnitude of the tangent vector is zero, the direction of tangency is not controlled directly; therefore, two curves so joined will not be C^1. The actual direction of the tangency at the point is determined by the tangency vector at the opposite end of the curve, as shown in Figure 9.33b.

Each application has continuity requirements, and each modeling scheme has continuity capabilities. The CAD developer must determine these and ensure that implementation satisfies the requirements. The CAD user must determine the limitations of the software available and ensure that either application requirements are satisfied, or if not, that the maximum continuity available is achieved. Without care, the continuity provided can easily deteriorate from that which is available in principle.

■ **EXERCISE 9.13:** Develop expressions for the local tangent, normal, and curvature for the parametric curves that have been presented: four-point cubic, hermite cubic, and Bézier. The tangent vector is $\{dx/ds \quad dy/ds \quad dz/ds\}^T$, and the curvature is measured by $\{d^2x/ds^2 \quad d^2y/ds^2 \quad d^2z/ds^2\}^T$.

■ **EXERCISE 9.14:** For the bilinear, lofted, Coons, bicubic, and Bézier patch, develop expressions for the local tangent and normal. At an internal location s, t, the tangent vectors are $\{dx/ds \quad dy/ds \quad dz/ds\}^T$ and $\{dx/dt \quad dy/dt \quad dz/dt\}^T$. If these are normalized to $\vec{n}_s$, $\vec{n}_t$, the local normal is $\vec{n}_n = \vec{n}_s \times \vec{n}_t$.

Intersection

Any detailed discussion of intersection is beyond the scope of this book; however, for implicit representations of geometry, intersection generally can be formulated as a root-finding problem.

In parametric geometry, intersection is a multiple-dimension root-finding problem. Consider two parametric curves: $x = g_x(s), y = g_y(s)$ and $x = h_x(t), y = h_y(t)$. Note that two different parametric variables are needed because the intersection will occur at different parametric coordinates on each curve. The intersection problem can be posed as

$$\text{find } s, t$$
$$\text{such that } g_x(s) - h_x(t) = 0$$
$$g_y(s) - h_y(t) = 0$$

■ **EXERCISE 9.15:** Formulate the intersection problem for two hermite cubic curves in 2-D. What are the mathematical indications for nonintersection?

Subdivision

Frequently the user will need to subdivide an entity into two "well-formed" entities. Here "well-formed" means that the resultant entities are represented in the correct data structure and that suitable operands exist for all possible operations. In manipulative operations, subdivision is an important step after intersection.

A straight line can be "broken" at $s = \eta$, resulting in two new parametric straight lines (A and B). Using the parametric expression for the straight line,

$$\begin{Bmatrix} x \\ y \\ z \end{Bmatrix} = (1 - s) \begin{Bmatrix} x_1 \\ y_1 \\ z_1 \end{Bmatrix} + s \begin{Bmatrix} x_2 \\ y_2 \\ z_2 \end{Bmatrix}$$

the new point is

$$\begin{Bmatrix} x_\eta \\ y_\eta \\ z_\eta \end{Bmatrix} = (1 - \eta) \begin{Bmatrix} x_1 \\ y_1 \\ z_1 \end{Bmatrix} + \eta \begin{Bmatrix} x_2 \\ y_2 \\ z_2 \end{Bmatrix}$$

The first new straight line is given by

$$\begin{Bmatrix} x \\ y \\ z \end{Bmatrix} = (1 - s) \begin{Bmatrix} x_1 \\ y_1 \\ z_1 \end{Bmatrix} + s \begin{Bmatrix} x_\eta \\ y_\eta \\ z_\eta \end{Bmatrix}$$

and the second, by

$$\begin{Bmatrix} x \\ y \\ z \end{Bmatrix} = (1 - s) \begin{Bmatrix} x_\eta \\ y_\eta \\ z_\eta \end{Bmatrix} + s \begin{Bmatrix} x_2 \\ y_2 \\ z_2 \end{Bmatrix}$$

Note that each new curve is still linear in s.

The temptation is to simplify the expression for the first line further by eliminating the coordinates x_η, y_η, z_η to yield

$$\begin{Bmatrix} x \\ y \\ z \end{Bmatrix} = (1 - \eta s) \begin{Bmatrix} x_1 \\ y_1 \\ z_1 \end{Bmatrix} + \eta s \begin{Bmatrix} x_2 \\ y_2 \\ z_2 \end{Bmatrix}$$

However, this is not a well-formed representation because it cannot be evaluated by the same procedure (subroutine) used to evaluate the "standard" parametric straight line. The standard data structure for a line cannot be used to store the preceding representation.

Consider a bilinear patch that is to be divided into four patches using coordinates η, ζ, as shown in Fig. 9.34. Find the new corners $\vec{P}_a$, $\vec{P}_b$, $\vec{P}_c$, $\vec{P}_d$, $\vec{P}_e$. For example,

$$\vec{P}_a = \vec{Q}(\eta, \zeta) = \{1 - \eta \quad \eta\} \begin{bmatrix} \vec{P}_{00} & \vec{P}_{01} \\ \vec{P}_{10} & \vec{P}_{11} \end{bmatrix} \begin{Bmatrix} 1 - \zeta \\ \zeta \end{Bmatrix}$$

Then form four bilinear patches, the first with points $\vec{P}_{00}$, $\vec{P}_a$, $\vec{P}_b$, $\vec{P}_e$, the second $\vec{P}_a$, $\vec{P}_{10}$, $\vec{P}_d$, $\vec{P}_b$, and so forth. For example the first new patch is given by

$$\vec{Q}(s, t) = \{1 - s \quad s\} \begin{bmatrix} \vec{P}_{00} & \vec{P}_e \\ \vec{P}_a & \vec{P}_b \end{bmatrix} \begin{Bmatrix} 1 - t \\ t \end{Bmatrix}$$

It is possible to develop patch subdivisions for which the parametric coordinates of the interior point differ from the parametric coordinates of the points on the edges. However, the new internal edges may not lie on the original patch. This degradation away from the original geometry should

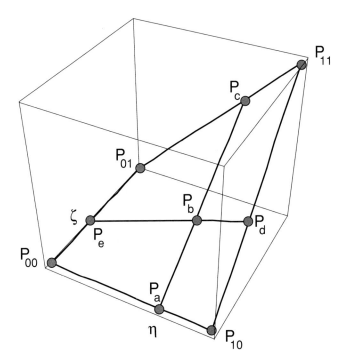

Figure 9.34 Subdivided bilinear patch.

be avoided because successive division may significantly corrupt the geometry.

■ **EXERCISE 9.16:** Develop equations to reparametrize a cubic curve, broken at $s = \eta$ into two well-formed cubics. It is important to maintain the maximum degree of continuity.

■ **EXERCISE 9.17:** Subdivide a Coons patch at location η, ζ.

■ **EXERCISE 9.18:** Subdivide a bicubic patch at location η, ζ.

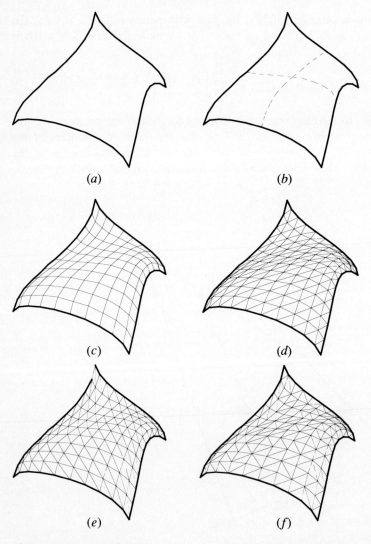

(a) (b)

(c) (d)

(e) (f)

Figure 9.35 Tesselation.

Tesselation

The display of patches within a graphics package can take on three forms: The simplest displays the boundary of the patch. The more complicated approach also displays some interior portion of the patch, still using lines (this has the option of using a hidden-line removal algorithm). The most complicated method displays a shaded continuous image of the patch. A wide variety of shading techniques has been discussed in Chapter 7.

Tesselation is the process of generating the information for the interior of the patch. The patch equation is used to generate internal points that are regularly spaced in parametric space. Then these points can either be connected to create a wire-frame model or be collectively grouped to form polygons that can be displayed with flat-shading or other shading algorithms. Flat shading assumes flat polygons and so a four-sided tesselation, as shown in Fig. 9.35c, is not precisely accurate. In most cases, the tesselation is small enough that any out-of-plane character for each facet can be neglected. However, complete accuracy will require three-sided facets, which can be generated as shown in Figure 9.35d and 9.35e. Note that in a line drawing, the diagonals will cause a visual bias to the patch. This bias can be avoided by randomly assigning the diagonal direction. However, often this is not aesthetically pleasing, as shown in Fig. 9.35f.

The CAD developer should note that speed of the tesselation procedure can be substantially increased by using algorithms other than a straightforward looping implementation; see Foley for details and pseudocode.

9.8 SOLID MODELS

The objective of solid modeling is the representation of real physical objects, referred to earlier as manifold modeling. The modeling package must provide the functionality of Tables 9.1 and 9.2, but as previously discussed, starting with manifold entities, these operations can lead to nonmanifold entities. Solid modeling packages limit representations to be 2-manifolds. Before discussing the representation schemes currently in use, consider the requirements for any scheme that proposes to represent geometry of physical objects (Table 9.4).

The most critical requirement is *validity*. A real 3-D object must exist for any model in the scheme. The scheme cannot produce "impossible" objects such as a Klein bottle. The scheme cannot allow isolated (or "dangling") lines or faces or something akin to an Escher drawing. Furthermore, manufacturing requirements may rule out the existence of internal voids.

The representation scheme should *span* the domain. This is the inverse of the validity characteristic. A model must be possible in the scheme for any 3-D object.

Two kinds of uniqueness are significant. *Uniqueness of interpretation* means that only one 3-D object corresponds to any specific representation.

Validity—A real 3-D object exists for any given model
Spanning—A model exists for any 3-D object
Uniqueness of interpretation—Only one 3-D object exists for any model
Uniqueness of Expression—Only one model exists for any 3-D object
Completeness
Conciseness
Efficiency
Ease of creation, modification

Table 9.4   Solid modeling requirements.

Interpretation is the downfall of most wire-frame modelers. From a wire-frame or line drawing, the object cannot be uniquely determined. *Uniqueness of expression* means that only one model is possible for any specific object. No modeling scheme in common use has uniqueness of expression; fortunately, a unique expression is generally not required. However, future developments in design methodology may impose a requirement for unique representation. For example, it is extremely difficult to compare designs effectively without unique representations.

The representation scheme should be *complete*. All operations supported should be applicable to all representations. That is, the operation should yield an entity that is "well formed" in the representation scheme and thus is a valid operand for all operations. Again, this is where non-manifold requirements raise difficulties.

Conciseness refers to the amount of information in the model. For example, pure spatial enumeration is a scheme with poor conciseness. Consider a volume of space divided into cubes, represented in a three-dimensional binary array, each element of which is 0 if void or 1 if filled. The array would represent a 3-D object, but would consume extreme amounts of memory to reach an acceptable resolution.

The major types of solid modeling schemes (as shown in Fig. 9.36) are: B-rep (boundary representation), c.s.g. (constructive solid geometry), sweep-based methods, octree, and primitive instancing. Each of these can be categorized by the characteristics listed in Table 9.5.

The CAD system designer and user must remember to distinguish between the internal representation of geometry and the user interface and displays. In this section let us focus on representation.

The *B-rep* scheme is most like the nonmanifold entities that have been discussed earlier in this chapter. The object is represented by a collection of faces. Different implementations will support various types of faces. Most B-rep modelers will support c.s.g. style input, even though the underlying representation is B-rep. The B-rep scheme has the advantage of quick, high quality graphical rendering. However, the scheme is not well suited for the analytical operations such as c.g. location. The B-rep is discussed in more detail in the next subsection.

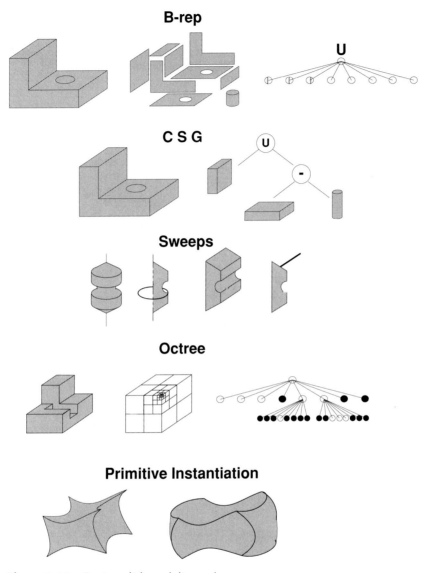

Figure 9.36 Basic solid modeling schemes.

The *c.s.g. scheme* stores the geometry as a binary tree of Boolean operations applied to a limited set of allowable fundamental primitives. It is well suited for unary analytical operations, and the manipulative operations are almost trivial. Design changes are easily made. For example, in Fig 9.36 the size of the cylinder can be changed simply by modifying the parameters of the primitive. However, the scheme is not well suited for display. In fact, rendering can be quite tedious. For this reason, many c.s.g. schemes maintain an equivalent B-rep model for rendering purposes. The

Primary representation scheme	B-rep
	C.s.g. bounded primitives
	C.s.g. half spaces
Domain defined by half spaces	Plane
	Quadric surface
	Sculptured surfaces
	Orthogonal positioning
Input style	C.s.g.
	Sweep
	Euler operations
Input modality	Driven by graphics menu
	Keyboard text input
	File text input (batch)
	Subroutine call

Table 9.5   Characteristics of solid modeling packages.

restrictions to 2-manifolds are very limiting for design purposes. Further-more, the scheme cannot handle deformations of bodies, which are of inter-est in stress analysis.

The *sweep methods* use an entity of a lower order plus sweep informa-tion. Sweeps take the form of either rotation or translation. For example, a surface will generate a solid, and a curve will generate a surface. The sweep models are easily stored (i.e., a cross-section, an axis, and a length). They provide fast, easy modeling for symmetric objects. However, because of the difficulties in handling asymmetric objects, they have not found wide use as an internal representation scheme.

The *octree models* are a form of "spatial enumeration." The 3-D space is broken into units, and the model consists of setting a flag to show if the unit is "occupied." Pure spatial enumeration is impossibly memory intensive for 3-D objects. However, a method of recursive subdivision has been developed that is known as a quadtree in 2-D and an octree in 3-D. Further discussion of the method is beyond the scope of this book, and the method is not often used in mechanical design. However, one of this method's strengths is its representation of complex irregular objects, such as those found in nature. In addition, it couples well to spatial sampling methods, although fast rendering requires the use of specialized hardware.

The *primitive instancing method* is based on analytical or parametric representations of single objects. In machining or analytical operations the method is useful for describing portions of objects; however, the user inter-face is often difficult and not straightforward. One example of a primitive is the parametric cubic hyperpatch, a 3-D extension of the parametric cu-bic curve, $x = f(s), y = g(s), z = h(s)$, and the parametric bicubic patch,

	1965–1972	1973–1978	1979–1984
Wire-frame Methods	2-D systems based on drafting principles Early NC from graphic databases	3-D systems Better NC More conveniences	Bounded surfaces Better analysis packages Color
Polygonal Schemes	Early hidden-line and visible-surface algorithms for polygonal faces Simulators	Better algorithms Polyhedral smoothing Faster simulators 3-D animation	Customized chips Improved displays Animation languages
Sculptured Surfaces	Aero, auto, and marine lofting Parametric polynomial and rational curves Coons patches Bézier surfaces	NC contour milling from lofted/digitized surfaces B-spline and surfaces	B-spline subdivision algorithms
Solid Models	ad hoc experiments using diverse approaches	Experimental B-rep, c.s.g., and sweep-based systems demonstrated Theoretical foundations emerge	Development of industrial prototypes Early production versions

Table 9.6   Development of 3-D object representation.

$x = f(s, t)$, $y = g(s, t)$, $z = h(s, t)$. The reader should refer to Mortenson (1985) for an excellent discussion of the hyperpatch.

The development of geometric modeling techniques is summarized in Table 9.6, after Requicha and Voelcker.

B-rep or Surface Models

The B-rep modeling schemes are based on collections of surfaces. Although commonly used, B-rep schemes have difficulty satisfying the solid modeling requirements in Table 9.4.

The first set of concerns with such modelers is the validity of the surface in the representation of a physical object. In general, an arbitrary B-rep will not be a 2-manifold and thus not a solid. In addition, B-rep models may suffer from continuity problems. Continuity is required if the surface model is intended to represent a manifold solid and completely enclose a three-dimensional volume. As discussed previously, on the boundary of a manifold solid, the small area around any point is homeomorphic to a disk or "locally two-dimensional." The boundary unambiguously separates the inside from the outside. Given a collection of patches, it is all too easy to have patches

388 Geometry

that have one or more edges unconnected to another patch. Given a "valid" solid represented by a B-rep, it is easy to modify it so that it is no longer valid. For example, the user might move a point or change a tangent vector so that the object is self-intersecting. Alternatively, the user might simply delete a point or a face, creating several dangling faces. The "raw edge" of a dangling patch is not homeomorphic to a disk. This dangling surface problem can be avoided by ensuring that each edge in the model belongs to two and only two patches.

The second problem is compatibility. The surface generated must be physically possible. This disallows self-intersection and orientation ambiguities. A surface that represents an object separates the inside from the outside. In other words, the surface has an inherent orientation, which is typically defined from the local surface normal at each point. Patches must not be assembled that will have common edges between patches but incompatible surface normals to either side of the edge. The Mobius strip and the Klein bottle are usually cited as objects with orientation problems.

Because of these potential problems, the user usually is not allowed access to the underlying geometric structures. Instead, the user sees a c.s.g. style interface.

Extensive treatment of the Boolean operations are beyond the scope of this text. However, it is possible to sketch ways that a B-rep scheme might implement the binary manipulative operations of Table 9.2. Consider the two B-rep's (A and B) shown in Fig. 9.37. For convenience, this is shown in two dimensions. The first step is to find the intersections between the two objects, which demonstrates the importance of intersection operations. Those components that intersect (patches) are subdivided at the intersection point, demonstrating the importance of the subdivision techniques discussed previously. Each B-rep is then divided into two collections of components, those outside the other object and those inside the other object (A_o, A_i, B_o, B_i). The inside/outside test is possible if each A and B is a 2-manifold. Note that at this point none of the four components are valid objects.

The result of the desired Boolean operation is a combination of one of the two parts of A and one of the two parts of B, with the additional possibility of a required inversion, or flipping of the normals. For example, if $\oplus$ denotes the combination and $(\ )^{-1}$ denotes reversing the normals, then,

$$A \cup B \Leftrightarrow A_o \oplus B_o$$
$$A \cap B \Leftrightarrow A_o \oplus B_o$$
$$A - B \Leftrightarrow A_o \oplus (B_i)^{-1}$$
$$B - A \Leftrightarrow B_o \oplus (A_i)^{-1}$$

The result is a valid solid that can be used in further operations. In principle, the preceding is sufficient to implement the Boolean operations. However, the developer should be aware of some potential complications. The inter-

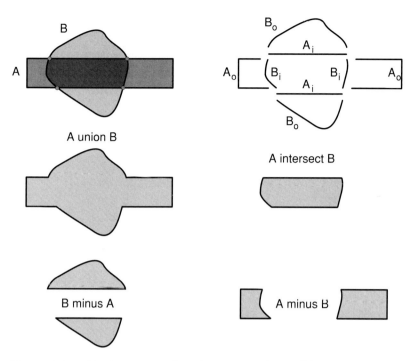

Figure 9.37   Boolean operations in constructive solid geometry.

section points for subdivision must be identical if the resulting object is to
be closed and not self-intersecting. Boolean operations applied to objects in
which faces are parallel and very close (as opposed to nearly perpendicular
faces in Fig. 9.37) can lead to numerical problems. Good test cases for solid
modelers are Boolean operations for cubes with adjacent faces. Alternatively,
test the modeler with the object shown in Fig. 9.38 and adjust the length
of the cylinder so that it is equal to the height of the block. The modeling
package must decide to produce either a clean hole or an extremely thin skin
of volume across either end.

Small parametric shanges in a c.s.g. representation can produce changes
in the structure of the B-rep. Figure 9.39 shows the effect of increasing the
diameter of the cylinder in Fig. 9.38. Compare the number of edges and
faces between Figures 9.38 and 9.39.

Constructive Solid Geometry

The phrase "constructive solid geometry" is frequently defined unclearly.
Sometimes it is used to describe the style of interface supported (e.g.,
Boolean operations) and sometimes it is used to describe the underlying data
representations. In this section we will briefly discuss the c.s.g. scheme for

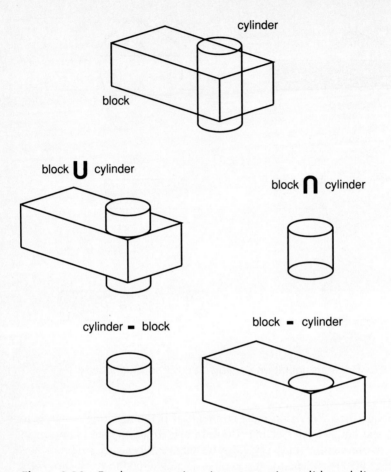

Figure 9.38 Boolean operations in constructive solid modeling.

object representation. A detailed discussion of the implementation of a c.s.g. modeler is beyond the scope of this book, however.

Fundamentally, the c.s.g. modeler is a combination of a binary tree data structure (for the c.s.g. tree) and a collection of geometric primitives. The c.s.g. tree is a binary tree in which the nodes represent operations and the leaves are primitives. Data structures for trees are discussed in the next chapter, and the analogy to parse trees will be seen in Chapter 11.

Modelers using c.s.g. schemes can be classified by the types of primitives supported and the underlying representation schemes for them. Most modelers support the sphere, circular cylinder, block, and cone aligned with the basic reference axes (x, y, z). Currently, most modelers will also support arbitrary rotations of these primitives relative to the x, y, z frame. A smaller subset of modelers will include the torus.

The primitives are represented by collections of analytical 2-manifolds. For example, a cylinder can be represented by two planes and an unbounded

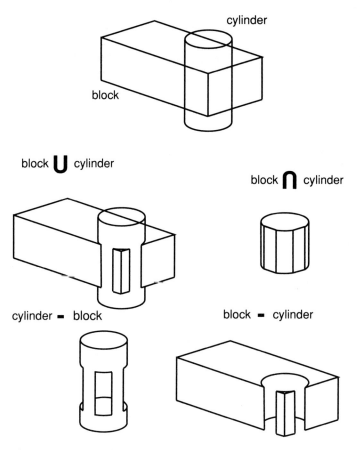

block **U** cylinder

block **∩** cylinder

cylinder **–** block

block **–** cylinder

Figure 9.39 Boolean operations in constructive solid modeling.

circular cylindrical surface: $z > 0$, $z < L$, $(x - x_c)^2 + (y - y_c)^2 - R^2 < 0$. In addition, it is important to remember that the underlying primitives are not represented by a B-rep scheme, which means that the systems usually are not extensible and do not allow for user-defined primitives.

The primary advantage of the c.s.g. representation is its inherent validity, completeness, uniqueness of interpretation, and conciseness. One cannot create impossible geometries. Furthermore, the resulting object is naturally parameterized, which is very useful for design purposes. The diameter or location of a hole is very easily changed in the c.s.g. tree. Of course, this doesn't change the image or the resulting volume and c.g. values until the c.s.g. tree is reprocessed.

The primary disadvantage is the computational complexity of evaluating the c.s.g. tree for graphical display. As a result, true interactive editing of the c.s.g. tree with graphical feedback is rare. Furthermore, the c.s.g. representation does not span all possible physical objects; for example, objects with sculptured surfaces cannot be represented. In addition, the c.s.g.

Figure 9.40   Instrument panel.

representation for any object is not unique. Although this is not a problem for most analytical operations, it may prove troublesome for design interpretations.

Example 9.6: C.s.g. Description of an Instrument Panel. The early work in c.s.g. models resulted in the PADL software package. The input modality for this program is text oriented. Figure 9.40 depicts the front panel for a standard instrument rack. The panel is created from a block by difference operations, forming four slots, three holes for switches, and a hole for a meter. The syntax is straightforward; the Boolean operations are UN, INT, DIFF, and the primitives used in the example are BLO and CYL. Note how each primitive is parameterized and then the instantiation is further parameterized. The switch holes all use the same primitive, but in different locations.

The programming used to create the panel follows:

```
Generic Panel (Panel);


Panel = Stock DIFF Cutouts;

Cutouts = S_Holes UN Meter_Hole UN Slots;

Slots = SL1 UN SL2 UN SL3 UN SL4;

S_Holes = S1 UN S2 UN S3


Stock = BLO (X = Stockwidth; Y = 6, Z = 0.125);

Stock2width = 19.5;


S1X = 6;   S1Y = 2;


S1 = Switch_Hole AT MOVX = S1x, MOVY = S1Y;
```

```
S2X = 6;   S2Y = 3;
S2 = Switch_Hole AT MOVX = S2X, MOVY = S2Y;


S3X = 6;   S3Y = 4;
S3 = Switch_Hole AT MOVX = S3X, MOVY = S3Y;


Switch_Hole = CYL (H = 0.125, D = 0.5);


Meter_Hole = CYL (H = 0.125, D = 3) AT MOVX = 3, MOVY = 3;


SL1 = Slot AT MOVY = 1;
SL2 = Slot AT MOVY - 5;
SL3 = Slot AT MOVY = 1, MOVY = Stockwidth;
SL4 = Slot AT MOVY = 5, MOVY = Stockwidth;


Slot = BLO(Y = 0.25, Z = 0.125, X = 1) AT MOVX = -0.5, MOVY
= -0.125;
```

Polyhedral Objects

The development of the surface and volume integral for a B-rep object is beyond the scope of this book. However, the reader may encounter the need for these operations when a complete geometric modeling package is not available. In that case it is useful to know how to analyze polyhedral objects. With some loss of accuracy, any B-rep model can be tesselated to form a polyhedral object whose faces are planes and whose edges are straight lines.

For a polyhedral body B with N_{poly} polygons and N_{pts} corners, the area, volume, and center of gravity can be found using the formulae that follows. The outward-directed unit normal vector of each polygon is denoted by $\vec{n}_i$, the jth point vector of the ith polygon is denoted by $\vec{p}_{ij}$ (ordered counterclockwise with respect to the outward normal), and the averaged point vector for the ith polygon is denoted by $\vec{\bar{p}}_i$.

$$A_b = \int_s dA = \frac{1}{2} \sum_{i=1}^{N_{poly}} \vec{n}_i \cdot \sum_{j=1}^{N_{pts}} (\vec{p}_{ij} \times \vec{p}_{i(j+1)})$$

$$V_b = \int_v dV = \frac{1}{6} \sum_{i=1}^{N_{poly}} \vec{p}_i \cdot \sum_{j=1}^{N_{pts}} (\vec{p}_{ij} \times \vec{p}_{i(j+1)})$$

$$\vec{p}_{cg} = \frac{\int_v \vec{p} \cdot dV}{V_b}$$

$$\vec{p}_{cg} = \frac{1}{24V_b} \sum_{i=1}^{N_{poly}} \sum_{j=1}^{N_{pts}} \Big(\vec{p}_i^2 + \vec{p}_{ij}^2 + \vec{p}_{i(j+1)}^2 + \vec{p}_i \cdot \vec{p}_{ij} + \vec{p}_{ij} \cdot \vec{p}_{i(j+1)}$$

$$+ \vec{p}_i \cdot \vec{p}_{i(j+1)} \Big) \Big((\vec{p}_{ij} - \vec{p}_i) \times (\vec{p}_{i(j+1)} - \vec{p}_{ij}) \Big)$$

9.9   FILE-DRIVEN INPUT FORMATS FOR REPRESENTING GEOMETRY

Any discussion of geometry should also consider storage and input/output techniques. (This material is closely related to the user interface material to be discussed in Section 11.3, because a data file is one form of user interface.) This section will discuss file-driven input formats for wire-frame and polyhedral objects. Parsing techniques for c.s.g. languages can be developed using the approaches discussed in Section 11.6.

Wire-Frame Data Structures

A wire-frame data structure can only support points and lines (limited straight line segments). For this case it is only necessary to store the endpoints, which can be thought of as the *move-draw form*:

file	cube example	
$x_1\ y_1\ z_1\ \hat{x}_1\ \hat{y}_1\ \hat{z}_1$	0.0 0.0 0.0	1.0 0.0 0.0
$\vdots$	0.0 0.0 0.0	0.0 1.0 0.0
$x_i\ y_i\ z_i\ \hat{x}_i\ \hat{y}_i\ \hat{z}_i$	0.0 0.0 0.0	0.0 0.0 1.0
$\vdots$	0.0 0.0 1.0	1.0 0.0 1.0
	0.0 0.0 1.0	0.0 1.0 1.0
$x_n\ y_n\ z_n\ \hat{x}_n\ \hat{y}_n\ \hat{z}_n$	1.0 0.0 0.0	1.0 0.0 1.0
	0.0 1.0 0.0	0.0 1.0 1.0
	0.0 1.0 0.0	1.0 1.0 0.0
	1.0 0.0 0.0	1.0 1.0 0.0
	1.0 1.0 0.0	1.0 1.0 1.0
	1.0 1.0 1.0	0.0 1.0 1.0
	1.0 1.0 1.0	1.0 0.0 1.0

```
do until end_of_file
  read x1, y1, z1, x2, y2, z2
  call insert_line(x1,y1,z1,x2,y2,z2)
  enddo
```

or

```
do until end_of_file
  read x1, y1, z1, x2, y2, z2
  call move(x1, y1, z1)
  call draw(x2, y2, z2)
  enddo
```

Note the repetition of data and the difficulty in detecting how many lines connect to a specific point (1.0, 1.0, 1.0). A better approach distinguishes between points and lines as separate entities:

file	cube example
file	**cube example**
npts	8
x_1, y_1, z_1	0.0 0.0 0.0
$\vdots$	1.0 0.0 0.0
x_i, y_i, z_i	0.0 1.0 0.0
$\vdots$	0.0 0.0 1.0
	1.0 1.0 0.0
$x_{npts}, y_{npts}, z_{npts}$	1.0 0.0 1.0
i j	0.0 1.0 1.0
i j	1.0 1.0 1.0
$\vdots$	1 2
	4 6
	7 8
	3 5
	$\vdots$
	6 8

```
read npts
do i = 1, npts
  read x(i), y(i), z(i)
  enddo
do until end_of_file
  read i, j
  call insert_line(x(i), y(i), z(i), x(j), y(j), z(j))
  enddo
```

Polyline Data Structures

A more advanced data structure is that of a polyline, or a collection of connected straight line segments. The number of segments per polyline is variable, as shown by the following:

file	cube example
npts	8
x_1, y_1, z_1	0.0 0.0 0.0
⋮	1.0 0.0 0.0
x_i, y_i, z_i	0.0 1.0 0.0
⋮	0.0 0.0 1.0
	1.0 1.0 0.0
$x_{npts}, y_{npts}, z_{npts}$	1.0 0.0 1.0
npolylines	0.0 1.0 1.0
i j k	1.0 1.0 1.0
i j k l	3
i j	1 2 6 4 1 3 7 4
	3 5 8 7
	6 8

Note that the cube example shown has taken care not to repeat or redraw lines.

Polygon Data Structures

If lines are considered as defined by endpoints, then surfaces are defined by lines. The simplest construct from this approach is a polygon. Once again, it is important to keep the point and line information separate from the polygon information. Most data structures, however, do not maintain a clean separation between the line and polygon information. In those systems, a polygon is, in some sense, a polyline with all of its line segments lying in a plane:

file	cube example
npts	8
x_1, y_1, z_1	0.0 0.0 0.0
$\vdots$	1.0 0.0 0.0
	0.0 1.0 0.0
x_i, y_i, z_i	0.0 0.0 1.0
$\vdots$	1.0 1.0 0.0
$x_{npts}, y_{npts}, z_{npts}$	1.0 0.0 1.0
npolygons	0.0 1.0 1.0
i j k	1.0 1.0 1.0
i j k l	6
i j k	1 2 6 4
	2 5 8 6
	1 3 5 2
	1 4 7 3
	3 7 8 5
	4 6 8 7

```
integer pt_list(4)
read npts
do i = 1, npts
   read x(i), y(i), z(i)
   enddo
read npoly
do ipoly = 1, npoly
   read pt_list
   do i = 1, 4
     poly(i, 1) = x(pt_list(i))
     poly(i, 2) = y(pt_list(i))
```

```
    poly(i, 3) = z(pt_list(i))

   enddo

 call insert_poly(4, poly)

 enddo
```

Of course, one could insert four lines instead of a single polygon. In that case, it is important to remember the implied draw from the last point to the first point, needed to close the polygon. The key question in these cases is the graphics supported. If filled polygons are impossible to draw, then only the boundary lines will be drawn, which means that each edge will be drawn twice, once for each polygon in which it appears. This motivates a data structure with points, lines, and polygons separated.

A remnant of the days of fixed record lengths (punch cards) is the practice of packing as much as possible onto one line. A very common structure (for instance, MOVIE-BYU) uses a minus sign to denote the start of a polygon:

file	cube example
npts	8
x_1, y_1, z_1	0.0 0.0 0.0
$\vdots$	1.0 0.0 0.0
	0.0 1.0 0.0
x_i, y_i, z_i	0.0 0.0 1.0
$\vdots$	1.0 1.0 0.0
$x_{npts}, y_{npts}, z_{npts}$	1.0 0.0 1.0
nrecords	0.0 1.0 1.0
$-i\,j\,k\,-i\,j\,k\,l$	1.0 1.0 1.0
$-i\,j\,k$	2
	-1 2 6 4 -2 5 8 6 -1 3 5 2 -1 4 7 3
	-3 7 8 5 -4 6 8 7

```
integer pt_list(16)

read npts

do i = 1, npts

read x(i), y(i), z(i)

enddo

read nrecords
```

```
do i= 1, nrecords
read pt_list
do i = 1, 16
    if (pt_list(i) > 0) then
    call draw(x(pt_list(i)), y(pt_list(i)), z(pt_list(i)))
    else
    call draw(x(istart), y(istart), z(istart))
    call move(x(pt_list(i)), y(pt_list(i)), z(pt_list(i)))
    istart = pt_list(i)
    endif
    enddo
enddo
```

With full screen editors, there is really no need for the minus sign notation. The best solution is to be able to read variable by variable rather than line by line; unfortunately, this is extremely difficult in FORTRAN.

9.10 SUMMARY

In this chapter a variety of representations for curves, surfaces, and volumes has been discussed. The focus has been on the underlying analytical expressions and the information required to define a specific instantiation of any representation. Design always requires a combination of entities—no single entity, not even an entire type of entity, is sufficiently complex. The issues of immediate importance to a CAD developer are determining which operations to support and the level of continuity required. These questions are also paramount to the CAD user attempting to use an existing geometric package. The next chapter discusses data structures that can be used to implement the concepts presented here.

9.11 ANNOTATED REFERENCES

Ball, A. A. "A Simple Specification of the Parametric Cubic Segment," *Computer-Aided Design*, Vol. 10(3)(May 1978), pp. 181–182.

A brief paper demonstrating the derivation of a parametric cubic segment from (the necessary and sufficient) three points and two slopes.

Barnhill, R. E., and Boehm, W. (eds.). *Surfaces in Computer Aided Geometric Design*. New York: North-Holland, 1983.

A collection of papers on a variety of surfaces, surface interpolation methods, and patch methods, including some industrial applications.

Barnhill, R. E., and Riesenfeld, R. F., *Computer Aided Geometric Design*. New York: Academic Press, 1974.

A collection of papers from the likes of Bézier and Forrest. An excellent presentation of splines.

Barnhill, R. E. "A Survey of the Representation and Design of Surfaces," *IEEE Computer Graphics and Applications*, Vol. 3(7)(October 1983), pp. 9–16.

A pragmatic examination of surface modeling in three-dimensions, with evaluation criteria for surface modeling methods.

Barsky, B. A. "A Description and Evaluation of Various 3-D Models," *IEEE Computer Graphics and Applications*, Vol. 4(1)(January 1984), pp. 38–52.

A computational perspective on three-dimensional surface and patch modeling, aimed specifically at computer graphics.

Bézier, P. *Numerical Control: Mathematics and Applications*. John Wiley & Sons, 1972 (English translation).

An application-oriented development of, for example, surface patches. Somewhat dated, but quite practical.

Bokowski, Jurgen, and Sturmfels, Bernd. *Computational Synthetic Geometry*. New York: Springer-Verlag, 1989.

A good introduction to abstract (not applied) synthetic geometry, with an extensive bibliography.

Brodlie, K. W. *Mathematical Methods in Computer Graphics and Design*. Academic Press, 1978.

An interesting collection of (short) papers, good on fitting and approximation. Contains a brief review of solid modeling as of 1978.

Brown, C. M. "Some Mathematical and Representational Aspects of Solid Modelling," *IEEE Transactions on Pattern Analysis and Machine Intelligence*, PAMI-3(4)(1981), pp. 444–453.

An overview of solid modeling that introduces some of the problems that persist to date.

Bu-Qing, S., and Ding-Yuan, L. *Computational Geometry: Curve and Surface Modeling*. New York: Academic Press, 1989.

Thorough development of splines and associated surfaces. Good, up-to-date bibliography.

Burton, F. W., and Huntbach, M. M. "Lazy Evaluation of Geometric Objects," *IEEE Computer Graphics and Applications*, Vol. 4(1)(January 1984), pp. 28–33.

Interesting computational technique for efficient quadtree utilization.

Catmull, E. E. "Computer Display of Curved Surfaces," *Proceedings of the IEEE Conference on Computer Graphics, Pattern Recognition and Data Structure*, 1975.

Historical value.

Chasen, Sylvan H. *Geometric Principles and Procedures for Computer Graphic Applications*. Englewood Cliffs, N. J.: Prentice-Hall, 1978.

Good development of curve fitting, but weaker on patches and surfaces. Predates much of current solid modeling, but uses a very practical approach in developments. Extensive examination of circle definitions.

Cohen, E. "Some Mathematical Tools for a Modeler's Workbench," *IEEE Computer Graphics and Applications*, Vol. 3(7)(October 1983), pp. 63–66.

Nonmathematical perspective on the use of mathematical tools in a real setting and some of the problems involved.

Coons, S. A. "Surface Patches and B-spline Curves," in *Computer-Aided Geometric Design*, R. E. Barnhill and R. F. Riesenfeld (eds.). New York: Academic Press, 1974.

Historical Value.

Coxeter, H. S. M. *Introduction to Geometry*. New York: John Wiley, 1961.

A good Introduction to pure geometry from a mathematical perspective, not geared towards computer implementation.

Coxeter, H. S. M. *Regular Polytopes*. New York: MacMillan, 1963.

A more advanced discussion of abstract geometries.

Coxeter, H. S. M., and Greitzer, S. L. *Geometry Revisited*. New York: Random House, 1967.

A very approachable introduction to the basic ideas of geometry, neither too abstract nor too applied.

Davis, Philip J. *Interpolation and Approximation*. New York: Blaisdell, 1963.

A good mathematical development of function approximations, fits, and interpolants through least squares and several polynomial systems.

Earnshaw, R. A. (ed). *Theoretical Foundations of Computer Graphics for CAD*. New York: Springer-Verlag, 1988.

A good collection of papers, comprising a sweeping snapshot of the state of the art circa September 1987.

Farin, G. *Curves and Surfaces for Computer Aided Geometric Design*. New York: Academic Press, 1988.

A development of Bézier and B-spline curves and patches.

Faux, I. D., and Pratt, M. J. *Computational Geometry for Design and Manufacture*, Chichester, U. K.: Halstead, 1979.

A good development of splines, including Ferguson's work with bicubic patches and parametric cubic curves. Painless development of B-splines and tensor product surfaces, as well as a treatment of degenerate patches.

Foley, J. D., Van Dam, A., Feiner S., and Hughes, J. *Computer Graphics: Principals and Practice*. 2nd ed. Reading, Mass.: Addison-Wesley, 1990.

Gasson, P. C. *Geometry of Spatial Forms*, W. Sussex, U. K.: Ellis Horwood, 1983.

Geometry developed from an engineer's perspective, from drawing and structure rather than automatic computation.

Hoffman, Christoph M. *Geometric & Solid Modeling*. San Mateo, Calif.: Morgan Kaufmann, 1989.

Knorr, Wilbur Richard. *The Ancient Tradition of Geometric Problems*. Boston: Birkhauser, 1986.

The history of ancient geometry is examined through Plato, Euclid, Archimedes and others. Centers on individual contributions to classical geometry.

Lord, E. A., and Wilson, C. B. *The Mathematical Description of Shape and Form*. W. Sussex, U. K.: Ellis Horwood, 1984.

A collection of mathematical topics that are indirectly useful and interesting to the CAD programmer.

Mandelbrot, Benoit B. *The Fractal Geometry of Nature*. New York: W. H. Freeman, 1977.

Fascinating work relating fractal geometry to the real world.

Mortenson, Michael E. *Geometric Modeling*. New York: John Wiley, 1985.

The standard text on geometry for computer modeling. Excellent bibliography of pointers into the extensive literature.

Noltemeier, Hartmut (ed.). *Computational Geometry and its Application*. New York: Springer-Verlag, 1988.

A modern collection of somewhat more specialized papers in the field.

Preparata, F. P., and Shamos, M. I. *Computational Geometry: An Introduction*. New York: Springer-Verlag, 1985.

Thorough and approachable, and strong on Voronoi diagrams. Presents pseudocode algorithms and practical methods.

Requicha, A. A. G. "Representations for Rigid Solids: Theory, Methods and Systems," *Computing Surveys*, Vol. 12(4)(December 1980), pp. 437–64.

The classic paper, laying the foundation for modern solid modeling.

Requicha, A. A. G., and Voelcker, H. "Solid Modeling: A Historical Summary and Contemporary Assessment," *IEEE Computer Graphics and Applications*, Vol. 2(2) (March 1982), pp. 9–24.

A general introductory paper that surveys state of the art at that time.

Rogers, D. F., and Adams, J. A. *Mathematical Elements for Computer Graphics*. New York: McGraw-Hill, 1976.

Somewhat dated, but develops practical graphics geometry from a strong engineering perspective, which may be more comfortable for the less computationally oriented.

Rogers, D. E., and Earnshaw, R. A. (eds.). *Techniques for Computer Graphics*. New York: Springer-Verlag, 1987.

Contains a good section on geometric modeling and computational geometry from a graphics perspective. Good paper by Forrest contrasting applied and theoretical viewpoints.

Semple, J. G., and Roth, L. *Introduction to Algebraic Geometry*. New York: Oxford, 1949.

A traditional course in standard classical geometry. Relatively approachable.

Tilove, R. B. "Set-membership Classification: A Unified Approach to Geometric Intersection Problems," *IEEE Transactions on Computers*, C-29(10) pp. 874–883.

Solid modeling is productively approached from an abstract, computer science perspective, providing insight into the nature of such geometric problems.

The following publications should be read regularly by CAD developers for geometry developments.

ACM Transactions on Graphics. Association for Computing Machinery, monthly.

Computer Graphics. Special Interest Group on Computer Graphics, Association for Computing Machinery, monthly.

ACM, *Proceedings of the Symposia on Computational Geometry*. Sponsored by ACM SIGGRAPH with ACM SIGACT, annual.

SIGGRAPH Proceedings. Association for Computing Machinery, annual.

9.12 PROJECTS

Project 9.1 Hull Geometry Representation

Problem Statement   Develop a geometry representation for the hull of the racing yacht *America*, first winner of the series named after it, the America's Cup Series.

Comments   The various crossections of the hull of the *America* are shown in Fig. 9.41. The hull can be modeled as a collection of patches. The coordinates are probably best obtained by enlarging this figure and using a digitizing process. Other than selecting the type of patch to use, the major aspect of this project concerns how to subdivide the hull into patches and what type of continuity to maintain.

Project 9.2 Sail Geometry Tesselation

Problem Statement   Develop a tesselated polyhedral model for the sail measurements given in Project 2.2.

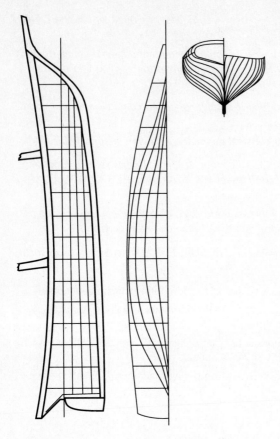

Figure 9.41 Lines of the schooner *America*.

Analysis   Discretize the arc cross-sections described in Project 2.2, given a collection of points in 3-dimensional space. Develop a tesselation for these points that gives a polyhedral model for the sails. Determine the local normal at each point for Gouraud shading.

Project 9.3   Sail Geometry, Patch Representation

Problem Statement   Develop a geometric model for the sail measurements given in Project 2.2.

Analysis   The sails can be modeled as a collection of patches. The assignment can be approached in many ways. Besides selecting the type of patch to use, the primary aspect of this project concerns how to subdivide the geometry into patches.

   Evaluate the geometric model developed by determining the error at various points inside the patches.

C H A P T E R

10

Databases and
Data Structures

10.1 INTRODUCTION TO DATA STRUCTURES

This text has continually emphasized the approach to the computer-aided design problem as one of data or as one of program code. However, this chapter will focus on the structures and techniques that are used internally to store and manipulate organized units of information. Eventually this chapter will conclude with a discussion of the formalized methods of using commercial databases, and thus will have once again come full circle, from data to program code (commands).

Most engineers who have worked with languages such as FORTRAN have no experience with the concepts of data structure. In fact, the only structure supported by FORTRAN is the array (albeit multidimensional). Many engineers have not studied that arrays of any order higher than one are ultimately dealt with as a single one-dimensional array.

Many algorithms are described in the language of specific data structures, and the CAD developer needs to work with the higher-order entities. This requires a brief but necessary digression into "toolsmithing." Once the concepts behind a specific structure are understood, a set of procedures can be developed to provide the basic functions, and the internal details are no longer visible. An example common to FORTRAN programmers is the multiplication of two rectangular arrays. This can be easily done in three nested loops, and many programmers will produce the appropriate source code as needed. However, the "toolsmithing" approach would require a standard subroutine library that is always used for array manipulation.

The required functions of general data structures are actually quite limited:

- Create/destroy
- Insert

- Delete
- Traverse
- Query entry

Other higher-order functions are combinations of these. For example, a *Replace* is simply a combination of *Insert* and *Delete*. Various kinds of *Sort* will be combinations of *Query* and *Replace*.

Many types of data structures have been developed. These are related to each other in Fig. 10.1. The most basic structure builds on individual data units (cells) and pointers (addresses). Then the simple constructs of stacks and queues can be employed. The actual implementation of these constructs will use the more general list structure and will make the first fundamental use of the pointer. Branching lists lead to trees of various kinds and multilinked lists. Arrays are a more restrictive form of list that finds frequent use in design analysis, and tables are a more general form of array. Finally, the general data file can be employed. This chapter will consider data structures and various lists before moving to a discussion of generalized databases.

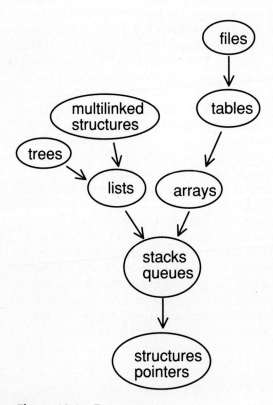

Figure 10.1   Data structures.

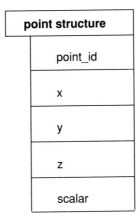

Figure 10.2   Point data structure.

10.2   STRUCTURES AND POINTERS

At this point in our discussion, all data is assumed to reside in the main computer memory (issues of page swapping should be reserved for a computer systems class). The most fundamental unit of computer memory is the bit, but such bits are always considered in some higher level of organization. For FORTRAN programmers, there is usually only the full-word integer, two-word integer, two-word float, and four-word float (I*2, I*4, R*4, and R*8). The more general programming languages consider the data cell to be the most fundamental addressable unit of storage; each data cell consists of named fields. When a data cell is represented in a figure, the value is in the center of the cell and the address or name of each cell is shown in the upper left-hand corner.

Figure 10.2 shows a data structure for a point, which consists of five named float fields (an identifier, x, y, z values, and a scalar for color or for a local variable such as temperature or pressure). Figure 10.3 shows alternative data structures for a line, as discussed in Section 9.5. The point coordinates

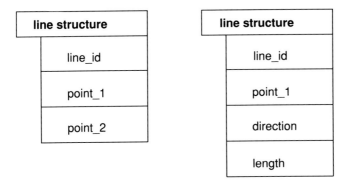

Figure 10.3   Alternative line data structures.

template   **instantiation**

circle   *left_circle*

float x_center	*x_center* 1.0
float y_center	*y_center* 1.0
float z_center	*z_center* 0.0
float n_x	*n_x* 0.0
float n_y	*n_y* 0.0
float n_z	*n_z* 1.0
float radius	*radius* 0.5

Figure 10.4   Data structure for a circle.

are not stored; instead, the address of the appropriate point structure is saved. (This is the address, not the point_id identifier.)

Figure 10.4 shows the data structure of a circle, which consists of seven named float fields. The instantiation of a particular circle is also shown. The value of left_circle.x_center is 1.0. In addition to float fields, there are

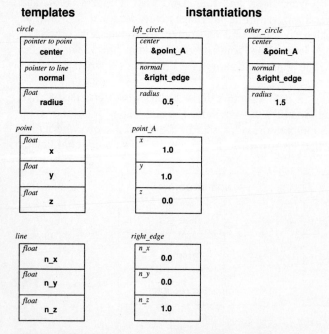

Figure 10.5   Data structure for a circle, using pointers to a point and a line.

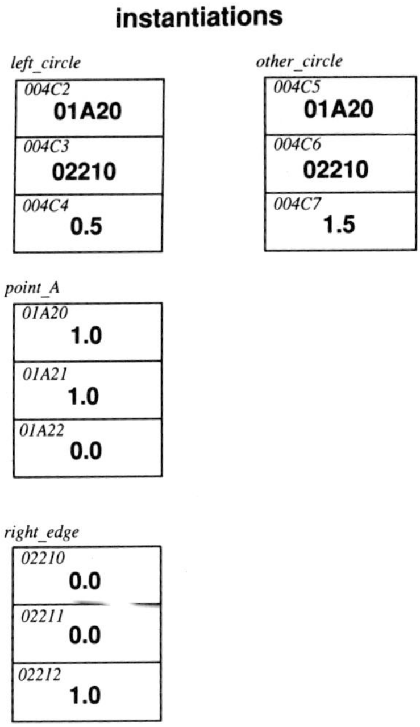

instantiations

left_circle

004C2
01A20
004C3
02210
004C4
0.5

other_circle

004C5
01A20
004C6
02210
004C7
1.5

point_A

01A20
1.0
01A21
1.0
01A22
0.0

right_edge

02210
0.0
02211
0.0
02212
1.0

Figure 10.6   Actual values in example data structure for circle.

also fields that contain addresses of other structures. For example, Fig. 10.5 shows three data structure templates for a circle, a point and a line. The center of the circle is identified in the circle structure by the address of a point data structure. The value of the x component of the center of the circle is left_circle.center->x, which is 1.0. Figure 10.6 depicts the values stored in each memory location (the address of each location is printed in the upper left-hand corner).

The advantage of using a pointer to the value instead of the value itself can be revealed after considering how two circles centered on the same point would be stored. In the method used in Fig. 10.4, the x, y, z components of the center would be stored twice, and to test if the circles were congruent would require three arithmetic if type tests. However, in the method used in Fig. 10.5, it is immediately clear that the two circles are congruent if left_circle.center = = other_circle.center. Similarly, the axis of orientation for the normal of the circle could be easily made parallel to the edge of another feature.

10.3   LISTS

The structures as developed in the preceding section can become quite complex but as presented are very situation specific. An extremely valuable generalization occurs when the field of a structure is allowed to be a pointer

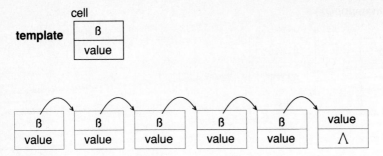

Figure 10.7 A linked list.

to another structure of the same type. This generalization permits data organization. The rest of this chapter will consider structures that have a local value and a number of pointers. It should be remembered that the local value can actually be an organized combination of floats, integers, characters, and so forth.

The most fundamental construct is the *linked list*. In this case, each structure contains a pointer to the next element on the list, as illustrated in Fig. 10.7. Characteristic of this structure is the head element and the tail element. The tail element may be formed by either a null terminated list as shown (with Λ, a null, as the address field for the final element) or by use of a sentinel, which is an additional element whose value is unique and acts to mark the end of the list. Note that the next pointer from the sentinel would be meaningless and not set to Λ. Useful information about the list includes the addresses of the head element (considered as the address for the entire list) and of the tail element (not necessary but useful).

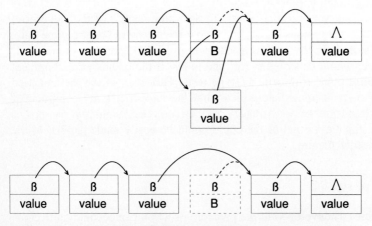

Figure 10.8 Structure insertion and deletion for a linked list.

The fundamental operations can now be considered. Creation of a list is simply a `malloc` of a single structure with a next pointer of Λ. Destruction of a list is accomplished by the freeing up of the memory used by this single structure. Structure insertion can take place as shown in Fig. 10.8. The address of a single structure of appropriate size is obtained by `malloc`, the value field is loaded, and then the pointers are appropriately rearranged. Note that this procedure is for an insertion after the structure with value B. Insertion before the structure with value B requires a bit more care because that structure does not have the address of its predecessor. One way to solve this problem is to use a double-linked list (which will be presented shortly). Another trick is to create a copy of the structure in question, change the value of the original structure to the new value, and insert the copied structure after the current structure, as shown in Fig. 10.9. Insertion at the head or tail of the list is a much simpler form of operation.

A stack can be implemented by only allowing insertion and deletion at the head of the list. For a stack, the tail address is not maintained. A queue

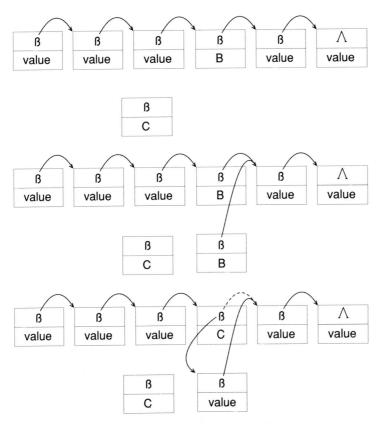

Figure 10.9 Structure insertion for a linked list.

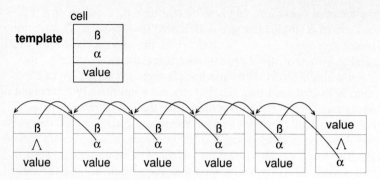

Figure 10.10   A double-linked list.

is implemented by only allowing insertion at the tail and deletion from the head of the list.

It is important to remember that the structures will not be as conveniently adjacent in memory as implied by Figures 10.7–10.9. The actual location in memory will be determined by the `malloc` procedure. In addition, the `free` procedure should be used when deleting structures from the list. Just because the pointer for the structure is no longer available does not allow the `malloc` procedure to reuse that portion of memory. In most CAD programs, if memory is not released as the program proceeds, the active use of lists can rapidly use up the available pool of free memory.

More elaborate structures are easily built using the concepts of the simple linked list. For example, if the tail of the list holds the address of the head of the list (rather than NULL) the structure is a ring.

In addition to a field for the address of the next structure, each structure can have a field for the address of the previous structure, as shown in Fig. 10.10. This is a double-linked list, and allows movement through the list (traversal) in both forward and backward directions. Connecting the head and tail structures produces a double-linked ring.

Each structure can refer to more than one structure further along. Figure 10.11 shows how both trees and graphs can be formed. The tree shown is binary because each structure leads to two other structures. The binary tree is useful for parse trees (discussed in more detail in Chapter 11) and the c.s.g. trees discussed in Section 9.8. Reference in a tree is always away from the root of the structure. The octree representation mentioned in Chapter 9 uses a fundamental structure with eight downstream references. Also shown in Fig. 10.11 is a general graph that can be formed from the same basic unit. In this case, structures are allowed to refer arbitrarily to other structures, possibly creating loops. The graph is a good representation of B-rep geometry.

Example 10.1: Winged-Edge Data Structure. As discussed in Chapter 9, surface models can be generated in several forms. One of these forms, shown in Fig. 10.12, is known as the winged-edge model. The object consists of

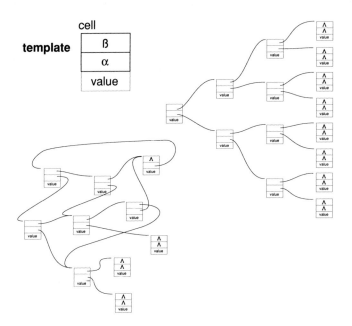

Figure 10.11 Multiple address references allow the
formation of trees and graphs.

points, edges, and polygons. The data structure focuses on the edge, which
connects two points and is the boundary for (at most) two polygons. Figure
10.13 shows the data templates for the two data structures required (the
edge and the point). Although the point coordinates could have been placed
within the edge structure, this would have created a large amount of repeated
information.

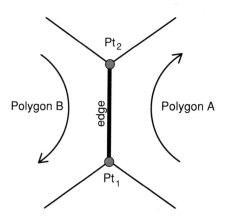

Figure 10.12 Winged-edge geometry.

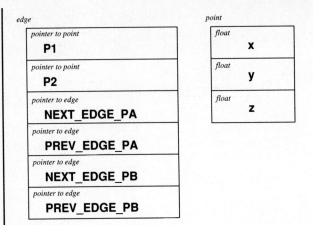

Figure 10.13   Data structure for winged-edge geometry.

The object is referenced by the pointer to one of the edge structures. Each edge references two points (P1 and P2) by pointers to point data structures. The edge forms the boundary for two polygons (PA and PB). The edge structure is doubly linked in the polygons, because both next and previous edges for each polygon can be reached directly. Of course, PREV_EDGE_PA could be reached by sequentially addressing NEXT_EDGE_PA and circuiting the polygon. Note that the outward normal for the polygon is defined by the direction in which the polygon is traversed. If the winged edge represents the surface of a solid body, polygons that share an edge will transit that edge in opposite directions. However, the edge structure has an explicit order (P1 versus P2) and this distinguishes polygon PA from polygon PB.

Example 10.2: Polyhedral Data Structure. Example 10.1, although sufficient for implementing a geometric processing package, can be improved substantially. Figure 10.14 illustrates the templates for an enhanced data structure for polyhedral geometry. This data structure contains more links and also provides locations for storing precalculated information.

A specific data structure is created for each polygon and these are connected into a double-linked list. This linkage is purely for ease in implementing algorithms that require actions to all polygons and require tests of all polygons. The double link is perhaps overkill but adds little complexity or expense. The polygon contains a pointer to a linked list of all points that lie on the boundary of the polygon. These could be accessed through the edge list but a direct link is useful. Note that the pt_list for each polygon is linked in a single direction. The points are placed in order based on the outward normal and the right-hand rule. Similarly, the polygon contains a pointer to a linked list of all edges forming the boundary of the polygon. These edges are also ordered by the outward normal and the right-hand rule. Finally, the polygon contains the coefficients

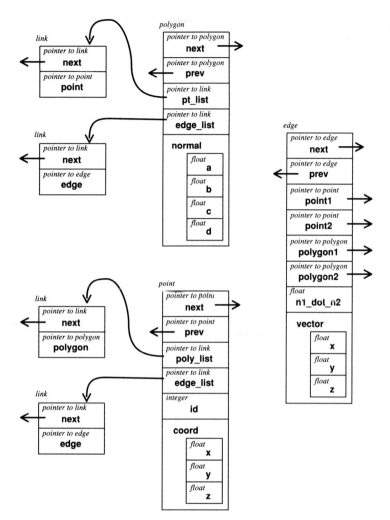

Figure 10.14 Enhanced data structure for polyhedral geometry.

for the plane normal form for the polygon, $ax + by + cz + d = 0$. This can be calculated from a cross-product of two edges, but if precalculated and stored, the normal is immediately available for use by algorithms such as the backside cull. Drawing the object on a color raster display could be achieved by a straightforward traversal, drawing all polygons which pass a backside cull filter. The polygon data structure could be expanded to include fields such as color, illumination intensity, point count, or visibility flag.

The edges form a double-linked list. Each edge points to two points and two polygon data structures. A field is included for the facet angle (n1_dot_n2), which is calculated from the dot product of the two polygon normals ($\vec{n}_1 \cdot \vec{n}_2$). The data structure also stores a unit vector along the edge, directed from point1 to point2 ($x\vec{n}_x + y\vec{n}_y + z\vec{n}_z$). A line drawing can be produced by traversing the edge list. Note that this avoids the double drawing caused by traversing the polygon list and drawing all edges.

The points also form a double-linked list. Each point contains a pointer to a list of polygons and a list of edges that share that point. Both of these lists are single linked. Each point has an identification number and coordinates. The point structure could be expanded to include fields for local normal, color, and illumination intensity. Note how link structures are used for the polygon's pt_list and edge_list and the point's poly_list and edge_list.

10.4   INTRODUCTION TO THE DATABASE

The database is a logical progression from the data structures discussed earlier. A database can be viewed as either a massive complex data structure or a large collection of simple data structures. For the typical CAD user, the distinction between a data structure and a database will be the characteristics of size, duration (length of time of existence), and speed.

Data structures such as linked lists may contain several thousand entities (such as the points, lines, or faces of a complex object), whereas a database may contain hundreds of thousands or millions of entries (such as part information, sales records, maintenance data).

A data structure rarely exists outside of the current program. The structure may be written to a file, but this involves some reformatting and flattening, and the file is a distinctly different entity from the structure itself. A database, on the other hand, exists separately from the user's program. The duration of a database is typically measured in years.

A data structure can be accessed rapidly; for example, CAD programs can easily traverse a linked list checking every element. A database has much higher overhead for access. Usually it is unreasonable to have a database return all records so that a variable can be checked (the procedure equivalent to the data structure traversal). Instead, commands are issued that instruct the database management system to perform operations, resulting in a substantial improvement in speed.

The need for database methods can be seen in the following examples:

- A company manufactures pneumatic-powered hand tools. Several components are to be manufactured on a Flexible Manufacturing System (FMS Workcell). Critical CAD/CAM activities include definition of part geometry, NC path generation, and factory floor scheduling. When multiple different parts exist, the company focuses on the scheduling of individual operations on each product part. The factory is assumed to be several FMS workcells with multiple tools in a tool magazine, although extra tools are available from the factory toolcrib. It will be critical to maintain information about the tools in the FMS magazines and in the factory tool crib. Potential activities are tracking the number of hours remaining for any particular tool, debiting hours as they are used, crediting hours for sharpening, and generating reports on statistical aspects of average tool breakage, usage, and so forth.

- A company designs and builds electromechanical devices (e.g., printers, copiers, and scanners). The product is a collection (assembly) of parts, most of which will be ordered from outside suppliers, along with a small number of custom parts. This company will need extensive vendor information about items such as bearings, motors, switches, clutches, power supplies, and so on.

- A design group uses concurrent engineering for vehicle design (automobile or truck). One concept being developed is an active suspension system. Nonlinearities of real systems preclude use of block diagrams and transfer functions, so the primary analysis technique is transient simulation as described in Chapter 5. Over the length of the project, this group will generate hundreds of simulation results for different designs and circumstances (initial conditions and loading). It may be too expensive or time consuming to regenerate these, if design alternatives need to be re-explored because of design changes mandated by manufacturing. These simulations will need to be organized in many ways: by parameters used in the model (actuator size and feedback gains), by performance indices (RMS ride quality, maximum suspension travel, and attachment point forces), and by inputs (transient bumps, sinusoidal, and random). A similar scenario could be created for a design group with a connection to an active test program that generates experimental data.

The CAD system designer may create data structures and write source code for the direct manipulation of these structures. (As stated earlier, the designer should apply "toolsmithing" instead of generating such manipulation code willy-nilly.) The CAD system designer is as likely to serve as the "toolsmith" for data structures. However, CAD system designers are as unlikely to write a database manipulation program as they are to write a compiler. Therefore, instead of exploring the internal details of database programs, let us focus on the terminology and functionality of database managers.

10.5 CHARACTERISTICS OF DATABASES

A commercial database program will provide the following characteristics that are extremely difficult to obtain from user-written data structures:

- Limited access
- Audit trail

- Formal backup procedures
- Integrity
- Simultaneous access

To the extent required by CAD, most of the desirable features listed above are easily delivered and are available in most commercial database programs. Limited access means parts of the database can be shielded from the view of specific users. For example, a company may have assembled a material properties database that it considers proprietary. The material properties can be shielded to prevent direct printing by most engineers; however, access can still be allowed to those application programs that use the material properties. An audit trail lists time, user, and action for all accesses and changes. The list of changes is the first step in acquiring the ability to undo changes. Also, in a design group it may be important to know who completed certain aspects of the design, which is the beginning of a design history. The system can perform automatic backup procedures at specified times or after a specified number of transactions. Experience continues to show that user-initiated backup is unreliable. Integrity checks are easily applied to maintain fields with appropriate values. For example, Young's modulus could not mistakenly be set to a value of 0.01 nor density to a value of 13.2×10^6.

Simultaneous access poses a significant challenge. It is relatively easy to provide multiple users with simultaneous read-only access to the database. However, when simultaneous write access is required, a number of difficult problems arise. For example, consider a database with part geometry information, where simultaneously one engineer is doing a stress analysis of the part while another is performing manufacturability analysis. Both engineers may wish to change aspects of the part during their work, for example, the diameter of a hole. Allowing multiple (sequential) changes to the database is possible. Advising other users of these changes is less feasible. Even more infeasible is to have each user work directly from the database. To show the absurdity of working directly from the database, every graphic update to the screen (pan, zoom, or rotate) would call for complete database access even if the user had not changed the underlying data. Furthermore, the two engineers may have conflicting goals regarding a parameter such as hole size: The database should not accept a change without calling it to the other users' attention for acceptance.

It should become obvious that the issue of simultaneous access is much more complex than simply keeping the database consistent. Currently, there are two accepted solutions for computer-aided design: single user write access and library check in/check out. In the former, only one user is authorized to change a particular field in the database. Although this alternative is relatively easy to implement, it may slow the design process unacceptably and frequently leads to secondary parallel (unofficial) databases. Alternatively, the library mode views the database system as a library that delivers large collections of data to the user. This data is converted to application-specific data structures that can be used quickly and modified. Simultaneous use is provided by providing clones of the library master copy to any user upon request. Difficulties with implementing this scheme relate to the check-in procedure. Obviously different versions cannot both be returned. This can be finessed to some degree by only returning data set changes, but even still some prioritizing scheme is required to allow for inconsistent updates.

10.6 DATABASE TERMINOLOGY

The database system is a collection of interacting programs, as shown in Fig. 10.15. The abstraction of the data types for a database is called the *scheme*. This is analogous to a structure definition for a compiler, (in C, struct point {int x; int y;};). The scheme describes the shape or form of the data. The actual data exists as an instance within the defined scheme. Creation of these instances is analogous to a declaration statement for a compiler (REAL* 4 KXX).

The database programmer uses the Data Definition Language (DDL) to express the descriptions of the scheme. The database management program

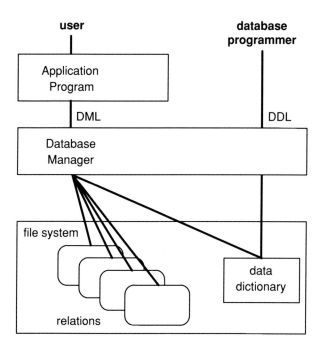

Figure 10.15 Database system architecture.

(DBMS) builds data tables, a data dictionary, and a directory of instances of each scheme. The users' application program uses the Data Manipulation Language (DML) to handle the data within each scheme. As will be seen, DMLs can be procedural or nonprocedural. To develop application programs, the CAD system programmer will have to use the DML. However, the CAD system programmer may or may not be able to function as database programmer and define new schemes. In any case, the user is shielded from the details of the scheme and the syntax of the DML.

The database manager (DBMS) is the go-between for the application programs and the database. Typically, the DBMS handles transactions or queries, interacting with the file manager to open and close appropriate data files and using information from the data dictionaries to enforce integrity and provide security. It is important to note here that the DBMS is a separate stand-alone program that exchanges data with the application program on request. Although a set of communication routines are provided to assist the application programs, the DBMS is not a library of routines for data structure manipulation. This characteristic is perhaps the primary conceptual difference between data structures and databases.

Given the high level of abstraction, the high degree of functionality provided, and the user insulation from detail, it should not be surprising that speed is adversely affected. At the present time, data structure codes are faster than commercial database management systems by a factor of 10 or 100 in response time.

Theoretical studies of database systems have identified three types of data models: object-based logical models, record-based logical models, and physical data models. Subtypes of each are listed below, including the most common object-based model, the E-R (entity-relationship) model. Although the other object-based models are not relevant to CAD, they are listed for completeness.

- Object-based models
  - Entity-relationship model
  - Binary model
  - Semantic data model
  - Infological model
- Record-based models
  - Relational model
  - Network model
  - Hierarchical model
- Physical data models

Most CAD applications have utilized record-based models. The relational model is a collection of tables consisting of columns with unique names. The next section will discuss this model in detail. The network model consists of records and links and is closely analagous to the structures and pointer in data structures. The hierarchical model is a network model in which the links are limited to forming only trees, rather than arbitrary graphs. Physical-based models are appropriate for file systems in which arrangements of disk cylinders, tracks, and sectors must be considered. As the name indicates, these models reflect the actual physical storage media.

The major focus of database systems has been on the entity-relationship and relational models. Most CAD applications have used relational databases. As with any data entity, the important issues concerning the programmer and user are creation, deletion, reading (value access), editing (value change), and access (obtaining one piece from many). We will look at these topics in the next section.

10.7 RELATIONAL DATABASES

A relational database is a collection of tables. Each table has a number of *attributes* (columns with names), and each attribute has a range of acceptable values D_i, its *domain*. The attributes and their ranges constitute the *scheme*. A row in a table is a *tuple* of values for each attribute $(V_1, V_2, \ldots, V_n)$.

It is important to note that the rows are not considered to be ordered and the ordering of columns is in some sense arbitrary. A tuple cannot be accessed by number and a column can only be accessed by name. Therefore, a table is not an array. The set of all possible rows is a cartesian product of a list of domains:

$$\mathop{\times}_{i=1}^{n} D_i$$

For example, let $D_1 = \{a, b, c\}$ and $D_2 = \{\alpha, \beta\}$. Then the cartesian product is the set

$$\{(a, \alpha), (b, \alpha), (c, \alpha), (a, \beta), (b, \beta), (c, \beta)\}$$

Mathematicians define a subset of all possible combinations as a relation. For example, $y = f(x)$ is a subset of all possible combinations of x and y. In the rest of this chapter, relation and table can be used interchangeably.

Example 10.3: Materials Database Scheme. Capitalization will denote names of schemes and lower case will denote relations or instances of a scheme. A scheme to store information about materials could be defined as

Material_scheme(density:float,
modulus:float,
cost:float,
supplier:string,
machinability:(high,low))

Note how each attribute is named and the domain is specified. A specific table or relation is declared by

> common_materials(Material_scheme)

Note that *common_materials* is a group of materials. Each row in the table is a particular material. If *t* denotes a tuple in *common_materials*, the notation for the value of a particular attribute of that tuple is *t[density]*.

Some other example schemes follow. Note that for brevity, the domain of each attribute has not been written.

> *FEM_problem(mesh_name,load_name,stress_name)*
> *Connectivity(element_number,node_1,node_2,node_3,node_4)*
> *Mesh(node_table_name, connectivity_table_name)*
> *Stress(node_number,sigma_x,sigma_y,sigma_xy)*

> *Tool_scheme(tool_no,cost,total_life,rem_life)*
> *Process_scheme (part_no,tool_no,machine_no,time)*

The finite-element example is limited to a particular element, because no element type is included in any table.

The last two relations will be used as a running example in the rest of this section, with particular relations:

> *tools(Tool_scheme)*
> *printer(Process_scheme)*

The name of the scheme has been explicitly denoted (e.g., *Tool_scheme*) for clarity to the reader. However, in the syntax as defined, the uppercase first letter is sufficient to differentiate a scheme from a relation.

The selection of the attributes, their domains, and the structuring of the attributes into tables is the database design phase. The primary question is how many schemes to include. Using several schemes can significantly reduce data repetition and avoid the need for *NULL* value entries. As we will see later, database design tries to avoid the need to enter *NULL* values for attributes. For example, when considering a tools database, where should the address of the tool supplier go? It could be added to *Tool_scheme*, but it would have to be repeated for each tool from the same supplier. If *NULLs* are strictly prohibited and addresses were part of *Tool_scheme*, then a tool could not be entered into the database without a supplier's address.

As previously stated, tuples in a relation are not numbered and cannot be accessed by position. *Keys* for a scheme provide unique selection of tuples. Consider a scheme R. Let K be a subset of R; that is, K is a subset of the attributes that comprise the scheme R. Then K forms a *super key*, if for tuples t_1 and t_2 ($t_1 \neq t_2$) and $t_1[K] \neq t_2[K]$. In other words, the set of values for columns K in row t_1 do not equal the set of values for columns K in row t_2. For the *nodes* scheme, $K = node\_no$ forms a key, but $K = x$ does not. Of course, a superset of K will also form a superkey. Therefore

$K = node\_no$, y or $K = node\_no$, x also are superkeys. The objective in most databases is to know the minimal superkey for each table. It should be noted that extraction of a tuple based on values for domains in the superkey may yield no tuples at all. However, it will never yield more than one tuple.

10.8   FORMAL QUERY LANGUAGES

Once a database has been defined, created, and filled with information, the next step is to consider the forms of interaction that are allowed. Formal query languages consider the situation from a programming aspect (i.e., which operations are allowed). The primary objective of Sections 10.9–10.10 is to discuss the semantics of database interaction. Although our objective is not to present any particular syntax, examples will require the introduction of syntax.

Methods of database interaction that are grammatical (the family of formal query languages) are divided into procedural and nonprocedural classes, which is highly analogous to the division of programming languages. Procedural query languages are similar to FORTRAN or C and focus on operations executed on data and the sequencing of those operations. Nonprocedural languages are less intuitive for engineers and concentrate on the data rather than the operations. Section 10.9 discusses an example of a procedural language, the relational algebra. In addition, Example 10.4 presents SQL, a commercial implementation of relational algebra. The relational calculus is discussed in Section 10.10 as an example of a nonprocedural language, with QBE (Example 10.5) as a specific commercial implementation.

10.9   RELATIONAL ALGEBRA

One procedural language applicable to a relational database is relational algebra. Data abstraction is a collection of tables; thus, the algebra will consist of operations on tables that produce other tables. These operations may be unary (with a single argument) or binary (with two arguments). The extension from a general algebra on the real numbers should be obvious. Real number algebra consists of unary operations, such as absolute value, negation, inversion, and so forth, and binary operations, such as addition and multiplication.

Five fundamental operations are needed to define relational algebra, although four other higher-order operations have proven sufficiently useful to warrant formal definition:

- Fundamental operations
  - Select
  - Project

- Cartesian product
- Union
- Set difference
- Higher-order operations
  - Set intersection
  - Theta join
  - Natural join
  - Division

The most primitive operation is the *select*, which will be denoted here as σ. Given a table a, *select* produces another table consisting of rows from a that satisfy some criteria p expressed in terms of the attributes of a:

$$\sigma_p(a)$$

A specific example is the selection of tuples for which the value in the *modulus* column is less than 13.9×10^6:

$$\sigma_{modulus < 13.9 \times 10^6}(common\_materials)$$

The predicate list p can be extended to include $=, \neq, <, \leq, >$, and $\geq$, as well as $\wedge$ (and) and $\vee$ (or). For example, assuming the definition of additional appropriate relations,

$$\sigma_{E > 10^7 \wedge \rho < 2.0}(metallic\_materials)$$
$$\sigma_{unit\_cost \leq 15 \wedge \rho > 1.5}(steels)$$

The predicate list allows comparison of fields

$$\sigma_{rem\_life > 0.5 total\_life}(tools)$$

A select operation shortens a table by retaining only specific rows. Which rows are retained depends on the data contained within each row. Because a relation (table) is considered to be unordered, it is meaningless to consider an operator such as "Keep the first 5 rows". Also, rows cannot be compared to each other with a select (keep the tuple with highest value of some attribute). Finally, table width (number of attributes and of columns) is not affected by a select.

The operation *project* (Π) is a unary operation to reduce the width of a relation. It copies the table, retaining only certain columns. If attributes are viewed as dimensions, then project produces a relation in a subspace of the original relation. For example, if the database represents the nodes of a finite-element mesh using a defined scheme, then the projection into the x, y plane can be formally specified as

Point_scheme(x:float,y:float,z:float)
all_nodes(Point_scheme)
$\Pi_{x,y}$ *(all_nodes)*

Note that for this example, after the projection, the z value is irrelevant. Specifically, the z value is not set to zero. It is gone and the table is a set of 2-tuples. As defined, the project operation can only work in the defining axes of this relation. It is not possible to project *all_nodes* onto an arbitrarily oriented plane ($x + y + z + 1 = 0$).

Formally, project (Π) operates on a table a, using a parameter list q that is a subset of the list of attributes of a:

$$\Pi_q(a)$$

For example,

$$\Pi_{density, unit\_cost}(steels)$$

The project operation can be used simply to reduce the size of a database by removing extraneous columns. It is also extremely useful if a relation has been produced with two identical columns. This will most likely happen from the richer operations yet to be described. However, a simple example would be

$$\sigma_{rem\_life \, = \, total\_life}(tools)$$

The result of this select is a relation with two identical columns. The redundancy can be eliminated by

$$\Pi_{tool\_no}(\sigma_{rem\_life \, = \, total\_life}(tools))$$

The preceding equation shows how operations are *concatenated* without defining names for the intermediate relationships, and it is a relational algebra translation of "find all new tools."

The remainder of the fundamental operations are binary, requiring two relations. Frequently the information required will be in two different relations, so a combined operation is required to generate the result. In the ongoing example of the machine tool database, consider the need to "find the cost of all tools used on part P_1 of the printer." The *printer* relationship has tool-part information; the *tools* relationship has tool-cost information. Because the tables have different lengths and widths, a straightforward combination is not possible. The proper operation is a cartesian product ($\times$), for example, $r = tools \times printer$. The scheme for r, denoted by R, can be described as

> $R(tools.tool\_no, tools.cost, tools.total\_life, tools.rem\_life,$
> $printer.part\_no, printer.tool\_no)$

Note how the origin for each column is denoted.

How can we "find the number of parts P_1 that can be made within the remaining life of tools on hand?" This would require the specific tools used to make P_1, their remaining life, and the amount of time each is used on part P_1. For specific data consider a tool selection of two tools, one of which is new:

tools			
tool_no	cost	total_life	rem_life
T_1	\$5	120 min	60 min
T_2	\$10	120 min	120 min

The product, a printer, has two parts that are made on two different machines:

printer			
part_no	tool_no	machine_no	time
P_1	T_1	M_1	10 min
P_2	T_1	M_1	2 min
P_1	T_2	M_2	30 min
P_1	T_1	M_2	10 min

Note that there are three entries for $P1$ because three processes are required. The cartesian product *tools* $\times$ *printer* is

tools $\rightarrow$ printer							
T_1	\$5	120 min	60 min	P_1	T_1	M_1	10 min
T_1	\$5	120 min	60 min	P_2	T_1	M_1	2 min
T_1	\$5	120 min	60 min	P_1	T_2	M_2	30 min
T_1	\$5	120 min	60 min	P_1	T_1	M_2	10 min
T_2	\$10	120 min	120 min	P_1	T_1	M_1	10 min
T_2	\$10	120 min	120 min	P_2	T_1	M_1	2 min
T_2	\$10	120 min	120 min	P_1	T_2	M_2	30 min
T_2	\$10	120 min	120 min	P_1	T_1	M_2	10 min

Note that *tools* $\times$ *printer* has all possible combinations of tuples even though some combinations may be inappropriate semantically. Specifically, tuples 3, 5, 6, and 8 are meaningless. These can be removed by a select operation:

$$\sigma_{tools.tool\_no \ = \ printer.tool\_no} \ (tools \ \times \ printer)$$

The select can further focus on the data relating to part P_1

$$\sigma_{printer.part\_no = P_1} \ (\sigma_{tools.tool\_no \ = \ printer.tool\_no} \ (tools \ \times \ printer))$$

The relation contains unnecessary columns so a project is used to remove duplicate or irrelevant columns:

$$\Pi_{tools.rem\_life, printer.time}$$
$$\left(\sigma_{printer.part\_no \ = \ P_1} \left(\sigma_{tools.tool\_no \ = \ printer.tool\_no} (tools \ \times \ printer) \right) \right)$$

The result is

tools.rem_life	printer.time
60 min	10 min
60 min	10 min
120 min	30 min

From this it would appear that the third tuple is the constraint and only four more P_1 parts can be manufactured. However, this is based on a misinterpretation of the results (i.e., 6 versus 6 versus 4). The first two tuples both use tool T_1 while the third uses T_2. The information about tool number has been lost during the project function. The more informative relationship is

$$\Pi_{tools.tools\_no,tools.rem\_life,printer.time}$$

$$\left(\sigma_{printer.part\_no \ = \ P_1} \left(\sigma_{tools.tool\_no \ = \ printer.tool\_no} (tools \times printer) \right) \right)$$

tools.tool_no	tools.rem_life	printer.time
T_1	60 min	10 min
T_1	60 min	10 min
T_2	120 min	30 min

Now it is clear that manufacture of three more parts will result in exhaustion of T_1 and leave T_2 with 30 minutes remaining. This example points out the pitfalls in database manipulation and shows that a database can be corrupted as easily as a data structure.

At this point it is worth a slight digression on the syntax of relational algebra. Note that the cartesian product is commutative: *tools* × *printer* is equivalent to *printer* × *tools*. Selects can be commutative with each other or combined. The following expression is equivalent to the previous select:

$$\sigma_{tools.tool\_no \ = \ printer.tool\_no \wedge printer.part\_no \ = \ P_1} (tools \times printer)$$

More generally, valid rewrite rules are

$$a \times b \Longleftrightarrow b \times b$$

$$\sigma_{P_1}(\sigma_{P_2}(a)) \Longleftrightarrow \sigma_{P_1 \wedge P_2}(a) \Longleftrightarrow \sigma_{P_2 \wedge P_1}(a) = \sigma_{P_2}\sigma_{P_1}(a)$$

The next fundamental binary operation is the union of two sets (∪). Consider the query, "list cost of all tools used on the printer or the disk drive." Postulating an additional relation *disk_drive* (*process_scheme*), the specification is

$$\sigma_{tool\_no \ = \ tool\_no} (\Pi_{cost,tool\_no} tools$$

$$\times \left(\Pi_{tool\_no}(disk\_drive) \cup \Pi_{tool\_no}(printer) \right))$$

Several aspects of the union must be observed. First, the relations must be compatible. This means that the arity is the same (number of columns) and the domain of the ith attribute must be the same. Second, since relations are sets, duplicates are eliminated. For example, Π_{tool_no} (*printer*) is

Π_{tool_no} (*printer*)
T_1
T_2

The reader is cautioned that many database packages will not eliminate duplicates automatically. Elimination of duplicates is a time-consuming step that is executed upon request.

The final binary operation is set difference $(A - B)$ which extracts tuples in A that are not in B.

To review, if a_1 and a_2 represent relations, then the four operations are defined as in Table 10.1. Furthermore, formal grammar studies have shown that these are sufficient for any query. In addition, there are four other common useful functions that can be expressed in terms of the fundamental operations.

Set intersection is specified as those tuples common to both r and s:

$$r \cap s = r - (r - s)$$

Frequently, the cartesian product is followed by a select:

$$\sigma_p(r \times s)$$

This combination has been named the *theta join*. It will occur when r and s have no common attributes.

$$r \bowtie_\theta s \iff \sigma_\theta(r \times s)$$

Usually the cartesian product will involve two relations with some common information. That is, there is some attribute (e.g., *tool_no*) common to each, and so the only meaningful tuples are those for which the values of common attributes are equal. The inappropriate tuples in *tools* $\times$ *printer* are removed by the *natural join* ($\bowtie$). Note that the repeated attribute is automatically identified; consistent tuples are retained, and the redundant attribute is dropped, as shown by the following table:

		tools $\bowtie$	*printer*			
T_1	$5	120 min	60 min	P_1	M_1	10 min
T_1	$5	120 min	60 min	P_2	M_1	2 min
T_1	$5	120 min	60 min	P_1	M_2	10 min
T_2	$10	120 min	120 min	P_1	M_2	30 min

The formal definition of the natural join is as follows. Let R and S be two attribute lists. The union of these two lists $(R \cup S)$, which will have duplicate attributes dropped, forms the scheme for the natural join. That is,

Fundamental Operations		Secondary Operations	
$\sigma_p(a_1)$	Select	$a_1 \cap a_2$	Set Intersection
$\Pi_s(a_1)$	Project	$a_1 \bowtie_\theta a_2$	Theta Join
$a_1 \times a_2$	Cartesian Product	$a_1 \bowtie a_2$	Natural Join
$a_1 \cup a_2$	Set Union	$a_1 \div a_2$	Division
$a_1 - a_2$	Set Difference		

Table 10.1   Relational algebra.

$r \bowtie s$ is a table in the scheme of $R \cup S$. Since one of the two columns with the same attributes will be dropped, it is logical to retain only those tuples for which the values of the common attributes are equal. This is a projection onto $R \cup S$ of $\bowtie_\theta$, requiring $r.A = s.A$ for each A in $R \cap S$. In other words, all common columns must be equal. This is the natural join of two relations and is central to all database theory and practice.

Consider the query, "find parts which use tool T_1 on all machines." A query with the flavor "find all" needs the final common operation, *division* ($r_1 \div r_2$). Using the fundamental operations, the query can be developed as follows. First, get a list of all machines and all part-machine pairs:

$$r_1 = \Pi_{machine\_no}(printer)$$

$$r_2 = \Pi_{machine\_no,part\_no}(printer)$$

Then determine which parts in r_2 use all of r_1.

Formally, if $r(R)$ and $s(S)$ are relations and $S \subseteq R$, then $r \div s$ is a relation on $R - S$. A tuple is in $r \div s$ if for every t_s there is a t_r such that

$$t_r[s] = t_s[s]$$

and

$$t[R - S] = t_r[R - S]$$

That is,

$$r \div s = \Pi_{R-S}(r) - \Pi_{R-S}\left(\left(\Pi_{R-S}(r) \times s\right) - r\right)$$

The algebraic statement of the query, "find parts which use tool T_1 on all machines," is

$$\Pi_{machine\_no}(printer) \div \Pi_{machine\_no,part\_no}(printer)$$

Just as word processing systems and graphics packages provide higher-order capability, a good database program will provide yet other higher-order functions and allow the user to define higher-order functions. However, the functions that have been discussed are the basic requirements and are sufficient for any query.

Example 10.4: SQL. The preceding discussion concerned the concepts of relational algebra and used a mathematical notation. One commercial implementation of a relational database is SQL (Structured Query Language). It is described here to highlight certain differences between theory and reality and to provide the reader with additional examples.

A typical SQL query has three clauses:

> **select** $A_1, A_2, \ldots, A_n$
> **from** $r_1, r_2, \ldots, r_m$
> **where** P

The first clause, *select*, is the projection operation (Π) from relational algebra. The terms A_i are the attributes desired in the result. The second clause, *from*, is the list of relations or tables (r_i) to be searched. The third clause, *where*, contains the selection predicate P that will involve attributes that appear in the same tables. Therefore, the preceding SQL statement is equivalent to

$$\Pi_{A_1, A_2, \ldots, A_n}\big(\sigma_P(r_1 \times r_2 \times \cdots \times r_m)\big)$$

The terminology can be confusing because unfortunately, the operation denoted by *select* in SQL represents the projection (Π) in the relational algebra. The **from** and **where** clauses represent the relational algebra **select** operation.

Of course, the full form of the generic statement is not always necessary. The attribute list can be replaced by the classic wildcard (*) or the predicate P can be eliminated (and assumed true). In the first case, the result is a "pure" select $\sigma_P(r_1)$:

> **select**   *
> **from** r_1
> **where** P

As discussed earlier, relations are built on set theory, and duplicate tuples should not occur. In most SQL implementations, duplicate removal is not automatic, but happens only if specifically requested as

> **select**   **distinct** A_1, A_2
> **from** r_1, r_2
> **where** P

Set theory is supported for relations, and union, intersect, and minus correspond directly to the relational algebra operation $\cup, \cap$, and $-$. In the predicate phrase the syntax for $\wedge, \vee$ and $\neg$ is **and**, **or**, and **not**. Many varieties of expressions are supported for the predicate, such as $>, \geq, \leq, =$, and $\neq$.

As previously described, the tuples in relations are inherently unordered. SQL allows for specific ordering with syntax such as

> **select**   *cost, tool_no*
> **from**   *tools*
> **where**   *rem_life = total_life*
> **order**   **by** *cost*

Additional richness is provided by the aggregate operations, which permit mathematical computations on groups of tuples. Some of the preceding relational algebra statements can be written as follows:
"Find all new tools"

> **select**   *tool_no*
> **from**   *tools*
> **where**   *rem_life = total_life*

"Find cost of all tools used on part P_1"

> **select**   *tools.cost*
> **from**   *tools, printer*
> **where**   *tools.tool_no = printer.tool_no*   **and**
>   *printer.part_no = P_1*

"Find all tools used on the printer and the disk drive"

> **select**   **distinct** *tools.tool_no*
> **from**   *disk_drive, printer*

10.10   RELATIONAL CALCULUS

Relational calculus formally describes the desired information, without specifying how to obtain the information. Relational calculus is therefore a nonprocedural language, as opposed to a procedural language such as relational calculus. This section will discuss the tuple relational calculus in which variables represent tuples. A similar calculus also exists in which variables represent values of domains (domain relational calculus).

The generic form for a query in tuple relational calculus is the set

$$\{t \mid P(t)\}$$

The expression represents the set of all tuples t such that predicate P is true for t. The value of tuple t on attribute A is $t[A]$ (i.e., *tools* [*tool_no*]) and $t \in r$ denotes that t is in relation r. Drawing on previous examples, "all new tools" is given by

$$\{t \mid t \in \text{ } tools \text{ } \land \text{ } t[rem\_life] \text{ } = \text{ } t[tot\_life]\}$$

This can be read as the set of all tuples in *tools* for which the value of *rem_life* is the same as the value of *tot_life*.

To find only the serial numbers of new tools requires the equivalent of the project.

$$\{t \mid \exists s \left(s \in tools \wedge s[rem\_life] \; = \; s[tot\_life] \wedge \; t[tool\_no] \; = \; s[tool\_no]\right)\}$$

This can be read as the set of all tuples t, for which there is a tuple s in *tools*, with *rem_life* $=$ *tot_life*. The value of *tool_no* is the same for s and t. Note that the scheme for t is not explicitly defined nor is the value of *tool_no* specifically copied from s to t.

More complex queries require a combination of relations. To find the "cost of all tools used on part P_1," find tuples t for which there exist two tuples, s from *tools* and u from *printer*. The value of *part_no* for u will be P_1 and s and u will have the same value for *tool_no*. Finally, t and s will have the same value for *cost*:

$$\{t \mid \exists s \, (s \in \; tools \; \wedge \; t[cost] \; = \; s[cost] \wedge \; \exists \, u(U \in \; printer$$
$$\wedge \; u[tool\_no] \; = \; s[tool\_no] \; \wedge \; u[part\_no] \; = \; P_1))\}$$

It should be clear from these examples that the richness of relational calculus lies in the formula for the predicate P. The grammar for a valid formula is built up from atoms that can take the following forms:

- $s \in r$
- $s[x] \, \Theta \, u[y]$
- $s[x] \, \Theta \, C$

These forms represent existence and comparison where C is a constant, and Θ is a comparison operation $(=, \neq, >, \geq, <, \leq)$. It is implicitly required that s and u be defined on attributes x and y and that those attributes be comparable.

Formulae are built up using the following combine rules for valid formulae P_1 and P_2, with possible free variable s:

- An atom
- $\neg P_1$ and (P_1)
- $P_1 \vee P_2$ and $P_1 \wedge P_2$
- $\exists s \; (P_1(s))$
- $\forall s \; (P_1(s))$

These combine rules are sufficient for parsing of relational calculus statements. As is common to powerful languages, expressions are not unique. Examples of equivalence include

$$P_1 \wedge P_2 \iff \neg(\neg P_1 \vee \neg P_2)$$
$$\vee t(P_1(t)) \iff \neg \exists t\big(\neg P_1(t)\big)$$

Given the nature of set theory, it is possible to generate an infinite relation. For example,

$$\{t \mid t \notin tools\}$$

There are an infinite number of tools not represented in the table *tools*. However, it is sufficient for the purposes of this text to caution the reader about using queries that may generate infinite results. Ways to handle and/or avoid such queries can be found in reference material.

Example 10.5: QBE. A commercial implementation of relational calculus is QBE (Query By Example). This software draws heavily on the concepts of graphical interfaces, visually oriented interfaces, interactive program control, and spreadsheets. The primary feature is the visual presentation of skeleton tables that show relation schemes, as in Fig. 10.16. These tables are loaded with example rows containing example domain values that can be constants or variables. Variables are denoted by a leading underscore (i.e., for *tot_life*, values could be 10, _x, or _y).

The skeleton table for finding the "cost of all new tools" is shown in Fig. 10.17. The $P._x$ in the *cost* column causes values of _x to be printed. Thus $P._x$ is similar in spirit to the project relation from relational algebra. Figure 10.18 shows the "tools that cost less than \$50."

Relations can be easily combined by simultaneous use of skeletons. For example, Fig. 10.19 represents the "cost of all tools used on part P_1." Multiple lines and variables can be used to express "and" and "or" queries. Figure 10.20 represents the "tools used on part P_1, costing between \$10 and \$50." Figure 10.21 represents the "tools used on part P_1 that cost less than \$50 or have a total life of greater than 20 h."

tools	tool#	cost	tot_life	rem_life

printer	part#	tool#	machine#	time

Figure 10.16   Skeleton tables for QBE.

tools	tool#	cost	tot_life	rem_life
		P._x	_y	_y

Figure 10.17   The table for the "cost of all new tools."

tools	tool#	cost	tot_life	rem_life
	P._x	<\$50		

Figure 10.18   The table for "tools that cost less than \$50."

tools	tool#	cost	tot_life	rem_life
	_y	P._x		

printer	part#	tool#	machine#	time
	P1	_y		

Figure 10.19   The table for the "cost of all tools used on part P_1."

tools	tool#	cost	tot_life	rem_life
	_x	< $50		
	_x	> $10		

printer	part#	tool#	machine#	time
	P1	P._x		

Figure 10.20   The table for the "tools used on part P_1, costing between $10 and $50."

tools	tool#	cost	tot_life	rem_life
	_x	< $50		
	_y		> 20 hr	

printer	part#	tool#	machine#	time
	P1	P._x		
	P1	P._y		

Figure 10.21   The table for "tools used on part P_1 that cost less than $50 or have a total life of greater than 20 h."

10.11 DATABASE DESIGN

The most important decisions regarding databases are made during the initial design stage, including choices about the number of relations and the scheme for each relation. It is beyond the scope of this text to adequately address the techniques for good database design; however, there are some significant pitfalls that can be described:

- Repetition of information
- Inability to represent certain information
- Loss of information

An excellent rule of thumb is to store information only once. This means that tables should not have common attributes besides those required for linkage. Repeated attributes are relatively easy to detect and remove. More common and more difficult to detect are attributes that can be calculated from others. In the example of *tools* and *processes*, the *tool_no* must be in both relations. It might be tempting to add a column to *processes* to represent unit operation cost:

process_scheme(part_no, tool_no, machine_no, time, unit_cost)

This is redundant information because *unit_cost* can be determined from tool cost, machine cost, and labor rates. Each of these attributes should exist elsewhere in the database. Developing the example sufficiently to illustrate the contribution of tool cost to unit cost for a particular part, leads to

$$unit\_cost \ = \ \frac{tools.cost}{tools.tot\_life} \cdot printer.time$$

Redundant data would appear to help increase the speed of database processing, but not without cost: It becomes extremely difficult to update the database. In the previous example, if the tuple *tool.cost* changes, then, *printer.unit_cost* values must be recalculated for those tuples that use *tool.cost*. Perhaps not so obvious is that if the tool used by a particular part (the tuple) is changed, then *unit_cost* must be changed also. Updates must be coordinated carefully, to prevent database corruption. The difficulty in commercial database systems lies in providing clear mechanisms for documenting and enforcing this kind of update.

If relations are not designed carefully, there will be some kinds of information that cannot be represented. For example, consider a single relation alternative to the *tools* and *processes* schemes. This alternative might have developed if tool life had not been relevant.

Other_scheme(part_no, tool_no, toolcost, machine_no, time)

Unfortunately, a tool that is not used on a part cannot be represented in this scheme. Specifically, if because of redesign, parts that used tool T_8 were removed from the printer, the existence of T_8 and its cost would be lost from the database. (Previous comments about redundancy apply to this scheme also with respect to the *tool_no, toolcost* pair that will probably be repeated several times.) A particular tool (*tool_no*) will always have the same cost (*toolcost*), and rather than repeating that information every time that particular tool is used, the *toolcost* should be in a seperate relation.

The NULL value is sometimes introduced to provide a way around this kind of problem. The tuple (P4, NULL, NULL, M6, NULL) represents a part for which the tool is not yet determined. The tuple to represent a tool not used by any part would be (NULL, T8, $18, NULL, NULL). Using NULLs makes database changes very difficult. Consider the operation of deleting a tuple from this last relation. Deleting a part will mean deleting all tuples representing operations for that part. However, when the last tuple that uses a particular tool is reached, the tuple is not deleted; rather, the *part_no* and *machine_no* fields are set to NULL.

Finally, manipulating a poorly designed database may result in loss of information. Remember that the natural join operation retains those tuples with common attributes. If the key for the relation is not in the common attributes, then $r \bowtie s$ will lose information because the key is necessary to distinguish between tuples.

The design of databases has been formalized and metrics are available to detect the preceding problems. In addition, a hierarchy of normal forms has been defined and the database is described by which form it satisfies. Two commonly used leads are the Boyce Codd Normal Form (BCNF) and the Third Normal Form (TNF). Although the BCNF is preferable, a database in either form can avoid the problems described, provide a lossless join, and presume all data dependencies.

10.12   SUMMARY

Useful computer-aided design applications depend on an algorithm applied to organized data with visualization and an interactive user interface. This chapter has focused on how data can be organized for use. At one extreme end of the spectrum are structured data types, which are formal definitions of data type beyond the common character, float, or array. Discussed in more detail was how these data types could use pointer information (addresses) to create higher-order data structures such as lists, rings, trees, and graphs. Much of a CAD programmer's activity revolves around the creation and manipulation of such data structures, and the creation of tools for this task.

A major part of a CAD user's actions are addressed at the generation and manipulation of data within these structures. As the amount of data, broad applicability, and duration increases, the focus moves to database management systems. The CAD user is seldom aware of the DBMS. The CAD programmer is now a user of existing commercial DBMS packages. At the DBMS level, the focus is often wider, including the entire enterprise and not just the design/analysis activities. The issues then pass over the threshold from CAD, CADCAM, CAM, CAE to CASE (computer-aided software engineering), PIM (product-information management), or CAEM (computer-aided enterprise management).

10.13   ANNOTATED REFERENCES

Aho, R.V., Hopcroft, J.E., and Ullman, J.D. *Data Structures and Algorithms.* Reading, Mass.: Addison-Wesley, 1983.

Ammeraal, L. *Programs and Data Structures in C.* New York: Wiley, 1987.

Date, C. J. *An Introduction to Database Systems.* 3d ed. (2 volumes). Reading, Mass.: Addison-Wesley, 1981.

Comprehensive introduction with numerous examples, and requires only a general background in computer science.

Boerstra, M. L. (ed.). *Engineering DataBases, Survey of Existing Engineering Database Management Systems, Criteria for Selecting a Database, and some Practical Experiences in Applying a Database System*. New York: Elsevier, 1985.

Encarnacao, J. L., and Lockemann, P. C. (ed.). *Engineering Databases: Connecting islands of automation through databases*. New York: Springer-Verlag, 1990.

Katz, R. H. *Information Management for Engineering Design*. New York: Springer-Verlag, 1985.

Korth, H. F., and Silberschatz, A. *Database System Concepts*. New York: McGraw-Hill, 1986.

Standish, T. A. *Data Structure Techniques*. Reading, Mass.: Addison-Wesley, 1980.

10.14 EXERCISES

■ **10.1:** Specify a data structure for a finite-element mesh consisting of a four-node tetrahedron.

■ **10.2:** Most multiple-patch surfaces are based on a rectangular grid of four-sided patches. Develop a data structure and file format to represent a multiple-patch surface consisting of an arbitrary arrangement of three- and four-sided patches.

■ **10.3:** Using a winged-edge geometry, describe an algorithm that can break an edge into two edges. Describe an algorithm that can split a polygon into two polygons.

■ **10.4:** Describe an algorithm for visiting every edge in a winged-edge geometry.

■ **10.5:** Describe an algorithm for visiting every polygon in a winged edge.

■ **10.6:** Describe an algorithm to cleave a winged-edge geometry with a cutting plane. The result should be one or two winged-edge geometries.

■ **10.7:** Consider an object described by a winged-edge geometry where the object does not form a closed volume. Describe an algorithm to draw the edges that are not interior to the surface.

■ **10.8:** Sketch an algorithm for determining if a winged-edge object is a closed object.

■ **10.9:** Sketch an algorithm for determining if a winged-edge object is convex.

■ **10.10:** Sketch an algorithm to determine if a winged-edge object is self-intersecting.

■ **10.11:** Specify a data structure for a cubic patch surface model.

■ **10.12:** Describe a data structure for segments of a tool path on a multi-axis mill.

■ **10.13:** Consider a body represented by a set of polygons. Group the polygons into sets constituting irregular but contiguous patches. Describe a hierarchical data structure for grouping these patches.

■ **10.14:** Specify a data structure for a "visualization image" for one of the entities in Table 8.1.

■ **10.15:** Show that the natural join does not require parenthesis to show ordering, as in the case of $r \bowtie s \bowtie t$.

■ **10.16:** Expand the *tools*, *processes* database to include information on machines and part production volume. Describe the *machine_scheme* and *production_scheme*. Design the database to handle queries such as

- "Capital cost for part P_3"
- "Unit cost for part P_3"
- "Time available on machine M_4"
- "Which machines are used to capacity"

■ **EXERCISE 10.17:** Use relational algebra to express the queries in Exercise 10.16.

■ **EXERCISE 10.18:** Use relational calculus to express the queries in Exercise 10.16.

■ **EXERCISE 10.19:** An individual part may require several processes on multiple machines. Replace the *process_scheme* with a *product_scheme* for containing part information and a *process_scheme* for each part. Consider how to include sequences dependent on *process_scheme*.

10.15 PROJECTS

Project 10.1   Rigging Database

A major manufacturer of sailboats has begun to computerize the design and manufacture process. The design, analysis, and engineering production for the rigging for the entire line of boats must be brought into the CAD/CAM system. Treat the rigging as an engineering system and describe the function and information that should be provided by the CAD/CAM system.

The goal of this project is not to write a program but to write the specifications (the first step in top-down design). The preceding description is deliberately vague so as not to prejudice your thinking.

1. Begin by listing the functionality you wish to provide.
2. Describe the data form to be used for items of information.
3. Show how information specified in (1) can be extracted from the data in (2).

Project 10.2   Surface Data Structure

Develop a data structure for a surface consisting of a collection of bicubic patches.

Project 10.3   Truss Data Structure

Develop a data structure for a class of truss problems that includes Example 3.1.

Project 10.4   Railroad Classification Yard Design

Develop a data structure for the switching yard in Project 5.2. This structure should include the physical locations of the track, switches, and retarders as well as the input line of cars and their destinations.

C H A P T E R

11
User Interfaces

11.1 INTRODUCTION

The speed of a program is determined by the algorithms used, and the versatility, by the data structures chosen, but it is the user interface that determines the usefulness of a program. The user interface is a two-way exchange. Recall that Chapters 7 and 8 discussed graphic output and how graphics can enhance information transfer. Now this chapter will focus on the input side of the exchange, considering two classes of user interface, textual and graphical. CAD programs utilize both, so the CAD designer must be familiar with them.

A CAD system designer must make many choices. The design of the user interface is quite literally a design problem. The designer must consider human factors, data handling, database design, code optimization, and menu structure. Interactive programs have many different sections that may be executed in virtually innumerable combinations, which is quite different from a batch-style analytical code executed from start to finish with only looping and some minor branching. The task of ensuring data and program integrity is much more complex for interactive programs.

This chapter begins with a discussion of keyboard interfaces. A significant advantage of a textual interface is the ability to store and replay the input stream, as discussed in Section 11.4. Computer science developments in compiler specification have provided the CAD developer with tools for easily creating language-based interfaces, which is discussed in Section 11.5. In many systems, graphics plays a central role in interactive programs. A major topic in this chapter is the discussion of the Graphical User Interface (GUI). Section 11.8 discusses the window management function of the GUI. The variety of tools (widgets) used in a GUI to provide interactive program control is discussed in Section 11.9. The chapter concludes with a brief section about human factors.

11.2 HARDWARE

As previously mentioned, the interface handles transactions between the user and the application program. The type of transaction involved can be used to classify devices into four generic categories:

- Text input
- Valuator
- Selector
- Locator

Text input devices produce a character stream ending with some prespecified delimiter (for example, a keyboard provides text input). The valuator produces a floating-point variable (a dial or sliding potentiometer is a valuator). The third, the selector (for example, a function box) produces a single choice from a predefined set. The locator produces a set of variables (usually two floats) that can be interpreted geometrically, most commonly as cursor location (for example, a mouse is a locator).

A variety of physical devices have been developed, each optimized for one of the preceding actions. Some of the more common physical devices include

- Keyboard
- Dials
- Function keys
- Function box
- Number pad
- Digitizing tablet (pen or multibutton puck)
- Mouse (one, two, or three buttons)
- Joystick
- Trackball
- Thumbwheels
- Touch-sensitive screen
- Wands (three and six degrees of freedom)
- Spaceball

The fundamental role of each device is usually clear, but some devices regularly serve multiple functions. For example, a set of dials is a multiple-channel valuator, but the cursor could be attached to two dials, thereby providing a locator function. The number pad can produce either a numeric character string (text input) or a float value (valuator), depending on how the input stream is read. Alternatively, the number pad acts as a selector in a keypad-driven editor.

The reader will find most devices have been developed to be locators. However, few are pure locators. The multibutton puck and even a single-button mouse are also selectors (in fact the minimal selector, choosing between off and on). Many other devices have been developed or proposed to meet specific needs. For example, in mechanical CAD, six-degree-of-freedom manipulation is often required. This manipulation can be achieved with one valuator, a multichannel valuator (e.g., six dials), or devices such as the Spaceball™ or Data Glove™.

It is important to remember that with very little effort, any device can be used to simulate any other. The CAD developer maximizes portability by designing the program to use the four generic devices. As the situation demands, specific physical devices can be used.

This chapter will not be concerned with the details of the interface between the CPU and the devices; rather, it will assume the existence of a software utility package to provide this connection. However, the more unusual devices typically use a standard RS-232 interface and the ASCII character set with the escape codes discussed in Section 7.5. The necessary interface software can be developed, if the developer can write to and read from the RS-232 port.

The basic actions can occur in one of three modes:

- Event queue
- Immediate poll
- Interrupt

Usually keyboard, selector, and valuator inputs go into a first-in first-out event queue, while the locator operates in immediate poll. Some selectors will go onto the event queue; others may operate in interrupt mode.

In most cases, a virtual circuit is already established between the locator and the cursor display. This circuit and the ability to read cursor location and indicator status is the most fundamental requirement for development of interactive CAD applications. However, more elaborate packages can allow the developer to establish other virtual circuits between a valuator and a graphics transformation such as "x-translation." Display manipulations are most often considered for soft wiring in an application. However, in design using parametric modeling (optimization, simulation, etc.) a circuit between a valuator and a design variable or parameter can be very useful.

Because of the connection to cursor tracking, the utilities for device polling and response queuing are usually included in the graphics support system.

11.3   KEYBOARD INTERFACE

Before considering the graphical interfaces, we will discuss the basic keyboard interface. Many CAD packages still use this mode and the ease of journal file creation and use (discussed further in Section 11.5) are a significant advantage. In fact, many graphical interfaces are simply an additional layer on a keyboard interface.

Initially, computer programs had all data coded within the program (hard coded). Since all execution was batch oriented and based on card decks, it was natural to change the program itself for different runs. Isolation of data into a separate *data deck* allowed the program to be stored elsewhere (on disk) and prevented accidental changes to the program caused by changing the data. However, this feature created the requirement that the user be able to control the program from the data deck. Previously, changes in logic flow could be achieved with simultaneous changes in the program and the data. Therefore the data deck includes information consisting of both commands and pure data. Many current analytical programs (finite-element, simulation, and optimization) maintain this "data deck" orientation, although the data decks are now virtual, existing as disk files.

Since FORTRAN was the original language, using a precise format was critical, and so data decks consisted of precisely defined data fields.

Example 11.1: Data Deck Definition. The PATRAN finite-element pre- and post-processor uses several kinds of interfaces (data decks, both ASCII and binary, keyboard, and menu-driven). The ASCII data deck is called a neutral file. The neutral file is written entirely in 80-character card images and all data are organized into small "packets" of two or more card images. Each packet contains the data for a fundamental unit of the model, such as the coordinates and attributes of a specific node or the definition of a specific finite element. A card contains several fields, and each field is defined by variable name, specific value (if required), format, and description. The packet for a grid (point) definition follows:[1]

first card

IT	31	I2	Packet Type
ID		I4	Identification number
IV		I4	Additional ID not applicable in this case
KC	1	I4	Card count (number of data cards in this packet)

second card

X, Y, Z   3E11.4   Cartesian coordinates

The packet for a line definition is as follows:

first card

| IT | 32 | I2 | Packet Type |
| ID | | I4 | Identification number |

---

[1]The format has been change slightly to satisfy page width constraints. All I4 formats should be I8 and all E11.4 should be E16.9.

IV		I4	Additional ID not applicable in this case
KC	3	I4	Card count (number of data cards in this packet)

remaining cards

B	5E11.4/5E11.4/2E11.4	A 4 × 3 matrix of geometric format line coefficients
IG	2I4	End point grid ID's

The following is an example of the data file for two points with coordinates $(0.0, 0.0, 0.0)$ and $(5.0, 1.0, 2.0)$ and a line connecting them:

```
31   1   0   1   0   0     0   0   0
  .0000E+00   .0000E+00   .0000E+00
31   2   0   1   0   0     0   0   0
  .5000E+01   .1000E+01   .2000E+01
32   1   0   3   0   0     0   0   0
  .0000E+00   .1000E+01   .1000E+01   .1000E+01   .0000E+00
  .0000E+00   .0000E+00   .0000E+00   .0000E+00   .0000E+00
  .0000E+00   .0000E+00   1   3
```

Observe that although the data file is easy to read (as opposed to binary representation), the data is very context-specific. The matrix of geometric format line coefficients requires intimate knowledge about the geometric data used within the program. Editing this data file can very easily cause data incompatibility. For example, the points could be changed to have identification numbers of 101 and 102 with the same coordinates. However, appropriate changes would be required in the 32 packet.

Because FORTRAN didn't handle character input well, alphanumeric data was not frequently used and operation codes or *op-codes* were common. These op-codes were not usually the escape sequences discussed in Section 7.5 but simply the integers chosen by the programmer to represent specific commands. For example, 99 was a frequently used op-code for EXIT. Example 11.1 discusses a data deck interface useful for batch processing or for storing a data structure as discussed in Chapter 10. Most interactive programs still maintain this style interface in addition to more advanced interfaces. It is difficult for users to generate data files directly (a process sometimes referred to as "hand-packing"), but data files are very easy to use as communication between programs.

One can develop a keyboard interface using the op-code approach, as shown in Example 11.2. Note the difficulty in precisely specifying the syntax of the interface, which increases with advanced keyboard interfaces and with GUIs.

Example 11.2: File Interface for a Dynamic Simulation. A simulator has been written for a specific differential equation that has three parameters:

$$m\ddot{x} + b\dot{x} + k_1 x + k_3 x^3 = F_0 \cos \omega t$$

Table 11.1 lists the allowable commands and the op-code values for each.

A sample data deck might be as follows. Comments have been annotated in *italic*.

2			*Set initial conditions*
0.2	4.0		$x_0, \dot{x}_0$
3			*Set time parameters*
0.0	35.0	0.2	t_0, t_{final}, dt
1			*Execute simulation*
2			*Set initial conditions*
0.2	2.0		$x_0, \dot{x}_0$
1			*Execute simulation*
99			*End*

Note that very specific knowledge is required about the structure of the data deck. For example, a 2 card must be followed by a card with two float values.

One difficulty with this kind of interface is the two-line pattern of

```
command
```

```
value(s)
```

This pattern is dictated by the differing number of values for various commands. The initial conditions require two values, the physical parameters require one, and the execute command requires none. It is extremely difficult in FORTRAN to read a line of input whose content is yet to be determined, so the two-line format is needed.

Opcode	Action
1	Execute simulation
2	Set initial conditions (requires two values)
3	Set time parameters (requires three values)
4	Set integration parameters (requires two values)
5	Set m
6	Set b
7	Set k_1
8	Set k_3

Table 11.1   Simulation program op-codes.

The two-line format can be avoided by structuring submenus, as shown in Table 11.2. At the highest level, single-line commands either execute the simulation or activate a submenu. Within a submenu, a valid command is a single line with an op-code/value pair. Note that a submenu is exited by entering an opcode and an arbitrary value. An alternative to this approach is to automatically exit the submenu after a single command. The latter approach is more useful if the user only changes one item per simulation run. The format shown in Table 11.2 is preferable, however, if the user can be expected to enter several commands before leaving the submenu. Also, note how the submenu op-codes are repeated and not unique. This makes the data file difficult to read and motivates the change to character variables rather than op-codes.

Note how easily values of parameters are changed; however, the differential equation can be changed only by editing a subroutine and recompiling. This is not a significant disadvantage for a program operating from a data deck.

As FORTRAN evolved to handle character input, the format rapidly changed to more explanatory input decks. For example, CHARACTER variables[2] can be used instead of integers to implement the interface of Example

Opcode	Action		
1	Run simulation		
99	Stop		
2	Change physical values		
	0	arbitrary	done
	1	float	set m
	2	float	set b
	3	float	set k_1
	4	float	set k_3
3	Change integration values		
	0	arbitrary	done
	1	float	set t_0
	2	float	set t_{final}
	3	float	set dt
	4	float	set nsteps
	5	float	set error
4	Change initial conditions		
	0	arbitrary	done
	1	float	set x_0
	2	float	set $\dot{x}_0$

Table 11.2   Hierarchical op-codes.

---

[2]A historical note: CHARACTER variables are a recent addition to the FORTRAN language.

11.2. However, many commercial programs still retain the basic orientation whereby the user prepares a "data deck" using the editor of choice and submits it to the program.

There is very little difference between reading a data deck or reading input from the keyboard. The program structure must change somewhat because sequential order is not as easily imposed. The order in which data is presented in a data deck can be rather rigid. The user can be expected to arrange the data deck as required. In the preceding example, setting initial conditions can be easily required before specifying integration parameters. In fact, with access to a full screen editor, the program can require the user to enter values for all variables (using no defaults) in a prescribed order. However, a user cannot be expected to be so constrained in keyboard mode.

As has been discussed several times, design is a series of small changes. Programs are therefore usually written to use mixture of data deck and keyboard input. The data deck begins the design formulation, setting variables to known or expected values. As design proceeds, keyboard input is used to make changes in the design values (or analysis parameters).

There are two generic types of data files that can be used to start a design study:

- Data deck
  - Flat file
  - Binary file
- Journal file

The first type (data deck) stores data in a specific format (which differs from the keyboard command syntax). There are two subtypes: flat file or binary. The flat file stores the data in a human-readable format that can be edited. The format, however, is not that of the keyboard interface. Example 11.2 describes such a flat file. On the other hand, the binary file stores the data structures themselves. Although this approach is more efficient, the flat file can be edited by the user, or more importantly, easily written by some other program.

At first glance, the journal file appears to be little different from the flat file. However, it is conceptually quite different, consisting of program commands in the syntax of the keyboard interface. Section 11.5 discusses journal files more extensively. Creating the syntax for the keyboard interface requires careful thought to both semantics and syntax. The interface semantics concerns the functions that will be provided; the interface syntax concerns the specific character sequences required (command names, order of arguments, etc.).

Choosing reserved words is a trade-off between short abbreviations that can be typed quickly and longer, more meaningful words. Even then, the programmer must choose between several possible alternatives. For example, consider the collection of words that are commonly used to terminate a program: *STOP, QUIT, EXIT.*

Error handling is critical for a keyboard interface, because even expert users will make typographical errors. At a minimum, the program must indicate that an error was detected. It is unacceptable to simply repeat the input prompt without comment. The HELP function is an extension of the error handling, and provides a sequence of increasingly detailed information. The creation and maintenance of HELP information is so important that frequently a separate database program is developed for this purpose.

The primary conflict in designing a keyboard interface is between the needs of the novice and the expert users. The novice user does not know the semantics of the program well and does not remember the commands specifically. The typical novice user makes typographical errors and needs (and will tolerate) more extensive prompts, cues, and help. The expert user is very fast, a better typist, and is willing to remember and use abbreviations. Also, the expert user will often submit commands faster than the program can execute them. This is sometimes referred to as "type ahead."

Example 11.3: Keyboard Interface for a Dynamic Simulation. A keyboard interface can be specified for the program in Example 11.2. This interface differs very little from the data file interface. Short character variables are used rather than op-codes. The commands are arranged into submenus as shown in Table 11.3.

A typical novice interaction follows. Note that the program-generated text is shown in a normal font and the user-typed text is shown in a bold font.

```
simulator > set
enter variable to set >m
enter value > 10.4
enter variable to set > help
the following variables can be set: m,b,k1,k3
enter done to return to main menu
enter variable to set > k1
enter value > 4.3
enter variable to set > done
simulator > go
simulator > plot
plot which variable ?x
plot which variable ?done
simulator >
```

On the other hand, a typical expert interaction might be as follows:

```
?>set, m, 10.4
?>set, k, 4.3
?>go
?>xplot, v, x
?>
```

go	Run simulation	
stop	Exit program and return to operating system	
set	Change physical values	
	done	done
	m	set m
	b	set b
	k1	set k_1
	k3	set k_3
int	Change integrator values	
	t0	set t_0
	tf	set t_{final}
	dt	set dt
	n	set nsteps
	e	set error
ic	Change initial conditions	
	x0	set x_0
	v0	set $\dot{x}_0$
		above are followed on next line by a float value
plot	Create a plot of variable versus time	
	x	add trace for x to plot
	v	add trace for $\dot{x}$ to plot
	a	add trace for $\ddot{x}$ to plot
	done	generate plot
xplot	Create a cross plot of two variables	
	v1,v2	two variable names, abcissa and ordinate

Table 11.3   Hierarchical commands.

The expert command processor requires more sophisticated parsing techniques to handle lines of variable length and is described in Example 11.6.

Editors are another prime example of interactive programs with keyboard interfaces. Usually such programs use the keyboard, numberpad, or function keys in selector mode, executing without awaiting the command delimiter (<cr> or enter).

Currently, operating systems provide the best examples of keyboard interfaces. In these environments, commands have parameters, good help facilities exist, and frequently the systems allow for novice and expert users. One example is the need to only type enough of the command to make it unique from the set of reserved words within the language. The commonality of most keyboard interfaces can be seen in the following examples of command lines from widely available programs.

Example 11.4: PADL 2 Command Line Example. The following few lines are taken from a constructive solid geometry modeling program, PADL 2 (see also Example 9.6).

```
Stock = BLO(X = Stockwidth, Y = 6, Z = 0.125);

Stock2width = 19.5;

Meter_Hole = CYL(H = 0.125,D = 3) AT MOVX = 3, MOVY = 3;

Panel = Stock DIFF Meter_hole
```

Example 11.5: ASCL Command Line Example. The following command lines are taken from Section 5.12:

```
PARAM H=0.,VA=100.

FINISH X= -10.

PRINT 0.05,X,Y

END

PRINT 0.01,X,Y

END

STOP
```

Example 11.6: PATRAN Command Line Example. The following few lines are taken from Example 11.7:

```
GRID,1,,0/-8/0

GRID,2,,40/-8/0

LINE,101,2GRID,,1,2
```

11.4 ERROR HANDLING

Error handling is often overlooked by CAD system designers, who focus more on application functionality. One advantage of an interactive program is the ability to detect errors and handle the situation before the application program receives inappropriate data. Error handling avoids arithmetic overflow, which is often due to format mismatch, data lines out of sequence, or minor syntax errors. Error handling is critical for a keyboard interface because even expert users will make typographical errors. A keyboard interface using a limited set of commands that branches by if-then-elseif constructions will never branch on an incorrectly typed command, and should not crash. At the minimum, the program must indicate that an error was detected; it should *not* merely repeat the input prompt without comment.

Most error handlers will produce a short description of the error detected. In many cases, the next user action will be a *HELP* query, so the text of the error message is the first level in a series of increasingly detailed information. The creation and maintenance of this textual information is so important that frequently a separate database program is developed for this purpose. This is yet another example of toolsmithing.

Interfaces with automatic corrective action can be developed with various techniques from the field of artificial intelligence. Such an intelligent interface would be an expert system. However, this topic is beyond the scope of this book.

11.5 JOURNAL FILES

A record of the commands which have been sent to a program is called a *journal file,* or sometimes a *history* or a *session file.* The journal terminology evokes the transactional nature of database management programs that maintain log files of all transactions. In a CAD environment, maintaining these files is properly the responsibility of the user interface rather than the application.

Journal files are clearly an outgrowth from the common practice of "echo printing" all program input. Echo printing is writing to the terminal immediately after the READ occurs. During debugging, this technique is useful to catch the user's typographical mistakes as well as input format problems. It is a minor change to write to a data file all user input before acting upon it.

Improved program debugging and maintenance is one important benefit from journal files. When a user detects an error, the journal file can be used to recreate the conditions leading to the error. In CAD programs with complex data structures, errors are often caused by unforeseen interaction between data structures or errors in pointers. These conditions are usually impossible to recreate without a journal file.

Journal files are useful in program maintenance by providing a means to automatically exercise program functions. Consider a large CAD program to which new functionality is being added, which requires modifications in the old data structures. A well-prepared journal file can be used to test that previous functionality has not been affected by the changes.

The user often looks at a journal file as analogous to the teach pendant for robotics programming. One mode for robotic programming is to manually drive the robot through the desired trajectory (e.g., spray-painting a fender) and save the resultant joint angles or locations. The robotic task is executed by replaying these values. The task can even be modified by editing the file.

Experienced CAD users can employ journal files in a similar manner. The designer first conceptually parameterizes the product and/or design process. The interactive aspects of the CAD tools (f.e.m., simulation, and optimization) are used to build the model. (This usually means using the graphical user interface, which will be discussed later in this chapter.) However, in this case the primary objective is not the model but the journal file saved by the program. The strategy is to make design changes with simple changes in the journal file, which is then used to create the new modified model.

Example 11.7: Journal File to Create Geometry in PATRAN. The following is a journal file from the PATRAN mesh generator for creating a hollow right circular cylinder with a circular hole. The cylinder has a radius of 12.5 mm and a length of 60 mm. The circular hole has radius of 8 mm. The objective of this example is not the particular commands of PATRAN but to show that a session file is more akin to a program than to a data file. The session file consists of the commands that the user would type directly to the program. The general syntax of a command is: entity, entity number, option, data, data. For example PATCH,101,ARC,0/0/0/1/0/0/90,101 creates patch number 101 with the circular arc function, rotating about an axis through the origin (0/0/0) aligned with the x-axis (1/0/0) by 90°, and line number 101 is the generator for the patch. The approach is to generate one quarter of the model, and then reflect twice to produce the entire hollow cylinder with a hole.

```
GRID,1,,0/-8/0

GRID,2,,40/-8/0

GRID,3,,12.5/0/0

GRID,4,,12.5/0/-30

LINE,101,2GRID,,1,2

LINE,102,2GRID,,3,4

PATCH,101,ARC,0/0/0/1/0/0/90,101

PATCH,102,ARC,0/0/0/0/0/1/-90,102

PATCH,3,ROTATE,0/0/0/0/0/1/-90,102

LINE,1T2,INTERSECT,2,P101,P102

LINE,5T6,PATCH,2T3,P102

PATCH,1/2,2LINE,102,1/2,5/6

LINE,101,DELETE

PATCH,101T102,DELETE

PATCH,4T6,MIRROR,Y,1T3

PATCH,7T12,MIRROR,Z,1T6
```

The diameter of the cylinder or of the hole can be changed by editing the session file, changing 12.5 or 8, respectively, to new values. The session file is analogous to a programming language. Note that a session file that can mesh the first object may be able to mesh the second as well. However, this depends on the degree of topological equivalence between the two objects. For example, consider a 12.5 mm cylinder with a 15 mm hole.

CAD designers who have become experienced in a specific program will often maintain a collection of files to perform various parameterized tasks, just as a computer programmer uses a collection of procedures or subroutines. This is another example of the toolsmithing approach.

The journal file is an excellent example of the dichotomy of data versus program, state versus history, or product versus process. What was once a sequence of program steps has been converted to a data file, which allows all of the data manipulation techniques to be applied. Specifically, data can be stored, retrieved, copied, modified, and deleted. How easily the data can be modified depends upon the syntax of the journal file. For example, numeric op-codes are more difficult to edit than alphanumeric commands. This is analogous to the increase in readability obtained by moving from machine code, to assembly language, to higher-level languages.

As previously stated, each journal file is in a particular language. These files have all aspects of formal computer languages; for instance, they have a set of reserved words and specific syntax restrictions. However, few journal files provide the richness of even the most simple languages. Few provide for data structures other than simple float variables, although a larger subset will provide for named variables. Few will provide for control structures (branching and looping) or subprocedures with arguments. Nevertheless, the formal techniques to evaluate languages are applicable to these rather limited languages. These techniques cannot be pursued in this book; however, the CAD developer is urged to learn more in this area.

If a CAD program provides all of the above (data structures, named variables, and control structures), then theoretically, any application such as simulation, optimization, or finite-element analysis can be developed within that CAD program. However, the novice user is cautioned that journal files as languages should be viewed as interpreted languages with all of the associated disadvantages of interpreted, as opposed to compiled, languages (primarily speed).

11.6 LANGUAGE-BASED INTERFACES

It can be difficult to describe a specific keyboard user interface. The final user documentation is a description, but during development a more concise description is needed. A common technique is an annotated example of a user session. Fortunately, the techniques developed for compiler description and analysis can be useful because of the rigor and formality that they imposed. Also, these techniques provide the abstraction to higher-level entities that is not available in an example session. This section will discuss how to describe and specify a keyboard user interface.

The user input will be a string of ASCII characters. The interface will parse each line (delimited by a <cr>). Parsing is the process of identifying words in the stream and branching using if-then constructions. The result is a specific path through the tree of all possible combinations.

The process is similar to that used by a compiler handling a series of lines of source code. The compiler will write object code, accept input, and generate output. The keyboard interface is an interpreter that accepts an input stream and executes actions determined by the content of the input stream.

One way of describing all possible valid input streams is to describe the language of the input stream. In this terminology, a language is made up of words, and an ordered collection of words is a sentence. The keyboard interface receives a line of input characters, identifies words, and then, based on word order, determines the action to take. This activity is known as parsing the input stream. Lexical analysis determines if the words are valid to the language; the parser determines if the sentence is valid within the language. In the context of Example 11.3, the input line set,z,54.0 contains an invalid word (z) and the line ic,b,3.5 contains valid words but is meaningless. Word order in a sentence is relatively easy to check for validity. On the other hand, sentence order is much more difficult to check. Again considering Example 11.3, ic,b,3.5 <cr> is easily identified as invalid; however, ic <cr> b <cr> 3.5 <cr> is much harder to detect as invalid.

Many types of grammars have been identified, including the context-free grammars, context-sensitive grammars, LL(k) grammars, and LR(0) grammars. The remainder of this discussion will focus on context-free grammar because of its direct applicability to CAD interfaces.

A context-free grammar is a set of variables or nonterminal entities. These entities are described recursively in terms of each other and fundamental entities called terminals. Note that a terminal is a fundamental item. A terminal is analogous to an atom in that, for purposes of grammar, it cannot be subdivided. Just as H_2O is a molecule, O is an atom, and an electron is a subatomic particle; then set,m,3.5 is a sentence, set is a terminal, and s is a character. Parsing is concerned with recognizing set, not the three characters s e t.

It is unfortunate that "terminal" evokes images of end of stream such as period, semicolon, or <cr>, which are terminators. The terminal concept applies to the parse tree that is being generated. A terminal cannot be parsed further.

The rules that define the grammar are called productions. The standard form for a production is

$$< a > \ \rightarrow \ < b >< c >$$

which should be read as the nonterminal on the left can be replaced by the nonterminals on the right. In this notation <> denotes variables. A common example of a set of productions is

$$< sentence > \rightarrow < action >< noun\ phrase >$$
$$< noun\ phrase > \rightarrow < adjective >< noun\ phrase >$$
$$< noun\ phrase > \rightarrow < noun\ phrase >< attribute\ phrase >$$

$$< attribute\ phrase > \rightarrow < attribute >< adjective >$$
$$< noun\ phrase > \rightarrow < noun >$$
$$< noun > \rightarrow \texttt{cylinder}$$
$$< attribute > \rightarrow \texttt{color}$$
$$< adjective > \rightarrow \texttt{largest}$$
$$< adjective > \rightarrow \texttt{blue}$$

Note that `cylinder`, `color`, `largest`, and `blue` are terminals. Also note that many more productions are necessary to include sentences such as `set largest cylinder color blue`. Originally, context, free grammars were motivated by the description of natural languages. However, they generally are not considered adequate to represent natural languages such as English. It is easy to generate sentences such as `set blue cylinder color left` that are syntactically correct but semantically meaningless. However, context-free grammars have proven extremely useful in describing computer languages (of which user interfaces form a subset).

Before proceeding, we can formalize the definition of a context-free grammar $G = (V, T, P, S)$. This grammar is based on a finite set of variables V, a finite set of terminals T, and a finite set of productions P of the form $A \rightarrow \alpha$, where A is a variable ($A \in \{V\}$), α, a string of symbols from $(V \cong T)$, and S, a special start symbol.

In computer science, the Backus-Naur Form (BNF) has developed as a slightly different notation for context-free grammars. This notation has been further affectecd by the LEXX and YACC utilities in UNIX. These two programs accept data files in BNF format and generate the C code for the parser. The YACC format for a production rule is

$$left : right1 \mid right2 \mid right3 ;$$

where *left* is a variable and *right1*, *right2*, and *right3* are valid productions. The "|" is read as "or" and the ";" as a statement terminator. The definition of a grammar is therefore

$$grammar : grammar\ rules \mid rules;$$
$$rule : rule\ "\mid"\ formulations \mid$$
$$non-terminal\ ":"\ formulations \mid$$
$$nonterminal\ ":"\ ;$$
$$formulation : formulation\ symbol \mid symbol;$$
$$symbol : nonterminal \mid terminal;$$

The procedure is to run the BNF file (xxx.l) through YACC, thereby producing two output files (y.tab.c and y.tab.h). The LEXX file (yyy.l) defines all of the terminals for the lexical analyzer. The general format is

```
definitions

%%

rules

%%

program
```

Passing `yyy.l` through LEXX produces `lex.yy.c`, which contains the C function `yylex()`. The parser uses `yylex` to identify terminals (tokens).

Example 11.8: Simple Grammar for a Point Language. A very simple language can be described for creating points. Note that the data structure questions of Chapter 10 are not considered. This code only provides the definition of the user interface:

$$
\begin{aligned}
\textit{point\_prog} &\rightarrow \textit{point\_prog statements} \mid \textit{point\_prog} \text{ exit} \\
\textit{statements} &\rightarrow \textit{statements statement} \mid; \\
\textit{statement} &\rightarrow \text{id} = \textit{function}; \\
\textit{function} &\rightarrow \textit{value} \mid \text{point } (\textit{spec}); \\
\textit{value} &\rightarrow \text{float} \mid \text{id}; \\
\textit{spec} &\rightarrow \textit{spec, spec} \mid \textit{spec} \mid \text{x} = \textit{value} \mid \text{y} = \textit{value} \mid \text{z} = \textit{value};
\end{aligned}
$$

A collection of valid sentences is

```
a = 5.0

b = 3.2

c = point (x = 3.5, y = 7.0)

d = point (x = 3.5, y = b)

exit
```

The reader will note several things about a program in *point_prog*. First, no end-of-line delimiter is required. Of course, the language could be changed to require ";" or any other delimiter of choice. The command `d = point (x=1.0, x=5.0)` is valid, but how the program would react is not determined. An *id* can be reused; that is `a = 5.0 a = point(x = 1.0, y = 3.4)` is valid. However, a sentence that seems both clear and likely to be used `d = point(x=y=1.0)`, is not valid. Finally, `b = a` will bind the value of b at execution and will not enforce future equality. Figure 11.1 shows a parse tree for a *point_prog*.

Note that the BNF definition of the language is not unique. An alternative definition follows:

$$
\begin{aligned}
\textit{point\_prog} &\rightarrow \textit{point\_prog statements} \mid \textit{point\_prog} \text{ exit} \\
\textit{statements} &\rightarrow \textit{statements statement} \mid;
\end{aligned}
$$

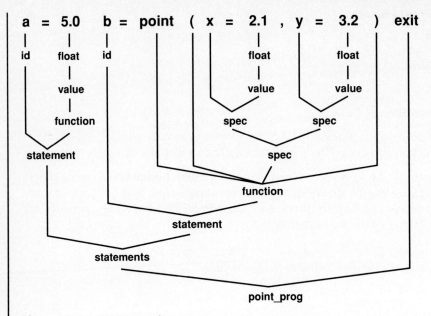

Figure 11.1 Parse tree for a *point_prog*.

$$statement \rightarrow \texttt{id} = \texttt{float};$$
$$\rightarrow \texttt{id} = \texttt{point}(spec);$$
$$value \rightarrow \texttt{float} \mathbin{!} \texttt{id};$$
$$spec \rightarrow spec, spec \mid spec \mid \texttt{x} = value \mid \texttt{y} = value \mid \texttt{z} = value;$$

As mentioned earlier, the UNIX programs LEXX and YACC accept a BNF definition of a language to produce C source code for a parser. The LEXX file for this interface follows:

```
#include "y.tab.h"

delimiter [ \t\n]+
alpha     [A-Za-z_/\.]
digit     [0-9]
float     -?{digit}+.{digit}*
name      {alpha}({alpha}!{digit})*

exit   { ECHO : return ( EXIT ); }
"="    { ECHO : return ( "=" ); }
"X"    { ECHO : return ( X ); }
```

```
"Y"    { ECHO : return ( Y ); }
"Z"    { ECHO : return ( Z ); }
point  { ECHO : return ( point ); }
{delimiter} { fprintf(yyout,"\n"): /* do nothing *? }
{name} { ECHO : /* yytext holds the text string */ ;
return ( ID ); }
{float}  { ECHO :  sscanf(yytext,"%f",&(yylval));
return (FLOAT); }
```

The skeleton of the YACC parser file, without any C code included is as follows:

```
/* definitions section */

%start point_program
%right '='
%token ID, FLOAT, POINT, X, Y, Z, EXIT
%%
point_prog:  point_prog statements
          ¦  point_prog EXIT
          ¦
          ;
statements:  statements statement
          ¦
          ;
statement :  ID '=' function
          ;
function  :  value
          ¦  POINT '(' spec ')'
          ;
value     :  FLOAT
          ¦  ID
          ;
```

```
spec      :   spec ',' spec

          |   'X' '=' value

          |   'Y' '=' value

          |   'Z' '=' value

          ;
%%
```

When the definitions and actions are included, the parser file is

```
/* definitions section */
%{
#include <stdio.h>
#include <math.h>
/* declare a structure with 4 fields, name, points,
float, next */
/* declare pointer to variable_table */
char name[256];
float the_value;
float x_loc,y_loc,z_loc;
/* declare the function insert(list, name, ptr, float);
*/
/* which puts something into a list */
/* declare long value (list, name) */
/* which returns floating point value associated with
name */
/* for completeness declare long prt (list, name) */
/* which returns point pointer associated with name */
define YYSTYPE float;
%}
%start point_program
%right '='
%token ID, FLOAT, POINT, X, Y, Z, EXIT
```

```
%%
point_prog: point_prog statements ! point_prog EXIT ! ;

statements:  statements statement ! ;

statement : ID {strcopy(name,yytext);

/* pick up name from ID */

pt_ptr= NULL ; the_value=0.0; /* set up defaults */ }

'=' function {

insert(variable_table, name, pt_ptr,the_value;

/* put info away in the table */ };

function  : value ! POINT '(' {

x_loc=0.0;y_loc=0.0;z_loc=0.0;

/* set default values  */}

spec')' {

pt_ptr = GEO$INSERT_POINT (x_loc,y_loc,z_loc):

/* function in geometry package to create a point */ };

value : FLOAT { the_value = yylval; /* use the float */ }

! ID  { the_value = value (variable_table, yytext);

/* use the value of the float associated with the name */ }

;

spec : spec','spec

! 'X''=' value { x_loc=the_value; /* change x_loc */ }

! 'Y''=' value { y_loc=the_value; /* change y_loc */ }

! 'Z''=' value { z_loc=the_value; /* change z_loc */ } ;
%%
```

Note how pieces of C code have been added. For instance, when x = 3.5 is identified, the parser will return 3.5 in location yylval, and the line of code x_loc=the_value; will be executed. Note that x = a will use the procedure value to look up the value of a in the table.

The preceding example is not intended to be a sufficient introduction to LEXX and YACC. However, it shows how a data file can be used by a code generator to produce an interactive program and isolate the CAD system programmer from many of the details of parsing an input stream. The CAD system designer is strongly encouraged to become familiar with the LEXX and YACC utilities.

Example 11.9: Alternative BNF for Example 11.4. The Backus-Naur-Form for the simulation interface in Example 11.4 can be written as

$simu\_prog \rightarrow simu\_prog\ statements \mid simu\_prog$ `exit`

$statements \rightarrow statements\ statement \mid\ ;$

$statement \rightarrow action1 \mid action2\ target\ value;$

$action1 \rightarrow$ `go`;

$action2 \rightarrow$ `set` $\mid$ `integ` $\mid$ `ic`;

$target \rightarrow$ `m` $\mid$ `b` $\mid$ `k1` $\mid$ `k3` $\mid$ `t0` $\mid$ `tfinal` $\mid$ `dt` $\mid$
`nsteps` $\mid$ `error` $\mid$ `x0` $\mid$ `v0`;

$value \rightarrow$ `float`;

This form has modified the interface slightly to make all interactions single-line commands. The multiple-line command is not a context-free grammar and cannot be written in BNF.

11.7 GRAPHICAL USER INTERFACES

Programs that do not use a keyboard interface rely on some form of screen interaction as the primary communication channel with the user. This interaction can be achieved with cursor control keys, digitizing tablets, touch-sensitive screens, or a mouse. In all cases, the programs are based upon some form of *graphical user interface* (GUI) or menu management system. The CAD programmer will always need to operate within a particular GUI. In most cases, this is provided as a system utility and used by the programmer. However, in some cases, the programmer will need to develop the GUI also. The utilities for managing the GUI should be segregated, just as the graphics package and numerical analysis package are segregated.

Overall, the GUI must serve as window manager and menu manager. These two tasks are becoming separated in most programming environments and will be discussed independently in Sections 11.8 and 11.9.

11.8 WINDOW MANAGERS

The GUI may use either the entire display screen or a virtual screen that is set in a subsection of the screen, and is commonly referred to as a window. The control of multiple windows is simply a higher-order function that can be developed within a GUI. Because individual windows may be attached to separate programs, the window control is usually located in a separate program, in effect, a higher-level GUI. A window manager is analogous to a compiler or database manager in that the CAD programmer will probably never have to develop one. However, the CAD programmer will need to learn the window manager for the target system. Although standards are developing in this area, a variety of environments exist.

Multiple-window graphical interfaces are tied to the concept of multitasking (simultaneous independent programs). A keyboard interface can handle multitasking by indicating separate programs or "sessions" in the user input prompt:

cedar>>

ash>>

One-DOF>>

In this fashion the user could interact with simultaneous programs. However, as output became graphic, the labeled prompt became unacceptable because programs could not use the same screen simultaneously.

An additional need for windows arises from the multiple images that may be needed from within one program. For example, in a drafting program the user may need the traditional three views (top, front, and side) as well as a perspective view. Although these views would be located in a fixed position on a traditional drafting sheet, the user benefits tremendously from the flexibility to pan and zoom these views independently and enlarge each to full screen when necessary.

Similarly, a simulation program can use separate windows for system parameter selection, integration parameter selection, animation, and response plotting. In response plotting, multiple plots are trivially generated by reusing the plotting program in several windows.

Finally, in the code development cycle, separate windows are used for the editor, compiler, debugger, and program execution. This method is formalized in most code management systems or Computer-Aided Software Engineering (CASE).

Window managers are newer than graphics packages, so the level of standardization is correspondingly lower. However, the X-windows program appears to be the most likely candidate for the industry standard. This section will discuss some of the fundamental aspects of window management as related to the user interface, specifically:

- Tiled versus overlapping windows
- Icons versus text

We will not consider the underlying data structures required for implementation or graphics questions. Similarly, the many questions relating to textual information and fonts in windows of varying sizes will not be discussed. Finally, this discussion is not intended as a complete taxonomy of the characteristics of window managers; rather, the intent is to address the usefulness of window managers to the CAD user.

The most immediately obvious characteristic to the user is whether multiple windows are allowed to overlap, as depicted in Fig. 11.2. Overlapping

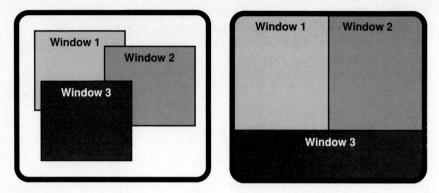

Figure 11.2 Examples of overlapping and tiled windows.

windows are often referred to as the "desktop metaphor," just as papers on a desk top can overlap. Tiled windows, on the other hand, are restricted to rectangular nonoverlapping segments of the screen.

In most cases choosing between the two is not difficult because the overlapping windows provide much more flexibility to the user and have become sufficiently common that the necessary user interface is easily obtained. On the other hand, the tiled system is much easier to manage. A programmer who must develop a window system with limited resources (both computer CPU power and programming time) should consider a tiled window manager.

The CAD programmer is always concerned with the aspect ratio of the target window. A graph can be distorted to fit any arbitrary aspect ratio. However, consider the graphics questions involved in drawing a circle into a window that is specified as square in the graphics calls but is then changed to rectangular by the window manager. Should the circle be drawn as a circle or as an ellipse? Many combinations of window systems and graphic packages will produce the ellipse. One role of the window manager is to insulate the program, and so ideally the program is unable to detect that the window is no longer square and pass this information along to the graphic display list program. Tighter coupling between the graphics processor and the window manager can solve this problem, but at the cost of flexibility. The best solution available to the CAD programmer is to enforce an aspect ratio on the window manager. Many readers probably already have used programs in which some windows are not adjustable.

For engineering applications, full use of overlapping windows can be computation-intensive and noticeably slow the program. All open windows must be completely updated, even if only a small portion of the window is visible. The graphics processor can spend a significant amount of time transforming, clipping, and projecting a complex geometry that is hidden by another window. Also, even slight changes to the location or size of a window might cause graphics in all windows to be regenerated. To minimize this computation, a sophisticated window management system can utilize information about windows that do not overlap. Thus users should arrange the desktop to minimize the overlap. In addition, closing windows can result in substantial speed increases.

At any one occasion only one window can be the input window. This window is referred to as the *listener*. Syntax issues concern how to show which window is the listener and how the user picks the listener. In some window systems, the listener is determined simply by the location of the cursor. In others, a "click" within the window is required for selection.

Icons serve as a graphical representation of both windows and data. A closed window must either become an icon or appear on a list of textual names. Usually the former is used for operating system actions; the latter, for accessing data files within a program. The graphical aspects of the icons can be used to convey both data and process information. The information about the data within the entity refers to the file type and to which programs might be able to use the icon. The information about the entity relates to whether or not the file is closed, open, requesting action, and so forth.

The fundamental actions that relate to windows are

- Select
- Create
- Delete
- Bring to top
- Push to bottom
- Move
- Reshape
- Force to full size
- Open
- Close

A syntax must be determined for each of these functions, but all of these actions are not required explicitly. Note that the "push to bottom" function expedites access to completely covered windows and can be achieved by several reshapes and moves to eventually uncover the target. In most systems, "select" and "bring to top" are combined. "Create" and "delete" are usually program actions rather than user interactions with a specific window. "Force to full size" is a convenience and can be achieved by the more general "reshape" function. Therefore the primary syntax questions relate to "move," "reshape," "full size," and "close." These are the functions that a user will need to know first when learning a new window system.

Many systems are designed to use various combinations of mouse button selections to control the "move" and "reshape" actions, which of course requires a system with a multiple-button mouse. It is also important to note that "move" and "reshape" are not dynamic. The contents of the window do not change during the process, but usually an outline of the window is used and the window contents are passed through the graphics pipeline only after the final size and location are chosen.

11.9   MENU MANAGERS

A program can use a keyboard interface between the user and the program and still use a sophisticated window manager to manipulate the screen layout. However, most programs need to allow the user to control the program from an interactive menu. The window manager can be viewed as a utility at the level of the operating system. In contrast, the menu manager is a utility at the level of an individual program. The distinction begins to blur when a program has several windows and utilizes the window manager to control them.

Standardized interface packages are not as well developed as graphics packages, geometry packages, or window managers. The CAD user will find many diverse styles of interfaces, and frequently the developer must produce a support package. In designing a menu, the CAD programmer must consider characteristics such as

- Pop-up versus pull-down
- Fixed location versus movable
- Hierarchical structure (submenus)
- Handling of illegal actions
- Use of command keys

From a graphics programming viewpoint, the menu design must consider the following:

- Graphics (icons, rheostat markings, and so forth)
- Text
  - Font
  - Color
  - Background color
  - Selected style (highlighted style)
  - Deactivated style

These characteristics will not be discussed in detail. The reader should refer to graphics programming literature for additional discussion.

A menu is simply a list of items (usually actions), any one of which can be selected. In that sense, the menu acts as a "selector." However, the menu can include selectable entities that are also valuators. A more extensive list of menu entities includes

- Actions
  - Positioning
  - Rotation
  - Color selection
  - Parameter input (float input)
  - Selection from list (text input)
- Buttons
- Switches
- Radio buttons (blender buttons)
- Sliders (rheostats)
- Joysticks
- Meters
- Keypads
- Stirrers
- Handles

The combinations of graphic screen entities and source code for implementing these interactions have been called widgets. Figure 11.3 shows a collection of some common widgets. Standardization in menu systems should lead to a standardization of a common set of widgets.

The menu management package must generate the graphic entities that form the menu, including the hierarchical structure, textual data, and iconic data. Sometimes, the available actions will not correspond to graphical entities on the display. For example, some CAD programs use an extensive menu overlay on the digitizing tablet, although the overlay does not appear on the screen. Ideally, all available actions should appear as selectable entities on the screen: The user should not be required to use a mixture of keyboard

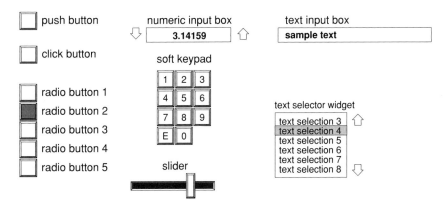

Figure 11.3   Widgets.

and menu-driven interaction. However, this is not to say that the alternative of keyboard versus menu should not be provided. Rather, if a menu interface is used, it should be used for all actions. For example, when prompted for a file name, the user should be provided with a list of names to select from instead of having to type the name.

The creation of menus provides an excellent example of the power of interactive graphical programs. The menu has a large amount of geometric information that must be specified. For example, locating text is much better done on the screen with a locator instead of sketching on grid paper and writing the accompanying source code.

This example leads to an interesting bootstrap procedure. A good menu-creation program inevitably will require a relatively complex menu. However, the CAD developer can write a very simple menu creation program, which can be used first (and probably only once) to create the more elaborate menus for the desired menu creation program.

This example shows the two roles for menu management systems: creation and use. In creation and management, the utilities are used by the CAD system designer either to make new menus or to change existing ones. In writing interactive programs, the CAD designer uses a subset of the menu utilities to display specific existing menus and manage the active sets.

There are two architectures for the menu systems, data oriented or program oriented. Figure 11.4 shows the data-oriented approach. Menus exist as data files, and the menu creator reads this file and writes a new version of this file. (Ideally, the file is a flat file, not binary, and can also be edited by any system editor.) Applications access menu utilities that read the file, create the graphic entities for the screen, and manage the active sets. In this architecture, small changes can be made to the menu using the system editor (for example, changing command names). Alternate menus can be provided in foreign languages simply by swapping the data file. Moreover,

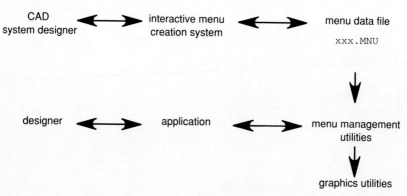

Figure 11.4   Data-driven menu architecture.

such changes are effective at the next execution because neither compilation nor linking is required. The existing executable statements can still be used. However, the menu data file must be present in the correct location for execution to occur. If the menu file is lost, the program is unusable.

In the alternate architecture, the menu creator/editor uses a code generator and the output is source code in the target language, as shown in Figure 11.5. In creating the application program, the source code is included as procedures to generate graphics structures and manage active sets. Therefore this output is specific to the target language and the graphics support package. Even in this architecture, a flat file format is required to enable the menu creator/editor to read in a menu, which also simplifies the code generator greatly. Unfortunately, in this architecture even small changes require rebuilding the program. Furthermore, alternate menus require separate executables. The program cannot be rendered unusable through loss of the menu file, but if the data file is lost, the menu manager will not be able to edit the menu from the source code files.

Example 11.10: A Menu Data File. The following is a sample data file for a menu management system. The system supports graphic structures in the menu as points, lines, text, and active rectangular areas called viewports. Each viewport includes a linear mapping so that floating-point coordinates within the viewport can be determined. This example is intended to illustrate the use of menu data files and to motivate the reader to use them. The example is drawn from a menu management system for calligraphic monochrome graphics systems. In using such a system, the reader would rapidly find the need to include features such as color, text font, and hierarchical menus.

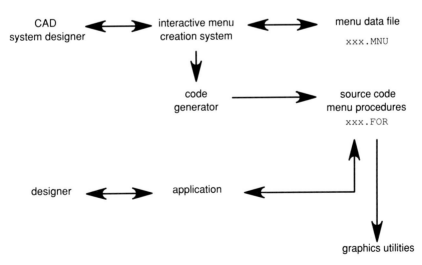

Figure 11.5 Code generator menu architecture.

```
numpts     tracelen num\ _text  num\ _pt
11         8       4       5
points
x          y          z
0.0        0.0        0.0
1.0        0.0        0.0
1.0        1.0        0.0
0.0        1.0        0.0
0.85000    0.00000    0.0
0.85000    0.15000    0.0
0.85000    0.30000    0.0
0.85000    0.45000    0.0
1.00000    0.30000    0.0
1.00000    0.45000    0.0
0.85000    1.00000    0.0
trace
-5     8     12     2     -6     10     -7     11
text       x          y
EXIT       0.92500    0.10000
ZOOM       0.92500    0.20000
-          0.87000    0.37500
+          0.98000    0.37500
viewports
0.85000    0.00000    1.00000    0.15000
0.85000    0.15000    1.00000    0.30000
0.85000    0.30000    1.00000    0.45000
0.00000    0.00000    0.85000    1.00000
0.00000    0.00000    1.00000    1.00000
11         maps       ur
```

−1.00000	−1.00000	1.00000	1.00000
−1.00000	−1.00000	1.00000	1.00000
−100.000	0.00000	100.000	0.00000
−0.85000	−1.00000	0.85000	1.00000
−1.00000	−1.00000	1.00000	1.00000

Figure 11.6 shows the menu for this data file. Note from the legend that points are shown as numbered circles, and windows are shown as dashed rectangles with the window number in a triangle in the upper right-hand corner. The actual unannotated menu is illustrated in Figure 11.7. Note that windows are identified by number rather than by name. In addition, observe that the lines on the menu are completely separate from the boundaries of the active areas (windows or buttons). A mapping has been used on window number 3 so that the value of the location of the cursor can be used to set a zoom gain. Of course, this feature also could have been done later by

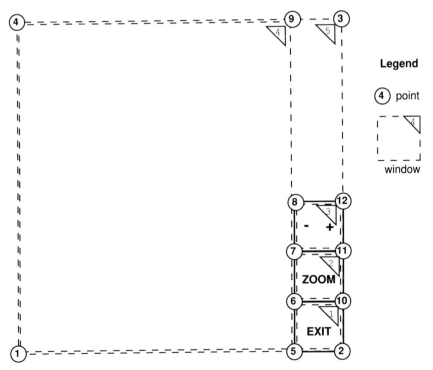

Figure 11.6 Sample menu (annotated).

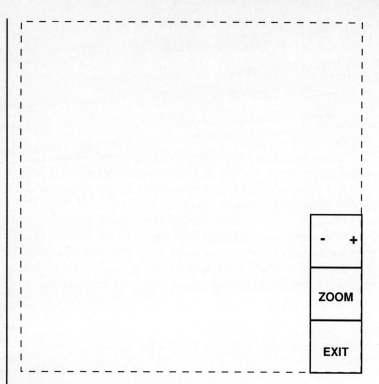

Figure 11.7 Sample menu.

software. Note, however, that the mapping on window number 4 has been set to represent the nonsquare aspect ratio of the window. What would have happened if this had not been done?

Further structuring of the user interface can ease the development of application software. For example, the developer may use the available window manager and structure the application around a collection of specialized windows such as the following:

- Data window(s) (graphical data from the application)
- Header window (useful information such as date, open file, etc.)
- Menu window
- Text window (scrolling screen of user-typed text)
- Message window (application specific messages)

Earlier, the importance of journal files was emphasized. If the application is to support journal files, it must inevitably support a keyboard interface. The developer must decide how to support both keyboard and menu-driven interfaces. For example, interactive menu programs can serve as front ends to language-based textual interfaces. Menu item selection simply generates an addition to the input character stream. This feature can make journal file creation and usage very easy for menu-driven programs and further isolates the application from the user interface.

11.10   HUMAN FACTORS

The literature on human factors for CAD programs is scattered and found mostly in journals. Instead of a detailed discussion here, this section will highlight a few key points. The interface consists of interaction between the human user and the machine. The interaction stream can be broken down into individual units that can be referred to as transactions. There are two similar forms for a transaction, as shown in Fig. 11.8. The following factors should also be considered when developing interfaces:

- As a rule of thumb, the transaction should be initiated and terminated within the same procedure.
- The interface should minimize distractions and discontinuities.
- The program should provide virtually immediate feedback (rapid response time)
- The interface must allow for recovery/cancellation.
- The user will be sensitive to command operand order. The choice of command operand order affects ease of use, ease of prompting, and ease of recovery/cancellation.
- The developer must consider physical environment of the user.

It is important to try to maintain subsecond response time. This doesn't mean the command must be executed within that time; however, the interface must provide some response to the user indicating that the command has been accepted.

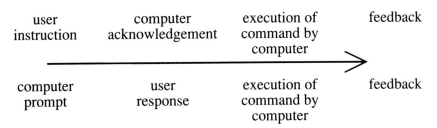

Figure 11.8   User interface transactions.

The processes of recovery and cancellation should be supported. If an image or a data structure can be changed, good human factors require that the user be able to undo the change. Actions that are difficult to undo (the deletion of large amounts of data, etc.) may require user confirmation. For example, quit may require a second selection before execution. During a transaction, the user will frequently be selecting from a list (even though the list is not visibly a list). For example, a set of menu buttons may appear to be a list, although an image with several lines will not appear to be a list. After a user selects from a list, a second selection from the list can be interpreted also as de-selection of the first. Of course, this raises the question of how to support selection of sublists: For example, the user may wish to delete five lines. This will require forming a sublist consisting of five lines from the list of all lines in the image. Finally, the user should not be forced to complete a transaction. If cancellation occurs, there should be no change to the data.

11.11   MULTITASKING OR TIMESHARING

Interactive interfaces and multitasking are an outgrowth of artificial intelligence research. Primitive mainframe computers used single program batch execution. Early AI researchers would use corporate mainframes after regular hours. In this research, small programs were used and the primary activity was a series of small changes made to the program (much as in the current software development cycle). Several researchers might wish to use the same computer; however, interactive programs wasted time waiting for interaction in a batch execution scheme with only one program loaded. Multitasking was required, which led to an environment that could support interactive interfaces.

Interestingly, personal computers are following the same evolutionary process from single tasking to multitasking. Workstations, perhaps because they have developed as reduced minicomputers, have always been multitasking.

CAD must be viewed as an environment rather than as a single program. CAD is a collection of programs and datastructures used to facilitate design. Programs communicate by exchanging data, but only if programs have journal files can one program execute or control another. Programs executing other programs increase extra capability by an order of magnitude.

11.12   SUMMARY

The user interface poses some of the greatest challenges to the CAD programmer. Both keyboard and graphical interfaces are widely used, and each has advantages. The primary advantage of the graphical interface is its enhanced human factors. However, it is interesting to note that in a program that allows the user to choose either interface, the expert user usually selects the keyboard interface. The primary advantage of the keyboard interface is the ease with which journal files can be accommodated. Journal files are critical to productivity in CAD programs. Also, journal files provide the basis for macro creation, which increases the user's programming powers and adaptability to applications.

The user interface is an excellent example of the continual issue of data versus program. Any user interface must eventually exist as computer code for execution. However, the menus can be viewed (and exist) as source code statements, hard-coded within the program, or the menus can be considered (and exist) as data files for use by a menu management system.

Some of the most difficult aspects of CAD program development are specifying and documenting the user interface. Unfortunately, CAD programs display little uniformity in this area. However, a primary objective of this chapter is to focus attention on the user interface and indicate to the reader that computer science developments provide a means to address these aspects.

11.13 ANNOTATED REFERENCES

Aho, Alfred V., Sethi, Ravi, and Ullman, Jeffrey D. *Compilers, Principles, Techniques, and Tools*. Reading, Mass.: Addison-Wesley, 1986.

Bass, Leo, and Coutaz, Joelle. *Developing Software for the User Interface*. Reading, Mass.: Addison-Wesley, 1991.

Baecker, R., and Buxton, W. *Readings in Human Computer Interaction*. San Mateo, Calif.: Morgan Kaufman Publishing.

Laurel, Brenda. *The Art of Human-Computer Interface Design*. Reading, Mass.: Addison-Wesley, 1990.

A collection of papers.

Coutaz, J. "Abstractions for User Interface Design," *IEEE Computer*, Vol. 18 (9)(September 1985), pp. 21–34.

Gayeski, D., and Williams, D. *Interactive Media*. Englewood Cliffs, N. J.: Prentice-Hall, 1985.

A discussion of modern and innovative forms of man/machine interaction.

Guedj, R. A., ed. *Methodology of Interaction*. New York: North-Holland, 1980.

Proceedings of an IFIP workshop on user/machine interaction, which is often the weak link in graphics programs.

Hopcroft, J. E., and Ullman, J. D. *Introduction to Automata Theory, Languages, and Computation*. Reading, Mass.: Addison-Wesley, 1979.

International Journal of Man Machine Studies, Academic Press, monthly.

Open Look Graphical User Interface Functional Specification. Reading, Mass.: Addison-Wesley, 1990.

OSF/Motif Style Guide Version 1.0. Cambridge, Mass.: Open Software Foundation, 1989.

Scheifler, R., and Gettys, J. "The X Window System," *ACM Transactions of Graphics,* Vol. 5 No. 2 (April 1986), pp. 99–109.

Sudkamp, T. A. *Languages and Machines.* Reading, Mass.: Addison-Wesley, 1988.

Sullivan, Joseph, and Tyler, Sherman. *Intelligent User Interfaces.* Reading, Mass.: Addison-Wesley, 1991.

NeWS Technical Overview. Mountain View, Calif.: Sun Microsystems, March 29, 1987.

11.14 EXERCISES

■ **EXERCISE 11.1:** As presented, Example 11.3 is a pure analysis program that generates a system response given input values. One crucial aspect of design is the comparison of designs (as represented by the associated responses) for design modification. Expand the syntax of Example 11.3 to allow the user to save an arbitrary number of responses and select a subset of responses to plot for comparison.

■ **EXERCISE 11.2:** Continuing from Exercise 11.1, expand the syntax to allow other ways to change parameter values besides set. Think about the ways in which values can be changed, not purely specified.

■ **EXERCISE 11.3:** Continuing from Exercise 11.1, expand the syntax of commands relating to responses so as to allow manipulation other than store and plot. Think about how a designer might need to use the response data.

■ **EXERCISE 11.4:** Discuss the advantages and disadvantages of maintaining textual information for *HELP* within and outside of the application program. How might *HELP* text be organized? Specify a set of procedure calls to access the textual information.

■ **EXERCISE 11.5:** Specify the file format for storing *HELP* text for a hierarchical keyboard interface (one that has multiple levels of prompts).

■ **EXERCISE 11.6:** Generate the *HELP* text for a small example keyboard interface taken either from a previous project or from Example 11.3.

■ **EXERCISE 11.7:** Specify a data structure for a multiple window manager that allows for overlapping windows. The listener is selected by a single mouse click and the listener cannot be covered. Pay particular attention to how closed windows are handled.

■ **EXERCISE 11.8:** Specify a data structure for a hierarchical menu. Write a menu creation program that can be used to graphically create and edit these menus. Use either a code generator or data file approach.

■ **EXERCISE 11.9:** Specify and implement a widget for selection of an item (text) from an arbitrarily long list of alternatives. As a demonstration, use it to select data files to open.

■ **EXERCISE 11.10:** Specify a grammar in BNF for a language that can define points and lines in two dimensions. An example of the target language is

```
a = 25.
b = 34.
c = 60.
pt1 = point(a, b)
pt2 = point(a, c)
ln1 = line(first = pt1, second = pt2)
left_hole_x = 2.6
left_hole_y = 5.5
right_hole_x = 6.8
right_hole_center = point(x = right_hole_x,
                          y = left_hole_y)
left_hole_center = point(x = left_hole_x,
                         y = left_hole_y)
line_of_action = line(second = right_hole_center,
                      first = left_hole_center)
exit
```

■ **EXERCISE 11.11:** Specify a grammar in BNF for a language to specify circles.

11.15   PROJECTS
Project 11.1   Polyhedral Viewing Program

Create (design and implement) an interactive viewing program for polyhedral objects. If possible, use an existing data structure for the geometry. Allow for multiple display modes (wire-frame, flat-shaded, Gouraud, transparent, ...) to the extent that your graphics package allows. Note that the program must support several objects simultaneously.

Project 11.2   Polyhedral Editor

Create (design and implement) an interactive program for editing a single polyhedral object.

Project 11.3   Hierarchical Display Tree Editor

As discussed in Chapter 7, a scene can consist of a hierarchically arranged collection of objects. This hierarchy can be viewed as a tree. Design and implement a GUI for editing this tree structure (i.e., for rearranging the structure of the subsegments of the scene). Allow the fundamental item to be a single geometric entity for which software utilities already exist on your system (possibly a polyhedron).

Project 11.4   Bicubic Patch Editor

Create a GUI for manipulating the control parameters for a single bicubic patch.

Project 11.5   Surface Editor

Create a GUI for manipulating a collection of bicubic patches to enforce different levels of continuity (C^0, C^1, and C^2).

Project 11.6   Dynamic Simulation GUI

Implement a GUI for Example 11.3 that includes the conditions given in Exercises 11.1–11.3.

Project 11.7   Simulation GUI

Implement a GUI for any of the projects in Chapter 5.

Project 11.8   Manipulation with Six Degrees of Freedom

Manipulating objects in space involves six degrees of freedom. A significant problem in CAD application design is how to vary six degrees of freedom from an inherently two-dimensional input (e.g., cursor location). Implement three different widgets (or a collection of widgets) to position and rotate a three-dimensional object. The extra degrees of freedom in scaling will not be considered. Then evaluate these widgets by user performance. Create an application that displays a reference object and a displaced and rotated version of the same object. Measure the time needed to align the displaced version with the reference object to within some tolerance level.

This project can be done without an extensive geometry package if limited to relatively simple shapes. Use a random number generator to determine the initial position, and use the system clock for timing. This project works best if several users can be tested increasing the amount of experimental data on each widget. Look for differences between large and small initial displacements. Does the tolerance level chosen affect the results?

Project 11.9 Primitive Feature Language

A product consisting of several parts (or objects) can be described by the geometry of each part. Alternatively, the product might be specified by how the parts interact with each other. One component of such a specification would be the geometry of each surface where interaction occurs. Interacting surfaces can be classified into generic types that can be parametrized.

One candidate set of interface features is

- Round pad
- Rectangular pad
- Cylinder
- Helix
- Sphere

Each set can be parametrized, and the location and orientation can be specified in terms of points and lines.

Determine a parametrization and a syntax for specifying each primitive and the defining points and lines. Describe the grammar and its syntax in BNF or YACC format.

A
Programming Guidelines

A.1 INTRODUCTION

The general rule of thumb is that the value of software exceeds that of the associated hardware. Also, since most engineering programming occurs in some group context, continuity is a significant problem. For these reasons, the importance of ease of maintenance cannot be overemphasized.

The intent of these guidelines is to familiarize you with techniques for producing software that is easy to develop and maintain, as well as robust (relatively insensitive to system changes). Although these guidelines are aimed at production systems that are to be used by others, they should be considered for personal programs (private use only). The distinction between the two types blurs over time. Following these suggestions will seem like more work than just sitting down and coding, but in the long run they will save time and aggravation.

A.2 LANGUAGES

Most CAD programs use FORTRAN-77, Pascal, or C. The latter two provide a richer programming environment, but FORTRAN is generally faster in compilation speed. Argument passing between languages is not too difficult to learn and so programs may actually be using several languages. For instance, many of the numerical method utilities that are available are written in FORTRAN.

A.3 SYSTEM COMMENTS

Learn the features and limitations of the full screen editor, and use programming tools such as the interactive debugger. When programming, write small modular programs spread into several files. Consider a target size of a page or two of listing, excluding initial comments. The size is affected by the overwhelming use of full screen editors. In addition, store functions/subroutines in separate files, and create subdirectories to keep files organized.

For declarations common to several files (or C EXTERNALs and TYPE-DEFs), keep a single copy of the declarations in the directory as a HEADER (.h) file, and refer to it from each file that requires it. The general rule is that every variable, constant, and entry point should be declared exactly once. For example:

```
FORTRAN:    include 'mydefs.for'
C:          #include <mydefs.h>
```

Create a file, BUILD.COM, containing the commands for building each program. Then the command @ build will compile and link the program. Of course, if only one subroutine is changed, @ build should only recompile the changed file and then relink everything.

A.4   DECLARATIONS

Always explicitly declare *all* variables, including loop counters, switches, and so forth. In addition, begin every FORTRAN subroutine or function with the line:

```
implicit none
```

or

```
implicit complex*16 (a - z)
```

The latter alternative is useful on compilers that do not accept `implicit none`. Then it becomes relatively easy to scan a compilation listing and pick out undeclared variables. Variables should be characterized as local (automatic), global (external), or arguments; arguments can in turn be described as input (given to the function/subroutine) or output (returned by the function/subroutine). Avoid using the same variable for input and output, even where allowed. Furthermore, make names mnemonic so that they describe the quantities they name. It is preferable to try to follow the "I through N" rule, whether using FORTRAN or not. Never use single-letter variables since they are difficult to search/replace using the editor.

Each variable should have an associated comment describing its use. Depending on individual style, the comments can be in-line or collected into a comment block, but be consistent. Use of a comment block is suggested for FORTRAN since alternating lines of comments and declarations are difficult to read. In addition, use comments to declare all called subroutines and functions with their argument list.

Use named constants rather than "magic numbers." Thus, for an array of points in FORTRAN use the following:

```
parameter npoints = 50
real* 4 graphpts(npoints,3)
```

In C use the following instead:

```
#define npoints   50
float graphpts[npoints][3];
```

A.5   FORTRAN STRUCTURE

The following guidelines relating to FORTRAN structure should be observed:

- Use modern flow of control structures such as DO ... ENDDO and IF ... THEN ... ELSE.
- Do *not* use the arithmetic IF statement.
- Collect all FORMAT statements at the end of the subroutine.
- No executable statement may have a label. Thus the only statements that can have labels are FORMAT and CONTINUE.
- Do not use the DIMENSION statement. Use in-line declaration instead.
- All common blocks must be labeled.
- Avoid the use of DATA statements to initialize COMMON variables.
- Indent all statements following DO or IF by at least three blanks.
- Use logical variables rather than numeric flags and use logical expressions to set the value of a logical variable as opposed to a complicated conditional branch.
- Initialize *constants* with nonexecutable statements, *variables* with executable statements.
- Separate system-dependent calls, especially I/O, into as few primitive level routines as possible.
- Use logical names with some mnemonic content for I/O devices and files. This will result in the fewest changes if a device must be reassigned. When in doubt, use more rather than fewer names, even if many have the same value. In this way, later separation is less error-prone.

A.6   C STRUCTURE

The following guidelines relating to C structure should be observed:

- Use the appropriate flow of control structures such as SWITCH and FOR instead of complex IF ... THEN ... ELSE clauses.

- Do not use GOTO.

- Indent *consistently*, by blocks and clauses, with at least three spaces.

- Provide thorough comments for compact and hard-to-read expressions.

- Capitalize *Constants* and place *variables* in lowercase.

- Separate nonstandard function calls into as few primitive level functions as possible.

- Use one function per file—compiling multiple files together will preserve the scope of variables just as if the functions were in the same file.

- Avoid duplicate variable names even when allowed.

- Use TYPEDEF for structures.

- Explicitly type pointers, and do not assign to an int pointer the address of a structure, character or float. Use UNIONs when flexible pointers are necessary.

- Leave a space when dividing by a dereferenced pointer; for instance, number/*number_ pointer is an unterminated comment.

- Always call functions with the appropriate number of arguments.

A.7   DOCUMENTATION

A complete documentation package consists of six elements:

- User's guide
- Internal documentation
- Internal organization (how the application works)
- Build instructions (how to construct the application from source files)
- Verification (how to verify the application works properly)
- Commented listing

Documentation of internal organization is basically a program logic manual that should include an overall description or flowchart illustrating the high-level flow of control. Key data structures should be described, including a specification of which routine(s) write/read them. INCLUDE files form much of this information. Also important is a description of the database, how it is accessed, and by which routines. References to variable and sub-routine names are important, as well as a cross-referenced list of all routines (identifying which ones call what routines).

A.8 BIBLIOGRAPHY

Material for these guidelines comes from several sources:

McCracken, D. *A Guide to FORTRAN IV Programming.* 2nd ed. New York: Wiley, 1972.

Herzog, B. *Programming Policy for FORTRAN Programmers*

Dill, J. *Programming Guidelines for Instructional Software.* Ithaca, N. Y.: Cornell University, 1982.

Conway, R., and Gries, D. *An Introduction to Programming.* Cambridge, Mass.: Winthrop Publishers, 1975.

Kernighan, and Plauger, *The Elements of Programming Style.* 2nd ed. Reading, Mass.: Addison-Wesley, 1978.

I N D E X